NORTH AMERICAN HOUSING MARKETS INTO THE TWENTY-FIRST CENTURY

NORTH AMERICAN HOUSING MARKETS INTO THE TWENTY-FIRST CENTURY

Edited by
George W. Gau and Michael A. Goldberg

Ballinger Publishing Company
Cambridge, Massachusetts
A Subsidiary of Harper & Row, Publishers, Inc.

Copyright © 1983 by Ballinger Publishing Company. All rights reserved. No part of this publication may be reproduced, stored in a retrieval system, or transmitted in any form or by any means, electronic, mechanical, photocopy, recording or otherwise, without the prior written consent of the publisher.

International Standard Book Number: 0-88410-880-5

Library of Congress Catalog Card Number: 82-18495

Printed in the United States of America

Library of Congress Cataloging in Publication Data
Main entry under title:

North American housing markets into the twenty-first century.

   Papers presented at a symposium held at the University of British Columbia in July 1981.
   Includes bibliographies and index.
   1. Housing—North America—Forcasting—Congresses.
2. Population forecasting—North America—Congresses.
3. Twenty-first century—Forecasts—Congresses.
I. Gau, George W. II. Goldberg, Michael A.
HD7292.A3N67 1982   381'.456908'097   82-18495
ISBN 0-88410-880-5

Contents

List of Figures

List of Tables

ACKNOWLEDGEMENTS

Developing a volume such as the present one requires the moral support and financial assistance of a great many people and institutions. This book has evolved from papers presented at a symposium that was made possible through the financial support of a number of organizations that we would like to acknowledge publicly. An endowment from the Daon Development Corporation of Vancouver provided us with much of the "seed money" to formulate and host the symposium. The organized real estate industry in the province also supported it through continuing research grants from the Real Estate Council of British Columbia. The British Columbia Real Estate Association is also to be thanked for their participation in the symposium, as well as for their ongoing close ties with the University of British Columbia Faculty of Commerce and Business Administration. Finally, the Social Sciences and Humanities Research Council of Canada provided a grant that allowed us to broaden greatly the geographic diversity of participants. Without such generous financial support it would not have been possible to host the symposium.

Although the funding of the symposium was a necessary condition for the creation of this book, the sufficient condition was met through the goodwill and efforts of all the authors, participants, colleagues, and staff who made things happen. Specifically, we would like to extend thanks to our colleagues in the University of British Columbia Urban Land Economics Division (Dennis Capozza, Stan Hamilton, Larry Jones, and Jon Mark), who gave us continuing guidance as we developed the plans for the symposium and who helped to make the symposium a stimulating and enjoyable experience. Peter Lusztig, dean of faculty, was most generous with his time. His enthusiasm for the project and his presence at a number of symposium events were also much valued. Professor Terry McGee, Director of the Institute for Asian Research at the University of British Columbia allowed us to use the institute's magnificent new facilities as the base for the symposium.

All of the foregoing made the symposium and the book possible. However, without the extraordinary ability, energy and dedication of Sheila Jones and Kathy Sayers, the "possibility" could not have reached the reality embodied in the symposium and the pages that follow. They were involved from the outset in planning and organizing all aspects of the symposium and upon completion of the symposium they were active in the editing of the revised papers and putting them into a consistent format. To both our heartfelt appreciation.

Finally, the faculty support staff have allowed us the achieve seemingly impossible deadlines without any sacrifice in quality. In particular, Nancy Schell and her colleagues in the faculty's word processing center provided us with remarkable turnaround in the midst of an exceptionally hectic workload. And last, but by no means least, Joan Ewer has helped us keep details (such as accounts) straight and also kept an eye on the numerous pieces of correspondence that floated through our offices.

To all of the above we express our deepest gratitude.

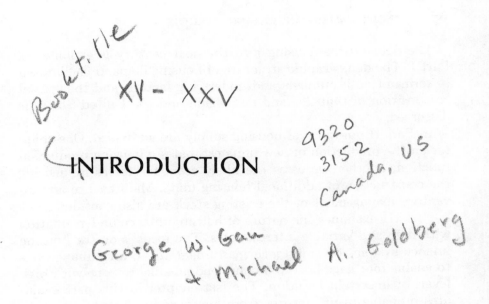

INTRODUCTION

The chapters in this volume were first presented at the University of British Columbia in July 1981 at a symposium designed to anticipate trends in North American housing markets into the next century. With less than two decades remaining before the start of a new century and significant demographic, supply, and financing changes foreseeable on the horizon, the time seemed appropriate to step back a bit from the pressing day-to-day research problems and policy issues and speculate on future housing markets in Canada and the United States. These symposium papers have been revised in light of discussions during the symposium sessions and suggestions from the editors.

The symposium and this volume compare the experiences of the United States and Canada with respect to demographics and housing demand, housing supply from both new and existing stocks, housing finance and mortgage markets, and government housing policy. This comparison may be the symposium's most important contribution, for the comparative approach allows researchers to gain valuable insights from other institutional settings into the general principles that appear to prevail in housing and mortgage markets.

The present introduction tries to make some sense of the history of behavior of housing and mortgage markets in both countries. The balance of the book is in four parts.

The demand for housing into the next century is explored in Part I. The demographic structure of housing demand is glimpsed in terms of both numbers and underlying factors, and the spatial composition of that demand in Canada and the United States is discussed.

In Part II questions of housing supply are addressed. One chapter on the production of new units estimates a housing production function; another discusses the likely economic forces influencing the construction of additional housing units. Maintenance and inventory management of the existing stock are also considered.

Part III examines the nature of housing finance under inflation with high and variable interest rates. The focus is on the housing finance system, the mortgage instrument itself, and innovations to enable mortgage borrowers and lenders alike to cope with high levels of uncertain inflation. The last chapter in this part evaluates probable future returns from housing investment.

Two perspectives for examining government housing policy are set out Part IV, one in terms of normative economic theory and the other in terms of the foundations of U.S. housing policy. Besides providing frameworks for studying policy and policymaking, these chapters look at the likely (and unlikely) directions of housing policy for the remainder of this century. Selected comments from panelists on government housing policy are included.

The concluding chapter of the book summarizes the major conclusions and issues from each of the four parts of the volume, and going further, it synthesizes their findings to reach more general conclusions than were possible from any particular discussion on a given topic. In treating these findings and the major unresolved issues, this final chapter sets out an agenda for future research. A comparative framework is argued for as providing a unique opportunity to develop rigorous analytic results that can simutaneously be broadened to more general principles about the functioning of housing and mortgage markets.

RECENT HOUSING AND MORTGAGE MARKET ACTIVITY IN NORTH AMERICA

Tables I–1 and I–2 provide some insight (albeit crude and aggregated) into the volatility of housing and mortgage markets during the past two decades. For example, over the period 1960–1979 annual housing starts in the United States ranged from a high of roughly 2.4 million (1972) to a low of 747,000 (1979). The 1970s typifies the recent problems faced by housing markets, with year-to-year fluctuations. These variations appear to be getting even more pronounced. Similar movement is evident in the mortgage market in the United States where rates have varied from a low of 7.7 percent for conventional mortgages (1972) to a high perilously close to 20 percent in summer and fall 1981.

Canadian housing and mortgage markets exhibited similar behavior. Over the period 1960–1979 housing starts moved generally upward, starting from a low of 108,900 in 1960 and reaching an all-time peak of 273,200 units in 1976. Starts have since fallen steadily from that peak, however, and in 1980 were down to 158,600, the lowest level since 1966. New mortgage originations reflect this activity, having peaked in 1977 after rising (with few interruptions) since 1960. Mortgage rates were at least as volatile in Canada as they were in the United States, achieving a low of 8.9 percent (1971) and rising to over 20 percent in summer and fall 1981.

One significant difference between the 1970s and the 1960s was the rate and stability of inflation in both countries. The 1960s were relatively stable years typified by inflation rates well under 6 percent per annum and rising moderately over the decade. The 1970s, however, saw the emergence of double-digit rates of inflation and enormous variability in the rates. In the United States in 1972 inflation was as low a 3.3 percent, based on the annual increase in the Consumer Price Index (CPI); by the end of the decade inflation was at 14.4 percent.

The situation in Canada was not appreciably different, though the timing varied, with inflation rates peaking in the mid-1970s and then climbing again in 1980–81. The Canadian CPI rose by merely 2.9 percent between 1970 and 1971, but between 1972 and 1973 prices increased at a rate of 15.7 percent; the rate slowed to 6.2 percent between 1978 and 1979, moving back into double-digits between 1980 and 1981.

Housing and mortgage markets are inextricably intertwined with the other capital and product markets in the economies of both countries. These economies absorbed major shocks in the 1970s, including dramatic increases in energy prices and decreases

Table I–1. U.S. Housing, Mortgage, and Economic Indicators, 1960–1979

	Housing Starts (Thousands of Units)	Residential Mortgages Outstanding ($Millions)	Multifamily Vacancy Rates (%)	Gov't Bond Yields (%)	FHA Mortgage Yields (%)	Consumer Price Index (1957–1959 = 100)	Unemployment Rate (%)	GNP (Billions of 1972$)	Median Sales Price for Single-family Homes ($)
1960	1,296.0	161,636	8.1	4.0	6.2	103.1	5.5	737	...
1961	1,365.0	175,895	8.7	3.9	...	104.2	6.7	...	...
1962	1,492.0	192,295	8.1	4.0	...	105.4	5.6	...	...
1963	1,635.0	211,229	8.3	4.0	...	106.7	5.7	...	...
1964	1,561.0	231,142	8.3	4.2	...	108.1	5.2	...	...
1965	1,510.0	250,120	8.3	4.2	5.5	109.9	4.5	926	20,000
1966	1,196.0	263,952	7.7	4.7	6.4	113.1	3.8	...	21,400
1967	1,322.0	279,970	6.8	4.8	6.6	116.4	3.8	...	22,700
1968	1,545.0	298,587	5.9	5.3	7.2	121.3	...	...	24,700
1969	1,499.5	318,984	5.5	6.1	8.3	124.9	3.5	...	25,600
1970	1,469.0	338,318	5.3	6.6	9.0	135.5	4.9	1,075	23,400
1971	2,084.5	374,649	5.4	6.1	8.3	141.3	5.9	1,103	25,200
1972	2,378.5	422,088	5.6	5.6	7.5	146.0	5.6	1,171	27,600
1973	2,057.5	470,041	5.8	6.3	8.2	155.1	4.9	1,235	32,500
1974	1,352.5	503,438	6.2	7.0	9.6	172.2	5.6	1,218	35,900
1975	1,171.4	540,317	6.0	7.0	9.2	187.9	8.5	1,202	39,300
1976	1,547.6	660,677	5.6	6.8	8.8	198.8	7.7	1,271	44,200
1977	989.8	768,419	5.2	7.1	8.7	211.7	7.0	1,333	48,800
1978	2,023.3	883,876	5.0	7.9	9.7	228.0	6.0	1,386	55,700
1979	746.6	1,003,005	5.0	8.7	10.9	253.8	5.8	1,432	62,900

Sources: Statistical Abstract of the U.S.; HUD Trends.

Table I–2. Canadian Housing, Mortgage and Economic Indicators, 1960–1979

	Housing Starts (Thousands of units)	Residential Mortgages Outstanding ($Millions)	Multifamily Vacancy Rates (%)	Gov't Bond Yields (%)	NHA Mortgage Yields (%)	Consumer Price Index (1961 = 100)	Unemployment Rate (%)	GNP (Billions of 1971$)	New NHA House Prices for Single-Family Homes ($)
1960	108.9	9,392	...	5.3	6.8	...	7.1	53.2	14,618
1961	125.6	10,641	...	5.0	6.5	100.0	7.1	54.7	14,727
1962	130.1	12,198	...	5.1	6.5	101.2	5.9	58.5	15,171
1963	148.6	13,910	6.1	5.2	6.3	103.0	5.5	61.5	15,544
1964	165.7	16,027	5.5	5.0	6.3	104.8	4.7	65.6	16,210
1965	166.6	18,618	4.5	5.4	7.3	107.4	3.9	70.0	16,955
1966	134.5	20,707	3.1	5.7	8.3	111.4	3.4	74.8	18,381
1967	164.1	23,027	1.3	6.5	8.8	115.4	3.8	77.3	19,784
1968	196.9	25,275	2.7	7.3	8.7	120.1	4.5	81.9	20,205
1969	210.4	27,929	4.0	8.3	10.0	125.5	4.4	86.2	21,058
1970	190.5	30,645	5.0	7.0	9.8	129.7	5.7	88.4	21,847
1971	233.7	34,109	5.0	6.6	8.9	133.4	6.2	94.5	21,979
1972	249.9	38,875	3.8	7.1	9.0	139.8	6.2	100.2	22,686
1973	268.5	46,083	2.2	7.7	9.9	161.7	5.5	107.8	24,802
1974	222.1	53,622	1.2	8.8	11.8	177.2	5.3	111.7	27,482
1975	231.5	62,371	1.2	9.5	11.9	202.0	6.9	113.0	33,289
1976	273.2	72,898	1.3	8.5	11.2	230.9	7.1	119.1	37,877
1977	245.7	86,390	2.3	8.8	10.2	256.5	8.1	121.9	41,542
1978	227.7	101,977	3.2	9.7	11.0	273.1	8.4	126.1	44,055
1979	197.0	115,703	2.9	11.3	12.9	289.9	7.5	129.8	49,024

Sources: Canadian Housing Statistics; Economic Review.

in productivity and in the rate of growth of real output in general. Unemployment rose dramatically over the 1970s in the United States and has remained high during most of the decade in Canada. The generalization that the western world is undergoing a major transition is reasonable.

In addition to and closely tied with these economic shifts, major changes have become apparent concerning the make-up and growth rate of the population base in both countries. Smaller families, later marriage, lower fertility rates, tighter immigration policies, and growing numbers of single-parent and single-person households all proved to be important demographic trends during the 1970s. The implications for housing and mortgage markets of these movements are at least as profound as any of the broader changes observed in North American economies.

It is in environment that the housing and mortgage markets must function during the last two decades of the twentieth century. These markets are increasingly unstable and particularly hard hit by volatile mortgage interest rates. The rapid pace of inflation and the uncertainty of its future course strongly affect housing and mortgage markets for three reasons. First, housing is very dependent on the avilability and cost of mortgage financing. Second, in uncertain and volatile times it is difficult to make long-term commitments such as those engendered in housing acquisition and development. Third, fluctuations in monetary policy expose both mortgage lenders and borrowers to greater interest-rate risk, a risk that borrowers are not used to absorbing and often unable to manage effectively.

Against such a background of change, uncertainty, and volatility, people who study housing must try to unravel market dynamics. The task is difficult in the best and stablest of times. The demands placed on housing and mortgage market researchers are considerable in light of the low level of housing starts in both Canada and the United States in the 1980s. Moreover, high mortgage rates paralyze housing markets, and finally, rising housing prices, falling vacancy rates, and shrinking inventories of unsold new housing in some areas augur very poorly for housing availablity over the next few years and more pessimistically in the longer run in many regions, while other regions suffer economic stagnation and shrinking housing demand.

GAPS IN CURRENT KNOWLEDGE ABOUT
HOUSING AND MORTGAGE MARKETS

The boom in housing and mortgage market research began in the early 1960s and has continued through to the present. Initial research such as that by Muth (1960) dealt with quantitative estimates of the demand for housing; more recent efforts go considerably beyond estimating demand and supply equations to apply models directly to assess impacts of actual and proposed housing policies (e.g. de Leeuw and Struyk 1975; Struyk, Marshall, and Ozanne 1978; Bourne and Hitchcock 1978; Kain and Apgar 1977; and Ingram 1980).

Despite great advances and technical sophistication, current knowledge is largely based upon the functionings of housing and mortgage markets in the 1960s and early 1970s. The utility of extending such findings and methodologies into the 1980s is questionable in light of the economic and demographic trends mentioned before. Changing relative prices for energy and capital also have serious consequences for the spatial composition of housing demand both within and among urban regions. Costs of land, infrastructure, energy, and credit directly affect the supply of housing by making new housing and land resources more expensive. Evidence exists that these forces are evolving. For instance, there is renewed interest among portions of the housing market (singles and professional couples) in central-city living and in revitalizing inner-city housing (Solomon 1980). The boom in transit investment is further evidence of the impact of energy costs on urban form and housing location in the longer run (Altshuler 1979).

As a result of these changing conditions it is unreasonable to expect knowledge based on cities, populations, and conditions of the 1960s and early 1970s to have the same utility in the 1980s as they did in an era of rapid population growth, suburbanization, abundant land and energy, and buoyant economic growth. In short, economists must take a fresh look at the stock of knowledge about housing markets in both the United States and Canada. Economic, political, demographic, behavioral, and broad environmental unknowns give cause to reflect on past research achievements and ask a new set of questions more appropriate for the present and the future.

Similarly, the impact of inflation on mortgage markets and housing finance systems is still not well understood. Although topics like alternative mortgage instruments have been extensively researched (e.g., Lessard and Modigliani Federal Home Loan Bank Board 1977), there are still significant gaps in knowledge of the instrument preferences of mortgage lenders and borrowers under conditions of high and variable interest rates. Why have borrowers been reluctant to adopt alternative designs for the residential mortgage? Further research is also necessary to examine how the financial intermediaries active in the mortgage market should evolve given turbulent capital markets and the foreseeable technological changes in our payments systems.

THE COMPARATIVE APPROACH: A DIGRESSION ON METHOD

In view of the major changes taking place today in North American society, the ability to assess these movements properly and cope with them in society is of pivotal importance. It is often difficult, however, to appreciate change from within an evolving system. New and fundamental insights into the behavior of the system and the dynamics of change can be gleaned by stepping back from the values, institutions, and culture of the society in question. This is precisely the strength of cross-national comparisons (Goldberg and Mercer 1980). By studying how two or more societies respond to similar changing circumstances, the analyst is in a position to generalize about the nature of change, not just in a single society but, more fundamentally, about how societies adapt to changing social, economic, political, and environmental conditions.

As one case in point for a cross-national perspective, high and variable inflation rates have meant that lenders are faced with significant interest-rate risk as well as with having their capital repaid in inflated (and therefore overvalued) dollars. As a response, lenders have sought new mortgage instruments to protect their capital and their profitability. To complicate matters, in the context of the U.S. mortgage market, institutional factors have historically limited the attractiveness of traditional passbook savings and have periodically put thrift institutions in illiquid positions. Elaborate institutional arrangements such as secondary mortgage markets have been developed in the United States to overcome these problems (e.g., Federal National Mortgage Association (FNMA) and Government National Mortgage Association (GNMA)).

An alternative route has been followed in Canada: simpler and less complicated institutional arrangements. The development of the rollover mortgage in Canada allowed financial institutions to match the term structure of their assets and liabilities and therefore hedge against adverse changes in interest rates. The ability of Canadian financial institutions to vary savings deposit rates as market forces dictate provides a simple and direct solution to the disintermediation problem faced by many U.S. thrift institutions. Thus two very different approaches to the related problems of interest-rate risk and liquidity are used in the two nations. Analysts in the United States could profit from studying the Canadian experience as they try to improve the efficiency of their own nation's mortgage markets.

Another virtue of comparative analysis can be seen in returning to the data in Tables I–1 and I–2. The broad observation that housing and mortgage markets were increasingly volatile over the 1970s masks some important differences. First, the Canadian housing market produced housing units at near record rates throughout most of the 1970s, experiencing dramatic growth since 1960. In contrast, the housing production system in the United States performed significantly better on average during the 1960's than it did during the 1970s. So two very different production profiles are apparent despite the fact that the Canadian and the U.S. economies were subjected to very similar forces during these two decades. Juxtaposing the performance of these two housing markets leads to a series of questions about deeper differences between the two economies and their housing markets. Probing beyond superficial similarities is necessary to get at the structural and dynamic properties of the systems in order to understand why these economies registered contrasting behavior.

To sum up, faced with growing uncertainty, change, and volatility in the housing and mortgage markets, analysts in both the United States and Canada need to enhance their understanding about the fundamental forces at work in these markets. The elucidation of common problems and issues faced by different social and economic systems provided by comparative work is great indeed. As the reader will see in the following set of papers which make up this book, there are some fundamental differences in the ways in which the United States and Canada have dealt with housing issues in the past, and there are some institutional and cultural reasons why future treatment will continue to be quite different. By understanding these differences we should be in a position to profit from the best and most appropriate responses of each system while avoiding many of the less effective and more inappropriate approaches.

REFERENCES

Altshuler, Alan. 1979. *The Urban Transportation System.*Cambridge, Mass. MIT Press.

Bourne, Larry S., and John R. Hitchcock, eds. 1978. *Urban Housing Markets: Recent Directions in Research and Policy.* Toronto: University of Toronto Press.

Canada Mortgage and Housing Corporation. *Canadian Housing Statistics.* Various years. Ottawa: Canada Mortgage and Housing Corporation.

de Leeuw, Frank, and Raymond Struyk. 1975. *The Web of Housing: Analyzing Policy with a Market Simulation Model.* Washington, D.C., The Urban Institute.

Department of Finance. *Economic Review.* Various Years. Ottawa: Department of Supply and Services.

Federal Home Loan Bank Board. 1977. *Alternative Mortgage Instruments Research Study,* volumes 1–3. Washington, D.C.

Goldberg, Michael A., and John Mercer. 1980. "Canadian and U.S. Cities: Basic Differences, Possible Explanations, and Their Meaning for Public Policy." In *Papers of the Regional Science Association* 45:159–183.

Ingram, Gregory K., ed. 1980. *The Economics of Residential Location and Urban Housing Markets.* New York: National Bureau of Economic Research.

Kain, John F. and William C. Apgar. 1977. "Simulation of the Market Effects of Housing Allowances, Volume II: Baseline and Policy Simulations for Pittsburgh and Chicago." City and Regional Planning Research Report R77-2, Harvard University, Cambridge, Mass.

Franco Modigliani, and Lessard, Donald R., eds. 1975. *New Mortgage Designs for Stable Housing in an Inflationary Environment.* Boston: Federal Reserve Bank of Boston.

Muth, Richard F. 1960. "The Demand for Non-Farm Housing." In *The Demand for Durable Goods,* pp.29-96. Edited by Arnold C. Harberger. Chicago: University of Chicago Press.

Solomon, Arthur P., ed. 1980. *The Prospective City.* Cambridge, Mass.: MIT Press.

Struyk, Raymond J.; Sue A. Marshall; and Larry J. Ozanne. 1978. *Housing Policies for the Urban Poor.* Washington, D.C.: The Urban Institute.

U.S. Department of Commerce, *Statistical Abstract of the U.S.* Various years. Washington D.C.: U.S. Government Printing Office.

U.S. Department of Housing and Urban Development, *HUD Trends.* Various Years. Washington D.C.: U.S. Government Printing Office.

DEMAND FOR HOUSING

Patterns of housing demand began to change dramatically during the 1970s, reflecting changing demographic structures and locational behaviors and preferences. At the societal level, the following demographic changes occurred in both the United States and Canada (and in most other western nations too, for that matter): declining fertility rates; delay of marriage; growth in the number of households composed of single parents and children, single individuals or unrelated individuals; the relative decline of the traditional family, comprising husband and wife and children living at home; rising divorce rates; the general aging of the North American population; and, finally, restrictions on legal immigration.

Whether or not these trends persist, increase in strength, or revert to the more traditional demographic patterns of the 1950s and 1960s obviously holds the key to the composition of housing demand in the remaining years of this century. These essentially behavioral issues interact closely with economic forces. Forecasting the stability of emerging patterns and forces is exceptionally difficult; yet without looking into the future, planners for the housing needs of North America's residents are at an enormous disadvantage.

Macrodemographic issues dominate all estimates of housing demand for the next several decades. They filter down to affect the next levels in the demand hierarchy: the spatial composition of housing demand among the major regions and urban areas of Canada and the United States and the spatial composition of housing demand within major metropolitan regions in both countries. The interregional flows of people and the intraurban distribution of housing preferences have enormous consequences for housing demand. To illustrate, even if there were absolutely no net population change across either the United States or Canada, the demand for housing still could be significant if the changing demographic and preference structures of the North American population favored different regions of the continent or different subareas within urban locations. The movements in the United States from the Frost Belt to the Sun Belt and from metropolitan to nonmetropolitan areas are examples of how changing preferences can have significant consequences both for the winners (growing need for infrastructure and services) and for the losers (maintaining fiscal stability in the face of declining revenue-raising capability).

The first four chapters of this book all consider these demographic and spatial questions for North America, although they approach the subjects in quite different ways. Philip Brown examines demographic trends in Canada and their implications for housing demand, whereas William Alonso analyzes the underlying socioeconomic factors influencing demographics and housing. Turning to spatial issues, Larry Bourne and Daniel Garnick explore the shifting patterns of population in Canada and the United States, respectively.

In Chapter 1, "The Demographic Future: Impacts on the Demand for Housing in Canada: 1981–2001," Philip Brown presents findings from a Canadian demographic and housing requirements projection model. The model developed by the Canada Mortgage and Housing Corporation (CMHC) is used to give projections of variables such as population, household formation, headship rates, and housing requirements by dwelling and tenure type. These forecasts suggest movements that will be less favorable to housing demand than in the past. Changes in the composition of housing demand are also anticipated, reflecting changes in the age structure of the population. To provide the reader with comparable demographic data for the United States, we have added an appendix at the end of the chapter with similar housing demand projections for that country.

Chapter 2, William Alonso's contribution, "The Demographic Factor in Housing for the Balance of This Century," provides a rich analysis of the principal demographic currents that influence the future directions of U.S. housing demand. Among the issues considered are compositional effects on household formation and housing demand, such as the passage of the baby boom crest across the years. Also examined are generational effects, the life-course behavior of different generations. Alonso also discusses the impact of declining populations on theoretical models of urban form that are premised on population growth.

The 1970s brought forth a number of challenges to conventional understanding of urban growth and population movements. Larry Bourne's "Living with Uncertainty: The Changing Spatial Components of Urban Growth and Housing Demand in Canada," Chapter 3, explores many long-term and short-term trends shaping the spatial structure of urban growth. He identifies the components and determinants of different urban growth patterns and population distributions in Canada, emphasizing disaggregating these components into their various spatial expressions and defining the complex web of relation among demographic, employment, and income growth within the urban system.

Long-term population and employment projections in the United States by region, state, metropolitan, and nonmetropolitan categories are reviewed by Daniel Garnick in Chapter 4, "U.S. Population Distribution into the Twenty-first Century." He presents recent forecasts, by the U.S. Bureau of Economic Analysis, of future population distribution and discusses the economic forces underlying these trends. He also considers the implications of technological changes on spatial patterns in the United States.

PP. 5-31

1 THE DEMOGRAPHIC FUTURE: Impacts on the Demand for Housing in Canada, 1981–2001

Philip W. Brown

Recent trends in Canada's population and household growth, housing markets, and residential construction industry have highlighted the importance of demographic factors to the performance of the housing sector and to the Canadian economy more generally. The "discovery" of these trends has been taken up by the media and by those segments of the economy most likely to be affected. Their existence is of course nothing new. The Canadian housing market offers a good example of the way in which the day-to-day operation of an economic system can obscure and conceal the importance of factors such as fertility, morality, and migration. In a boom period, when there is excess demand, a product's planning and construction proceed on the assumption that it can be sold to a consumer in the short run, often without explicit recognition that demand may decline as a result of demographic factors in the longer run. The trend in the residential construction industry until the middle of the 1970s was toward an ever-increasing supply of housing, fueled by a seemingly insatiable housing demand. From 92,500 housing starts in 1950, produc-

I wish to acknowledge the invaluable assistance of Anica Divic and Nicholas Waloff in the preparation of this chapter. The views expressed are mine and do not necessarily reflect the views of Canada Mortgage and Housing Corporation.

tion rose to 190,500 in 1970 and to an all time peak of 273,203 in 1976 (Figure 1–1).

With the continuing decline in housing starts since 1976, both industry participants and industry observers produced a plethora of economic explanations rather than demographic ones. Inflation, interest rates, energy costs, and declining productivity were among the causes of economic malaise cited. One effect was a reappraisal of Canada's demographic future in the context of limited or zero economic growth and its implications for long-term changes in housing requirements. Awareness of the impact of demographic factors came about as a result of nonhousing concerns. School closings because of decline in school enrollment is one example. The increasing preoccupation of geriatric and health care organizations with a looming elderly boom also resulted from a gradual realization that the baby boom contained within it the promise of a very different set of demographic conditions.

In order to explore the demographic future in Canada, the findings are presented here from a demographic and housing requirements projection model developed at Canada Mortgage and Housing Corporation (CMHC), the federal agency responsible for

Figure 1–1.   Dwelling Starts in Canada, 1960–1980 (Thousand Units)

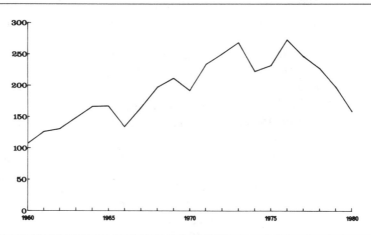

Source: Canadian Housing Statistics 1980: table 1.

housing, together with an assessment of their implications for housing demand. Constraints and caveats are attached to the model and to certain lacunae circumscribing its usefulness. Because the findings can be interpreted several ways, the views expressed in this chapter are offered as much to stimulate debate as to pinpoint specific trends and areas that should be considered in the development of policy recommendations.

Whatever interpretations are placed on these findings, there is little doubt that the demographic characteristics of the Canadian population and its households are changing and will produce a different set of housing requirements in the not too distant future. The prospects beyond 2001 are also explored, because it appears likely that the impact of trends in housing and social capital will be felt well beyond the turn of the century.

MODEL OVERVIEW AND RESULTS

The CMHC housing requirements model provides projections of population, households, and housing requirements at the provincial, metropolitan (Census Metropolitan Area), and major urban area (Census Agglomeration) levels. Population projections are made by five-year age and sex cohorts for the 1976 to 2001 period. The cohort census survival ratio method is used. Intercensal estimates are derived by linear intracohort interpolation. Household projections are made from 1976 to 2001 for all households and for both family and nonfamily households by age and sex groups. The headship rates are obtained by extrapolation using a modified exponential method. Housing requirements by age groups are calculated for each geographic area. Occupancy patterns by age, tenure, and family type are used to determine housing requirements. Since the projections are only as good as the assumptions upon which they are based, special attention will be given to the assumptions used. A more detailed explanation of the model is available elsewhere (Divic 1979, 1981).

The projection period, 1981–2001, will be characterized by declining population growth rates, a slowing down of metropolitan and urban concentration, declining rates of household formation, and an expanding elderly population, all of which have profound implications for housing demand in Canada.

Population Growth

A continuing decline in Canada's population growth rate is projected by the model, down 25 percent in terms of average annual growth rate over the twenty-year period. Canada is projected to enter the twenty-first century with 28.86 million inhabitants, an increase of 19 percent from 24.18 million estimated for 1981 (Table 1–1). Reasons behind this decline in growth include continuing low fertility rates, a slowing in survival rate increases, and lower levels of international immigration. The absolute volume and rate of growth of Canada's population will continue to be determined more by natural increase than by immigration.

The fertility rate is at an all time low for Canada.[1] In the absence of significant trend changes in the recent past, the model assumes that the 1978 rate will stay constant over the period. Although small fluctuations may occur, the anticipated increases in the participation rates of females in the labor force together with the fact that the fertility rate has already dropped below levels only previously anticipated by 1991 suggest that major shifts are unlikely in the future. This experience is supported by that of other western nations (Lavoie 1979). If natural increase does indeed remain the major source of population increase, identification of future rate changes and contributory factors will be even more critical to determining future projections.

The model also assumes that 1976 mortality levels will remain constant to 2001. Existing low rates and their slow rate of change imply that further reductions will likely be small or negligible (for a discussion of mortality rates and mortality projections see Gnanasekaran 1979). Improved medical knowledge and health

Table 1–1.   Population Projections for Canada, 1976–2001

Census Year	Population (thousands)	Average Annual Growth Rate
1976	22,992.6	1.29 (1971–1976 Actual)
1981	24,184.0	1.02 (1976–1981)
1986	25,405.5	0.99 (1981–1986)
1991	26,619.4	0.94 (1986–1991)
1996	27,784.5	0.86 (1991–1996)
2001	28,860.6	0.76 (1996–2001)

service advances may result in higher life expectancy levels and thus in a larger population than anticipated, however.

Of all the components of population growth in Canada, net immigration is perhaps the most difficult to project to 2001. Gross immigration to Canada has fluctuated widely since 1945 with no clear trends evident (Figure 1–2). Gross immigration has ranged from a high of 149,429 in 1976 to a low of 86,313 in 1978 and back up to 143,117 in 1980.[2] The large number of refugees admitted to Canada in 1979 and 1980 is also a recent development. Emigration from Canada is difficult to estimate since Canada does not keep an exit register or require exit visas or other controls. An assumption of 75,000 emigrants per year is currently used to derive estimates of net immigration (Employment and Immigration Canada 1981).

Based upon an assessment of recent immigration patterns (1976–1980) and of the federal government's planned immigration levels for the next three years (Employment and Immigration Canada 1981), international immigration is assumed to be a net 65,000

Figure 1–2. Gross Immigration to Canada, 1945–1980 (Thousands)

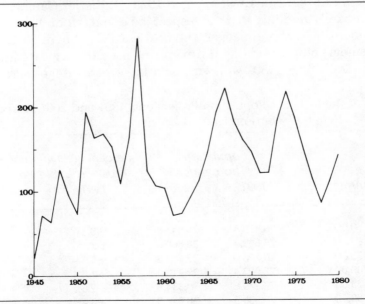

Source: Employment and Immigration Canada 1979.

people per annum over the next twenty years.[3] Unforeseen disruptions in the world situation notwithstanding, this assumption appears particularly appropriate for at least the medium terms in Canada. The characteristic volatility of international immigration, however, makes any longer term projection more tenuous.

Variation of the net immigration assumption clearly results in different population estimates. Table 1–2 presents population estimates for Canada for 1991 and 2001 based on various levels of average annual net international immigration. Depending upon the assumption employed, Canada's population in 2001 ranges from a low of 28.54 million to a high of 30.83 million. In terms of population growth, however, variation of the net immigration assumption could increase population growth in the 1981–1991 period by as much as 38 percent, and in the 1981–2001 period by as much as 42 percent.

Age Distribution of the Population

Canada is an aging country, as demographers have observed (Stone and MacLean 1979; Wargon 1979; Statistics Canada 1979). The model's findings in this respect bear out what has already been identified: the impact of the postwar baby boom on Canadian demographic trends as its members pass through middle age (Table 1–3). The 1980s will witness a large percentage increase in

Table 1–2.   Population Projections, 1991 and 2001, Based on a Range of Net Immigration Levels

Average Annual Net Immigration	Population (Thousands)		Percentage Difference from Most Probable Population	
	1991	2001	1991	2001
50,000	26,469.4	28,541.8	−0.6	−1.1
65,000	26,619.4	28,860.6	. . .	. . .
75,000	26,758.0	29,102.8	+0.5	+0.8
100,000	27,007.4	29,719.4	+1.5	+3.0
125,000	27,279.6	30,334.5	+2.5	+5.1
150,000	27,536.3	30,827.9	+3.4	+6.8

the number of 35– to 44-year-olds and those over 65, which will be followed in the 1990s by a large increase in the number of 45- to 54-year-olds and a smaller increase in the number of 55- to 64-year-olds. The rate of increase in the number of persons over 65 will, however, be lower in the 1991–2001 period than in the earlier decade. Declines in the number of people in the younger age groups are also expected over the period: a 21 percent decline in the 15- to 24-year-olds is projected for 1981–1991 and a similar 21 percent decline in the 25–34 age group for 1991-2001. The latter decline is in stark contrast to the 13 percent increase in numbers experienced by this age group in the previous decade. Looking at the percentage changes over the whole 1981–2001 period, the largest increases will be in the 45–54 age group (70 percent) followed by the 35–44 age group (65 percent) and the 65 + group (41 percent). By 2001, people under 14 and over 65 will form almost one-third of the entire population, the same percentage as estimated for 1981 (Table 1–3).

Taken in isolation these trends suggest some basic impacts upon housing demand for the period. Ignoring household formation rates, the fast growing numbers of middle aged imply that they will form the dominant market of the 1980s and 1990s and that attention will focus primarily on their predilections. The rise in the number of elderly suggests that greater consideration will have to be given to the provision of housing and associated health

Table 1–3. Projected Age Distribution, 1976–2001

Age Group	1976 No.	%	1981 No.	%	1991 No.	%	2001 No.	%	Percentage Change 1981–2001
0–14	5,896.2	25.6	5,479.3	22.7	5,832.5	21.9	6,274.5	21.7	+14.5
15–24	4,479.1	19.5	4,605.1	19.0	3,662.9	13.8	3,827.9	13.3	−16.9
25–34	3,620.5	15.7	4,271.4	17.7	4,830.4	18.1	3,815.8	13.2	−10.7
35–44	2,597.0	11.3	2,957.1	12.2	4,314.2	16.2	4,881.1	16.9	+65.1
45–54	2,473.1	10.8	2,468.9	10.2	2,864.6	10.8	4,197.6	14.5	+70.0
55–64	1,924.4	8.4	2,128.7	8.8	2,271.6	8.5	2,650.4	9.2	+24.5
65 +	2,002.3	8.7	2,273.4	9.4	2,843.2	10.7	3,213.4	11.1	+41.3
Total	22,992.6		24,183.9		26,619.4		28,860.7		+19.3

care appropriate to their needs. The smaller number of younger persons implies that there may be a shift away from child-oriented housing as resources are redeployed to meet the needs of aging consumers, particularly those whose disposable income is likely to be high during this period. Notable by its absence is any evidence of an impending second baby boom or boomlet. An echo effect from the postwar baby boom has long been awaited, but with depressed fertility rates, it does not appear to be materializing.

Looking beyond 2001, the wave effect as the baby boom cohorts move through the years will culminate in a large increase in retired persons after 2010 as they begin to reach age 65. By that date some 12 percent of Canada's population will be over 65; longer run projections suggest this proportion might rise to 17 percent in 2026 before starting to fall again. The predicted low fertility rates of the 1980s and 1990s will mean that this geriatric boom will be paralleled by a continuing dearth of children, barring any marked change in influencing factors. If the children from these decades do not restore their depleted numbers in the 2010s and 2020s by increases in fertility rates, this will certainly happen. The imbalance of the baby boom may well only work its way out by the 2030s and 2040s. If these trends continue, then deaths may exceed births and Canada may actually experience negative population growth toward the middle of the twenty-first century. In any event, mortalities will become a much more important component of change over the period 2010–2040.

Household Formation

The model identifies a number of distinctive trends affecting Canadian households over the next two decades. Age- and sex-specific headship rates by family type, from which future households are calculated, are estimated to increase overall by 14 percent over the period 1981–2001. The first decade displays a more rapid rate of increase than the second for all age groups, in large part a reflection of the model's use of modified exponential curves to estimate likely increases (Figure 1–3). The assumption is made that headship rates will increase but at a decreasing rate between now and the year 2001.

Figure 1–3.   Total Household Headship Rates, by Age Groups, for Canada 1976–2001

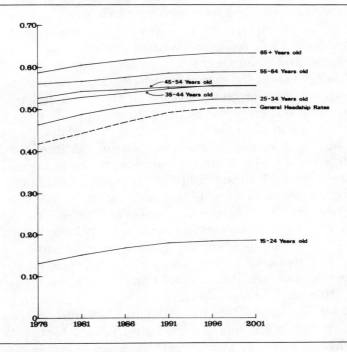

Source: Statistics Canada 1979.

By far the largest increase in headship rates over the period is estimated for the 15–24 age group at 25 percent, although by 2001 they will still be at only 30 to 35 percent of the rates for older groups. It has often been suggested that those under 25 may be particularly compelled to remain at the parental home for financial reasons in the future. This might suggest that the modest increases in headship rates assumed here may be optimistic. Indeed Miron's (1980) research on one-person households in Ontario led him to conclude that demographic factors alone could explain only one-third of these household formations during the period 1966–1976, and that the main contributing factor to household formation over this period was increasing affluence.

The male and female elderly combined have historically enjoyed high headship rates, and this trend is assumed to continue in the future. Whether it will continue into the next century will depend in part upon whether the members of the elderly boom will prefer to maintain independent households given financial ability to do so, will opt for congregate living in the face of high shelter costs, or will choose to live with younger relatives. The implications of these scenarios, which may be related as much to sociocultural and economic factors as demographic ones, are considered later. The experiences of the baby boom generation in living in single-person or group settings in the 1960s and 1970s may result in radical departures in either direction.

In terms of headship rates by family and nonfamily categories, the model's assumptions produce a 9 percent increase in the family headship rate and a 31 percent increase in the nonfamily headship rate between 1981 and 2001. By the year 2001, however, the nonfamily headship rate will still only be at 37 percent of the family rate, up from 30 percent in 1981. The rising number of separations and divorces together with a possible general increase in the desire for independent living on the part of seniors support this trend. Adverse economic conditions in the future may reduce the appeal of nonfamily household situations, however. Applying the headship rates to the population projections gives an estimate of 10.24 million households by 1991 and 11.39 million households by 2001, a 38 percent increase over 1981 (Table 1–4).

The average annual growth rate in households declines over the period although it is at all times in excess of the average annual growth rate in population. Family households are projected to increase by 31 percent over the 20-year period, while nonfamily households are projected to increase by 58 percent. Despite the large increase in the number of nonfamily households, 73 percent

Table 1–4.   Household Projections, 1976–2001

Census Year	Households (Thousands)	Average Annual Growth Rate
1976	7,166.1	3.40 (1971–1976 Actual)
1981	8,278.6	2.93 (1976–1981)
1986	9,329.7	2.42 (1981–1986)
1991	10,236.9	1.87 (1986–1991)
1996	10,895.0	1.25 (1991–1996)
2001	11,387.9	0.89 (1996–2001)

of all households in 2001 will still be family oriented, a reflection of the large number of people in the older age groups. Throughout the 1980s, therefore, the emphasis will be on households that are proceeding through the life cycle of childbearing, child rearing, and release. The impact of reduced numbers of young persons coming into the household formation age groups in the 2000s will perhaps tend to inhibit nonfamily household growth after that date, although this may be offset by the rising number of elderly.

Household size will also be affected by these trends: A continued decline is projected from an observed 3.2 persons per household in 1976 to 2.6 persons in 1991 and 2.5 persons in 2001, primarily due to the low fertility levels and the increasing proportion of nonfamily households.

Variation of the net immigration assumption results in different estimates of the number of households in Canada. Table 1–5 presents household estimates for Canada for 1991 and 2001 based on various levels of average annual net international immigration.

Depending upon the assumption employed, the number of Canadian households in 2001 ranges from a low of 11.26 million to a high of 12.15 million. In terms of household growth, however, variation of the net immigration assumption could increase household growth in the 1981–1991 period by a as much as 18 percent over the most probable estimate and in the 1981–2001 period by as much as 25 percent (Table 1–5).

Table 1–5.   Household Projections, 1991 and 2001, Based On a Range of Net Immigration Levels

Average Annual Net Immigration	Households (Thousands)		Percentage Difference from Most Probable Households	
	1991	2001	1991	2001
50,000	10,176.9	11,261.5	−0.6	−1.1
65,000	10,236.9	11,387.9	. . .	. . .
75,000	10,294.8	11,493.5	+0.6	+0.9
100,000	10,358.4	11,676.6	+1.2	+2.5
125,000	10,452.0	11,874.4	+2.1	+4.3
150,000	10,590.5	12,149.7	+3.5	+6.7

Housing Requirements

Total net addition to Canadian households per year provides an estimate of the total number of "new" houses required as a result of demographic change. Net yearly additions to households decline over the period from 210,000 in the 1981–1986 period to less than half that number in the 1996–2001 period. Quantitative housing requirements due to demographic factors alone will thus decline dramatically over the next 25 years.[4]

In order to estimate housing requirements by tenure and dwelling type for family and nonfamily households by age groups, the distinct occupancy patterns by unit type and tenure for different age and household types that existed in 1976 are calculated from the 1976 Canadian census and applied to the demographic projections. The assumption is made that while the nature of household growth over the projection period will change considerably, the distinct occupancy patterns that existed in 1976 will continue over the projection period (Table 1–6).

Existing values in Canada place a very high priority on homeownership, and it is generally assumed that current housing tenure preferences will continue into the foreseeable future. Whether the current high costs of homeownership will change these occupancy patterns to any considerable degree is a question that needs to be carefully monitored and analyzed as new data, such as the 1981 census, become available. Based on these assumptions,

Table 1–6. Propensity to Own and Rent by Age and Household Type, 1976

Age	Own			Rent		
	Family	Nonfamily	Total	Family	Nonfamily	Total
15–24	.274	.062	.190	.726	.938	.810
25–34	.586	.151	.516	.414	.849	.484
35–44	.753	.272	.709	.247	.728	.291
45–54	.795	.376	.743	.205	.624	.257
55–64	.789	.473	.719	.211	.527	.281
65+	.755	.493	.643	.245	.507	.357

Source: 1976 Census

the model predicts that requirements for ownership will drop by 41 percent over the period from 123,600 units per annum in 1981–1986 to 72,600 in 1996–2001 (Table 1–7). More dramatic is the 70 percent decline in rental requirements from 86,600 in 1981–1986 to a mere 26,000 in 1996–2001. Out of all housing requirements, however, the proportion of owner-occupied dwellings will increase from 59 percent to 74 percent. Rental housing requirements consequently decrease both relatively and absolutely.

As can be seen from Table 1–8, the 1980s are characterized by a large decline in requirements for owner and rental accommodation from the 15–24, 25–34, and 55–64 age groups. The most marked decline is from the 25–34 age group as it moves forward into the next cohort. This group has traditionally contained the bulk of the first-time homebuyers. The decline in both rental and owner requirements continues throughout the period for this age group although it appears to "bottom out" at the end of the century. The slight upturn in the 15–24 housing requirements after 1991 (primarily rental) may result in a subsequent turnaround in this group in the next century. It will likely be some considerable time, however, before either of these two age groups plays a major role in the Canadian housing market again. This is in sharp contrast to their importance during the 1970s. In comparison to the above two groups, the 55–64 age group, having experienced a decline in the 1980s, markedly increases its housing requirements in the last decade and shows the beginnings of a high upturn to 2001 and beyond.

Requirements for seniors will peak slightly in the 1986–1991 period before falling during the 1990s—a short-term decline before the 2000s. In the 1986–1991 period almost one-quarter of all housing requirements will be for households over age 65. In the 1980s the largest number of housing requirements will be for the 35–44 age group and in the 1990s for the 45–54 age group, again reflecting the baby boom passing through middle age.

Housing requirements by dwelling type reveal, not surprisingly, a declining demand for all types over the next 20 years. A 46 percent decline in requirements for ground-oriented housing is projected along with a 64 percent decline in apartment requirements.[5] Ground-oriented housing, however, increases its share of all requirements from 61 percent in the 1981–1986 period to 71 percent in 1996–2001. Within the ground-oriented housing cate-

Table 1–7. Average Annual Housing Requirements, by Tenure, Dwelling Type and Household Type, 1976–2001 (Thousands)

	1976–1981	%	1981–1986	%	1986–1991	%	1991–1996	%	1996–2001	%
Tenure										
Homeownership	118.5	53	123.6	59	117.4	65	93.9	71	72.6	74
Rental	104.0	47	86.6	41	64.0	35	37.7	29	26.0	26
Total	222.5	100	210.2	100	181.4	100	131.6	100	98.6	100
Dwelling type										
Single Housing	108.8	49	112.9	54	106.2	59	85.1	64	66.3	67
Semidetached	9.6	4	9.4	4	8.0	4	5.0	4	2.7	3
Row houses	7.2	3	7.0	3	5.5	3	2.6	2	0.9	1
Apartments	77.5	35	64.6	31	49.4	27	31.5	24	23.2	24
All other types	19.4	9	16.3	8	12.3	7	7.4	6	5.5	5
Total	222.5	100	210.2	100	181.4	100	131.6	100	98.6	100
Household type										
Family	142.3	64	135.7	65	118.0	65	84.5	64	58.0	59
Nonfamily	80.2	36	74.5	35	63.4	35	47.1	36	40.6	41
Total	222.5	100	210.2	100	181.4	100	131.6	100	98.6	100

Table 1–8.   Average Annual Housing Requirements, by Age of Household Head (Thousand Units)

Age Cohort	1981–1986	1986–1991	1991–1996	1996–2001
15–24	1.8	− 8.6	2.9	9.0
25–34	60.3	22.3	−44.0	−55.1
35–44	82.2	78.8	55.5	15.5
45–54	7.6	41.0	79.7	72.2
55–64	20.9	4.2	6.0	38.7
65+	37.4	43.7	31.5	18.3
	210.2	181.4	131.6	98.6

gory, the model predicts that by 1996–2001 requirements for single-detached houses will have risen to 95 percent of all units from 87 percent in the 1981–1986 period. The continuing strength of the attraction of single homes is in large measure a reflection of the large proportion of 35- to 54-year-old buyers on the market during the 1980s and 1990s and the fact that they will likely be moving to second or third homes. Whether the single-detached home will indeed increase its share of housing requirements as projected depends in large part on the relative attractiveness over the period of other house types, such as row houses and semidetached houses and high-rise condominiums, to the increasing number of older buyers. Beyond 2001 the retirement of very large numbers of elderly is likely to place different strains upon the market. The majority will likely be owner-occupants living in single-detached homes and fitting the description of overhoused "empty-nesters." The implications of this are discussed later.

IMPLICATIONS FOR HOUSING DEMAND

Although changes in any of the model's parameters will influence the projections to some extent, the unique age distribution of the population in 1981 ensures that the major trends already outlined will be irreversible and that a longer term perspective on the Canadian housing market is required in order to appreciate their effects. Some of the more obvious implications of these trends are as follows:

Existing Housing Stock Management

Housing requirements are often compared directly with new housing starts. This is not necessarily appropriate, however, as "new" units to satisfy requirements may be provided through the conversion of older homes to additional units, the conversion of nonresidential buildings such as churches or warehouses to residential use, and through the reclamation and rehabilitation of abandoned units. A major problem in ascertaining whether in fact housing requirements have been satisfied in the medium term is determining the net additions or net deletions to the stock provided through these means. Given the increasing importance attached to the renovation and modification of older buildings in Canada, the contribution that these processes make to changes in the existing housing stock is likely to increase.

If it is assumed that the quantitative housing requirements detailed here will be satisfied between now and the end of the century, then it is important to note that approximately 73 percent of Canada's housing stock in the year 2001 is already built. This observation supports the hypothesis that the near future will largely resemble the present and that the ramifications of the demographic changes over the next 20 years will to a large extent be worked out within the existing housing stock. It is not therefore unreasonable to assume that the housing choice in 20 years time will not be so very different from that in 1981.

By the early 2000s, however, the increase in numbers of elderly will mean that a sizable mismatch may well occur between their needs and the characteristics of the single-detached home. As a result, there may be a significant fall in demand for this type of housing. What type of response is made in the face of such a mismatch will clearly depend on the aspirations of the elderly and their income and asset situation in relation to the costs of running a home.

This situation may be exacerbated to some degree by the fact that 35 percent of the total housing stock will be over 40 years old in 2001, compared to 23 percent in 1981 (as estimated by CMHC). Houses of this vintage usually require upgrading of structure and major facilities. The aging of the housing stock in concert with the population could result in major investments being required in a large number of dwellings at a time when they do not meet the needs of the fastest growing segments of the population. Even though renovation and repair activity is increasing in Canada at the present time, it does not necessarily follow that the older renovated units of today will meet the presumably higher renovation standards of 2001. Even the stock in the 20–39 age group, built 1961–1981, may require modification and upgrading in the light of higher standards at that time.

Residential Mobility

Essential to the effective operation of the housing market is residential mobility which allows households to adjust their housing conditions to suit their changing needs: People move to form households, to select new residences, and to "move up" to bigger and better ones (Clark and Moore 1980). It is well known that mobility rates are higher for renters than for owners and that they also vary with age. The elderly homeowners are often the least mobile in society, staying many years in a house that may no longer suit their needs.

Given the trend toward an aging population, it is likely that average mobility rates will decline, thus restricting the flow of younger households among the existing housing stock. It is precisely because of low mobility rates among the elderly that a possible mismatch of dwellings and households after 2001 will occur. The inability of households to adjust their housing needs through residential mobility may well turn out to be a housing problem in its own right over the next 20 years.

It is also well known that a large number of residential moves within an area are initiated by the construction of new houses: A chain of moves as a result of new construction is said to occur (Sharpe 1978). Over the next 20 years the volume of new construction will be a much smaller percentage of the total housing stock. New housing starts as a percentage of total stock are projected to decline from 2.5 percent in 1981 to 0.9 percent in 2001. The contribution that new residential construction can make to residential mobility will thus be reduced significantly, households may be faced with restricted housing choices as a result.

Dwelling Size, Type, and Design

Suggestions are often made, particularly by the media, that declining household size and increasing housing costs are likely to result in a demand for smaller sized units. There is no doubt that the former two trends are occurring: Average household size in Canada is expected to fall from 3.2 persons per household in 1976 to 2.5 in 2001, and the costs of owning and running a home have been increasing rapidly for some time now. Projections indicate that the decline in household size is likely to lessen toward the end of the century, however. If this is the case, dwelling size may show much less of a decline than some observers would have us believe. Cost considerations will probably play a more important role than the demographic composition of the household in determining future dwelling size.

An increasing number of small units for nonfamily households will probably be supplied over the next 20 years, but even here minimum space standards exist that individuals are prepared to accept and indeed that are specified in local building codes. With respect to family housing, rising energy costs are frequently cited as being considerable for larger dwellings. Yet to date, residential construction companies have preferred to maximize energy efficiency within the constraints of existing house types and sizes. Player (1981) notes that with modern energy-conserving methods it is possible to achieve savings without reducing house size although, inevitably, cost factors enter into the ability of households to pay for this facility. It seems likely that the consumer will continue to support energy-conservation expenditures rather than reduce space expectations.

Dwelling types may similarly remain relatively constant over time. Housing requirements are strongly oriented toward existing dwelling types, particularly single-detached homes. Row and semidetached houses and high-rise condominiums may increase in popularity, however, especially in desirable locations such as the inner city. So far, conventional homes have been mass produced by the residential construction industry without much concern for longer term needs. On the other hand, it is unlikely that radically different dwelling types will prove attractive to consumers who are essentially conservative and whose propensity to replicate previous expectations is high. The question still remains whether the type of units produced over the next 20 years may be inappropriate for household needs in the twenty-first century.

Dwelling designs are likely to change over the next two decades in response to demographic and life-style shifts. Design changes will be facilitated by the nature of wood frame construction, which lends itself to adaptation in this regard. In response to the baby boom there have been alterations in design such as his-and-her studies, recreation rooms, and dens. Further adaptations include, for example, studios located off the master bedroom ("Single Family Housing in the 80's" 1981). Such adaptations are likely to continue in the future. The decline in the number of younger persons living at home has led to a reduction in the number of bedrooms and the consequent labeling of space for other functions. The number of two- and one-bedroom houses will therefore increase in the future. The concept of the single-family home is thus likely to be challenged over the next 20 years.

The Future of the Rental Market

The major problem area of the 1980s and 1990s will almost certainly be the rental market. Rental housing requirements are projected to decrease from 86,600 per annum in 1981–1986 to 26,000 in 1996–2001, a drop of 70 percent. Although the demographics project a large decrease in rental requirements, comparative costs of owning and renting may well serve to ameliorate this situation. Wellman (1981), for example, asserts that homeownership has often been viewed as a means of holding one's shelter costs relatively constant rather than paying gradually increasing rents. Fluctuations in interest rates and rapidly rising energy costs have removed much of the sense of security that comes with ownership. Households in rental accommodation, especially if it is rent controlled, are relatively insulated from these economic uncertainties. In addition, the costs of owning and running a home have increased so much more rapidly than rents over the last five years. The gap between the two has widened considerably, thus making it more difficult for renters to achieve homeownership status. Lower and middle income potential housebuyers may be faced with a situation in which entry into the housing market is not feasible. As a result a pent-up demand may inflate the figures postulated by the model for housing requirements in the rental sector. It is unlikely, however, that these economic factors will outweigh the implications of the demographic trends.

As rental housing requirements decline over the next two decades, the market for the limited number of units that will be produced will also be changing. In the period 1976–1981, 41 percent of rental requirements were for households in the 25–34 age group. In 1986–1991 this group will require only 19 percent of all rental requirements, whereas households in the 35–44 and 45–54 age groups will require 39 percent and 19 percent respectively. In 1996–2001 almost all the rental requirements are for the 45–64 age group. This change in market has considerable implications for the type of rental accommodation provided and the services that they offer.

Life-styles of the Baby Boom

It will have become evident that the phenomenon of the baby boom is and will be responsible for dramatic changes in Canada's demographic trends. One feature of this boom that has attracted much speculation is the preferred life-style and resulting consumption patterns of this major consumer group.

The question of levels of expectation is critical. It has frequently been suggested that the baby boom generation displays highly hedonistic, individualistic values in spite of what has been termed a strong "caring" component. The buoyant economies of the 1950s, 1960s, and early 1970s created a generation of consumers anticipating ever-increasing standards and availability, of products and services whose expectations have been compounded by higher education levels and job and income expectations. By the time this generation faces retirement, the strain upon the national economy of pension provision may be considerable unless expectations with respect to living standards are reduced or people continue to work after 65.

Realization that erosion of expectations is imminent or threatened may result in a search for means to curtail household expenditures besides the usual steps to increase income. In this connection the possibility of other forms of housing tenure in addition to conventional ownership or rental may become the subject of increased interest. The third or nonprofit sector may become a particularly attractive vehicle for curbing the uncertainty inherent in shelter costs over the next two decades and beyond. It has the advantages of homeownership security and private rental flexibility together with the prospects of containment of servicing and utility charges. An upsurge of interest in cooperatives and nonprofit housing corporations may occur—over the remainder of the twentieth century as "inflation psychology" becomes endemic.

The life-styles of the baby boom generation will inevitably leave a legacy to those following, both in terms of values and housing forms. The single homes already referred to that will likely be built over the next 20 years will probably feature unprecedented standards of luxury, convenience, and comfort. By 2001, an "exclusive" pool of housing may well exist for which demand is lacking in the 2000s.

SUMMARY AND EVALUATION

In the next 20 years housing requirements and housing demand will most likely be considerably lower than in previous decades. This decline will be accentuated toward 2001 and will clearly have profound implications for the residential construction industry. The onset of the twenty-first century, however, will see an upsurge in housing requirements in specific age sectors and for different forms of housing. By conventional standards, the term "crisis" would be much more appropriate for the year 2001 and onward, judged by sheer magnitude and duration.

Although strategies to accommodate the changing demographic trends are clearly necessary, it would be inappropriate to adopt them as if they were written in stone. One of the major problems with projecting the long-term future is the large impact that small changes in model parameters may have on the end results. Sensitivity analysis is useful in assessing the possible variance in demographic projections, but only through the continuous updating of the model's parameters, as new data become available, will the projections be able to incorporate the most recent trends. Four major areas deserve careful scrutiny.

The first concerns the propensity to own by the elderly: The model assumes that this will stay at its present high level. In many cases this tendency has been the consequence of entry into and continuance in the ownership market under very different conditions than those pertaining today. When the elderly are faced with rapidly rising utility and maintenance costs and rising property taxes and with increasing pressures on overall disposable income, their propensity to own homes may decline, perhaps considerably. The result might be a substantial upturn in the appeal of the rental sector to the elderly and a substantial increase in rental demand over and above that predicted by the model. On the other hand, removal of rent controls may negate such a change.

Another possibility is that the model has overestimated the ownership propensities of the 25- to 34-year-olds and 35- to 44-year olds. Causes of a decline in the propensity to own might include, as discussed previously, a continued escalation of interest rates, house prices, and utility costs. Again, the existence and demonstration of viable alternatives such as nonprofit forms of housing might lead to a realization that other options exist besides conventional tenure types. The performance of Canada's economy and the rate of growth of real disposable income will obviously have a critical bearing upon any such changes insofar as people accept thresholds beyond which they are not prepared to allocate funds for shelter costs. The circumstances and dimensions of the affordability issue are thus of great relevance to the directions that might be taken vis-á-vis homeownership propensities. As mentioned previously, a downturn in the propensity to own could offset to some degree the projected decline in rental housing requirements.

On the demographic side, an increase in the fertility rate could have a major impact upon housing demand toward the end of the century and upon household size as of now. If a gradual increase occurred, housing demand from first-time homebuyers in the 2000s might be considerably inflated.

Finally, the unknown factor over the next two decades is international immigration. Although a lower level of international immigration has been assumed in this model compared to previous projections, this area is particularly prone to intervention and is indeed primarily under government control. A scenario in which immigration might increase considerably in the face of an economic upturn to provide an enlarged skilled work force could be postulated. This in turn would likely have effects upon the fertility rate in that immigrants tend to be in the reproductive age groups destined for the work force. This could reduce the decline in the proportion of younger persons in the 1990s and 2000s. Another perhaps more likely scenario is that of a large increase in the number of people admitted to Canada on social and humanitarian grounds in the face of world unrest. It is unlikely, however, that we will see levels of immigration such as those achieved in the late fifties and sixties.

Instead of the growth anticipated during the sixties and early seventies, the focus of activity in the eighties and nineties will be reoriented toward modest changes in the status quo and to the allocation and reallocation of limited resources. These will be far smaller in scale and importance prior to 2001 than after that date. The period, as some observers have commented, may be regarded as a breathing space before the demographic upheaval of the 2000s.

Appendix 1A.
Projections of U.S. Population and Housing
Consumption: 1980–2000

There is no shortage of alternative estimates of U.S. population and housing demand over the coming two decades (e.g.: Jones 1972; Sternlieb and Burchell 1978; and U.S. Bureau of the Census 1979). The projections included in this appendix are chosen on three grounds: their recency, the technique used to generate them, and their comparability to the Canadian estimates in the foregoing chapter.

The forecasts that appear in Table 1A–1 are taken from Pitkin and Masnick (1980). Pitkin and Masnick employ a new methodology to develop their estimates of future housing demand, an approach that directly relates housing consumption by dwelling size and tenure type to age cohorts and then follows these cohorts (and their resulting housing consumption patterns) through time. Because of the flexibility of their technique and the wide range of assumptions that it can consider, a great diversity of forecasts is

Table A1–1. Summary of Projections of U.S. Population and Housing Consumption, 1980–2000

	Total Households	Tenure		Structure Type			
		Owners	Renters	Mobile	1-Family	2- to 4-Family	5 + Family
All Households (thousands)							
1975	72,482	46,894	25,588	3,368	49,737	8,901	10,510
1980	79,114	50,535	28,578	4,188	52,346	9,990	12,623
1985	86,338	55,052	31,286	5,049	55,830	10,862	14,628
1990	92,717	59,468	33,249	5,818	59,099	11,368	16,461
1995	97,513	63,546	33,967	6,557	61,839	11,578	17,568
2000	101,697	67,275	34,423	7,301	64,284	11,688	18,455
Percentage							
1975	100.0	64.7	35.3	4.6	68.6	12.3	14.5
1980	100.0	63.9	36.1	5.3	66.2	12.6	16.0
1985	100.0	63.8	36.2	5.8	64.7	12.6	16.9
1990	100.0	64.1	35.9	6.3	63.7	12.3	17.8
1995	100.0	65.2	34.8	6.7	63.4	11.9	18.0
2000	100.0	66.2	33.8	7.2	63.2	11.5	18.1
Five-year change (thousands)							
1975–1980	6,632	3,641	2,990	820	2,609	1,089	2,113
1980–1985	7,225	4,517	2,708	861	3,484	872	2,005
1985–1990	6,379	4,417	1,962	769	3,269	506	1,653
1990–1995	4,796	4,077	719	739	2,739	210	1,107
1995–2000	4,184	3,729	456	744	2,446	110	887
Five-year change (%)							
1975–1980	9.1	7.8	11.7	24.3	5.2	12.2	20.1
1980–1985	9.1	8.9	9.5	20.6	6.7	8.7	15.9
1985–1990	7.4	8.0	6.3	15.2	5.9	4.7	12.5
1990–1995	5.2	6.9	2.2	12.7	4.6	1.8	6.7
1995–2000	4.3	5.9	1.3	11.3	4.0	0.9	5.0

Source: Pitkin and Masnick 1980: table 1.3

possible. Reproduced here is a middle-range projection predicated on a total fertility rate of 1.8 births per woman and extrapolation to the year 2000 of cohort housing choice trends typical of the 1960–1970 period. The estimates should provide a reasonable basis for comparison with the Canadian projections in Table 1–7.

Some similarities are immediately apparent in the trends exhibited by these projections for Canada and the United States. First, the early 1980s are seen as being the peaks in both countries for increases in housing demand, with sharp drops expected in the 1990s. Second, homeownership rates are expected to climb steeply over the next 20 years across North America, with nearly 90 percent of the projected rise of housing consumption in the United States forecasted to be in the owner-occupied category by the closing years of the century. This figure compares with an estimate of roughly 73 percent owner-occupied housing for the 1966–2001 period in Canada.

Turning to some of the significant differences in the housing trends between the two countries, projected housing requirements relating to structure type contrast markedly. In the United States single-family homes constitute the vast bulk of housing demand over the next two decades, starting at 68.6 percent of all structures in 1975 and falling to 63.2 percent in 2000. In contrast, single-family housing is only 49 percent of the housing requirement in Canada during the 1976–1981 period and then rises sharply to 67 percent of the 1996–2001 housing demand. This trend is paralleled by a decline in apartment demand in Canada from 35 percent in 1976–1981 to only 24 percent in 1996–2001, while U.S. demand for multifamily housing (five or more units) rises from 14.5 percent in 1975 to 18.1 percent in 2001. Thus, over the next two decades preferences in the United States are expected to shift only marginally, whereas rather striking changes in structure-type choices are envisioned in Canada.

NOTES

1. The total fertility rate in Canada was 1.76 in 1978, the year for which most recent data are available. In contrast, the total fertility rate in 1956 was 3.86.

2. Gross immigration to Canada in 1981 was expected to be approximately 122,000 (Employment and Immigration Canada 1981).
3. The federal government announced gross immigration levels of 130,000 to 135,000 for 1982, 134,000 to 144,000 for 1983, and 130,000 to 145,000 for 1984 (Employment and Immigration Canada 1981).
4. The model does not attempt to estimate or project either the number of dwellings required to compensate for net stock losses due to conversion, abandonment, or demolition or the number of dwellings required to maintain a satisfactory vacancy level. No assumptions are therefore made about the existing housing stock.
5. Ground-oriented housing includes single-detached, semidetached, and double houses and row houses.

REFERENCES

Canada Mortgage and Housing Corporation, 1980. *Statistics.* Ottawa: Canada Mortgage & Housing Corporation. Table 1, p.1.

Clark, W.A.V., and E.G. Moore, eds. 1980. *Residential Mobility and Public Policy.* Urban Affairs Annual Reviews, vol. 19. Beverly Hills: Sage Publication.

Divic, A. 1979. *Population, Households and Housing Requirements for the Census Metropolitan Areas of Canada, 1971–2001.* Ottawa: Program and Market Requirements Division, Central Mortgage and Housing Corporation.

———. 1981. *Population, Households and Housing Requirements Projections for Canada, the Provinces and the Census Metropolitan Areas, 1976 –2001.* Ottawa: Market Forecasts and Analysis Division, Canada Mortgage and Housing Corporation.

Employment and Immigration Canada, 1979. *Immigration Statistics.* Cat. WH-5-006. Ottawa.

———. 1981. *Annual Report to Parliament on Immigration Levels, 1982.* Cat. WH-5-019. Ottawa.

Gnanasekaran, K.S. 1979. "Revised Mortality Projections for Canada and the Provinces, 1971–1986." Unpublished paper, Population Estimates and Projections Division, Statistics Canada, Ottawa.

Jones, D. 1972. "Projections of Housing Demand to the Year 2000 Using Two Population Projections." In *Economic Aspects of Population Change,* vol. 2. Washington, D.C.: U.S. Government Printing Office.

Lavoie, Y. 1979. "Fertility Projections for Canada and the Provinces, 1976 –1991." Unpublished paper, Population Estimates and Projections Division, Statistics Canada, Ottawa.

Miron, J.R. 1980. "The Rise of the One-Person Household: The Ontario Experience, 1951–1976." Research Paper 116, Centre for Urban and Community Studies, University of Toronto.

Pitkin, J., and G. Masnick. 1980. *Projections of Housing Consumption in the U.S., 1980 to 2000, by a Cohort Method.* Washington, D.C.: U.S. Department of Housing and Urban Development.

Player, R.A. 1981. "Is There Scope for Further Innovation in Housing Energy Efficiency?" Notes prepared for the All Sector National Housing Conference, Ottawa.

"Single Family Housing in the 80's. Target Marketing with the New Demographics." 1981. *Canadian Building* 31,213 –17.

Sharpe, C.A. 1978. "Vacancy Chains and Housing Market Research." Research Note 3, Department of Geography, Memorial University of Newfoundland.

Statistics Canada. 1979. *Canada's Elderly.* Cat. 98 –800. Ottawa: Census Characteristics Division.

Sternlieb, G., and R.W. Burchell. 1978. *Multifamily Housing Demand: 1975–2000.* Washington, D.C.: U.S. Congress Joint Economic Committee.

Stone, L.O., and MacLean, M.J. 1979. *Future Income Prospects for Canada's Senior Citizens.* Institute for Research on Public Policy. Toronto: Butterworth.

U.S. Bureau of the Census. 1979. "Projections of the Number of Households and Families: 1979 to 1995." *Current Population Reports,* Series P–25, No. 805. Washington, D.C.: U.S. Government Printing Office.

Wargon, S.T. 1979. *Canadian Households and Families: Recent Demographic Trends.* Cat. 99-753. Ottawa: Census Analytical Study, Statistics Canada.

Wellman, A. 1981. "The Outlook for Rental Markets in the 1980's". Paper prepared for the All Sector National Housing Conference, Ottawa, March.

2 THE DEMOGRAPHIC FACTOR IN HOUSING FOR THE BALANCE OF THIS CENTURY

William Alonso

Traditionally, demography has been viewed as the basic provider of numbers for estimating future housing demand. In the simplest case the demand for housing rises in simple proportion to population. In slightly more sophisticated approaches such Factors as the age distribution of the population and trends in headship rates are taken into account.

It is not uncommon to find such an approach used to determine housing needs over some projected period. The number of people or of households is projected, then converted to some quantitative objective, in terms of total housing needed (dwelling units in some countries, square meters in others). The difference between this needed total and the present housing stock (sometimes adjusted for demolitions and other expected losses) is taken as a measure of housing demand into the future or as a target for housing policy.

Sketched in this chapter are some of the complexities beyond this simple view. The observations apply, in one or another form, to all of the developed countries, but they are based on the country I know best, the United States. The first topic is the three principal demographic currents at play in these countries, with some comments on their geographic aspects. The second topic is the implicit assumptions of the major working theories of housing and urban

33

form, which no longer hold and thus necessitate both new theory and applied research. The possibility of a new baby boom and its housing consequences are discussed next and finally, some observations and opinions are offered on demographics and housing.

PRINCIPAL DEMOGRAPHIC CURRENTS

Although demography is not necessarily destiny for housing, a review of the principal demographic currents for the direction of their effects is worthwhile. There are three principal purely demographic currents: (1) a complex of female roles, family, and fertility, which I will call the *family factor*; (2) the *age factor*, which includes the rising number of old people, the diminishing number of children, and the march of the baby boom generation across recent and future history; and (3) the *migration factor,* which includes international refugees and illegal immigrants, as well as internal migration among central cities, suburbs, and nonmetropolitan areas, and among regions within the United States.

The Family Factor

By the *family factor* I mean the changes in the ways in which people organize themselves into households and their reproductive behavior. These have been changing, as we all know. The traditional family is becoming less dominant and less permanent, as marriage is postponed, divorce rises, fertility drops, and living alone or in nontraditional households becomes more common.

At the root of this change is the need of advanced societies to rationalize and make efficient their use of resources, including people. In sociological terms, there is a shift from ascribed to achieved status. In economic terms, some market imperfections are reduced and the economy becomes more integrated.

Simply put, it is in the end irrational and inefficient to categorize workers by gender or other criteria (such as race, religion, or sexual preference) rather than by what they can do. And so advanced societies integrate. Obviously this integration is not complete or perfect; women and minorities are paid less, are subject to discriminatory behavior, and so on. But the general trend, in mores, law, and institutional practices, is in the direction of integration and away from ascribed statuses. This integrative drive has deep effects throughout society, but for the purpose at hand I will focus on one: the changing situation of women and some of its consequences.

Women have been joining the labor force at an extraordinary rate for the past quarter-century. This has been the result both of the integrative drive and of the shift to a postindustrial sectoral composition, which specializes in occupations that have been traditionally female.

As women have come to be wage earners, they have left behind their position as socially defined dependents on men. As they earn their own paychecks they break the pattern that made them economically dependent, first on the father and later on the husband. As this independence grows, so do the options of life-style and life course. Marriage can be postponed because it is a personal decision, not an economic necessity; it can also be broken, through divorce, because the separating parties are self-sufficient. Further along in this spirit, marriage as a contract becomes less important as its clauses become less binding. And so more consensual unions are made and broken, because the partners rightly regard them pragmatically: Will they work, and if they do, for how long?

If women can choose to be something else than daughters first and then wives and mothers, it stands to reason that many will exercise these options. Moreover, the obligations of men have been the other side of the coin to the dependency of women. As women gain their independence so do men, because of the mutuality of the relationship. And so marriage rates will slow down and divorce and singleness will rise. Fertility will drop because, as alternatives increase, the opportunity cost of having children rises.

The results on housing of these changes in the family factor are many and well known by now. I will mention only a few:

- Headship rates have risen for all groups of the population and this, together with the sharp decline in fertility, has reduced markedly the average size of households. Thus even where population has been declining (an increasingly common phenomenon), the number of households has been rising.

- Although I have not seen data on this, it stands to reason that the real investment and housing space per capita must have risen faster yet. Even a small unit for one of two persons typically has, in western societies, bathroom, kitchen, circulation space, and these do not rise proportionally with the number of people in the unit.
- As the number of nontraditional households increases, the structure of the demand for housing changes. Yards for children become less important, for instance. Time becomes a scarcer commodity in households where every grownup is employed. One may expect an increasing substitution of capital for labor, in the form not only of machinery such as dishwashers but also in the form of household inventory of semidurables and of the purchase of goods embodying prior preparation. Housing sizes and design must accommodate these.
- As people change their household affiliation and composition more frequently, new forms of tenure become common. The scarcity of time in the fully employed household would pull in the direction of apartment living, where upkeep demands on the householder's time are reduced by the nature of the unit and the institutionalization of several of these functions. However, the financial attractiveness of owning, particularly in these inflationary times, is such that the popularity of the condominium becomes quite an understandable response.
- Location preferences are also likely to change. Not only are there two journeys to work in an increasing proportion of households, but other factors change in importance as well. In childless homes the quality and racial composition of the schools play no role. Many of the middle class find central-city housing attractive both in price and location, convenient to services and entertainment—thus the rising wave of gentrification.

The Age Factor

The age of the populace is changing for three reasons: the rise in the elderly population, the progress of the baby boom generation across history, and the decline in the number of children. Let us consider these briefly in reverse order.

The effects of childlessness on locational preferences have already been mentioned. Having no children or few obviously also affects such matters as the number of bedrooms wanted and the disposition of discretionary income by the household. One may also note that it is not only the number of children born in a lifetime that is in question but also the timing; although timing and spacing are tricky matters, it may be said in summary that childbearing is being delayed more than before. This should also affect the demand for housing both through the differences in equity position of older parents and because attitudes and preferences change with age.

The rise in the elderly population reflects primarily the extended life expectancy at later ages, as well as the size of the cohorts born 60 or 65 years ago. For the balance of this century it will be the parents of the baby boom generation who will be entering this category. They were the ones who populated the suburban explosion in metropolitan areas. Their choices and their actions over the coming years, as their children leave home and later as they retire, will greatly determine the availability to the younger population of the vast stock of housing they built and occupy. Clearly it would be wise to develop policies and instruments that will avoid trapping them in their present housing and that can provide them with other options. Otherwise they will continue to occupy and underutilize a very substantial portion of the housing stock, precluding its use by younger households, at considerable expense and inconvenience to themselves.

The big story in age composition is, of course, the baby boom generation. Although any choice of cut-off dates for the boom is necessarily arbitrary, let me set them from 1947 to 1971, the last year in which the total fertility rate was above replacement in the United States. This generation in 1980 ranged in age from nine years old to thirty-three and at the turn of the century will range from twenty-nine to fifty-three. It was the rearing and schooling of this generation that led to the suburban explosion of the 1950s and 1960s. Because this generation is so very large and diverse in its life-styles, as it comes of the age of household formation it can contribute to gentrification, suburbanization, and migration to nonmetropolitan areas all at the same time. But clearly its commitment to early monogamy and sustained childbearing is less than that of its parents, and so the composition of its housing demand will be different. Virtually all discussions of the baby boom are focused exclusively on the white population. By most criteria, however, the boom was even more marked among blacks, who were then moving from rural areas to central cities and definitely not suburbanizing. The reason for the black baby boom is even more uncertain than that for whites and its consequences less explored.

As the baby boom generation makes its way into the housing market it is bound to jostle other groups. There is already concern about displacement of minorities and working class people in the central cities as a result of gentrification. One may construct several scenarios as to what may happen as this generation ages and a larger proportion starts to form families and look for single-family suburban housing, which is presently occupied (and underutilized) by their parents' generation. This competition will be made more severe by the high price of housing, high interest rates, and the unavailability of buildable land in many places. Sometime early in the next millenium, this giant generation will begin to enter the elderly category and will undoubtedly have further strong effects on housing at the same time that it brings about a crisis in the Social Security System.

The Migration Factor

Migration plays an important demographic role as well. To suburbanization, gentrification, and migration out of metropolitan areas should be added the continuing urbanization of the Old South and the migration to the Sun Belt. Although each of these is a fascinating and important phenomenon of relevance to housing, I will concentrate instead on international migration into the United States.

In the 1980s the issue of immigration has achieved a public prominence comparable to that of the great political debate on this subject earlier in this century. Refugees and illegals dominate the image of immigrants, and the total flow into the United States may at this moment be larger than the rate of natural increase. Although numerical estimates of stocks and flows vary by as much as one order of magnitudes, this issue has begun to capture national attention and promises to grow in importance.

It is necessary to step back a little to understand this process, a common one among the more industrially advanced countries, although in differing forms. Just as changes in the family are a consequence of the internal integrative logic of advanced societies, so this migration is the result of the unequal development or dualism of the advanced countries with respect to poorer ones. It is a curious contradiction that, while advanced societies progress internally toward integration, contradictorally their international position creates a new internal dualism, in the form of these new immigrants.

It will be useful to distinguish between economic migrants and refugees, although in practice the line is often blurred. Economic migrants come, in part spontaneously and in part through recruitment by the host country, as a form of cheap and docile labor, to fill positions that are unattractive to the native labor force. In this sense immigrants may be considered the complement of native workers, filling the meanest and lowest paid jobs. In addition to this structural aspect, there sometimes is a cyclical one as well (most explicitly in Northern Europe) whereby the host country in effect tries to export its cyclical unemployment to the poorer countries. In practice, however, many of these migrants and their children become permanent residents, with legal rights including those of family completion, which in the end may account for more immigrants than the original arrivals.

Refugees are a different expression of the international dualism. Those advanced countries whose geopolitics have led them to establish international empires are faced with the periodic collapse of one or another province. This generates waves of refugees, most dramatically of boat people (Vietnamese, Cuban) but more commonly (if numerically fewer) of members of client elites from these countries. The occurrence of any one wave may be difficult to predict, but they are stochastically quite certain. Thus the United States has received Indochinese, Cubans, Iranians, Salvadorans, Haitians, and more and may look forward in the future to receiving Philipinos, Chinese from Taiwan, and sundry others.

Obviously this immigration, of both types, has enormous repercussions at both the economic and the political level. The current levels of immigration are as great as those of the great European immigration earlier in this century, although they are lower in rate because of the larger base of the native population.

Three aspects of this immigration merit special attention. First, most of these migrants are rural in origin, and therefore we are witnessing the third great rural-to-urban migration (the European immigration peaked in the first decade of this century; the second, domestic immigration, principally black, peaked simultaneously with the baby boom). The second aspect of note is that most of the recent immigrants are colored according to American cultural perceptions: mulatto, mestizo, or Asian. Third, a majority of the immigrants are Hispanic in culture.

These facts should be cause for alarm that history will be allowed to repeat itself. Will we witness once again the formation of slums, with their burden of discrimination, exploitation, poverty, crime, disease, and racism? Will class conflict once again express itself as ethnic conflict; will those nearest and thereby most threatened by the new immigrants express themselves through riots, such as the black riots in Liberty City, Miami, in 1980 or the Irish riots in New York more than one century ago? Will racism, both redneck and scientistic, find expression both in everyday life and in local and national politics? Social attitudes and economic interests, often misguided, will express themselves, to our common grief. The beginnings can already be seen.

What have we learned, in housing as in other areas, that might help us to avoid repeating the social tragedy of the other great urbanizing migrations? What policies can help us avoid the ghetto and the formation of a new underclass? Even if mere self-interet is involved, how can those among us who are privileged avert this social trauma for ourselves and for our children?

THEORIES AND ISSUES

Two further issues on the interaction of demographics and housing are important: the role of demographic growth and decline in housing theory, and fertility and housing.

The Role of Demographic Growth and Decline in Housing Theory

How applicable are existing theories under new regimes? Two workhorses of theory in housing and urban form have been the filtering theory and the concentric theory. These theories have evolved and been refined, to be sure, into later models of considerable sophistication, but their essential insights have proved remarkably durable. This is probably because they are easy to grasp and partly true, at least under certain circumstances.

Their steadfastness is manifested in many ways. Elaborate econometric models of vintages, reinvestment, and disinvestment only dot the *i*s and cross the *t*s of the basic idea of housing markets that operate by building new houses for the rich, with filtering of the older stock down the economic ladder. The powerful grasp of Earnest Burgess's concentric image of urban areas across more than a half-century is stunningly attested to by the way geographic statistics are used for both analysis and policy: The world consists of central cities, their suburban complement in metropolitan areas, and a residual category of nonmetropolitan areas; this in spite of a common awareness of how poorly this simple geometry describes the patterns of today.

Of course, the explanatory (as opposed to the morphological) side of Burgess's concentric theory is merely the spatial expression of the filtering theory of housing markets. The center is filled, so new housing can be built only at the rural edge. The rich are those who can build and want new housing, and so they live in the outer reaches of the urban area; their hand-me-downs filter down the socioeconomic ladder in ripples that reach to the inner areas of the central city.

Clearly these twin theories are neither quite untrue nor a full description of what happens. Complications and exceptions not withstanding, the explanatory mechanism of these theories is based on some unstated relation of various rates: the rate of population growth, the rates of physical and economic depreciation, the size of various socioeconomic classes and household types, and the rate of social mobility among them. The great chain of being in both these theories is based on the balance among various rates in the system. In this sense they are identical in logic to the stable rate systems of demographers and ecologists. Because of the dependence of these theories on the continuity and specific levels of these rates, I suggested nearly two decades ago that they be termed *historical* (Alonso 1964).

The question now is: what happens if important changes occur in these rates? What happens, for instance, if there is a slowdown of entrants at the bottom to soak up the last drops from the filter

... of if the income distribution is changed; or if social processes change the structure of preferences, so that newness is prized less, antiquity more, grounds less, accessibility more. And, most crucially, what happens if the rate of population growth (or, more strictly, household growth) slows down? Who then will pay for the used dwellings, enabling the well-off to trade up to new ones?

Whether or not life-styles and tastes are changing, whether or not income distribution is changing, what is clear is that in a great many housing markets the rate of population growth has changed from positive to negative. For the first time in modern history the population of entire metropolitan areas (principally the largest) is shrinking in absolute terms. This is partly from outmigration but largely from a decline in fertility.

Great publicity has been given to the outmigration from the largest and older urban areas. Their population decline is commonly attributed to this outmigration. It is a factor, of course, but the decline in fertility is a greater one. Human fertility in these areas has dropped dramatically, standing today at less than half of what it was twenty years ago. Even without outmigration most of these areas will soon be experiencing population decline.

The total fertility rate (TFR) at a given time is the measure of the total births that a statistical woman would have over her lifetime if she bore children at the age-specific rates then prevailing. In other words, it is the rate at which women are currently reproducing themselves. A statistical woman would need to bear slightly more than two children to reproduce herself; two because of the nearly even chances of having a boy or a girl, and slightly more because some women die before they complete this statistical fertility course. But these adjustments are minor, and a statistical woman under current demographic regime needs to bear only 2.1 children to reproduce herself.

The total fertility rate now stands at 1.8 in the United States (14 percent below replacement) and slightly lower in Canada. This means that, should this fertility regime continue, the native population would shrink by 14 percent per generation, or about 0.5 percent per year. Moreover, in certain regions, such as Southern New England, the TFR now stands at 1.4, or 33 percent below replacement. Births continue to exceed deaths in the United States and Canada only because of the large numbers of peoples currently in the prime reproductive ages; even at low rates, their numbers are sufficient to produce a slight increase in total births over the next few years. But in countries such as Britain, West Germany, and Austria, where the baby boom was not as marked, deaths already exceed births and total population is in absolute decline. In major urban areas of North America, fertility is lower, and thus even without migration their population will begin to decline in a few years.

For the Burgess filtering process to operate, population or household increase is necessary or else a hole will appear at the center. For the time being, as noted concerning the family factor, even urban areas undergoing population decline grow in households because of falling household size. But clearly this compensation cannot go on much longer (mean household size in certain areas is already below 2.0); fairly soon the number of households will begin to diminish in a great many metropolitan areas.

How then will housing markets work? The answer cannot be simple because the same social processes that lead to population decline and eventual household decline result as well in a changing composition of types of households and of the mix of tastes and budgets among them. No one has in hand either theories or practical rules of thumb to handle this new situation. It is obviously not sufficient to put the concentric filtering model into reverse: The path downward cannot be the same as the path upward. Hysteresis obtains because of both the nature of housing capital and demographic processes.

A challenge thus exists to develop new theories or modes of thought. The models need not be totally new, but at the very least a rethinking of the behavior of the old workhorses under different circumstances or parameters is called for. Although the form of this reformulation is uncertain, it will require more attention to the opportunity costs of investment in new housing versus reinvestment in old, compared with the old theories, which focused on investments in new housing.

The new rural-to-urban flow of the new foreign immigrants may in certain regions and urban areas postpone population decline from lower fertility and outmigration, and provide central demand at the end of the filtering tube, as did the earlier migrations. But it is very unlikely that it will be large enough or geographically prevalent enough to avert over the next two or three decades the issues of demographic decline in an important proportion of urban areas. In sum, the basic conceptual models of housing have presumed demographic growth but how is decline to be handled?

Fertility and Housing

There are those who believe that a new baby boom is around the corner: not just a slight increase in the yearly number of births, because there are now so many young and fertile people born a generation ago during *the* baby boom, but a genuine rise in the fertility rate itself. The principal argument for this view has been made by Richard Easterlin in various works over two decades, most recently in *Births and Fortunes* (1980); the argument goes thus: Large generations are at a lifetime disadvantage in labor markets because of oversupply and therefore have relatively low wages and few children. Small generations (such as those that grew up or were born during the Depression) are by contrast in short supply and thereby advance rapidly and command high wages throughout their lifetimes; being happy and rich, they procreate. As the peak of the baby boom occurred slightly more than twenty years ago, the young people now entering the labor force and the age of having children should (other things being equal) have better prospects and security and for this reason be more fecund.

A key assumption of this theory, as Easterlin himself stresses, is that what people really want to do, when they can afford it, is to have the man earn the wages and the woman stay home and care for children. In this view more women are working now only because their potential mates cannot afford to support them at home and, by working, these young women make the situation worse by increasing the supply of labor and driving wages lower. I do not subscribe to this theory for two reasons. The first is the view I advanced earlier, that advanced societies rationalize and integrate, shifting from ascribed to achieved status; thus I distrust Easterlin's emphasis on traditional sex roles. The second reason is that, from what I can see around me, there is no chance of today's young women going back to kids and kitchen as the principal avenue for their lives. This is a personal opinion, of course, but I believe it is supported by many attitudinal surveys and most of all by the behavior of young women.

But since, despite all my good reasons, I may be wrong, I want to explore the implications of a possible new baby boom. These would be many, of course. For instance, a new boom would provide in time the necessary swelling of the labor force to prevent the Social Security crisis now projected for about the year 2020. It would, in the shorter run, sharply curtail the growth of the labor force (as young women opt for the hearth), especially in the industries and occupations that have been growing fastest. The American labor force would decline in absolute numbers, and its industrial and occupational composition would undergo radical changes.

What would be the consequences for housing? The key effect would not be, at first, the faster population increase from higher birth rates, but a sharp reduction in the rate of increase of households. This is because a baby boom can occur only if people begin again to marry early and stay married, which is what people did during the baby boom; this would reverse the trend of rising headship rates and declining household size of the past two decades. There would be a decline in one and two-person households, a rise in households composed of husband and wife with children present. The U.S. Bureau of the Census, in its rather conservative projections of households to 1995, projects a mean yearly increase in all households ranging from 1.0 and 2.0 percent and of husband-wife households of 1.3 and 0.9 percent for the most and least family-oriented projections, respectively; but the range of these projections does not include a baby boom, which would reduce further the rate of total household formations and increase that of husband-wife households (1980: table 65). For comparison, during the baby bust of the 1970s total households grew yearly by 2.2 percent and total married couples by 0.7 percent.

Geographically, there would be an acceleration of suburbanization, both because of the strong cultural tradition that the single-family house is the proper place to raise children and because more people would be including considerations of school quality, social class, and race in their location decisions.

Because much of the suburban housing stock is still occupied, if underutilized, by the parents of the earlier baby boom, much of the demand for such housing would have to be accommodated by new construction, and the associated facilities (roads, schools) would also have to be built. This would take place against the grain of local growth control, which has grown much more effective since the 1960s and which redoubled its conservationist zeal for the environment as local school taxes began to go through the roof. It is to be expected that growth control would be successful in many places so that, overall, the development would be more scattered than that of the 1950s and 1960s. This might be partly alleviated if successful policies are adopted to ease the relocation of older people out of the existing suburban housing stock, providing them with attractive financial terms, housing types, and locations.

Of course, in the central cities almost the reverse scenario applies. It was the family orientation of the time that made urban renewal in the 1950s and 1960s fail in its attempt to bring the middle class back to the city, just as now it is the increase in childless households that feeds the gentrification process. The market is accomplishing what public programs could not do because the demand exists now and did not them. If a new baby boom started, it would dry up the wave of gentrification.

As middle class demand for central city housing dropped, housing prices and rents would decline. The city would be left again to the rich and the poor. This would have the virtue, where foreign immigration is slight, of providing the city's poor and working class with relatively inexpensive housing, which was one good thing about the plight of the city as it used to be, albeit at the cost of disinvestment through low maintenance and abandonment. A further aspect of this scenario is that it would slow down the currently accelerating black middle class suburbanization, because the relative price of suburban housing would rise.

Since I am extremely skeptical of a new baby boom, the foregoing scenario seems to me basically improbable. Much more likely, I think, is a slightly oscillating low fertility pattern that might at times be lower than today. This possibility may strike some as unlikely, but Canadian and United States' fertility has been at a historic low in recent years and standing 14 percent below generational replacement, compared with the peak of the baby boom, when it was 71 percent above replacement and with the low fertility bottom during the Great Depression, when it was at about replacement levels. Today certain regions of the United States are one-third below replacement, at about the level of West Germany;

and although exact data are not available, certain social groups in the United States, such as Jews and the black middle class, seem to have even lower replacement rates. Thus, although oscillations in fertility are likely because of economic and generational factors, it would not be surprising to see the total fertility rate drift lower in the coming decades.

The correlates of a low fertility are more parity in sexual roles, more flexibility and change in households, smaller households, and a different pattern of incomes and preferences. If the present demographic path is held, most of today's trends can be expected to continue, though they cannot all continue indefinitely, of course. For instance, household size cannot diminish without limit, and therefore many areas will begin to experience a decline in the total number of households, as noted earlier.

Rather than speculating on the effects of demographics on housing, I will conclude this chapter with some speculations on the effects of housing on demographics. It is not uncommon today to see reports that young couples, faced with rapid inflation in housing prices and high interest rates, quite explicitly face the option of postponing childbearing in order to be able to afford to buy a house or even a condominium. It is quite credible that today's housing situation is contributing to low fertility.

Over the past twenty years most of the concern about population has been in the shadow of Malthus and the population bomb. Yet for the past decade the population of the United States and Canada has been failing to reproduce itself. This very low fertility rate has been masked by the age composition resulting from the postwar baby boom, so that births still exceed deaths.

We must therefore contemplate the likelihood that national concerns will turn to the consequences of low fertility a few years from now, when the echo of the baby boom fades and the situation becomes more apparent to the public. Bills have been introduced in the U.S. Congress with the explicit purpose of encouraging the traditional family, including the bearing of children. While concern over depopulation is quite rare today in the United States and Canada, it is quite common in European countries, from France to the Soviet Union (with respect to its European, not Asian population). There is worry about the aging of the population, about the shrinking labor force and military manpower, about the loss of vitality with the loss of youth and the dangers of a gerontocracy.

Earlier in American history when fertility was well above replacement but declining, concern about "the suicide of the race," was so grave that Theodore Roosevelt referred to it in his inaugural address. This concern had a strong racist tinge linked theoretically with social Darwinism and eugenics and was fueled by the Slavic and Mediterranean immigration at the turn of the century, and by the higher fertility of these immigrants and of the black population.

A comparable concern was experessed by many during the Great Depression, including John Maynard Keynes and Gunnar Myrdal. American and European fertility was falling, and to the worries of the consequences of an inverted age structure were added more global concerns. For instance, it was speculated that a declining population would fail to provide sufficient demand for the internal product of capitalist nations, so that they would be drawn to an aggressive policy of imperialism to capture foreign markets, and that the conflicting imperial interests would lead to armed conflicts.

The world is somewhat different today, and so are some of our ideas. But it does not take much imagination to see the convergence of several streams into a clamor to strengthen the traditional family and its reproductive role in society. Reaction has already arisen to the changed life courses of so many of the population, as have significant social and political movements in favor of family and traditional women's roles, and against abortion, homosexuality, nonmarital sex, and pornography. These appear linked with notions of national economic and military power as well as with morality.

Moreover, as noted earlier, the United States is experiencing a substantial immigration of people who are regarded as colored by the dominant culture, and who typically have high reproductive rates. A number of polls already reveal a preponderance of sentiment to cut off this immigration. It seems to me quite likely that in the coming years the profamily and anti-immigration sentiments will be joined and become a powerful social and policitical force. Although this phenomenon, if it comes about, will undoubtedly be troubled and complex, it is reasonable to speculate on the implications for housing policy on the basis of past history.

The profamily, pronatalist interest would express itself, as it does already in several European countries, in a number of policies that make having children easier and more attractive. These include labor legislation providing paid maternal leaves with preservation of seniority, family allowances, and baby bonuses, and even medals and awards for the very prolific. More to the point here, these policies also include the provision of housing in attractive terms to encourage marriage and childbearing.

The anti-immigration sentiment is likely to express itself in many forms, but concerning housing and spatial distribution responses are likely to be conflicting. On the one hand, prejudice and discrimination are likely to deny the newcomers many housing choices that might be within their economic reach. This will produce segregation, as it did in U.S. history and in current European experience.

But on the other hand, the concentration of unassimilated groups will be seen as dangerous because it facilitates the preservation of their culture, their foreigness. Geographic concentration makes it easier for them to maintain their language and not learn English, to have radio stations and newspapers, cafés, restaurants, churches, and all of the other elements of community life. In the United States there is already open resentment about this alien presence in New York, Miami, and Los Angeles; nationally, there has been an explicit policy of trying to disperse the Cuban immigrants. In France, in the interval between the two World Wars, there was a similar concern about the clustering of the large number of Italian and Polish immigrants. Similar reactions are also found today in Britain, Sweden, and West Germany. And so we are likely to see the contradictions of segregation and dispersal, of separateness and acculturation. The Liberty City riots in Miami and those in many British cities in 1980–81 repeated the earlier experience of riots such as those of Harlem in 1934 and 1943, and are likely a rehearsal for similar expressions of conflict in the coming years and decades.

In the matter of housing quality, a similar dialectic is likely, as occured at the turn of the century. Most of the new immigrants inherited, naturally, the dregs of the housing market. Racists then, with the sanctifying accompaniment of the eugenicists and the Social Darwinists, pointed to the squalor as evidence of inferiority. Such thinking also occurs today, of course, and lurking in the wings are genetic theories of racial differences in intelligence and other attributes; some of these, with great mathematical display, tell us that cultural traits can become genetically inheritable within fairly short historical periods.

But the other side will also play a part, as it did then, in the form of housing reform. Its advocates promised that better housing and well-designed parks would instill in these unfortunates civic and private virtues, elevated sentiments, and civilized behavior. The extraordinary promises of the reformers can only be understood in their context: as one side of the polemic between nature and nurture, in opposition to the heritability argument. Here too history is likely to repeat itself, leading to new efforts in housing reform. The arguments will be slightly different, based more on social and psychological perspectives and less on simple environmental determinism, but it is fairly safe to predict that an important part of housing policy about twenty years from now will be to do something about the *barrio* or the *kampong*.

CONCLUSION

Speculation about the future is an uncertain business. In this chapter I have speculated on demographics and the future of housing not by using technical projections, but by structural and historical reasoning. I will remind the reader of Robert Merton's important distinction between the styles of European and American sociology: The European does not know if what he says is true, but he is sure it is important; the American is certain that what he says is exact, but he does not know what it means.

REFERENCES

Alonso, W. 1964. "The Historical and the Structural Theories of Urban Form: Their Implications for Urban Renewal." *Land Economics* 40 (May).

Easterlin, R. 1980. *Births and Fortunes.* New York: Basic Books.

U.S. Bureau of the Census. 1980. *Statistical Abstract.* Washington, D.C.: U.S. Government Printing Office.

3 LIVING WITH UNCERTAINTY: The Changing Spatial Components of Urban Growth and Housing Demand in Canada

Larry S. Bourne

Aggregate statistics on changes in population inevitably conceal a myriad of continuing redistributions within that population. Shifts in household composition, age structure, fertility levels, socioeconomic class and net foreign immigration are perhaps the most obvious components of population change at the national level. These components not only derive from differing sources, but they vary over time and from place to place within a nation. In combination with net internal migration—increasingly the most volatile source of differential population growth in Canada—these components can substantially alter the character and distribution of urban and regional growth within a relatively short time. These changes in turn shape the location and schedule of demand for public services, labor, consumer goods and housing, as well as the future political map of the country.

This chapter examines the changing importance and variability of these components over time and by location and speculates briefly on the future configuration of urban and regional growth in Canada. It is not an exercise in forecasting or in projecting future housing needs. These statistics are available elsewhere (Canada Mortgage and Housing Corporation (CMHC) 1980; Statistics Canada 1980; Smith 1980). Instead, the intention is to lay a basis for more cautious and spatially sensitive forecasting. Emphasis is placed on the inherent complexity and increasing unpredictability of trends in population growth and redistribution, the contrasting processes evident at different spatial scales, and the failure of existing research models to account for past trends. The discussion is largely descriptive, drawing on but not replicating empirical analyses of urban growth in Canada for the 1971–1976 period (Bourne and Simmons 1979; Simmons 1981a; Robinson 1981). Scattered data for the post-1976 period are included wherever possible, but these data sources are extremely limited and of poor quality. The concluding sections draw out some of the implications of these recent trends for cities, housing, and public policy through to the end of the century.

URBAN AND REGIONAL GROWTH

Recent Trends: Urbanization and Population Distribution

In a country as large and diverse as Canada, marked differences in rates of growth among regions and urban places are to be expected. Given the intensity of regional economic specialization, long-standing cultural differences, a decentralized system of policy controls and the country's relative openness to external influence, it is not surprising that such differentials in growth rates exist. The question is not simply why such differentials exist but how, where, and why some persist while others do not.

The decade of the 1970s did indeed see a dramatic reordering of the components of urban and regional growth in Canada. Slower overall population growth—due primarily to declining fertility levels and lower rates of foreign immigration—combined with massive structural shifts in the national economy, set the stage. The annual national growth rate in population for 1971 to 1976, continuing the postwar decline began in the 1950s, was 1.1 percent and has since dropped below that level. This is roughly the rate prevailing in the economic depression of the 1840s, 1890s, and 1930s. In fact, the 1970s can be seen historically as a return to growth rates more typical for Canada, the 1950s and 1960s having been the aberration. Unfortunately, it is the aberrant period on which most of our urban images and growth models are based.

On the regional scale the rate of population redistribution has remained remarkably stable, but its pattern has not (Table 3–1). In contrast to the well-established image of a central or heartland region draining people, wealth, and resources from an exploited periphery, in fact the reverse was the case in Canada during the 1970s. The provinces of Ontario and Quebec, after a half-century of increasing their share of the national population, began to decline after 1970 (as in the decade from 1900 to 1910), losing population and jobs to the western region and, for the first time this century, to the eastern provinces.

As in earlier periods, urban and regional declines have become more evident as overall growth rates dropped. In 1971–1976, 35 of 157 urban places in Canada (with over 10,000 population) showed absolute population declines, including two Census Metropolitan Areas (CMAs)—Windsor and Sudbury. Both of these CMAs are industrial centers, the former specializing in automobiles, the latter smelting. Here perhaps is the beginning of metropolitan decline so typical of older industrial cities in the northeastern United States and Western Europe (Buhr and Fredrick 1982).

As Alonso (1978) argues, however, population decline is not necessarily a problem. Indeed it may in some instances help to alleviate specific problems. Nevertheless, it poses difficulties for particular groups of firms and households and puts additional pressures on both public and private sectors which are already having difficulty adjusting to technological changes, fiscal imbalances, and shifts in their economic base.

At the same time the rate of growth of Canada's entire system of urban places has dropped below that of the nation as a whole. In the 1971–1976 period, for example, the twenty-three CMAs accounted for 57 percent of national population growth, down from 62 percent in the earlier census period. In later years (to 1980) the proportion has declined to 54 percent. In particular, the most marked declines have been in the growth rates of the largest metropolitan areas, notably Montreal and Toronto. The highest order urban places have both the lowest rate of natural increase and negative net migration. The aggregate level of urbanization of the Canadian population, as a result, has stabilized at about 76 percent (Table 3–1). Clearly, metropolitan concentration, at least by

Table 3–1. Percentage Regional Distribution of Population and Levels of Urbanization, by Province, 1951–1981

Region	1951 Can. Pop.	1951 Urban[b]	1961 Can. Pop.	1961 Urban[b]	1971 Can. Pop.	1971 Urban[b]	1976 Can. Pop.	1976 Urban[b]	1981[a] Can. Pop.	1981[a] Urban[b]	1981[a] Total Population (Thousands)
Newfoundland	2.6	42.7	2.5	50.7	2.4	58.9	2.4	58.9	2.4	n.a.	583.6
Prince Edward I.	0.7	25.1	0.6	32.4	0.5	38.9	0.5	37.1	0.5	n.a.	124.1
Nova Scotia	4.6	55.3	4.0	54.3	3.7	58.0	3.6	55.8	3.6	n.a.	856.1
New Brunswick	3.7	42.6	3.3	46.5	2.9	54.5	2.9	52.3	2.9	n.a.	709.1
Atlantic	11.6		10.4		9.5		9.5		9.4		2,272.9
Quebec	28.9	67.0	28.8	74.3	27.9	79.5	27.1	79.1	26.3	n.a.	6,325.1
Ontario	32.8	73.4	34.2	77.3	35.7	81.8	36.0	81.2	35.7	n.a.	8,600.5
Central	61.7		63.0		63.6		63.1		62.0		14,925.6
Manitoba	5.5	56.6	5.1	63.9	4.6	70.1	4.4	69.9	4.3	n.a.	1,027.0
Saskatchewan	5.9	30.4	5.1	43.0	4.3	52.7	4.0	55.5	4.1	n.a.	957.7
Prairies	11.4		10.2		8.9		8.4		8.4		1,984.7
Alberta	6.7	48.0	7.3	63.3	7.5	73.6	8.0	75.0	8.9	n.a.	2,135.9
British Columbia	8.3	70.8	8.9	72.3	10.1	79.7	10.7	76.9	11.2	n.a.	2,687.0
West	15.0		16.2		17.6		18.7		20.1		4,822.9
North	0.2		0.2		0.3		0.3		0.3		64.3
All Canada		62.9		69.9		76.0		75.5		n.a.	24,088.7

a. Preliminary estimates

b. Defined as the proportion of the population living in incorporated places of 1,000 or more or in unincorporated places with a population of 1,000 or more and a density of 1,000 per square mile.

Source: Statistics Canada, 1980.

standard definitions, has also stopped or decreased, and nonmetropolitan areas have undergone a resurgence of growth. Urbanization as such has ceased, but urban growth, in terms of the
expansion of individual cities, has not.

Within metropolitan areas the dominant impression from an
analysis of the 1971–1976 data is the massive thinning out of population in the inner and the older inner suburbs. On average, inner city populations in Canada dropped by 12.2 percent in this
period, compared to a decline of 4.3 percent in the preceding five
years.[1] In older and higher density cities the decline was in the
order of 20 percent. Here the impacts of the demographic transition—smaller families and more nonfamily households—as well as
those resulting from nonresidential land-use succession and the
changing location of jobs and residences accompanying improvements in transportation, higher incomes and environmental decay, are most evident. This combination of processes, of thinning
out and decentralization, appeared in every city and region regardless of the size of the city or the condition of local housing
and labor markets. Only those cities with a strong central core
and an earlier start on inner city revitalization (as in Vancouver
and Toronto) were able to modify the trend.

In many instances decentralization has spread well beyond the
Census Metropolitan Areas into essentially rural surroundings.
This phenomenon, again well documented in heavily urbanized
regions of the United States and Western Europe (Berry and
Silverman 1980), not only has transformed the local housing markets of many Canadian cities but also has removed any remaining
utility in the differentiation of urban and rural.

Within some regions and provinces and in distinct contrast to
the trend at both the national and interurban level, population
concentration has been the dominant expression of change. In Ontario and in most other provinces that are growing slowly, population and employment growth has become more concentrated in
selected metropolitan regions, although not within the immediate
boundaries of the metropolitan area themselves. During the 1976–
1980 period nearly 90 percent of all population growth took place
within the central region of southern Ontario, in what is essentially the Toronto urban field. Only the Kitchener, London, and
Ottawa suburban fringes registered any significant growth. Most
of the rest of the province is now in decline (Bourne 1981).

Mobility and Migration

As the rate of natural increase has stabilized, again at historically low levels, foreign immigration and interregional and interurban migration have become relatively more important mechanisms of adjustment. In other words the "flow" of population growth has increasingly become the crucial variable to explain urban and regional growth. Interestingly, each component of population mobility (immigration, emigration, net immigration) and the various indices of internal migration (in, out, gross, and net) has its own momentum over time and its own calculus of movement over space. Each responds to a particular set of circumstances, each exhibits its own leads and lags, and each mirrors a complex web of interrelations (Simmons 1979). This complexity makes the task facing any forecaster more difficult and the results more uncertain.

The degree of stability in recent years in aggregate rates of population movement in Canada has been surprising (Figure 3–1). But again, the balance and direction of net aggregate flows have shifted. In effect only three regions of the country are growing through net in-migration: Almost all areas (both urban and rural) west of the Saskatchewan–Alberta boundary; the outer fringe areas around Toronto, Ottawa, and Montreal; and isolated locations in the Atlantic region. Although it is not clear who these recent migrants are or what motives they have for relocation, movement to the west is obviously linked closely to the availability of jobs and to the investment boom there, whereas the other movements contain a larger proportion of migrants and retirement population, combined with a lower rate of out-migration than prevailed in earlier decades.

To date no consistent and convincing analytical framework has emerged to explain these flows. Most forecasting models treat net internal migration as a given or as a residual, rather than as a variable. The difficulties of accounting for these flows statistically and especially for changes in the rate of population mobility over time from place to place have been amply demonstrated in recent studies by Stone (1978), Termote (1980), Termote and Frechette (1980), Simmons (1978, 1979), and others. Simmons' study, for example, shows that despite the stability in overall migration rates, any explanations that formerly existed for net migration no longer pertain. The best predictors of in- and out-migration flows in one period are the flows in the previous period. Only 27 percent of the interurban variation in net migration in 1971–1976 could be accounted for by variables measuring initial (1971) conditions in the pair of urban places involved. Net migration was negatively associated with population size and surprisingly with average wage rates, and positively, albeit modestly, with the level of employment and amenity variables. Adding change variables for 1971–1976, notably employment growth, improved the explanatory power of the equations. A growth in wages or income, in con-

Figure 3–1.   Mobility Status: Canada, 1966–1971 and 1971–1976

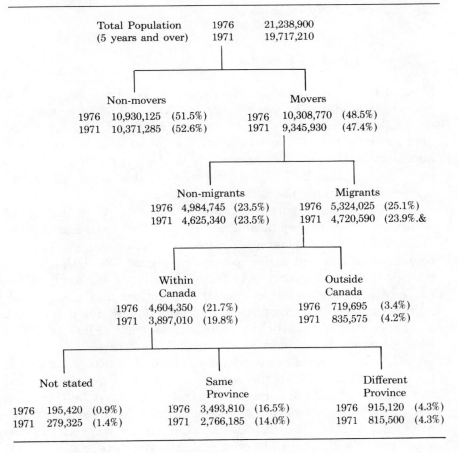

	Total Population	1976	21,238,900
	(5 years and over)	1971	19,717,210

Non-movers
1976 10,930,125 (51.5%)
1971 10,371,285 (52.6%)

Movers
1976 10,308,770 (48.5%)
1971 9,345,930 (47.4%)

Non-migrants
1976 4,984,745 (23.5%)
1971 4,625,340 (23.5%)

Migrants
1976 5,324,025 (25.1%)
1971 4,720,590 (23.9%.&

Within Canada
1976 4,604,350 (21.7%)
1971 3,897,010 (19.8%)

Outside Canada
1976 719,695 (3.4%)
1971 835,575 (4.2%)

Not stated
1976 195,420 (0.9%)
1971 279,325 (1.4%)

Same Province
1976 3,493,810 (16.5%)
1971 2,766,185 (14.0%)

Different Province
1976 915,120 (4.3%)
1971 815,500 (4.3%)

Source: Statistics Canada. 1980.

trast, was of little value; both appear to retard out-migration rather than to attract in-migrants. Combined, the traditionally strong variables of employment, income and wages, accounted for less than 50 percent of the variance in net migration, even allowing for distributed lag effects.

These complex interrelations are far too cumbersome and variable to be discussed in detail here, however. It will suffice to note that although many of the expected determinants of migration rates do emerge as significant variables, the volatility in the urban system is such that far more empirical research and refined, spatially sensitive models are necessary. Without such models, accurate predictions of future population flows and thus housing demand are simply impossible.

The Post-1976 Period

Most of the trends noted for the earlier periods have continued, if not accelerated, in the years following 1976. Here, of course, the national data base for Canada is more restricted and more suspect in accurancy. For urban areas disaggregate data are almost nonexistent. Nevertheless, since this is the period of interest to most readers and the last stepping stone to discussions of the future, we must make use of what we have.

As background, Figure 3–2 provides a matrix summarizing the dominant flows of population among the ten provinces for the years 1976–1980. The annual rates for these same regions are compared to those of earlier periods in Figure 3–3. Although the provinces are not particularly suitable as units for analysis because of the wide variation in their populations and areas, parallel flow matrices for urban areas are not available for this period.

The evidence, nonetheless, is relatively clear. The net movement of population to the west, from all other regions, has accelerated. The principal net exporter to all regions except Quebec is now Ontario (it is also the largest importer of population and the major recipient of foreign immigration). The Atlantic region had by 1980 reverted to its traditional role as a source of out-migrants, but in this case destination was now primarily the west, notably British Columbia and Alberta, rather than Ontario and Quebec. The rate of out-migration from Quebec in fact has slowed or at least returned to the level of earlier (pre-1971) periods. The principal destination of those migrants, although at a declining rate, is still Ontario; in fact without the large net gain from Quebec, the latter's net population balance would have been negative.

Figure 3–2. Net Population Movement, by Region, 1976–1980

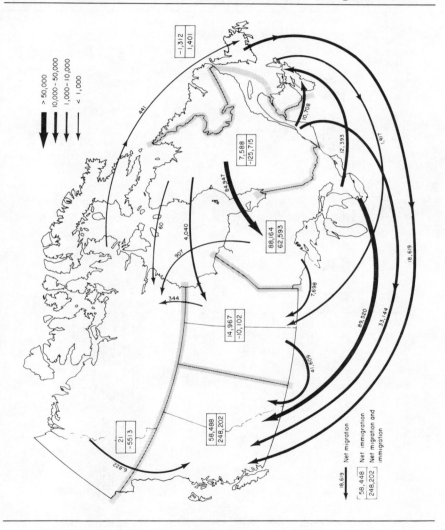

Source: Statistics Canada. 1980.

At the scale of individual metropolitan regions the direction of trends and the sources of variability in growth are even more evident. Table 3–2 illustrates the different contributions to population growth of each component for all of the country's CMAs for 1971–1976 and 1976–1978.[2] Note that the rates of natural increase vary widely, from a low of −0.2 (per 1,000 population) in Victo-

Figure 3–3.   Net Migration, by Region, 1961–1980

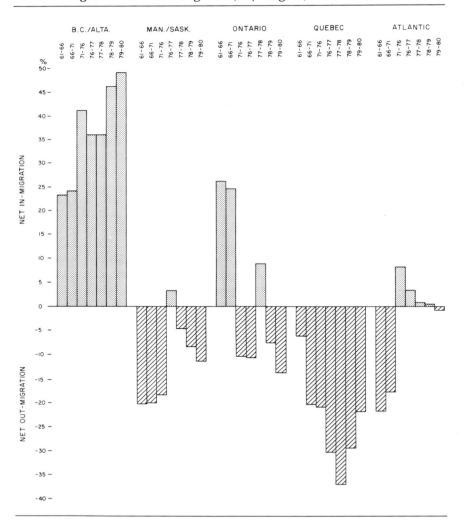

Source: Statistics Canada. 1980.

Table 3–2. Components of Population Growth: Census Metropolitan Areas, 1971–1978 (thousands)

	1971–1976			1976–1978			1971–1978			Per 1,000 Average Population 1971–1978			Distribution of Components of Population Change (%) 1971–1978		
	Natural Increase	Net Migration	Population Change	Natural Increase	Net Migration	Population Change	Natural Increase	Net Migration	Population Change	Natural Increase	Net Migration	Population Change	Natural Increase	Net Migration	Population Change
Calgary	25.0	41.6	66.6	10.8	24.2	35.0	35.8	65.8	101.6	11.4	20.8	32.0	35.2	64.8	100.0
Chicoutimi-Jonquiere	6.9	-4.7	2.2	3.1	-2.0	1.1	10.0	-6.7	3.3	11.2	-7.5	3.7	303.0	-203.0	100.0
Edmonton	32.4	25.8	58.2	13.9	13.3	27.2	46.3	39.1	85.4	12.3	10.4	22.7	54.2	45.8	100.0
Halifax	13.2	4.2	17.4	5.1	-1.9	3.2	18.3	2.3	20.6	10.0	1.3	11.3	88.8	11.2	100.0
Hamilton	19.6	6.7	26.3	3.9	0	3.9	23.5	6.7	30.2	6.5	1.8	9.1	77.8	22.2	100.0
Kitchener	14.0	19.6	33.6	5.8	2.1	7.9	19.8	21.7	41.5	10.9	12.0	22.9	47.7	52.3	100.0
London	12.6	4.8	17.4	3.8	-0.1	3.7	16.4	4.7	21.1	8.9	2.5	11.4	77.7	22.3	100.0
Montreal	85.8	-12.5	73.3	38.0	-17.5	20.5	123.8	-30.0	93.8	6.4	-1.5	4.8	132.0	-32.0	100.0
Oshawa	6.5	8.4	14.9	2.8	1.3	4.1	9.3	9.7	19.0	10.2	10.7	20.9	48.9	51.1	100.0
Ottawa-Hull	28.4	45.0	73.4	10.9	22.2	33.1	39.3	67.2	106.5	8.3	14.3	22.6	36.9	63.1	100.0
Quebec	23.1	17.7	40.8	9.5	2.8	12.3	32.6	20.5	53.1	8.8	5.6	14.4	61.4	38.6	100.0
Regina	8.6	1.9	10.5	3.5	5.3	8.8	12.1	7.2	19.3	11.5	6.8	18.3	62.7	37.3	100.0
St. Catharines-Niagara	9.9	6.2	16.1	3.0	1.1	4.1	12.9	7.3	20.2	6.2	3.5	9.7	63.9	36.1	100.0
St. John's	9.0	2.6	11.6	3.1	0	3.1	12.1	2.6	14.7	12.4	2.7	15.1	82.3	17.7	100.0
Saint John	5.1	1.2	6.3	2.1	2.1	4.2	7.2	3.3	10.5	9.2	4.2	13.4	68.6	31.4	100.0
Saskatoon	6.6	0.8	7.4	2.6	2.8	5.4	9.2	3.6	12.8	9.9	3.9	13.8	71.9	28.1	100.0
Sudbury	11.4	-12.1	-0.7	3.6	-5.6	-2.0	15.0	-17.7	-2.7	13.7	-16.2	-2.5	...	...	100.0
Thunder Bay	3.7	0.9	4.6	1.3	0.1	1.4	5.0	1.0	6.0	3.0	0.6	7.3	83.3	16.7	100.0
Toronto	128.4	72.6	201.0	45.6	7.8	53.4	174.0	80.4	254.4	9.1	4.2	13.3	68.4	31.6	100.0
Vancouver	28.8	55.1	83.9	12.0	-5.0	7.0	40.8	50.1	90.9	5.2	6.3	11.5	44.9	55.1	100.0
Victoria	-0.1	22.6	22.5	-0.2	4.4	4.2	-0.3	27.0	26.7	-0.2	18.4	18.2	-1.1	101.1	100.0
Windsor	11.1	-12.2	-1.1	3.4	-4.7	-1.3	14.5	-16.9	-2.4	8.4	-9.8	-1.4	...	...	100.0
Winnipeg	22.3	6.1	28.4	8.1	2.8	10.9	30.4	8.9	39.3	7.7	2.2	9.9	77.4	22.6	100.0
Total CMAs	512.3	302.3	814.6	195.7	55.5	251.2	708.0	357.8	1,065.8	8.1	4.1	12.2	66.4	33.6	100.0
Distribution (%)	62.9	37.1	100.0	77.9	22.1	100.0	66.4	33.6	100.0	66.4	33.6	100.0	...	...	...

Source: Statistics Canada. 1980.

ria, British Columbia, to a high of 13.7 in Sudbury, Ontario, and the rate of net migration varied from −16.2 in Sudbury, to 20.8 in Calgary, Alberta. As a proportion of metropolitan population growth between 1971 and 1978, the contribution of net migration ranged from 101 percent in Victoira to −203 percent in Chicoutimi-Jonquiere, Quebec. Overall, net migration contributed 34 percent to total metropolitan growth.

Urban Growth and Population Redistribution: A Summary

The various tendencies outlined can be summarized in terms of four broad processes operating at four different spatial scales:

1. National decentralization. The shift in population (and in jobs and wealth) from the central industrial region to the west and to a lesser extent to the east.
2. Hierarchical decentralization. Within the national system of urban places, the relative shift in growth from the larger metropolitan centers to medium and smaller centers.
3. Intraregional concentration. The increasing concentration of population in one or a few regions (that is, within an urban subsystem), particularly those containing the larger metropolitan areas.
4. Intrametropolitan decentralization. The continued spread of population (and jobs) beyond the boundaries of metropolitan areas into outer fringe areas (the urban field).

The first two and the last two of these processes of population redistribution are obviously interrelated, and the scale and intensity of the latter varies from region to region. Regions that are growing rapidly in both Canada and the United States tend to be the resource-based, retirement, and recreational regions. They also tend to contain newer and smaller cities, reflecting lower levels of urbanization in those regions and more weakly developed urban subsystems. The few rapidly growing cities outside of the resource regions are most frequently residential and industrial outliers of the larger metropolitan complexes, or they are political capitals.[3] The latter attests to the growing importance of the public sector in shaping patterns of urbanization. The society is not, as has been said, throwing away the old metropolis; it is simply building new ones.

Similarly, the growth of the outer fringes of the larger metropolitan areas reflects both out-migration from the core into rural retreats and small-town retirement locations, as well as in-migration from other regions or abroad that is now bypassing the older parts of the urban area. Even without these actual migrations, however, population shifts at the intraurban scale would still have been substantial due to large and localized differences in demographic structure. Migration, in fact, acts to shift the location of the demographic transition over both space and time.

Ironically, these trends are also in contradiction to those that might be anticipated in a world of rapidly rising energy prices and concern over losses of agricultural land, regional inequalities, environmental conservation, improvements in public transportation, and limits on public expenditures. All but the third tendency are, in broad outline at least, high on energy use, the consumption of agricultural land, environmental destruction, and new public expenditures. They may also lead to even greater regional inequalities in income and living standards.

Alternative Explanations

Although space does not permit a detailed examination of the various explanations that have been advanced for the complex trends outlined thus far, a few generalizations are possible. From previous empirical analyses of net migration, it is known that a large number of variables are needed to achieve even modest levels of statistical explanation of interregional and interurban population redistribution. The problem is not due to a misspecification of the models (although that may be true) but to a lack of understanding of the processes involved.

Clearly no single or simplified explanation of these trends will suffice. Pulling together threads in the preceding discussion, at least four major sets of explanatory variables may be hypothesized (see Bourne 1980):

1. Structural change in the economy, the boom in resource demand, the recession in manufacturing, pressures from international competition and technological change.
2. Social change, rising incomes and aspirations, the desire for changes in life-styles and for higher levels of environmental amenities.
3. The demographic transition, including an overall aging of the population and substantial shifts in the size and composition of specific age cohorts.
4. The unintended effects of public policy, to the extent that public policies have favored new regions over old, relocations over rebuilding, external demands over local initiatives, and private development over public.
5. The random or stochastic elements typical of a diversified space economy undergoing change in a turbulent and highly unpredictable world.

Clearly all five of these sets of variables have made a contribution to the changing spatial distribution of population and economic growth in Canada. In the first set the changing pattern of urban growth is treated essentially as the mirror image of the economy, and the shifts in production, investment, and employment from manufacturing to resource-based sectors (Termote 1980). In the second and third sets urban changes are seen primarily as household-led, following demographic trends and social preferences (Berry and Silverman 1980; Robinson 1981). The fourth introduces the role of governments and the public sector generally in designing the nation's landscape, primarily through policies whose spatial imprints are unintended (Glickman 1979; Simmons 1981a), while the fifth sees random disturbances acting on a highly differentiated economic and social system that is relatively open to exogenous influences.

In what proportion, at what scale, and with what long-term implications these variables are combined remains unclear, however. Some of the relations carry the same sign; while others work in conflicting directions. Some reflect the short-term perturbations that are characteristic of urban systems such as Canada's (Simmons and Flanagan 1980). Others produce effects that are only evident over a generation or two.

Whatever set of arguments one subscribes to, the policy implications and the projections of future patterns that flow from these arguments will be very different. The immediate challenge faced by analysts is to attempt to integrate elements from each of these approaches and to develop a series of integrative hypotheses for future research and decisionmaking.

Implications for Housing

The specific housing implications that follow from these assertions are neither novel nor unique but in combination are likely to be substantially different from those in the past. As other chapters in this volume will be reviewing future housing requirements in detail (see those by Brown, as well as Clayton and Hobart), the following discussion will present only a brief summary of some of the major issues that could emerge.

Although a reasonable idea may exist of the magnitude of new housing needs over the next decade or two, given a number of critical (but largely untested) assumptions, there is much less of an idea of the distribution of those needs by type and location. Aggregate housing demand in Canada is estimated to fall from 240,000 in the early 1970s to about 160,000 in the 1990s, based primarily on estimates of the rates of net household formation and foreign immigration (CMHC 1980). Traditionally it has been assumed that the number of new starts is a sufficient criterion by which to measure the response of the market to changing needs. Distributional questions have remained relatively untouched.

In a context of slower overall growth but of relatively large demographic shifts and an even more rapid redistribution of population, the latter questions increase in importance and in analytical difficulty. Access to housing does depend in part on where one lives. Why else would housing problems appear to have worsened, allowing for media exaggeration, precisely at a time when the macrolevel supply problem seems to have diminished? The demand for housing, as a consequence of migration flows and income instability, is certainly going to be more volatile and unpredictable in the future.

What is very likely to occur in an urban system such as Canada's, in which urban areas differ so markedly and in which readjustment is rapid, is that contrasts among region, cities, and neighborhoods may well increase. Rapidly growing areas will have continuing housing shortages, high and rising prices, low vacancies and hurriedly built and poorly planned subdivisions. Declining areas, in contrast, will have housing surpluses, low and falling prices, high vacancies, and low levels of investment. Under this scenario, we will witness a greater tendency to write off housing resources and infrastructure in declining areas while reducing living standards for all.

The point is that housing—the stock, the industry, and the investment institutions—is not easily adaptable to rapid change. Some of the problems of soft or declining markets, admittedly, may be seen as short-term difficulties resulting from a disequilibrium in the market, but more likely they will persist while changing their nature and location. Indeed, such problems have existed for a long time and will almost certainly exist into the next century.

In several large U.S. metropolitan areas, housing production has exceeded household formation by as much as 50 percent for more than a decade. As a result, large areas of the inner city are now depopulated and the housing derelict. This process of deterioration is both a cause and an effect of suburban overbuilding, augmented by racial transition, poverty, and the downward spiral of disinvestment. In Canada there are as yet few examples of similar overbuilding and the collapse of demand within the major cities, although there are numerous examples in smaller centers in declining resource- or industrial-based regions.

TOWARD THE FUTURE

Will these trends in urban development continue? Most readers would agree that any projections made for the interregional and interurban distribution of population in Canada for the next ten or twenty years are almost certainly going to be wrong. There are numerous examples of widely erroneous forecasts in the past, recently and notably those made between 1972 and 1975 before the release of the 1976 census results. Since that census, in fact, most forecasts have had to be extensively revised, for the most part downward. They will likely be revised again.

The problem is not only that the components of growth are unstable—migration now contributes more to the variance than natural increase and immigration combined—but that they are subject to frequent surprises and extensive exogenous influences. Moreover, forecasters tend to overreact to the tide of recent events by failing to place these events in their proper long-term context.

Whether the four dominant tendencies persist or not obviously depends on a mix of factors deriving from both internal and external sources. Each mix requires that a somewhat different scenario for the future form of urban and regional growth in Canada. One scenario that is very unlikely, however, is a linear extrapolation of past trends.

Many of the unpredictable factors in estimating the future distribution of population are well known. The price of specific commodities—lumber, fish, wheat, potash, coal, or oil—which are largely set in international markets, will delimit the growth potential of the west and to a lesser extent the east coast. The viability of the manufacturing sector, in the face of rapid technological change and rising competition from abroad, will shape the growth of cities in Ontario and Quebec. Changes in lifestyle, household composition, labor market conditions, and in intergovernmental relations, to name but a few, will benefit one or a few regions and groups of cities over others.

Some of these changes will be of long duration; others will be short-lived. The latter factors are reflected in the massive swings from year to year in production, household income, net migration and job creation endured by most smaller and specialized communities in Canada (Simmons and Flanagan 1980). Pressures that persist in technology, employment shifts, and demography will become part of the longer term reordering of the space economy and social morphology of the country.

The easiest scenario to draw is no doubt the projection of a composite of recent and historical trends for at least the next ten years, with some readjustment of feedback as the urban system attempts to compensate. In Canada the redistribution of population (and power) to the west will almost certainly continue through the 1980s, although at somewhat reduced rates due to restrictions at the destinations and relative improvements at the points of origin. Overall population growth will also be slow, excluding the unlikely events of a new baby boom or renewed waves of foreign immigration. This of course means that fewer new households (and fewer service jobs) are available to redistribute. Under these conditions the rate of internal migration not only becomes more unpredictable, but its impacts at both origin and destination become larger and more immediately evident. Inequalities in living conditions and housing opportunities between growing and declining cities and regions may then increase.

At the same time numerous factors, such as barriers to intermetropolitan and especially interprovincial migration, may act to slow the process of population redistribution in the future. The relative decline in the size of age cohorts with high migration propensities; increased restrictions on employment and goods movements across provincial boundaries; the substantially higher costs of relocation (in terms of the costs of social disruption, transportation, and differential living standards); improvements in communication technology and the integration of nonmetropolitan areas into the prevailing metropolitan culture; and the inevitable progression toward a guaranteed annual wage, which will facilitate adaptations to fluctuating incomes in place, may combine to reduce both the need and the incentive to migrate.

Counterbalancing forces of course could alter this scenario. The continued expansion of the retirement population (to 13 percent by the year 2000), assisted by higher incomes, portable pensions and fewer family-based households, may add to the flows of population into rural, amenity-rich, or familiar regions. Continued sharp economic decline in parts of the country (including the eastern prairies, the older industrial areas of Ontario and Quebec, and rural areas in the east) could force further out-migration from these regions. The difficult question is one of anticipating the balance of these different pressures.

At the scale of the individual city the form of the metropolitan region of the future still hangs in the balance. There are two contrasting scenarios: an empty and deteriorated inner city surrounded by a massive and low-density suburban and exurban sprawl or a centrally oriented, higher density city with far outer suburbs subject to deterioration and depopulation. Neither of these forms are likely to occur in Canada. Instead, individual cities will follow different and at times contrasting routes between these extremes over the next two decades, with the actual route depending on the local chemistry of growth and change. The ability to predict which route urban form will follow has not been very good.

At the national scale, however, the Canadian urban fabric is remarkably stable and resilient. The distribution of urban population in the year 2000 will not be dramatically different from what it is today. The urban system is now so firmly implanated, so diverse, and grouped into quasi-independent regional subsystems with differing economies and social structures, that the capacity for adjustment to change without altering the extant urban system is immense. Change will occur, nevertheless, and at the margin some of these changes will be dramatic.

Some cities will certainly face severe problems in providing jobs, adequate standards of public services, and housing, notably in those cases where growth or decline is too rapid. Many more cities will need to deal directly with declines in population and reductions in their economic base. Although the demographic transition toward a stable population has largely been completed, its effects on the demand for public services, housing and employment will be felt for two or three decades to come. The challenge is to identify the leading sectors and firms and households that will influence future population and employment movements in general and the operation of individual housing markets in particular and to translate these actions into their social and economic impacts.

CONCLUSIONS

This chapter has documented a few of the modifications in the form and direction of urban growth and population redistribution in Canada during the 1970s and speculated on the future configuration of growth and decline. The critical assertions relate to the diversity and instability of the individual components of population growth over time and at different spatial scales.

In a slow-growth environment, the mechanisms of population redistribution, notably net internal migration, become the most important variables determining shifts in the location of demand for social services and housing. Unfortunately, migration among cities and regions, as noted, is also the most volatile and unpredictable of these components (Termote and Frechette 1980). It also appears to be only weakly related to the demographic and employment mix and is only partly collinear with employment growth. In the latter relation migration is both a dependent and an independent variable, exhibiting substantial temporal lags and high spatial variability.

This means that analysts and policymakers must live with considerable and increasing uncertainty (Simmons 1981b). Aggregate population figures can be forecast that, given the overall stability in the Canadian urban system, have a reasonable chance of being accurate. From these national housing requirements can be estimated, but with considerably less accuracy. Further down the spatial scale to the level of individual regions or urban areas, understanding of the processes involved decreases and the degree of uncertainty increases. Forecasting models become increasing insensitive, if not irrelevant, and the error functions in the equations explode.

This does not mean, however, that we throw up our arms in despair. Instead it suggests the need for more flexible models, for disaggregation of the major data sources, for continuous monitoring of urban growth trends over time, and the necessity of varying both the indices and spatial scales used for analysis. Knowing how many Canadians there will be in the year 2000 is of little value if we do not also know where and how they will live.

NOTES

1. The inner city was defined by the Ministry of State of Urban Affairs as including all census tracts where the percentage of housing built before 1946 was more than twice that for the entire metropolitan area.
2. These figures are preliminary estimates and therefore should be treated with considerable caution. The estimates are based on two principal sources: changes in address for family allowance payments and changes in address for driver's licences. Both sources are subject to substantial errors, including an inevitable time lag.
3. Among the ten most rapidly growing metropolitan areas in Canada during this period, seven were political (provincial) capitals or public administration centers.

REFERENCES

Alonso, W. 1978. "The Current Halt in the Metropolitan Phenomenon." In *The Mature Metropolis*, edited by C. Leven. Lexington, Mass.: D.C. Heath.

Berry, B.J.L., and L.P. Silverman, eds. 1980. *Population Redistribution and Public Policy*. Washington, D.C.: National Academy of Sciences.

Boisvert, M. 1978. *The Correspondence between the Urban System and the Economic Base of Canada's Regions*. Ottawa: Economic Council of Canada.

Bourne, L.S. 1980. "Alternative Perspectives on Urban Decline and Population Deconcentration." *Urban Geography* 1:39–52.

_____. 1981. "Designing the Future: A Perspective on Recent Trends and Emerging Issues in Ontario's Urban Environment." Research Paper 129, Centre for Urban and Community Studies, University of Toronto.

Bourne, L.S., and J.W. Simmons. 1979. *Canadian Settlement Trends: The Spatial Pattern of Growth, 1971–76*. Major Report 15, Centre for Urban and Community Studies, University of Toronto.

Buhr, W., and P. Friedrick, eds. 1982. *Planning in Stagnating Regions*. Baden-Baden, West Germany.

Canada Mortgage and Housing Corporation. 1980. *The Long Term Outlook for Housing in Canada*. Ottawa: CMHC.

Foot, D.K. 1979. *Public Policy and Future Population in Ontario*. Toronto: Ontario Economic Council.

Glickman, N. 1979. *The Urban Impacts of Federal Policies*. Baltimore: The Johns Hopkins University Press.

Miron, J. 1979. "Migration and Urban Economic Growth." *Regional Science and Urban Economics* 9:159–83.

Norrie, K.H., and M.B. Percey. 1981. "Westward Shift and Interregional Adjustment: A Preliminary Assessment." Discussion Paper 201, Economic Council of Canada, Ottawa.

Robinson, I. 1981. *Canadian Urban Growth Trends: Implications for a National Settlements Policy*. Vancouver: University of British Columbia Press.

Simmons, J.W. 1978. "Migration and the Canadian Urban System. Part II. Simple Relationships." Research Paper 98, Centre for Urban and Community Studies, University of Toronto.

_____. 1979. "Migration and the Canadian Urban System. Part III. Comparing 1966–71 and 1971–76." Research Paper 112, Centre for Urban and Community Studies, University of Toronto.

_____. 1981a. "The Impact of Government on the Canadian Urban System: Income Taxes, Transfer Payments and Employment." Research Paper 126, Centre for Urban and Community Studies, University of Toronto.

_____. 1981b. "Population Forecasting: How Little We Know." Mimeo, Centre for Urban and Community Studies, University of Toronto.

Simmons, J.W., and P. Flanagan. 1980. "The Movement of Growth Impulses through the Canadian Urban System." Research Paper 120, Centre for Urban and Community Studies, University of Toronto.

Smith, L. 1980. "Housing in the Eighties." Mimeo, Department of Political Economy, University of Toronto.

Statistics Canada. 1980. *Population Projections for Canada and the Provinces 1976–2000.* Cat. 91-520. Ottawa: Statistics Canada.

Stone, L. 1978. *The Frequency of Geographic Mobility in Canada.* Ottawa: Statistics Canada.

Termote, M. 1980. *Migration and Settlement: 6. Canada.* RR-80-29. Laxenburg, Austria: IIASA.

Termote, M., and R. Frechette. 1980. "Le Renversement Recent Des Courants Migratoires Entre les Provinces Canadiennes. Essai d'Interpretation." *Canadian Journal of Regional Science* 3 (Autumn):163–92.

PP. 73-88

8 4 10
9 4 12
U 5

4 U.S. POPULATION DISTRIBUTION INTO THE TWENTY-FIRST CENTURY

Daniel H. Garnick

In the space of one hundred and seventy-six years the Lower Mississippi has shortened itself two hundred and forty-two miles. That is an average of a trifle over one mile and a third per year. Therefore, any calm person ... who is not blind or idiotic ... can see that in the Old Oolitic Silurian Period, just a million years ago next November, the Lower Mississippi River was upward of one million three hundred thousand miles long and stuck out over the Gulf of Mexico like a fishing rod. And by the same token any person can see that seven hundred and forty-two years from now the Lower Mississippi will be only a mile and three-quarters long, and Cairo and New Orleans will have joined their streets together and be plodding comfortably along under a single mayor and a mutual board of aldermen. There is something fascinating about science. One gets such wholesale returns of conjecture out of such a trifling investment of fact.

—Mark Twain

The author is indebted to his colleagues, E. R. Janisch, K. P. Johnson, J. R. Kort, E. I. Steinberg, and A. H. Young of the U. S. Department of Commerce Bureau of Economic Analysis and to S. G. Machado of Abbott Laboratories, for incisive comments leading to improvements on an earlier draft. The views expressed in this chapter are not necessarily those of any of these persons nor of the Bureau or the Department of Commerce.

73

Long-term regional economic projections by the Bureau of Economic Analysis (BEA) of the U.S. Department of Commerce indicate that U.S. areas that grew relatively fast or slow in recent history will continue to grow relatively fast or slow into the twenty-first century. The projections do not portray empty holes developing in the northern and central states, however, or "black holes" in the South and West. Self-limiting forces confounded the prognostications of the exploding metropolis in the 1960s, and the BEA projections assume such forces in the future will similarly limit the extent of the emptying metropolis. This is not to say, however, that the metropolitan-nonmetropolitan growth reversal of the 1970s was a temporary phenomenon (Garnick 1978a, 1978b). The growth reversal reflects industrial and residential locational preferences, and these, in turn, reflect internal costs as well as economic and social externalities.

The agricultural revolution beginning in the 1940s and the subsequent reallocation of redundant farm labor were responsible for much of the net outflow of population from nonmetropolitan areas during the quarter-century following World War II. The positive growth during the 1970s in the nonmetropolitan areas is attributable to a decreasing rate of loss due to both the slowdown in the agricultural employment decline and the decreasing share of agriculture in total nonmetropolitan employment. Mining employment has increased in contrast to declines in the middle decades of this century. Manufacturing employment continues to disperse out of the large metropolitan areas. In general, there has been a continuing extension of exurban growth involving commuting to metropolitan areas as well as job dispersal. This trend has been reinforced by employment growth and retirement and semiretirement migration to lower cost and high amenity nonmetropolitan areas. These forces for dispersion are expected to continue beyond this century but with decreasing intensity as returns to labor and the costs of doing business become geographically less disparate.

This chapter reviews the recent BEA projections and the economic forces underlying the long-term trends. The implications of advances in technology and energy costs will provide a basis for evaluating the projections and will be extended to implications for the future of housing markets.

LONG-TERM PROJECTIONS

State-level projections of income, employment, and population to the year 2000 were published in the November 1980 issue of the U.S. Department of Commerce *Survey of Current Business*. Additional projections to the year 2030 are available from BEA on computer tape for states, Standard Metropolitan Statistical Areas (SMSAs), and BEA economic areas. A set of eleven volumes containing all of the projected data and detailed discussion of methodology is currently being published. Tables 4–1 and 4–2, showing regional projections of population growth rates and levels, respectively, by metropolitan and nonmetropolitan areas, are summarized from the data tapes. At the state level, a single "best" projection is published. At the substate level, such as the metropolitan-nonmetropolitan split included in these tables, alternative projections are made based on three different assumptions with respect to the trends in areas' shares of their parent states. The alternative adopted for this chapter is the one that most nearly reflects the 1970s differentials between the metropolitan and nonmetropolitan growth rates.[1]

Tables 4–1 and 4–2 show that the less densely populated regions, particularly in the South and West, are characterized by higher growth rates than the more densely populated regions in the Northeast and central portions of the country.[2] The generally inverse relation between population density and growth rates is also reflected within regions; for example, the three northernmost states of New England are projected to grow much faster than the more densely populated three southernmost states. In most cases the rank order of projected regional population growth rates remains the same both before and after the year 2000, although the range substantially narrows between the former and latter periods (see Table 4–3).

The projections for metropolitan and nonmetropolitan areas reflect considerable leveling of growth rates, particularly after the year 2000. Nonmetropolitan areas continue overall to grow faster than metropolitan areas, but this is not the case for the less densely populated states in the Plains, Rocky Mountain, and southern regions, where metropolitan areas are generally small relative to the rest of the country and continue to grow faster

Table 4–1. Regional Average Annual Population Growth Rates, SMSA-nonSMSA, Historical and Projections

	1969–1978	1978–2000	2000–2030
United States			
Total	.89	.80	.48
SMSA	.80	.78	.47
NonSMSA	1.14	.85	.49
New England			
Total	.48	.51	.32
SMSA	.32	.43	.28
NonSMSA	1.33	.90	.52
Middle Atlantic			
Total	.03	.05	.10
SMSA	−.12	−.01	.09
NonSMSA	1.03	.41	.15
Great Lakes			
Total	.36	.48	.27
SMSA	.24	.45	.27
NonSMSA	.77	.58	.28
Plains			
Total	.55	.59	.42
SMSA	.64	.66	.45
NonSMSA	.45	.51	.39
Southeast			
Total	1.42	1.09	.67
SMSA	1.60	1.20	.73
NonSMSA	1.18	.93	.58
Southwest			
Total	1.97	1.44	.68
SMSA	2.23	1.60	.72
NonSMSA	1.30	1.01	.59
Rocky Mountain			
Total	2.30	1.67	.76
SMSA	2.39	1.80	.81
NonSMSA	2.16	1.48	.68
Far West			
Total	1.46	1.25	.64
SMSA	1.31	1.21	.63
NonSMSA	2.53	1.54	.72
Hawaii, Alaska			
Total	2.41	1.79	.84
SMSA	2.25	1.65	.80
NonSMSA	2.79	2.10	.90

Source: BEA, U.S. Department of Commerce.

Table 4–2. Regional Population Levels, SMSA-nonSMSA, Historical and Projections (Thousands)

	1969	1978	2000	2030
United States				
Total	201,298	218,051	259,845	299,817
SMSA	148,667	159,768	189,632	218,522
NonSMSA	52,631	58,283	70,213	81,295
New England				
Total	11,735	12,256	13,716	15,112
SMSA	9,858	10,143	11,143	12,108
NonSMSA	1,877	2,114	2,573	3,004
Middle Atlantic				
Total	42,111	42,224	42,653	43,961
SMSA	36,829	36,431	36,313	37,332
NonSMSA	5,282	5,793	6,340	6,630
Great Lakes				
Total	39,904	41,233	45,818	49,714
SMSA	30,945	31,631	34,926	37,884
NonSMSA	8,959	9,600	10,893	11,830
Plains				
Total	16,202	17,018	19,367	21,957
SMSA	8,298	8,785	10,150	11,604
NonSMSA	7,904	8,233	9,218	10,353
Southeast				
Total	43,440	49,334	62,612	76,490
SMSA	25,026	28,873	37,546	46,659
NonSMSA	18,414	20,461	25,067	29,831
Southwest				
Total	16,328	19,460	26,665	32,689
SMSA	11,586	14,133	20,020	24,767
NonSMSA	4,742	5,328	6,646	7,921
Rocky Mountain				
Total	4,943	6,064	8,734	10,954
SMSA	2,905	3,594	5,322	6,770
NonSMSA	2,038	2,469	3,413	4,184
Far West				
Total	25,596	29,175	38,376	46,498
SMSA	22,494	25,289	32,943	39,784
NonSMSA	3,102	3,886	5,433	6,714
Hawaii, Alaska				
Total	1,039	1,287	1,903	2,443
SMSA	727	888	1,272	1,616
Non SMSA	312	400	631	827

Source: BEA, U.S. Department of Commerce.

78 DEMAND FOR HOUSING

Table 4–3. Index of Projected Population Growth Rates by Region, 1978–2000, 2000–2030 (U.S. = 100)

Region	1978–2000	2000–2030
Rocky Mountain	209	158
Southwest	180	142
Far West	157	133
Southeast	136	140
Plains	74	88
New England	64	67
Great Lakes	60	56
Middle Atlantic	6	21

Source: BEA. U.S. Department of Commerce

than the nonmetropolitan areas. The result of the differential growth among regions and, for the most part, between metropolitan and nonmetropolitan areas is to distribute population geographically more evenly over time in correspondence with a more even geographic distribution of employment and income.

Before we turn to the underlying trends and projections of employment, several observations with respect to the population levels and area delineations presented here need to be made:

1. In October 1980, BEA completed its regional projections for the years 1985–2030. The population projections were based on U.S. Census Bureau estimates through 1979. The 1980 population projection implicit in the projections for the United States was 221.6 million. The Census Bureau certified its April 1, 1980, counts of the U.S. and state populations, however, on December 31, 1980. Its count for the United States was 226.5 million. The 4.9 million difference at the national level is spread unevenly among the states, much of it in the faster growing states of the South and West. Thus, the projected rates and levels of population are probably somewhat understated for these fast-growing regions.
2. The metropolitan areas are those designated by the Office of Management and Budget in 1977, with the exceptions of Burlington, Vermont, and Cheyenne, Wyoming, which were postulated by BEA in order to give each state an SMSA or its

equivalent for purposes of the projections. Over the time horizon of these projections, nonmetropolitan growth may result in more (or more broadly defined) metropolitan areas as the deconcentration of population from city centers and inner suburbs continues (see Leven 1978; Garnick and Renshaw 1980; Long and De Are 1980). Thus metropolitan growth may be greater than that projected here, but that would be the result of changed SMSA designations rather than reflect the areas noted here.

3. Since the BEA data are based on county building blocks, no similar split as that for metropolitan and nonmetropolitan areas is made for cities and suburbs. SMSAs are generally composed of counties; in almost all cases cities are subcounty entities. Nevertheless, some mention will be made of the decentralization of jobs from cities to suburbs and beyond.

UNDERLYING EMPLOYMENT TRENDS

The foregoing population projections are based on state-level birth and death rates and the assumption that interstate (and interarea) migration of the working-age population is mainly determined by economic opportunity. Economic opportunity, in turn, is based on projections of employment and earnings by detailed industry. Interstate dispersion of employment for virtually all nonfarm industries has occurred throughout the entire half-century for which BEA has prepared state estimates of income. And interarea deconcentration of employment from city-core counties to outlying suburban counties (and beyond) has occurred over much of the past quarter-century.

Whatever impact government policy may have had on industrial location patterns (data inadequacies make it difficult to resolve controversy on the question), few would argue against the proposition that changing technology has had a large impact on interregional dispersion and intrarea deconcentration. The shift over time to lightweight materials, miniaturization, and, more generally, the widespread substitution of electronic for mechanical processes and developments in microcircuitry have directly and indirectly reduced the role of transportation costs and of large, skilled labor-pool requirements in the production and distribution processes. The advances in telecommunications, more efficient transmission of power, and, until recently, relatively cheap but still fast and convenient transportation have increasingly overcome the impedances of distance in the provision of producer services—business, financial, professional, transportation, and communications services— as well as in the production and distribution of goods. Overall, economies of proximity have been weakening. Cities built during an earlier period of industrialization required larger labor pools and denser concentrations than current production and distribution processes appear to warrant.

As an example, NCR (formerly National Cash Register) reduced its work force in Dayton, Ohio, from a peak of 20,000 to 5,000 between 1969 and 1977. This reduction resulted from adapting microcircuit technology in its product lines, shifting from mechanical cash registers to point-of-sales data terminals and a full line of computer systems. The changing composition of its output was reflected in dropping the manufacture of 5,000 mechanical parts, requiring large, skilled labor pools, for the production of cash registers in favor of simpler assembling of several hundred smaller electronic components, many of which are manufactured in areas of low labor cost in the United States and abroad. Not only are the size and skills of the area labor force requirements reduced, but plant requirements are also reduced and floor space layouts changed (see "NCR's New Strategy Puts It into Computers to Stay" 1977 and McInnis 1978). Thus, dense multistory plants are increasingly giving way to more extensively spaced single-story plants, which tend to be located where land rents as well as labor costs and market and supply-source access costs are minimized overall.

Manufacturing employment had been the major portal for entry into the work force, as well as to upward mobility, for generations of migrants to the cities prior to the 1960s. But the decline of cities as centers of manufacturing diminished such opportunities after midcentury, particularly in northern and central regions. Manufacturing employment fell, not only in the cities but in most metropolitan areas overall, throughout the northern and central regions during the late 1960s and 1970s. Nonmetropolitan areas in these regions better maintained and sometimes (especially in the case of the Plains states) improved their manufacturing job situations, often at the expense of the cities and even the suburbs. For the most part, however, manufacturing employment growth accelerated in the southern and western regions during these years in both metropolitan and nonmetropolitan areas. The metropolitan areas on the average did somewhat better than the nonmetropolitan, except for the more densely populated areas in California.

Manufacturing employment was not a significant source of growth in the U.S. economy overall in the 1970s, although it was substantial in the southern and western regions as well as in the Great Plains. In fact, the commodities-producing industries as a whole offered little opportunity for employment to the large group of new labor force entrants in the 1970s. Service industry growth was the major source of employment opportunities in the private sector in all regions of the country. Here again, the South and West (and, to a lesser extent, the Plains) grew at significantly higher rates than the national average, and the earlier industrialized states of the Northeast and Great Lakes grew at well below average. The faster growth of services in the South and West is related to the growth of manufacturing and to the catch-up in per capita income in these regions as well as to energy-related production growth.

Population projections are in part related to projections of employment. Table 4–4 presents historical and projected average annual total employment growth rates by region and by metropolitan-nonmetropolitan areas. Population and employment growth rates are not entirely commensurate however, although employment growth rates will better approximate the rate of growth of new households. Because new entrants to the labor force in the projected period will stem from cohorts born during a period of low birth rates (following the postwar baby boom), employment growth is projected to drop from the mid-1980s on. Although the national average annual growth rate for total employment was more than twice that for population growth during the 1970s, it is projected to be only 50 percent higher in the period to the year 2000. Moreover, the employment growth rate will fall to almost 50 percent lower than the population growth rate in the period from 2000 to 2030, as the average age of the population increases. The South and West are projected to maintain significantly higher shares of total employment growth, as well as population growth, over the entire projections period. And nonmetropolitan employment and population growth rates

Table 4–4. Regional Average Annual Total Employment Growth Rates, SMSA-nonSMSA, Historical and Projections

	1969–1978	1978–2000	2000–2030
United States			
Total	1.89	1.18	.25
SMSA	1.80	1.16	.24
NonSMSA	2.19	1.26	.27
New England			
Total	1.19	.83	.08
SMSA	1.09	.73	.04
NonSMSA	1.74	1.31	.28
Middle Atlantic			
Total	.36	.47	−.11
SMSA	.23	.42	−.11
NonSMSA	1.40	.83	−.06
Great Lakes			
Total	1.21	.90	.08
SMSA	1.11	.88	.08
NonSMSA	1.59	1.00	.09
Plains			
Total	1.90	.96	.16
SMSA	2.03	1.03	.19
NonSMSA	1.74	.86	.13
Southeast			
Total	2.63	1.50	.39
Total	2.80	1.56	.41
NonSMSA	2.33	1.40	.35
Southwest			
Total	3.51	1.75	.49
SMSA	3.76	1.88	.52
NonSMSA	2.70	1.31	.39
Rocky Mountain			
Total	4.13	2.04	.55
SMSA	4.26	2.17	.59
NonSMSA	3.93	1.80	.49
Far West			
Total	2.85	1.55	.39
SMSA	2.75	1.50	.38
NonSMSA	3.65	1.87	.46

Source: BEA, U.S. Department of Commerce.

are projected to exceed metropolitan rates, but not in the South and West (excluding California).

ON THE FUTURE GEOGRAPHIC DISTRIBUTION OF HOUSING

As noted at the outset, while the southern and western regions of the United States should grow faster in the future than the northern and central regions (and nonmetropolitan faster than metropolitan areas), the latter are not projected to become empty quarters. The national 1978 population is projected to increase by 82 million by the year 2030 (and nonmetropolitan areas to increase by 23 million). New England is projected to increase by 2.9 million (of which nonmetropolitan areas will account for nearly 0.9 million); the Mideast, or Middle Atlantic states, 1.7 million (nonmetropolitan 0.8 million); the Great Lakes 8.5 million (nonmetropolitan 2.2 million); the Plains 4.9 million (nonmetropolitan 2.1 million); the Southeast 27.2 million (nonmetropolitan 9.4 million); the Southwest 13.2 million (nonmetropolitan 2.6 million); Rocky Mountain 4.9 million (nonmetropolitan 1.7 million); and the Far West (not including Alaska and Hawaii) 17.3 million (nonmetropolitan 2.8 million).

These projections of population are in part based on Bureau of Census Series II national projections of population; the subnational distribution of the projected population is based mainly on regional economic projections. The BEA regional economic projections are based on an extension and some modification of the U.S. Bureau of Labor Statistics national employment and gross national product (GNP) projections (*Falim and Fullerton* 1978). BEA projects states' growth as shares of the national industrial growth by "constrained" extrapolations of past relations and share growth rates. The limiting assumption of decelerating regional growth advantages was imposed on the projected trend lines to reflect underlying equilibrating forces (changing mixes of positive and negative externalities) at work in the regional economies. Still, the methodology may very well understate the extent to which technological change promises to permit even more footloose industrial location patterns than heretofore and even less constraints to residential location choice.

During the projected period, five jobs will be created in service industries and government for each job created in goods-producing industries. Many of the jobs in the former category will be connected with the information industry. Even now wage employees in this industry are able to do at least some of their work in their own homes via portable computer terminals and connecting telecommunications. Moreover, self-employment in general (*Fain* 1980) and in the information industry in particular has been growing rapidly in recent years, reversing the quarter-century decline following World War II. The pace of improvements in microcomputer technology is breathtaking. Not only is the microcomputer becoming increasingly powerful, but it will become virtually ubiquitous. Toffler (1980) foresees, among changes stemming from this, the reconstitution of the household as the place of production—technological cottage industries. And this, clearly, will remove work commutation field constraints on residential location choices significantly.

Work commutation fields appear to have expanded progressively, at least since the end of World War II. By the mid-1970s, one-third of all workers commuted outside their areas of residences, designated by metropolitan suburban and city, and nonmetropolitan areas (*Wescott* 1979). Hamilton (1981) finds that the average distance of the journey to work is surprisingly higher than would be predicted by the standard models of urban form, that no apparent difference exists in the average commuting distance between compact cities of the East and their less compact counterparts in the West, that the volume of commuting is up to ten times higher than optimal, and that an assumption of random behavior is a much better predictor of urban form than standard optimizing models. The concept of optimality employed by Hamilton entails only the minimization of land rents plus transportation costs. The two job commutation studies cited were based on mid-1970s Annual Housing Survey journey-to-work data. It might be assumed that the effect of the rising real costs of commutation following the sharp oil price increases after 1974 had not yet fully worked its way into the residential-location calculus of utility. Yet the migration of persons to nonmetropolitan areas and outer suburban counties actually accelerated in the latter half of the 1970s. Many surveys have shown continuing household preferences for exurban and small-town residential locations. In addition, a future such as that foreseen by Toffler (1980) would permit an even more substantial fraction of the population to benefit from the positive externalities they appear to perceive in exurban residential location.

In summary, a preference has been clearly revealed for deconcentrated residential location within areas, manifested increasingly over the entire post World War II period, as well as longer term interregional dispersion. Decentralization of jobs has also proceeded apace. Not only have manufacturing and consumer service employment moved out from city centers and interregionally, but producer service employment has increasingly followed this pattern. Even considering rising real costs of energy, technology appears to support further deconcentration and interregional dispersion. And the BEA regional projections appear to have captured these trends for the most part. They might possibly overstate the potential for employment and population growth in the Great Lakes states, especially until the year 2000, owing to the impact of further advances in electronics and robotics in the automobile and machinery industries. Not sufficiently accounting for the reversal in self-employment and the more recent acceleration of exurban migration, not to mention Toffler's cottage industries of the future, the projections may overstate the growth potential for presently constituted metropolitan areas in the South and West. The offset would be understated growth in the nonmetropolitan areas of these regions, especially in light of the historical pattern of metropolitan growth retardation and even reversal elsewhere, as diminishing returns set in. To a lesser extent, the same may be true for the Northeast and central regions. Thus even more deconcentration and dispersion than given in the projections might be likely beyond the start of the twenty-first century. The implications of these projections for housing markets, even with the aforementioned qualifications, seem clear. The large increment in new housing requirements will evidently be sharply felt in the growing areas in the South and West. But the housing industry in the Northeast and central regions will also have a very substantial workload.

About one-third of the current U.S. housing stock is over forty years old. Much of this stock is in the earlier established and slower growing Northeast and central regions. Even though these regions will not be the major beneficiaries of the increased population over the next fifty years, between 50 and 70 percent of the existing housing stock will have to be replaced or substantially restored. In the Middle Atlantic states alone this will entail 8 to 12 million housing units replaced or restored versus approximately 750,000 new housing units to accommodate the projected increment of 1.7 million in population between 1978 and 2030. Clearly, the housing market in the twenty-first century is not merely a market of increments. And, for all the high percentage growth of population, in the Rocky Mountain region and the low percentage in the Mid-Atlantic region—the fastest and slowest growing regions—the latter remains a much larger market.

It was noted in the preceding discussion that nonmetropolitan growth is likely to occur even somewhat faster than given in the overall projections. Clearly much of this growth will be in the form of incremental housing construction rather than replacement and substantially rehabilitated housing stock. Two groups in particular are likely to seek housing in these areas: two-parent families with children and retirees. Both will tend to seek out places where housing is cheaper and which they perceive to be safe spaces and close to natural amenities, as has been the trend increasingly over the 1970s and longer. Moreover, mineral-related industries will offer continuing additional employment opportunities in nonmetropolitan areas over the period. Information-industry growth combined with cheaper data transmission to and from remote terminals will also permit the dispersion of two-worker families. Slow-growing manufacturing will also continue its dispersion, providing even more economic base to small-town growth in nonmetropolitan areas among all the regions of the country. Still most of producer services and a large part of government employment will be based in existing cities and suburbs, and most of the gainfully employed members of households, both small and large, will continue to reside in these areas as reflected in the projections.

NOTES

1. The substate population projections were computed as follows: For each substate area the population/employment ratio in 1978 was multiplied by the projected growth rate in the parent-state popula-

tion/employment ratio. This result was then multiplied by the sub-state area total employment projections for the given time period to get projected substate area population. The three alternative sets of population projections were based entirely on a mathematical procedure relating historical and future trends. For each of the industries upon which total employment and population growth were based, the projections were made in terms of the substate area's share of the state's employment. The alternative projection presented here was computed as follows: For each industry, the substate area's share of the state's employment was projected to change from 1978 to 1980 at an annual rate of change equal to 85 percent of the annual rate of change in the share from 1969 to 1978; from 1980 to 1985, at an annual rate equal to two-thirds of the projected annual rate for 1978 to 1980; and for each succeeding five-year period, at two-thirds of the projected rate for the preceding five-year period. See the November 1980 issue of the *Survey of Current Business* for a summary description of the state and, therefore, regional methodology.

2. The states and the District of Columbia are divided among the nine regions as follows: New England: Maine, New Hampshire, Vermont, Massachusetts, Rhode Island, Connecticut; Mideast, better known as Middle Atlantic: New York, New Jersey, Pennsylvania, Delaware, Maryland, District of Columbia; Great Lakes: Michigan, Ohio, Indiana, Illinois, Wisconsin; Plains: Minnesota, Iowa, Missouri, North Dakota, South Dakota, Nebraska, Kansas; Southeast: Virginia, West Virginia, Kentucky, Tennessee, North Carolina, South Carolina, Georgia, Florida, Alabama, Mississippi, Louisiana, Arkansas; Southwest: Oklahoma, Texas, New Mexico, Arizona; Rocky Mountain: Montana, Idaho, Wyoming, Colorado, Utah; Far West: Washington, Oregon, Nevada, California. Hawaii and Alaska are listed separately.

REFERENCES

Fain, T. Scott. 1980. "Self-Employed Americans: Their Number Has Increased." *Monthly Labor Review* (November): 3–8.

Falim, Paul O., and Howard N. Fullerton, Jr. 1978. "Labor Force Projection to 1990: Three Possible Paths." *Monthly Labor Review* (December): 25–35.

Garnick, Daniel H. 1978a. "The Northeast States in the National Context." In *The Declining Northeast, Demographic and Economic Analyses*, edited by Benjamin Chinitz. New York: Praeger.

————. 1978b. "Reappraising the Outlook for Northern States and Cities in the Context of U.S. Economic History." Working Paper 51, Cambridge, Mass: Joint Center for Urban Studies.

Garnick, Daniel H., and Vernon Renshaw. 1980. "Competing Hypotheses on the Outlook for Cities and Regions: What the Data Reveal and Conceal." *Papers of the Regional Science Association* 45:105–24.

Hamilton, Bruce H. 1981. "Wasteful Commuting." Working Papers in Economics, no. 74, The Johns Hopkins University, Baltimore, Md.

Leven, Charles. 1978. "Growth and Nongrowth in Metropolitan Areas and the Emergence of Polycentric Metropolitan Form." *Papers of the Regional Science Association* 41:101–12.

Long, Larry H., and Diana De Are. 1980. *Migration to Nonmetropolitan Areas: Appraising the Trend and Reasons for Moving.* U.S. Bureau of the Census, Special Demographic Analyses.

McInnis, D. 1978. "How Technology Altered NCR and Dayton." *Washington Post* (January 8):F2.

"NCR's New Strategy Puts It into Computers to Stay." 1977. *Business Week* (September 26):100–4.

"Regional and State Projections of Income, Employment, and Population to the Year 2000." 1980. *Survey of Current Business* (November):44–70.

Toffler, Alvin. 1980. *The Third Wave.* New York: Morrow.

Wescott, Diana N. 1979. "Employment and Commuting Patterns: A Residential Analysis." *Monthly Labor Review* (July):3–9.

▌▌ SUPPLY OF HOUSING

One of the dominant features of housing markets is the role the standing housing stock plays in the marketplace. This role derives from the durability and fixed location aspects of real estate. Even a buoyant housing market will add only 4–5 percent to the stock each year. Hence, even if the North American housing production sector is very active for the duration of the century, more than half of all of the housing units in the year 2000 are already built and in place. If slower rates of growth, in the 2–3 percent range, are assumed then as much as 75 percent of the year 2000 housing stock is presently in existence. Accordingly, when looking at issues relating to the supply of housing we must consider both new supply and the management of the existing stock.

Focusing first on some of the principal issues relating to the standing stock, we find the following important questions to be addressed: How can the stock be managed so as to maximize the flow of housing services? What kinds of repair, maintenance, and renovation policies . . . and expenditures should be pursued? What opportunities exist to provide more or better housing services by reusing residential structures (both single- and multiple-family dwellings) in innovative ways? What opportunities exist for providing housing services from nonresidential building stock? How well will a housing stock built largely in the 1950s, 1960s, and early 1970s suit the needs of the changing demographic structure of North America's population? Is the stock located appropriately given changing locational preferences?

Concerning the new supply a somewhat different set of questions present themselves. Will land and infrastructure be sufficient to accommodate future residential construction? Will the growth and environmental controls of the 1960s and 1970s continue, diminish, or strengthen during the 1980s and beyond? Will the costs of new construction (including mortgages, materials, labor, and land) permit new housing units to be built economically? What kinds of units will be built in the future; specifically, what bundles of amenities, size, fixtures, and so forth will be needed to serve the changing spatial and demographic composition of demand?

Two of the chapters in this part of the volume consider aspects of the production of new housing supply. The study by Robert Edelstein, "The Production Function for Housing and Its Implications for Future Urban Development," estimates a housing production function using a data base of residential sales from five major areas in the United States. His approach is firmly rooted in microeconomic models of production and in the growing urban economics literature on this topic. The findings of his study suggest that the elasticity of substitution of land and nonland inputs is greater than previously recognized. Frank Clayton and Robert Hobart in Chapter 6, "The Supply of New Housing in Canada into the Twenty-first Century," take an alternative approach in this area and provide an overview of the likely changes in the supply side of Canadian housing markets over the next two decades. The availability of land, labor, and energy, as well as the effects of government policies, are assessed as factors that may affect new housing supply.

With respect to the existing housing stock and its management, Peter Chinloy's "Housing Repair and Housing Stocks," Chapter 7, analyzes repair and maintenance policies in the Canadian housing market. After describing the relevant institutional context of such policies, Chinloy develops a model for estimating net depreciation and maintenance rates based on demand projections of the Canadian Mortgage and Housing Corporation's housing requirements model (see Chapter 1). He also considers the cost/benefit relation of repair and maintenance expenditures. Ira (Jack)

Lowry in Chapter 8, "Managing the Existing Housing Stock: Prospects and Problems," examines the effect on the supply of U.S. housing services of changing preferences for location, size, and features of the dwelling, and preferred tenure arrangements. He argues that the most difficult problems in the area of inventory management are local housing surpluses created by population movements.

5 THE PRODUCTION FUNCTION FOR HOUSING AND ITS IMPLICATIONS FOR FUTURE URBAN DEVELOPMENT

Robert H. Edelstein

Many urban economics models have been devised to explain land use and the structure of urban space. Among the more important and respected examples are works by Muth (1969), Mills (1967), Smith (1976), Kau and Lee (1976 a,b), and Fallis (1979). An element crucial for drawing meaningful conclusions from these models about urban structure is the assumed properties of the production fuction. Elasticity of substitution between land and nonland improvements for housing is usually the key production function parameter for determining the long-run housing supply function and location equilibrium. Despite extensive research efforts attempting to estimate the value of the elasticity of substitution for housing factor inputs, a final answer is far from universal agreement. The confluence of data and estimation problems as well as conceptual-statistical modeling issues have engendered a lingering, thorny theoretical and empirical debate.[1]

While this research project has evolved over several years, the principal support for the empirical analysis has been provided by the Federal Home Loan Bank of San Francisco. I also have benefited from earlier research support for this work from the Federal Reserve Bank of Philadelphia, the Finance Department of the Wharton School at the University of Pennsylvania, and the School of Business at the University of Southern California. I would like to express my special thanks to Karen Alpert and Bruce Besecker for their willingness and expertise as my research assistants. I have benefited from conversations with many people; especially I wish to thank James Follain and Richard Muth for their comments. Of course, all errors remaining in the paper are solely my responsibility as author.

93

This chapter has two principal purposes. First, a new set of alternative empirical estimates is developed for the elasticity of substitution between land and nonland improvements for single-family residential parcels. These estimates are shown to be superior to those of earlier efforts because of theoretical and methodological research improvements. Second, a perspective is created pertaining to the effects of the elasticity of substitution on urban spatial structure. Using the estimates for the elasticity of substitution for housing within a model that is a variant of traditional urban economic analyses, the structure of the supply function for housing and the input-factor demand functions are explored.

In brief, this chapter concludes that the elasticity of substitution for housing inputs is sensitive to model specification, estimation procedures, and data base. It is highly likely that the elasticity of substitution is a variable function, differing from one geographic area to another. This result may be true because of technological, taste, and institutional differences across geographic areas as well as statistical-methodological estimation problems. If these claims are true, urban economics researchers using analytic models need to take great care in expounding the impacts of public policy and other factors on urban spatial development.

The discussion proceeds as follows: First the relation between the housing production function and the elasticity of substitution is outlined, then the basic issues and problems that pervade the estimation of the elasticity of substitution are catalogued and several important prior studies reviewed. The third section presents and discusses the present study's alternative estimates for the elasticity of substitution for housing inputs. The fourth section integrates estimates for the elasticity of substitution and a theoretical model for urban spatial structure in order to derive the urban housing supply function. An attempt is also made to place the elasticity of substitution estimation and urban economic models into a useful perspective for future research.

HOUSING PRODUCTION FUNCTIONS

In general, the housing services production function is of the form

$$Q = f(L,K),$$

where

Q = *the capacity of housing to generate the output of housing services per period;*

K = *the stock of nonland (improvements) inputs; and*

L = *the stock of land (building site) inputs.*

As is usual in these studies, the physical and price input data are measured as stock variables rather than economic flow variables. Presumably, the values and quantities of the stocks relate to (and correlate with) the corresponding flow variables.[2] Technically, therefore, the output measure Q is the capacity of a housing dwelling to provide a flow of housing services, which is a combination of the "quality" and "quantity" of housing. Although Q will be analyzed as an output from a technical production function, it should be recognized that Q is an aggregate and surrogate index, reflecting tastes as well as technology for producing a complex output, *housing shelter.*

This model of housing production assumes that returns to firm size are constant at a given location. This assumption seems consistent with the empirical fact that the residential construction industry is composed of many variable-sized firms. Furthermore, it seems neither plausible nor necessary to assume constant returns for the residential construction industry as a whole. For instance, at a given location the average cost for producing a given quality and quantity of housing is likely to be independent of the builder's size. However, similar houses built at other locations within a city, because of locational differences in land prices, would not necessarily be produced at the same average costs. If this is true, the assumption of constant returns to the residential construction industry appears *not* to be warranted.

If the production function has convex isoquants, the marginal rate of technical factor substitution between L and K and the input ratio of L/K will both decline as L is substituted for K along an isoquant. The elasticity of substitution between land and nonland improvements (σ) is a pure nonnegative number that measures the rate at which substitution takes place and is defined as the proportionate rate of change of the input ratio divided by the proportionate change of the marginal rate of technical factor substitution:

$$\sigma = \frac{d \log (K/L)}{d \log (f_L/f_K)} = \frac{f_L/f_K}{K/L} \cdot \frac{d(K/L)}{d(f_L/f_K)} .$$ 5-1

Under the normal assumptions of convex isoquants, σ will be non-negative.[3]

The elasticity of substitution, σ, will be the principal focus for this study's theoretical and empirical analysis. As will be shown, important features about urban spatial structure hinge on the precise value of σ. Appendix 5A discusses the technical relations among the estimating equations for the elasticity of substitution and alternative functional forms for the housing production function.

ESTIMATION PROBLEMS AND THE ELASTICITY OF SUBSTITUTION

The objective of this section is to delineate and to the extent possible resolve the apparent problems that pervade empirical estimation of the elasticity of substitution between land and nonland inputs for housing. A comprehensive review of prior empirical studies of the elasticity of substitution, including a discussion of empirical problems, has been presented by McDonald (1981, especially sections 4 and 5). He emphasizes the potential importance of measurement error bias and differences in specification of the proper functional form for estimation in existing σ estimates. Without retracing unnecessarily the same materials he covers, it is useful to clarify several of his conclusions. Additional empirical issues, not explored by McDonald, do merit review and explanations. After reexamining measurement error and specification bias problems, this section examines the estimation issues relating to the Federal Housing Administration (FHA) data base, surrogate variable definition errors, data aggregation, and statistical simultaneity.

Measurement Error and Estimating Functional Form

In the estimation of the elasticity of substitution for housing, Clapp (1980) and MacDonald (1981) observe that serious measurement error is likely to exist in the independent variable, especially the price of land inputs. Depending on the functional form of the estimating equation, this bias produces statistically inconsistent estimators that typically yield lower value than the true

parameter σ. McDonald (1981:208) claims, and there is good reason to concur, that if the estimating function form uses the *ratio*
of inputs prices as the independent variables, there may be offsetting measurements errors in R (the input price per unit of improvements) and W (input price per unit of land). When this
chapter uses different housing production functions for estimating
σ (see Appendix 5A), the independent variable for each case is the
ratio of input prices, which accordingly should mitigate the measurement-error bias problem.

Without denying that measurement error may impair the statistical estimating process, there is a more fundamental objection
to this argument as it is raised. In the estimation of the elasticity
of substitution with microparcel data, as in the instant case, Mc-
Donald states that "It is likely that appraisals of land value by
tax assessors or real estate appraisers are made with appreciable
error" (1981:203). This claim is proffered without substantial evidence, and, given the context, may put the issue out of proper
perspective. "Comparable" methods for many real estate markets
may generate very reasonable estimates of land prices for single-
family homes, with *relatively* small measurement error.[4] The
land-price estimates by appraisers probably have similar levels of
accuracy vis-a-vis building costs per square foot for new construction or estimates of *total* fair market value for new single-family
houses.

Furthermore, the observed selling price for housing, a variable
used directly or indirectly in many of the studies of σ, is a mar-
ket-observed "estimate" of fair market value and in that sense is
not likely to be free of measurement error. If one were therefore
to rearrange the estimating function in order to use "value" as
the independent variable, it would be unlikely to avoid measurement-error bias. In sum, measurement-error bias in many of the
studies would conceivably be minimized by using the input prices
as the independent variable rather than other variables.

FHA Data Base

As in many of the earlier studies of σ, the data consist of new
single-family houses sold under the auspices of the Federal Housing Administration Department-Housing and Urban Develop-

ment (FHA-HUD) 203 program (Appendix 5B provides details about the data base).[5] In contrast to many of the prior studies, this analysis uses individual single-family transactions as the unit of observation instead of census tract of Standard Metropolitan Statistical Area (SMSA) averaged data. Despite limitations of the FHA data noted by Muth (1971) among others, at the microindividual parcel level it is likely to provide reasonably accurate reflections of market behavior. The principal restriction inherent in the FHA-HUD 203 market program data is the sales price ceiling for eligible sales transactions, which delimits the range of observations.[6]

The data for each FHA microparcel in the sample were combined with census tract data. The FHA data have detailed information about the parcel characteristics, the financial arrangements of the sales transactions, and the financial and personal circumstances of the buyer. The census tract data were chosen to reflect neighborhood amenities and important socioeconomic and locational characteristics of the parcel. This data base is relatively comprehensive and rich and is needed to address properly the statistical problems of simultaneity and surrogate-definition error.[7]

Surrogate Variable Definition Error

Several prior studies have used data from a cross-section of SMSAs to evaluate the elasticity of substitution. Muth 1971, Sirmans and Redman 1979, Polinsky and Ellwood 1979, and Rosen 1978 are typical. All of these studies use FHA-HUD housing data, the first two employ average data for each of several SMSAs whereas the latter two use individual parcel observations from various SMSAs. In each study it is recognized that the cost of construction (the price of nonland inputs) may differ across SMSAs, and a Boeckh index for each SMSA is used as a surrogate for measuring relative nonland costs. The Boeckh index reflects the cost of construction for a "typical" structure for each SMSA and does not represent clearly the cost of construction for the *mix* of housing in the FHA-HUD programs either within an SMSA or between SMSAs.

Other earlier estimates of the elasticity of substitution for land and nonland for housing were based upon data from a single SMSA or housing market. For example, McDonald (1979) used a sample of single-family housing sales for Chicago. Sirmans, Kau, and Lee (1979) . . . and McDonald (1981) use the same sample of census tract averaged data for housing in Santa Clara County, California. As do various others, these studies claim that the cost of construction is constant within the specific housing market. Though conventional and plausible, this claim is true only if one were to control for possible quality differences per unit of housing improvements. As will be discussed under statistical simultaneity problems, within a housing market the quality and quantity of housing may differ between neighborhood locations, a likelihood that should be accounted for by a location-construction cost function for R.[8]

Data Aggregation

McDonald, summarizing earlier studies, avers:

> Estimates of σ based upon data from a single metropolitan area tend to be greater than the estimates obtained from a cross-section of metropolitan areas. Can this be explained by "aggregation bias"? A little reflection and consultation with Theil (1971: 556–562) will convince one that this cannot be the case. Since all of the studies of a cross-section of metropolitan areas are simple OLS [ordinary least squares] regressions (only one independent variable), the estimates of σ produced are the simple means of σ for each of the metropolitan areas in the sample. (1981:202–3)

McDonald (1981) appears to misunderstand the limitations and inapplicability of Theil's (1971) presentation. There is good reason to suspect that aggregation bias, to the contrary, could have a significant impact on the value of the elasticity of substitution estimated from cross-sections of either SMSA-averaged data (e.g., studies by Muth (1971) or Sirmans and Redman (1979)) or census tract averaged data as in studies by McDonald (1981) or Sirmans, Kau, and Lee (1979)).

Aggregation of data for SMSAs or census tracts is likely to introduce a serious statistical problem referred to as "pure aggregation bias" (Feige and Watts 1972). If the *independent* variable is used (explicity or implicitly) as the basis for aggregation, the coefficients of a regression estimated using OLS will be biased. Consider the properly specified model

$$Y = a + bX + e,\qquad\qquad 5\text{-}2$$

where a and b are the parameters to be estimated and e is the stochastic error term with the appropriate statistical properties. The means $\overline{Y}_i$ and $\overline{X}_i$ are calculated from the data that have been classified into intervals i, according to the value of the dependent variable Y. As the number of observations in each interval increases, X_i approaches $E(\overline{X}_i / \overline{Y}_i)$. Hence the explanatory variable X will not be statistically independent of the OLS regression error term e, causing a "simultaneity" bias. This will cause the absolute value of the estimated parameter to be overstated (biased upward).

In terms of the elasticity of substitution studies, the aggregation of data for several SMSAs or within SMSAs or census tracts is likely to cause implicitly this classification aggregation bias. This happens because SMSA or census tract data aggregation takes means of sample data that are likely to be considerably more homogeneous than the population data as a whole. To counter this problem, instrumental variable, simultaneous equation methods for estimation are necessary.

Another possibility, one usually related to the aggregation issue, for explaining the systematic variation in the values estimated from cross-section data versus single housing market data is that the elasticity of substitution may vary across metropolitan and even submetropolitan areas such as neighborhoods.[9] As can be seen in Figure 5–1, if the correct level for analysis were subgeographic, analysis conducted at a larger geographic level could disguise the true relation irrespective of whether data were aggregated (as in Muth 1971) or not (as in Rosen 1978). In Figure 5–1 the "true" parameters (assuming the constant elasticity of substitution is the correct form of the production function) are σ_1, σ_2, and σ_3, corresponding to subgeographic areas 1, 2, and 3, respectively. The circles represent the data concentrations for each area. The elasticity of substitution (Agg σ) estimated from a sample of either subarea aggregate average data or the combined subarea microdata will be too low vis-à-vis the true parameters. This bias essentially is caused by the pooling together of data that belongs to subgroups (different functional populations). Of course, if microdata were available, one could use standard statistical tests to examine this possibility.

Simultaneity

It is reasonable to expect that W, the price of land inputs, varies systematically with parcel location because of neighborhood and localized private and public amenities and because of different plot features. The cost of construction (nonland) inputs R may vary by location because the quality and the quantity of housing supplied are likely to be related to parcel location.[10] In the analysis using microparcel data, the levels of nonland to land inputs are represented by the relative number of square feet of each in the real estate parcel. Obviously, there are qualitative differences

Figure 5–1.   Aggregation and Estimation of Elasticity of Substitution

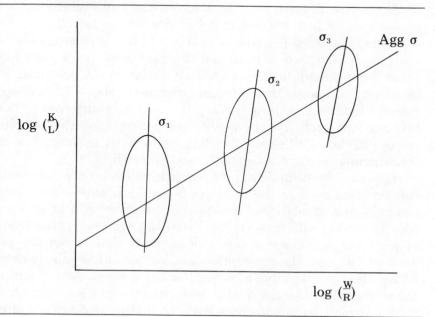

in both improvements and land inputs, which should be reflected in factor price differences across dwelling units.

In the case of nonland improvements, three types of relations appear to affect the cost and price per square foot for nonland inputs. First, if one were to control for the quality differences among dwellings, as a technical matter, the cost per square foot (the nonland improvement factor price) decreases as the dwelling square footage increases. This occurs because as the square footage increases (with quality controlled), the ratio of floor area to wall area increases, thereby reducing the effective cost of production per square foot of floor area. Similarly, certain basic dwelling equipment cost is allocated over a larger square-foot area as a dwelling's floor area increases. Second, controlling for dwelling-unit quality, the design of the floor plan affects the cost per square foot. The more closely a building conforms to a square, *ceteris paribus*, the lower is its cost per square foot. In general the lower the ratio of the dwelling's perimeter footage to its total floor area (square footage), the lower the cost of production per square foot of living space. Third, and in contrast to the first point, the *total* cost per square foot tends to increase as the floor area increases, because dwelling quality is usually related to dwelling size. That is, a larger house usually has additional and higher quality features not found in smaller houses.

Hence, the price per square foot for building is a function of both the total square footage and the quality of each square foot, these factors tend to be interrelated variables. In principle, the usual way to handle this problem econometrically is to develop a hedonic index for housing quality. The index is supposed to take into account explicitly the quality differences (and their implied prices effects) of different dwelling units, such as fireplaces, air conditioning, garages, basements, and so forth.

However, the hedonic index approach by itself may not resolve this problem because the producer is simultaneously determining the amount and quality of inputs *and* the price per unit of inputs (due to quality differences). Put somewhat differently, the theory of producer optimization behavior suggests that, given the production function, the input prices and output prices jointly determined the optimal input choices. For the present data the input prices are related to the quality of input choices (land and physical improvements are *not* homogeneous inputs) and in turn affect the price of output. Therefore, temporarily abstracting from land cost differences, the cost and market value per square foot of non-land improvements are likely to be optimally determined *simultaneously*.

Similarly, turning to land inputs, and as it is well documented in the real estate appraisal and urban economic literature, site values (the prices of land inputs) are influenced by locational-neighborhood characteristics, including public and private local amenities, and physical-legal features, such as lot area and land use zoning controls, property policies, and so forth. For empirical analysis, one needs to utilize properly the explanatory variables for site values that reflect locality differences. However, it is likely for producer optimizing behavior that because of location variables (including public services and tax capitalization effects), the size of the site used to build and the price of land inputs are simultaneously determined. In summary, the physical input ratio (K/L) and the input price ratio (W/R) plausibly are simultaneously determined variables. Econometrically, using OLS would generate inconsistent parameter estimation. In the empirical models to be described, in order to avoid this problem estimation has been conducted by using two-stage least squares (TSLS), a simultaneous-equation method.[11]

EMPIRICAL ESTIMATES

Using alternative production functions, the derived elasticity of substitution estimators was statistically fitted using a sample of 815 new single-family home transactions from the FHA-HUD 203 market program from nine counties in five different SMSAs. Tables 5–1 to 5–3 present the empirical estimates for the elasticity of substitution between land and nonland inputs for housing based upon three forms of the production function. As developed in Appendix 5A, the estimating functional forms are Eq. (5A-2), (5A-3), and (5A-6), which correspond to the CES (constant elasticity of substitution), VES (variable elasticity of substitution), and TRANSLOG) (transcendental Logarithmic) formulations for the production functions.

From the discussion in the preceding section, it is likely that substantial empirical problems may persist in estimating the

Table 5–1.   CES Production Function Estimates for the Elasticity of Substitution Between Land and Nonland, σ^a

Geographic Area	OLS Estimate for σ	TSLS Estimate for σ^b	Number of Observations
Los Angeles–Long Beach SMSA	.60 (.12)	.36 (.15)	39
Three New Jersey counties in Philadelphia–Camden SMSA[c]	.94 (.07)	.93 (.09)	51
Two San Bernardino SMSA counties[d]	.80 (.03)	.52 (.07)	325
San Diego SMSA	.59 (.13)	.89 (.14)	246
Two San Francisco SMSA counties[e]	1.00 (.04)	1.11 (.08)	154
Aggregate Nine-county data from the five SMSA's	.77 (.09)	.67 (.12)	9

a. Standard errors of the coefficients are in parentheses below the estimated coefficient.

b. The exogenous, excluded instrumental variables were a combination of census tract data and individual FHA purchaser and PHA parcel data. The instruments used in each SMSA varied; for a complete list of variables see Appendix 5B.

c. Camden, Burlington, and Gloucester Counties.

d. Riverside and San Bernardino Counties.

e. Alameda and Contra Costa Counties.

elasticity of substitution. Depending upon the data base and the estimating equation functional form, measurement error bias, aggregation bias, specification bias and simultaneity bias are all likely to be present, and the impact of these biases collectively is likely to be unclear either a priori or ex post facto. Nonetheless, to the extent possible the use of microdata and instrumental variable estimating techniques should tend to mitigate these econometric problems.

The value of σ derived from the CES (Table 5–1) and VES (Table 5–2) production functions have been estimated using OLS and

Table 5–2. VES Production Function Estimates for the Elasticity of Substitution Between Land and NonLand, σ[a]

Geographic Area	OLS Estimate for σ	TSLS Estimate for σ[b]	K L Ratio[c]
Los Angeles–Long Beach SMSA	−.08 (.08)	.02 (.10)	.21
Three New Jersey counties in Philadelphia–Camden SMSA	.55 (.11)	.65 (.14)	.16
Two San Bernardino SMSA counties	.01 (.04)	−.01 (.14)	.15
San Diego SMSA	.04 (.20)	.08 (.40)	.19
Two San Francisco SMSA counties	.17 (.09)	.68 (.20)	.37
Nine county aggregate estimator	.35 (.21)	.31 (.23)	.19

a. Standard errors of the estimates are directly below each estimate for σ.

b. See footnote b in Table 5–1 regarding choice of instruments for two-stage least squares estimation.

c. The ratio of nonland improvements measured in square feet to land (lot size) measured in square feet.

TSLS. The TRANSLOG (Table 5–3) estimators for σ were estimated by constrained-coefficient-TSLS methods. Given the inherent econometric problems, TSLS estimates for σ are preferred. In Tables 5–1 and 5–2 the TSLS and OLS generated estimates of σ often differ substantially. In all tables the estimates for σ by geographic area tend to differ significantly as well. This suggests, as hypothesized, that the production function for housing is likely to vary from place to place.

After estimating the statistical relation for σ, each observation can be checked for the quasi-concavity of the production function. In the case of the two inputs, L and K, this is equivalent to checking that the "estimated" value of σ is positive for each observation. Since σ is a function of the relative input prices and the estimated parameters from the multivariate statistical regressions, it is possible to solve for the input price ratio region in which σ is positive, and, therefore, within which the "implied"

Table 5–3. TRANSLOG Production Function Estimates for the Elasticity of Substitution Between Land and Nonland.

Geographic Area	$\sigma^{a,b}$	$\rho_{L}{}^{c}$	$\rho_{K}{}^{d}$
Los Angeles–Long Beach SMSA	.58 (.15)	.24	.76
Three New Jersey counties in Philadelphia–Camden SMSA	1.43 (.17)	.16	.84
Two San Bernardino SMSA counties	.38 (.11)	.21	.79
San Diego SMSA	1.19 (.11)	.27	.73
Two San Francisco SMSA counties	.90 (.07)	.22	.78
Nine-county aggregate estimator	.31 (.33)	.21	.79

a. σ has been estimated by using parameter estimates derived from the constrained two-stage least squares estimator described in the text. See footnote b, Table 5–1 about instrument variable choice.

b. The standard error of the estimate for each σ is in parentheses directly below.

c. ρL is the average value of the share of land to total value for the corresponding geographic area.

d. P K is the average value of the share of nonland to total value for the corresponding geographic area.

production function has the desired curvature (convexity) properties.

This test was done for each of the microdata production function estimates for σ. In brief, the convexity test suggests that the TRANSLOG estimator is superior in terms of data fit to either the CES or VES microdata estimators. The VES estimator is from a statistical perspective substantially inferior to either CES or TRANSLOG estimators for σ.[12]

The last estimate of σ reported in each table is based upon a cross-section of the sample aggregate average data for each county. In general, the aggregate nine-county estimates for σ are lower than the microdata estimates for each geographic area. As discussed in conjunction with Table 5–1, these findings reinforce the suspicion that the pooling of data across geographic areas engenders aggregation and subgrouping data problems. This has been confirmed by using Fisher–Chow statistical tests for groupings of data.[13] In particular, the estimates for σ for each geographic area were found to be uniformly statistically different from each other and from the pooled regression findings.

The estimates of σ should be considered tentative because of the wide spectrum of empirical estimation difficulties. On theoretical grounds and on a statistical performance basis, the TRANSLOG estimator would seem to be the more reliable functional form for estimating σ. Using the TRANSLOG estimators from Table 5–3 for this sample, the elasticity of substitution between land and nonland for housing appears to be greater than unity for two geographic areas, San Diego and the three New Jersey counties from the Philadelphia SMSA. The estimate of σ is not statistically different from unity for the two counties in the San Francisco SMSA. Finally, σ for the Los Angeles SMSA and San Bernardino SMSA sample appears to be statistically less than unity. The low-σ areas have average values of about 0.5 and the high areas have average values of about 1.3. These findings indicate that σ varies more widely from place to place than suspected in earlier studies[14]; any may be greater than unity for several sub-geographic areas.[15]

SUMMARY AND IMPLICATIONS

The elasticity of substituion between land and nonland improvements is a fundamental parameter describing the structure of the housing services production function. This elasticity is a measure of the relative ease with which these factors may be substituted in the production of "housing services." For this reason it plays a crucial role in many modern partial and general equilibrium models of urban spatial structure, patterns of urban growth, urban residential-employment choice, property tax incidence, and the long-run housing supply function. The process of factor substitution is basically microeconomic, and it occurs at the firm or housing site level. As has been demonstrated, it is not always clear how the relevant microelasticities are related to those estimated from cross-sections of average data either for geographically diverse SMSAs or for socioeconomically diverse neighborhoods or census tracts within an SMSA. Using microparcel data, this study concludes that the elasticity of substitution between land and nonland for housing frequently appears to be numerically greater than had been assumed previously. Not so surprisingly, it also appears that σ may vary considerably from one geographic subarea to another. In this study, for SMSAs the value of σ ranged from less than 0.5 to greater than 1.3.

Housing Price Effects on the Land Density Supply Function

The value of the elasticity of substitution impacts directly upon the density of land use. Equations (5-3) and (5-4) are well-known microeconomic relations:

$$\frac{\partial \log (L)}{\partial \log (W)} = -\rho_K \sigma \qquad \text{5-3}$$

$$\partial \log (P) = \rho_L \, \partial \log (W) \qquad \text{5-4}$$

Equation (5-3) is the derived demand for land as a function of the price of land inputs, holding other input prices and the output of housing constant (Allen 1938:373).[16] Equation (5-4) indicates that percentage incremental land price changes affect the percentage changes in the price of housing (output) proportionally to the ratio of the share of land to all costs. Solving Eq. (5-3) and Eq. (5-4) will yield Eq. (5-5):

$$\frac{\partial \log (L)}{\partial \log (P)} = \frac{-\rho_K \sigma}{\rho_L} \qquad (5\text{-}5)$$

The density of land use for single-family houses D in the sample is by definition the reciprocal of the land variable, lot size: $D = 1/L$. Substituting density into Eq. (5-5) and denoting the partial elasticity of the housing supply of land use density at a location with respect to housing value (price) changes as $E(D,P)$, yields Eq. (5-6).

$$E(D,P) = \frac{\partial \log (Dd)}{\partial \log (P)} = \frac{-\partial \log (L)}{\partial \log (P)} = \frac{\rho_K \sigma}{\rho_L} \qquad (5\text{-}6)$$

Using the sample mean values for $\rho_K = 0.79$ and $\rho_L = 0.21$, and the range of estimates for σ of 0.50 and 1.30, Eq. (5-6) can be used to calculate $E(D,P)$. The range of estimates for $E(D,P)$, the partial elasticity of land-use density, supplied at a location with respect to the market price per unit of housing, is 1.88 to 4.89[17] This result implies that housing price changes at a location, *ceteris paribus* note especially that housing quality at the location is held constant), will have a significant impact on the long-run land-use density of housing supplied.[18] Since the expected changes in land-use density are proportional to the value of σ, this chapter's relatively high-valued estimates of σ indicate that the land-density effects of changing housing prices are substantially greater than believed previously. Since there appear to be important density land-use effects, as Smith (1976) implies, researchers may need to take into account density (as well as housing quality) variables much more carefully than has been done traditionally.

Housing Price Effects on the Value of Housing Supplied per Unit of Land

The value of housing supplied per unit of land at a given location is defined as V/L where $V = P \cdot Q$, and obviously is related to the density of land use D just discussed. The elasticity of value of housing supplied per unit of land with respect to changes in housing prices can be shown to be Eq. (5-7):

$$E(\frac{V}{L},P) = 1 + E(Q,P) + E(D,P), \qquad (5\text{-}7)$$

where $E(Q,P)$ is the partial elasticity of housing supply at a location (measured in terms of the number of units of housing quality supplied, holding density constant) with respect to housing prices, and, as before, $E(D,P)$ is the partial elasticity of housing density supplied at a location with respect to housing prices. From Eq. (5-7) it is clear that the value of housing supplied per unit of land at a location is determined by the quality of housing supplied per dwelling unit as well as the density of dwelling land use.

De Leeuw and Ekanem (1971) estimate that $E(Q,P)$ is in the interval 0.3 to 0.7 for rental housing; Smith (1976) estimates that $E(Q,P)$ for a sample of single-family homes is greater than 5.0.

For the sake of argument assume that $E(Q,P)$ is about 3.0 and $E(D,P)$ is about 3.0. Then using Eq. (5-6), the partial elasticity for the value of housing supplied per unit of land with respect to changes in the price of housing would be about 7.0; the range for $E[(V/L)P]$ would be about 2.3 to about 11. This is considerably less than the value of about 20 found by Muth (1969).

The Elasticity of Substitution, the Value of Density Relation, and Spatial Equilibrium

It is interesting to ask how the elasticity of housing value supplied per unit of land with respect to housing price might differ between locations. This is an especially salient question because the price of housing and land are differentiated spatially. To answer this question, as is wont it is assumed that the price of non-land inputs, controlling for quality-quantity of inputs, is invariant with location changes within the housing market, and in contrast, housing and land prices are expected to have location premia.[19]Under these assumptions, Eq. (5-7) can be rewritten as follows:[20]

$$E(\frac{V}{L}, P) = 1 + \frac{\rho_K \sigma}{\rho_L} \qquad (5\text{-}8)$$

Taking the derivative of Eq. (5-8) with respect to location, t, will yield under these assumptions Eq. (5-9) which can be used to evaluate changes in land-use intensity (value and density) with respect to changes in location:[21]

$$\frac{\partial}{\partial_t}(1 + \frac{\rho_K \sigma}{L}) = [\sigma(\sigma-1)(\frac{\rho_K}{\rho_L})] \partial \log(W) \qquad (5\text{-}9)$$

It should be clear that the elasticity of housing value per unit of land varies over space according to the change in the price of land inputs and the bracketed term in Eq. (5-9). Assume for the sake of argument that σ does *not* vary with location (which with the presumed findings of this chapter is an uneasy assumption), changes in the elasticity of housing value per unit of land with respect to housing prices caused by changes in location will depend on σ; that is,

$$\frac{\partial}{\partial t} \left(E\left(\frac{V}{L}, P\right) \right) \gtrless 0 \quad \text{depending on whether} \quad \sigma \gtrless 1.$$

Given the empirical findings for σ, many cities may have "perverse" land-use intensity gradients as a function of distance from the center city. This being true, "perverse" rent-price gradients might be observed simultaneously. McDonald and Bowman (1979) offer evidence of an estimated "nonstandard" rent-price gradient for land in Chicago; in light of our analysis, this fact is readily consistent with Smith's (1976) findings that σ for Chicago is greater than unity.

Put somewhat differently, urban saptial theory concludes that prices of housing and the value of housing per unit of land should fall with distance from the center city. Unfortunately, the assumptions these models make about key parameters such as σ may be suspect. Furthermore, the implied theoretical growth–urban sprawl relations of these theories, also, may not be correct for the same reason.[22]

Finally, in an epoch of anticipated continually increasing energy costs, the cost of transportation is likely to be affected significantly. In that scenario, given urban spatial theory and the part transport costs play, land-location premiums should be expected to change drastically, especially in the inner city easy-access locales. If, in general, the elasticity of substitution between land and nonland inputs for housing is greater than believed previously, the analysis presented in this chapter suggests that urban areas are likely to become more compact, with a general diminution of the suburbanization-sprawl phenomena.

Appendix 5A
Estimating the Elasticity of Substitution for Alternative Functional Forms of the Production Function

The empirical estimates for σ in this chapter will be based upon three different underlying functional alternatives for the housing production function: CES (constant elasticity of substitution), VES (variable Elasticity of substitution), and TRANSLOG production functions. The relation for estimating σ is derived from production equilibrium optimization conditions for each production function and assumed market conditions.

CES: A form of the CES function is

$$Q = \gamma\,[\delta K^{-\rho}\,(1 - \delta)L^{-\rho}\,]^{\,-\mu/\rho}$$

where δ, γ, μ, ρ are parameters. Under proper assumptions regarding cost minimization[A1] and market conditions, the marginal conditions can be arranged to yield

$$\left(\frac{K}{L}\right) = \left(\frac{\delta}{1 - \delta}\right)(1/1 + \rho)\left(\frac{W}{R}\right)(1/1 + \rho),$$

with W = input price per unit of improvements and R = input price per unit of land. Taking logarithms of both sides of this equation produces Eq. (5A–1):

$$\log\left(\frac{K}{L}\right) = A + B\,\log\left(\frac{W}{R}\right) \qquad (5A\text{–}1)$$

where $A = \sigma\,\log[\delta/(1-\delta)]$ and $B = \delta = [1/(1+\rho)]$. In this form, given data for the ratios of the physical input factors and the input factor prices, Eq. (5A–1) can be used to estimate σ, the elasticity of substitution between land and nonland housing.[A2]

As the name implies, the CES function has a constant elasticity of substitution along an isoquant. Although the CES is easily estimated using Eq. (5A–1) (or simple transformations thereof), it may not be reasonable to assume that σ is constant for all levels and ratios of factor inputs. This is a potential weakness for the CES function and requires empirical verification.

VES: The variable elasticity of substitution production function, developed by Revanker (1971) among others, recognizes that σ may vary depending on output and/or factor input combinations.[A3] The VES production may be written as

$$Q = \gamma K^{\,\alpha(1-\delta\rho)}\,[L + (\rho - 1)K]^{\alpha\delta\rho},$$

where $\gamma > 0$, $\alpha > 0$, $0 < \delta < 1$, $0 \le \delta\rho \le 1$ are all parameters and

$$\frac{L}{K} > \frac{(1 - \rho)}{(1 - \delta\rho)}\,.$$

It can be shown that

$$\sigma = \sigma(K,L) = 1 + \frac{(\rho - 1)}{(1 - \delta \rho)} \left(\frac{K}{L} \right) . \qquad (5A\text{--}2)$$

Hence, from Eq. (5A–2), σ is a linear function of the ratio of non-land to land inputs. If one assumes constant returns to scale for the VES production function ($\alpha = 1$), competitive conditions in factor and product markets, and cost-minimization behavior, the marginal conditions can be rearranged to create Eq. (5A–3)[A4]:

$$\frac{L}{K} = G_0 + G_1 \left(\frac{R}{W} \right), \qquad (5A\text{--}3)$$

where $G_0 = \dfrac{(1 - \rho)}{(1 - \delta\rho)}$ and $G_1 = \dfrac{\delta\rho}{(1 - \delta\rho)}$.

If one were to estimate the parameters of Eq. (5A–3) and utilize the conditions of Eq. (5A–2), σ would be

$$\sigma = 1 - G_0 \left(\frac{K}{L} \right).$$

The VES form reduces to the Cobb–Douglas production function for $G_0 = 0$. *In general, if $G_0 = 0$, the CES and VES production functions differ because the former has a constant σ at all points along an isoquant and is independent of the level of output. For the VES production function, in contrast, σ is directly related to the factor input mix, thereby varying along an isoquant, σ is the same along any ray from the origin in $K\text{-}L$ space. Unfortunately, while the VES has the advantageous property of variable σ, it does represent a restrictive functional form, whose usefulness depends ultimately on its empirical validity.

TRANSLOG: The TRANSLOG production function is the most general functional form considered in this study. It assumes that the production function for housing is twice differentiable and strictly quasi-concave with the characteristics of being homothetically weakly separable for an appropriate partitioning of input factors. This latter assumption has been made implicitly by all previous studies of housing production functions.[A5] That is, the inputs can be subdivided into mutually exclusive and exhaustive subsets such that the production function may be written as

$$Q = F(L,K,T,0),$$

where T is location and ϕ represents other inputs, exclusive of L, K, and T. Further, it is assumed that F can be rewritten such that it is in the same form as Eq. (5A–1).[A6,A7]

$$Q = F^*(g(L,K),T,0) = f(L,K). \tag{5A–4}$$

Under the assumptions of the model, the dual of the production function maximization problem, Eq. (5A–4) can be derived as the optimizing minimization-cost function, Eq. (5A–5).[A8]

$$C = C(Q,W,R), \tag{5A–5}$$

where C is the total cost of housing services.

The empirical form for Eq. (5A–5) in this model resembles a second-order Taylor expansion:

$$\log C = \log a_0 + a_1 \log Q + a_w \log W + a_R \log R \frac{1}{2} b_{ww} (\log W)^2 + b_{WR} (\log W)(\log R) + \frac{1}{2} b_{RR} (\log R)^2$$

The TRANSLOG cost function linearity-homogeneity in prices imposes the following conditions:

$$C = WL + RK$$
$$a_W + a_R = 1$$
$$b_{RR} + b_{RW} = 0$$
$$b_{RW} + b_{WW} = 0$$
$$b_{WR} = b_{RW}$$

The cost-minimization solution, under the conditions of competitive markets and given factor prices, yields

$$\rho_L = \frac{W \cdot L}{C} = a_w + b_{ww} (\log W) + b_{wR} (\log R), \tag{5A–6}$$

$$\rho_K = \frac{R \cdot K}{C} = a_R + b_{RR} (\log R) + b_{RW} (\log W),. \tag{5A–7}$$

where ρ_L and ρ_K are factor shares for land and nonland inputs, respectively. C, the total cost, under the assumed conditions, is identical to $P{\cdot}Q$, the stock value for housing (the current market value for houses).

Equations (5A–6) and (5A–7) represent the empirically testable functional forms derived from the TRANSLOG production function model. Usually, instead of assuming that the underlying cost and production functions generating Eqs. (5A–6) and (5A–7) are exact, it is preferred to assume that the model represents a second-order local approximation. In this way, the stochastic error term can be added to either Eq. (5A–6) or (5A–7) for randomness in the approximation of the functional form as well as market and optimizing behavior.[A9]

Finally, if either Eq. (5A–6) or (5A–7) is estimated empirically one can use the parameters to estimate σ by Eq. (5A–8):

$$\sigma = 1 + \frac{{}^{b}WR}{\rho_K \rho_L} = 1 + \frac{{}^{b}RW}{\rho_L \rho_K} . \qquad (5A\text{--}8)$$

Notes to Appendix 5A

A1.   Moroney (1970) demonstrates that for the development of a model for empirical estimation, it is preferred to assume cost-minimization behavior rather than profit maximization; the latter behavioral assumption necessarily requires the assumptions of perfect product and input markets (see Nerlove 1967).

A2.   According to Moroney (1970) and McDonald (1981), estimation in this functional form, with the independent variable being the ratio of the factor input prices, tends to mitigate measurement-error bias.

A3.   Several other alternative "variable" elasticity production functions have been proposed (see Revanker 1971 and Nerlove 1967). The other variable models usually require nonlinear econometric estimation, which reduces their attractiveness for empirical work.

A4.   There are several alternative ways to rearrange the marginal conditions for estimation purposes. See, for examples, Sirmans and Redman (1979) or Sirmans, Kau, and Lee (1979).

A5.   This point has been recognized earlier, perhaps usually in only a back-handed fashion; see Muth (1969:18) and Arnott (1978:296). Only McDonald (1981:192-93), in essence, explicitly recognizes this issue.

A6.   Under the assumption the underlying "base inputs" follow the rule of separability such that

$$\frac{d \left[\dfrac{F_i{}^*}{F_i{}^*} \right]}{dX_n} = 0 \text{ for } i, j \ \lambda K, L \text{ and } X_h \ \& \ L, K$$

A7. For fuller explanation of the separability assumptions see Berndt and Christensen (1973 a, b).

A8. Diewart (1971) and Christensen, Jorgenson, and Lau (1973) discuss the solution of the production function–cost function duality problem. Basically, under the proper assumptions, there is a direct correspondence between production function and cost function so that, given one, the other can be readily derived.

A9. Also, because it is assumed that there are more than two inputs in the production function, one can conceptually view this analysis of the factor shares as a multiequation system. For that reason, among others, one would need to estimate the model with simultaneous-equation methods.

Appendix 5B
Data Base

The data base used for this study consists of single-family houses that were sold between 1974 and 1978 in five FHA housing regions, essentially corresponding to SMSAs, under the auspices of the FHA-HUD 203 program. The SMSAs were Los Angeles–Long Beach, San Bernardino Riverside–Ontario, San Diego, Philadelphia–Camden and San Francisco–Oakland. There were 11,446 individual property sales taken from the FHA-HUD 203 files for 1974 through 1978 for the five SMSAs; sales on *non*new construction or where relevant data were missing were eliminated from our sample. Unfortunately, for many of the parcel sales, and especially in the years 1974, 1975, and 1976, the census tract code was either not recorded or incorrectly recorded. In the case of the Pennsylvania counties in the Philadelphia SMSA, the census tract code was *not* recorded at all. After all data eliminations were performed, the sample consisted of 815 parcels:

Area	Number of Complete Observations
Los Angeles–Long Beach SMSA	39
Three New Jersey counties in Philadelphia–Camden SMSA	51
Two San Bernardino SMSA counties	325
San Diego SMSA	246
Two San Francisco SMSA counties	154

As discussed in the text, the sample of FHA market sales of new homes was matched to the appropriate 1970 census tract data. The following list itemizes basic variables available and used in the study:

Parcel Characteristics Available
Age of building
Building type
Construction type
Exterior finish
Number of stories
FHA condition code
Basement present
Bedrooms
Bathrooms
Rooms
Garage and capacity
Public water and sewer
Underground electrical supply
Extra features
Air conditioning
Lot frontage, depth, and area
Neighborhood code
Census tract code
Replacement cost of improvements
Living space area
Market price of land
Taxes and special assessments
Total operating and maintenance expenses

Sales Transaction Data
Data of sale transaction
Market value
Closing costs
Total acquisition costs
Mortgage loan
Loan-to-value ratio
Loan maturity
Monthly mortgage payments
Loan interest rate

Type of mortgage
Equipment included in sale

Buyer Household Characteristics
Mortgagor and comortgagor age
Years married
Number of dependents
Several measures of net effective income
Sources of income
Other assets and liabilities

Matched Census Tract Data
Several measures of housing crowdedness and condition
Several measures of educational levels attained
Population counts by age distribution and income levels
Housing unit counts, by rental and owner-occupied, by age of
    unit, by vacancy rates, by values or rentals
Use and availability of public transportation

NOTES

1. McDonald (1981) provides an excellent survey and evaluation of recent empirical studies of the elasticity of substitution for housing; some limitations of this survey are discussed in the second section.
2. In theory the stock value for housing is $V = P \cdot Q$ where P is the price per unit of housing services capacity. This in turn should be the risk-adjusted discounted value of the housing services over the life of the asset. Similarly the value of the stock-input and flow-input variables should be related via a time-discounted function. Koenker (1972) found, as would be expected if these assumptions were true, that property value (the stock value) and gross property rental (the flow value at a point in time) were highly correlated ($R^2 = {}^0.96$ in his sample).
3. Given the definition of σ, substitute for

$$d(\frac{K}{L}) = \frac{(LdK - KdL)}{L^2}$$

and for

$$d\left(\frac{f_L}{f_K}\right) = \frac{d\left(\dfrac{f_L}{f_K}\right)}{dL} \cdot dL + \frac{d\left(\dfrac{f_L}{f_K}\right)}{dK} \cdot dK.$$

The marginal rate of technical substitution can be expressed as dK = $(f_L/f_K) \cdot dl$. Therefore, we can express σ by substitution as

$$\sigma = f_L f_K (f_L L + f_K K)/L \cdot K \cdot D,$$

where

$$D = 2f_{LK}f_L f_K - (f_L)^2 f_{KK} - (f_K)^2 f_{LL} > 0$$

because of the assumption of convex isoquants. Since f_L, f_K, L, K, and D *are all nonnegative, the elasticity of substitution is nonnegative.*

4.   Smith (1976:399–401) finds land-value appraisals for his sample of Chicago single-family home sites are statistically good estimates, without systematic bias.

5.   For example, four studies use microparcel data. Polinsky and Ellwood (1979) use a cross-section of about 10,000 FHA single-family homes from thirty-one SMSAs. The identical data base is used by Rosen (1978) in his study. The objections to these studies relate to estimating σ across all SMSAs and the use of the price of land, which may inadvertently introduce problems of simultaneity and definition error. Clapp (1980a) uses non-FHA microsales data for office buildings; the objection to his study relates to the functional form of the estimating equation with only W (not the ratio of W/R) as the independent variable. Also Clapp uses the CES production function as the underlying behavior of builders. McDonald (1979) uses microdata from Chicago single-family homes to estimate the elasticity of substitution; but he fails to recognize that the price of construction (R) cannot be treated as a constant across the observations in his sample.

6.   At the time FHA-HUD 203 program loans were limited to $60,000 for single-family homes; they typically have higher than conventional financed loan-to-value ratios. In the West Coast SMSAs of San Francisco, San Diego, and Los Angeles, the mortgage limitation is likely to affect the potential universe of home sales that are eligible. Hence, controlling for neighborhood-locational features might be extremely important.

7.   Although the data contained in each parcel observation are rich, unfortunately, the sample is smaller than was initially hoped. This

was caused by the fact that some census tract coding was missing from the FHA data files. See Appendix 5B for data discussion.

8. Smith (1976) is aware of this problem in his study of individual property sales from Chicago and solves it through an indirect (and ingenious) set of transformations of his basic model.

9. Interestingly, McDonald (1981:193) poses the hypothesis of σ varying across geographic areas, although on p. 202, where he discusses aggregation effects, he ignores the potential impacts of this hypothesis.

10. Sirmans and Redman (1979) may inadvertently correct for simultaneity bias caused by input choice–input price; however, their use of the Zellner seeming-unrelated-regression method was proposed to control for interperiod cross-correlations. Similarly, McDonald (1981) uses an instrumental-variable method to correct for measurement problems, which inadvertently may correct for the simultaneity bias as well.

11. The effect of simultaneity bias on the estimated coefficients and ultimately on the elasticity of substitution estimator depends upon the production function and estimating equation functional form. For the CES estimating form, the estimate of σ will be overstated; for the VES and for the TRANSLOG forms simultaneity bias could cause either overstated or understated values for the estimate of σ, depending on the sign of the key coefficient.

12. Clapp (1980b) indicates that his findings and data are *not* inconsistent with several functional forms for the production function; however, he considers his evidence relatively weak. He admonishes researchers that "This conclusion implies that urban theoretical models should approach alternative functional forms with extreme caution. Occam's razor should be liberally applied." Using Clapp's (1980b) argument would indicate that the TRANSLOG functional form, given its flexibility, generality, and simplicity of assumptions, would be the appropriate choice.

13. See Chow (1960) and Fisher (1970) for the exposition on how to conduct these tests.

14. Sirmans and Redman (1979) find the elasticity of substitution varies with the capital/land ratio (using the VES production function) across fifty-two SMSAs. However, their analyses utilize a sample of average SMSA data and are likely to suffer from aggregation, measurement error, pooling, and functional specification problems. Also, their findings for all SMSAs indicate the σ is less than unity.

15. For reasons that will become apparent shortly, the value of unity for σ is a theoretically crucial threshold. For example, see Muth (1969: chap. 3).

16. The net input price elasticities of derived demand for land with respect to land input prices and for nonland inputs with respect to land input prices, respectively, holding output constant, are

$$E(L,W) = -\rho_K\sigma \quad \text{and} \quad E(K,W) = \rho_L\sigma$$

17. Following note 16, the net price partial elasticities for land inputs with respect to land-price changes $E(L,W)$ range from -0.40 to -1.03. Similarly, the net price partial elasticities of nonland inputs with respect to land-price changes $E(K,W)$ range from 0.11 to 0.27.

18. One would expect, in general, that increasing housing prices would affect optimal decisionmaking in terms of the amount of quality of housing per dwelling unit as well as the density. This will *a fortiori* reinforce the argument developed here.

19. Assuming that R, the price for the nonland inputs, is constant within the housing market area, is *in theory* a reasonable approximation for, say, an SMSA. The objection lodged in the empirical analysis of this paper is that one must control for quality differences in dwelling unit inputs when collecting data for R.

20. See Muth (1969: chap. 3) for the derivation of this formula. In this form $E[(V/L),P]$, using the sample means of $\rho_K = 0.79$ and $\rho_L = 0.21$ and the ranges for the estimates of σ of 0.5 to 1.3, will be in the range of about 2 to 6. This value is considerably less than Muth's estimate of 20 and is attributable basically to his assumed value $\rho_K = 0.95$, which is clearly incorrect for our data.

21. Equation (5-9) can be derived by noting that

$$d \left(1 + \frac{\rho_K}{\rho_L}\right) = \sigma d\left[\left(\frac{R}{W}\right)\left(\frac{K}{L}\right)\right]$$

and by substituting in the right-hand side

$$d \log \left(\frac{K}{L}\right) = \sigma d\left(\frac{W}{R}\right).$$

22. Contrary to what Muth (1969) finds, as construction costs *(R)* increase, the value-intensity of land use may decrease. If one assumes the following systems of equations:

$Q = F(P)$,   the consumer demand function;
$Q = G(K,L)$,   the production function;
$L = H(W)$,   the land supply function.

Totally differentiating the system of equations, assuming perfect markets and maximization by builders, will produce

$$E(\frac{V}{L}, R) = \frac{\sigma_K \left[(1 + E^* (Q,P) \sigma + (1 - \sigma) E^* (L,W) \right]}{(\rho_K \sigma - \rho E^* (Q,P) + E^* (L,W)}$$

where E^* (L,W) is the supply elasticity of residential land with respect to land prices and E^* (Q,P) is the *demand* elasticity for housing. It is reasonable to assume that in the long run E^* (L,W) > 0 and / $E^*(Q,P)$/ < 1 (see Polinsky 1979b). If these assumptions were true and if $\sigma > 1$ and $E^*(L,W)$ were large, two likely possibilities for many cities, then $E[(V/L), R] < 0$.

REFERENCES

Allen, R. 1938. *Mathematical Analysis for Economists*. New York: St. Martin's Press

Andrieu, M. 1974. "Derived Demand, Returns to Scale and Stability." *Review of Economic Studies* 41 (July): 405–17.

Arnott, R. 1978. "The Reduced Form Price Elasticity of Housing." *Journal of Urban Economics* 5 (July): 293–304.

Arnott, R., and F. Lewis. 1979. "The Transition of Land to Urban Use." *Journal of Political Economy* 87 (February): 161–69.

Berndt, E., and L. Christensen. 1973a. "The Internal Structure of Functional Relationships: Separability, Substitution and Aggregation." *Review of Economic Studies* 40 (July): 403–10.

———. 1973b. "The Translog Function and the Substitution of Equipment, Structures, and Labor in U.S. Manufacturing 1929–1968." *Journal of Econometrics* 1 (March): 81–113.

Bronfenbrenner, M. 1961. "Notes on the Elasticity of Derived Demand." *Oxford Economic Papers* 13 (July): 254–61.

Buchanan, J., and C. Goetz. 1972. "Efficiency Limits of Fiscal Mobility: An Assessment of the Tiebout Model." *Journal of Public Economics* 1 (April): 25–44.

Chow, G. 1960. "Tests of Equality between Sets of Coefficients in Two Linear Regressions." *Econometrica* 28 (July): 591–605.

Christensen, L., D. Jorgenson, and L. Lau. 1973. "Transcendental Logarithmic Production Frontiers." *Review of Economics and Statistics* 60 (February): 28–45.

Clapp, J. 1979. "The Substitution of Urban Land for Other Inputs." *Journal of Urban Economics* 6 (January): 122–134.

———. 1980a. "The Elasticity of Substitution for Land: The Effects of Measurement Errors." *Journal of Urban Economics* 8 (September): 255–63.

————. 1980b. "Production with Land and Non-land Factors: Which Functional Form?" *Journal of Urban Economics* 8 (July): 32–46.

de Leeuw, F. 1971. "The Demand for Housing: A Review of Cross Section Evidence." *Review of Economics and Statistics* 53 (February): 1–10.

de Leeuw, F., and N. Ekanem. 1971. "The Supply of Rental Housing." *American Economic Review* 61 (December): 806–7.

Diewert, W. 1971. "An Application of Shepard Duality Theorem: A Generalized Leontief Production Function.' *Journal of Political Economy* 79 (May/June): 481–507.

Edel, M., And E. Sclar. 1974. "Taxes, Spending, and Property Values: Supply Adjustment in a Tiebout–Oates Model". *Journal of Political Economy* 82 (September/October): 941–54.

Edelstein, R. 1974. "The Determinants of Value in the Philadelphia Housing Market: A Case Study of the Main Line 1967–1969." *Review of Economics and Statistics* 56 (August): 319–28.

Fallis, G. 1979. "Factor Substitution, Employment Density-Suburbanization." *Journal of Urban Economics* 6 April): 156–75.

Farebrother, R. 1979. "A Group Test for Misspecification." *Econometrica* 47 (January): 209–10.

Feige, E., and H. Watts. 1972. "An Investigation of the Consequences of Partial Aggregation of MicroEconomic Data." *Econometrica* 40 (March): 343–60.

Ferguson, C. 1966. "Production, Prices, and the Theory of Jointly Derived Input Demand Functions." *Economica* 33 (November): 454–61.

Fisher, F. 1970. "Test of Equality between Sets of Coefficients in Two Linear Regressions: An Expository Note." *Econometrica* 38 (March: 361–66.

Grieson, R. 1973. "The Supply of Rental Housing: Comment." *American Economic Review* 63 (June): 433–36.

Hamilton, B. 1976. "The Effects of Property Taxes and Local Public Spending on Property Values: A Theoretical Comment." *Journal of Political Economy* 84 (June): 647–50.

Johnston, J. 1972. *Econometric Methods,* 2nd ed. New York: McGraw-Hill.

Kain, J., and J. Quigley. 1975. *Housing Markets and Racial Discrimination: A Microeconomic Analysis* New York: National Bureau of Economic Research.

Kau, J., and C. Lee. 1976a. "Capital-Land Substitution and Urban Land Use." *Journal of Regional Science* 16 (April): 83-92.

————. 1976b. "Functional Form, Density Gradient and Price Elasticity of Demand for Housing." *Urban Studies* 13 (June): 193–98.

King, A. 1976. "The Demand for Housing: A Lancastrian Approach." *Southern Economic Journal* 43 (October): 1077–87.

124   SUPPLY OF HOUSING

Koenker, R. 1972. "An Empirical Note on the Elasticity of Substitution between Land and Capital in a Monocentric Housing Market." *Journal of Regional Science* 12 (August): 299–305.

Maddala, G. 1971. "The Use of Variance Components Models in Pooling Cross-Section and Time-Series Data." *Econometrica* 39 (March): 341–58.

McDonald, J. 1979. *Economic Analysis of Urban Housing Market.* New York: Academic Press.

———. 1981. "Capital-Land Substitution in Urban Housing: A Survey of Empirical Estimates." *Journal of Urban Economics* 9 (March): 190–211.

McDonald, J. and H. Bowman. 1979. "Land Value Functions: A Reevaluation." *Journal of Urban Economics* 6 (January): 25–41.

Mills, E. 1967. "An Aggregate Model of Resource Allocation in a Metropolitan Area." *American Economic Review* 58 (May): 197–210.

Moroney, R. 1970. "Identification and Specification Analysis of Alternative Equations for Estimating the Elasticity of Substitution." *Southern Economic Journal* 34 (July): 287–99.

Mundlak, Y. 1968. "Elasticities of Substitution and the Theory of Derived Demand." *Review of Economic Studies* 35 (April): 225–36.

Muth, R. 1964. "The Derived Demand Curve for a Production Factor and the Industry Supply Curve." *Oxford Economic Papers* 16 (July): 221–34.

———. 1969. *Cities and Housing: The Spatial Pattern of Urban Residential Land Use.* Chicago: University of Chicago Press.

———. 1971. "The Derived Demand for Urban Residential Land." *Urban Studies* 8 (October): 243–54.

———. 1972. "The Demand for Non-Farm Housing." In *Readings in Urban Economics,* edited by Matthew Edel and Jerome Rothenberg. New York: Macmillan.

Nerlove, M. 1967. "Recent Empirical Studies of the CES and Related Production Functions." In *The Theory and Empirical Analysis of Production,* edited by M. Brown. New York: National Bureau of Economic Research.

Oates, W. 1969. "The Effects of Property Taxes and Local Public Spending on Property Values: An Empirical Study of Tax Capitalization and the Tiebout Hypothesis." *Journal of Political Economy* 77 (November/December):957–71.

Polinsky, A. 1977. "The Demand for Housing: A Study in Specification and Grouping." *Econometrica* 45 (March): 447–61.

Polinsky, A. 1979. "The Demand for Housing: An Empirical Post-Script." *Econometrica* 47 (March): 521–23.

Polinsky, A., and D. Ellwood. 1979. "An Empirical Reconciliation of Micro and Grouped Estimates of the Demand for Housing." *Review of Economics and Statistics* 61 (May): 199–205.

Revanker, N. 1971. "A Class of Variable Elasticity of Substitution Production Functions." *Econometrica* 39 (January): 61–71.

Rosen, H. 1978. "Estimating Inter-city Differences in the Price of Housing Services." *Urban Studies* 15 (October): 351–55.

Rydell, C. 1976. "Measuring the Supply Response to Housing Allowances," *Papers of the Regional Sciences Association* 37:31–53.

Sato, R., and T. Koizumi. 1970. "Substitutability, Complementarity and the Theory of Derived Demand." *Review of Economic Studies* 37 (January): 107–18.

Schmidt, P., and R. Sickles. 1977. "Some Further Evidence on the Use of the Chow Test under Heteroskedasticity." *Econometrica* 45 (July): 1293–98.

Sirmans, C., J. Kau, and C. Lee. 1979. "The Elasticity of Substitution in Urban Housing Production: A VES Approach," *Journal of Urban Economics* 6 (October): 407–15.

Sirmans, C., and A. Redman. 1979. "Capital-Land Substitution: Some Inter-urban Estimates." *Land Economics* 55 (May): 167–76.

Smith, B. 1976. "The Supply of Urban Housing." *Quarterly Journal of Economics* 65 (August): 389–405.

Smith, B., and J. Campbell, Jr. 1978. "Aggregation Bias and the Demand for Housing." *International Economic Review* 19 (June): 495–505.

Theil, H. 1971. *Principles of Econometrics.* New York: J. Wiley and Sons.

Tiebout, C. 1956. "A Pure Theory of Local Expenditures." *Journal of Political Economy* 64 (October): 416–24.

Witte, A. 1975. "The Determination of Inter-urban Residential Site Price Differences: A Derived Demand Model with Empirical Testing." *Journal of Regional Science* 15 (December): 351–74.

————. 1977. "An Examination of Various Elasticities for Residential Sites." *Land Economics* 52 (November): 401–9.

6 THE SUPPLY OF NEW HOUSING IN CANADA INTO THE TWENTY-FIRST CENTURY

Frank Clayton and Robert Hobart

This chapter previews changes on the supply side of the new housing market in Canada over the next three decades. Most longer term housing studies devote considerable effort to documenting future demand or new housing requirements but either ignore or only briefly examine the implications for the supply side of the new housing market (for example, refer to Clayton Research Associates 1979). The implicit assumption appears to be that demand determines the supply response over the longer term, a premise we would generally support.

Although demand is clearly a dynamic force in the new housing marketplace, future supply considerations are also of major importance. Besides examining some of the more important factors likely to affect new housing supply over the next three decades, this chapter looks at the structure of the housing industry, characteristics of new housing, and house price prospects for the future. Factors affecting new housing production, including the availability and cost of real estate financing, energy supplies and price, land availability and price, labor availability and productivity as well as government policies and price, land availability and price, labor availability and productivity as well as government policies and regulations, are assessed first.

127

FACTORS AFFECTING NEW HOUSING SUPPLY

Financing

The explosion in mortgage interest rates that began in Canada in late 1979 is generally regarded as a one-time shock to the real estate financing system.[1] It is anticipated that over the next three decades mortgage interest rates will bear some more or less stable relation to the underlying inflation rate plus an allowance for the financial market supply and demand conditions. In all likelihood real mortgage interest rates—the differential between nominal rates and the consumer price index—will rise from the 300–400 basis points experienced on average over the past two decades to closer to the present 600 basis points. The wider gap in large part reflects the impact of the large energy projects planned in Canada on the demand for funds.

The expected presence and volatility of inflation in the Canadian economy will mean that mortgages will continue to carry high nominal interest rates. It is well known that the use of traditional level-payment mortgages in an inflationary environment creates a problem of "tilt" with respect to mortgage payments. The tilt problem arises because the inflationary premium incorporated into mortgage interest rates means the home purchaser must pay a relatively high proportion of income to meet mortgage payments in the early years (see Lessard and Modigliani 1975 as well as the Carr and Smith and Cappozza and Gau in this volume for more detail on this problem). Numerous mortgage instruments, such as graduated-payment mortgages and price-level-adjusted mortgages, have been developed to overcome the tilt problem. Lenders have been slow to introduce these instruments for a number of reasons.[2]. If inflation persists or accelerates and lenders continue to resist the implementation of these alternative mortgage instruments, new housing production will be curtailed to some extent. Should inflation continue, however, competitive pressures on lenders will probably result in a much broader use of these alternative mortgage instruments.

Interest rates have also become considerably more volatile during the past several years. Carr and Smith (Chapter 10) have attributed this increase in interest-rate volatility to the current inflationary climate and the speed with which changes in inflationary expectations become incorporated into interest rates. Because inflation is likely to endure in the foreseeable future, mortgage interest rates can be expected to remain volatile.

The uncertainty associated with this volatility increases interest-rate risk to lenders using the traditional five-year term, level-payment mortgage. Hence lenders have attempted to shift these risks to borrowers by shortening mortgage terms from five years to one to three years. In fact, residential mortgages are now being issued for terms as short as six months. Moreover, lenders are attempting to shift the interest-rate risk to builders by fixing mortgage interest rates to home purchasers at the time of closing rather than at the time of sale.[3]. If interest rates rise significantly between the time of sale and closing, home purchasers may no longer qualify for the loan, and builders may lose sales. Similarly, the relatively long period required to construct rental apartment projects may mean that a project considered viable at interest rates prevailing when construction was commenced may not be profitable when construction is completed, if interest rates have risen significantly over the construction period. Thus the uncertainties associated with interest-rate changes do have an impact on the supply of new residential construction.

It is likely, however, that markets will adjust to the interest-rate uncertainty. For example, a financial futures market based on expected movements in mortgage interest rates allows builders and other housing market participants to shift the interest-rate risk to others at a relatively modest cost. Another method of shifting risk that can be used for rental construction is a partnership agreement between mortgage lenders and investors where equity profits are shared with lenders in order to secure financing at reasonable and fixed interest rates.

The housing market will probably make institutional adjustments to offset the impacts of volatile interest rates. Even with such adjustments, however, volatile rates do represent a real cost to the various participants in the housing markets. Some of these costs will be borne by the suppliers of new housing.

Energy

Rising energy prices are a fact of life, and it is almost certain that real energy prices will increase during the next decade and perhaps the next three decades. In Canada the shock in energy prices will occur over the next several years because of the current imbalance between Canadian and world energy prices. Under the energy agreement recently signed by the Province of Alberta and the federal government, the price of gasoline, home heating oil, and natural gas are expected to more than double by the end of 1986.[4]

Although it is clear that energy price increases will occur in the immediate future, the long-term prospects with respect to energy price increases is less certain. The current level of prices has been effective in reducing demand and is serving to encourage the development of new energy-producing projects and energy-saving technology. Indeed, in 1981 there would appear to be a surplus of oil in the marketplace. Therefore, while real energy prices may increase after 1986, it is highly unlikely that the massive increases of the 1970s and early 1980s will occur again.

Rising energy prices affect the new housing market in three ways. First, higher heating (cooling) costs will result in homeowners attempting to reduce energy usage. This reduction can be done by a variety of methods including incorporating energy-efficient features during construction, reducing the size of single-detached home, and producing more multiple housing forms.

Second, rising commuting costs will shift housing demand to more accessible locations. This generally is taken to mean a shift from the suburban fringe to locations closer to the central core with less suburban development. The future pattern of any remaining suburban construction will also be more efficient. For example, the "urban village," where employment opportunities are tied in with commercial, retail, and residential areas in compact suburban locations, is already beginning to emerge.

Third, higher heating costs could shift demand from existing to new housing. To the extent that energy-conserving features can be incorporated into new houses less expensively than into existing housing, there could be some shift in demand to new housing. They therefore may sell at a slight premium relative to existing houses.

The net result of energy considerations will be the production of smaller and fewer single-detached houses and more medium-density forms and more housing closer to employment centers, both in the central city and in suburban subcenters. The overall impact in the total urban spatial context, however, should not be exaggerated for a number of reasons: (1) The majority of the 2001 urban structure is already in place; (2) the massive energy price increases of the 1970s and early 1980s are unlikely to repeat after the mid-1980s; and (3) the increased energy efficiency of automobiles is likely to more than offset the increased real costs of the energy required for commuting. In the short run, automobile owners are unlikely to purchase a new automobile in response to increases in fuel prices, especially if these prices are capitalized into the trade-in value of their existing vehicle. Upon replacement, however, the purchaser will acquire a car that is more fuel efficient. The current efficiency of new cars, combined with the prospects for further increases in fuel efficiency, tend to suggest that the increasing real prices of petroleum products will not result in massive changes in urban structure but, rather, in changes in the type of automobile driven.

Land

Massive changes in urban structure are not anticipated, but energy price increases will tend to augment the demand for land in areas close to employment opportunities. Of equal importance are expected increases in commuting costs, resulting from expected increases in real income and hence in the value of time.[5] This too will tend to augment the demand for land in areas close to employment opportunities.

The shift in locational preference will increase the demand for land located close to employment opportunities, which in turn means that land prices will rise in the central area and new suburban employment subcenters relative to other areas. This rise in land prices will in turn encourage higher density development, providing municipalities allow this development to take place. Many inner-city municipalities are reluctant to allow higher densities in older neighborhoods, composed of single-detached houses. An an alternative to the rezoning of older residential areas, many of these municipalities (like the cities of Toronto, Vancouver, and Edmonton) are offering incentives such as density bonuses to real estate developers for including a residential component in new commercial office developments in the inner core. Another policy being pursued by municipalities is the reuse of obsolete downtown industrial areas for housing. These policies, no rezonings in residential areas and bonus incentives, generally mean that the central core of the cities will increasingly become the home of the affluent.

In the suburbs one can anticipate more concentrated housing development around existing employment/retail regional centers. This development will include a range of housing from apartments to small lot singles. New suburban developments will have to be comprehensively planned to compete with the advantages of existing employment subcenters.

Labor

An adequate supply of skilled labor for the residential construction industry is not anticipated to be a general problem over the next three decades because residential construction will be a declining industry. Specific shortages could occur because of the competition for construction manpower from the energy projects and the reduction in the inflow of skilled tradespeople from other countries. For example, Clayton Research Associates (1981) found current shortages in bricklayers, formers, and carpenters in the Toronto area caused largely by reduced immigration.

Over the decade 1971–1980, increased output per person employed (labor productivity) averaged 0.8 percent per annum in the construction industry. As can be seen from Table 6–1, this

Table 6–1   Labor Productivity Growth, 1971–1980[a]

	Percentage Average Annual Growth in Output per Person Employed
All nonagricultural industries	0.7
Goods-producing industries	1.5
Manufacturing	1.7
Service industries	0.4
Construction[b]	0.8

a. Measured by changes in Gross Domestic Product (GDP) in 1971 dollars per person employed.

b. Includes both residential and nonresidential construction.

Source: Bank of Canada Review, various issues.

was very similar to the productivity gains recorded by all nonagricultural industries in Canada but significantly less than productivity gains in the manufacturing and goods-producing industries.

It is anticipated that gains in productivity will continue in the residential construction industry over the next three decades but at a pace greater than other sectors of the economy. This is because the decline in the demand for new residential construction coupled with the competitive nature of the building industry will create an environment conducive to increasing productivity. Marginal firms that do not adopt new techniques, such as a greater use of modular building, will be forced to leave the industry. Only the most efficient firms will survive.

Government Policies and Regulations

Governments in Canada have a long record of interventionism with market forces, especially with respect to housing. Because residential construction is an important component in the Canadian economy, the expected future reduction in the demand for new construction may elicit cries for government support. It is unlikely that such support will be forthcoming because of the financial constraints now faced by the federal and most provincial governments. The present climate of government restraint is expected to prevail. Thus, less government intervention with respect to new residential construction is anticipated for the future.

At the municipal level, however, greater restrictions may well be placed on the supply of new housing, at least in inner-city and inner-suburb municipalities. Although residential development in central urban areas will tend to increase somewhat, inner-city municipalities can be expected to attempt to preserve the status quo with respect to existing residents or at least to ensure that new residential development is compatible with the existing neighborhood. The result will be the implementation of stronger controls with respect to inner-city residential development, and prolonged periods of negotiation between developers and municipal officials with respect to specific projects.

In contrast, municipalities at the suburban fringe may provide incentives for residential development. Many fringe municipalities have already constructed costly infrastructure in anticipation of residential development. For these municipalities increased residential development is financially attractive because the costs of infrastructure have already been met.

THE STRUCTURE OF THE NEW HOUSING INDUSTRY

The future structure of the homebuilding and land development industries depends on a number of considerations. The major factor will be the shrinking of the overall market for new housing, the result being that buyers will be able to be more selective. To survive, a builder will have to be more capable of providing a salable product relative to the boom years of the 1970s. Local market intelligence will be a necessity. Small firms have the advantage of being local in nature but often lack the skills to adjust their product mix quickly to changes in demand. Large firms, on the other hand, have the problem of slow decisionmaking due to larger bureaucracies; yet many of the large real estate firms have effectively decentralized decisionmaking so that their response is more immediate. In addition to being able to identify the market, the survivors in the industry will need to have considerable financial expertise to obtain the best financing possible in a highly uncertain and complex financial environment. Survivors will also have to become astute negotiators with municipal officials to ensure that municipal concerns can be met while still maintaining a competitive price for the final product.

The industry survivors over the next three decades are thus likely to be small firms headed by astute entrepreneurs with expertise in marketing and finance and the very large firms who have a flexible, decentralized decisionmaking ability. Medium-sized and larger firms trying to cover a multitude of markets with centralized controls will not survive.

On the land development side there will always be opportunities for smaller land developers on underutilized and well located infill sites. In suburban locations, an expansion of large-scale land assemblies is envisaged, with comprehensive planned communities that incorporate employment opportunities, housing, other amenities, and generally good highway or transit access to other employment centers in a large metropolitan market. One can anticipate land development companies specializing solely in the creation of large planned communities. This has happened in Toronto, for example, and it is now happing in centers such as Winnipeg, Calgary, and Edmonton. The land developer will then sell serviced land to builders who agree to a large number of restrictive covenants concerning the type of housing that can be built. One can also envisage new partnerships emerging between the traditional mortgage lenders, and land developers may also have to share profits with lenders in order to secure financing at reasonable costs as long as inflation remains at high levels or the inflation outlook remains uncertain.

THE CHARACTERISTICS OF NEW HOUSING

A sizable proportion of the new housing production over the next two decades in major urban markets is likely to be single-detached and semidetached houses. However, by the early years of the twenty-first century, with the sizable growth of the empty-nester and elderly segments of the market, there will be a marked shift away from these low-density housing forms. Since single-detached and semidetached housing is a heavy land consumer, these houses will generally be built in suburban locations. The recent trend toward smaller lot sizes and smaller houses is expected to continue, with houses being built close to employment subcenters and major highway and transit routes. There certainly will be considerable production of new medium and higher density housing (and increased renovation activity) in existing built-up areas, particularly in the central part of the metropolitan markets. The extent to which this takes place will be limited by municipal zoning restrictions against higher densities in existing single-detached housing neighborhoods.

A significant amount of new medium-density construction in older upper income suburban locations over the next two or three decades is also envisaged, particularly after the year 2000 when the empty-nester age group expands rapidly. Many of this group will want to downgrade from the large single-detached house but will not want to move from their general neighborhood. New housing on infill land and underdeveloped sites will accommodate this demand.

House Price Trends

Housing prices are very difficult to predict since they vary so much by location within a particular urban market. Nevertheless, it is very evident that as real energy prices rise and real incomes increase, prices in more accessible, more central locations will rise more rapidly than overall price levels. Municipal restrictions on new development in central areas will reinforce these price trends. Conversely, prices in fringe suburban locations will rise less rapidly than the overall average. Beyond the next ten to fifteen years, what happens to house prices will depend on many factors. Among the important ones are changes in transportation technology and transportation improvements in an urban area. If major improvements are made in the time taken to commute between two points in an urban market, then land prices will not rise as rapidly in the more central part of the community and will rise more rapidly in suburban locations.

Some softening in the overall level of house prices is anticipated over the next two or three decades in the larger markets across Canada because of the productivity increases anticipated in the construction industry. House prices in general will likely rise slightly less than inflation but with the qualification that better located property will rise faster than the average, whereas suburban fringe locations will rise less rapidly.

CONCLUSIONS

This chapter's new housing supply scenario for the next three decades implies the following:

1. The current gap between nominal mortgage rates and the inflation rate is expected to persist over the longer term but not significantly affect the supply side of the new housing market. It is expected, however, that the volatility of interest rates will continue. Although the market will adjust to this volatility, the adjustment mechanisms available are not costless and will increase the price of housing to a modest extent.

2. The net result of energy considerations will be smaller single-detached houses, fewer single-detached houses and more me-

dium-density forms of housing, and more housing closer to employment centers, both in the central city and in suburban subcenters.

3. Land costs in the central city will increase at a more rapid rate than less accessible locations. Central cities, as a result, will increasingly become areas for the affluent.

4. An adequate supply of skilled labor is not anticipated to be a general problem over the next three decades since residential construction is a declining industry. Shortages in specific trades could become a problem because of competition from energy projects and reduced immigration of skilled tradespeople. Labor productivity in residential construction is expected to increase at a faster rate than for other sectors in the economy as marginal firms leave the construction industry.

5. It is unlikely that government policies will be introduced to offset the slowdown in residential construction. However, municipal regulations with respect to redevelopment in central areas are likely to become more rigorous.

6. The survivors in the homebuilding industry over the next three decades will be small firms headed by astute entrepreneurs and large firms who have a flexible decentralized decisionmaking ability. On the land development side, large firms specializing in the creation of large planned communities are anticipated to grow in importance. There will always be opportunities for smaller land developers on infill sites.

7. A slight decline in overall real house prices is likely during the next three decades because of the exit of the least efficient firms from the construction industry and because of severe competition for declining market. House prices are expected to rise more rapidly in central locations relative to suburban locations not closely situated to subarea employment centers or major transportation routes.

NOTES

1. Interest rates on conventional mortgage loans were as low as 13 percent in June 1980. By August 1981 interest rates on conventional mortgage loans had increased to nearly 22 percent.

2. Lenders' views on Canadian Mortgage and Housing Corporation's graduated-payment mortgages are documented in Clayton Research Associates (1980).
3. Some lenders, however, are offering a fixed interest rate at the time of sale if the closing date is within sixty to ninety days of the sale date. In this case the lenders' bear the interest-rate risk.
4. Donner (1981) estimates that gasoline prices will increase by 114 percent, home heating oil 125 percent, and natural gas 108 percent during the period September 1981–January 1987.
5. As real incomes increase, the opportunity costs associated with the time spent in commuting also increase.

REFERENCES

Bank of Canada. Various issues. *Bank of Canada Review.*
Clayton Research Associates, Ltd. 1979. *Long Term Demographic Trends in Canada: Their Implications for Housing and Related Industries.* A study Prepared for McLean, McCarthy & Company Limited.
_____. 1980. *Lender Attitudes to Graduated Payment Mortgages and Social Housing Loans.* A Report Prepared for Canada Mortgage and Housing Corporation.
_____. 1981. *Housing Demand and Constraints on Residential Construction in Toronto in the 1980's.* A Report Prepared for Toronto Home Builders' Association.
Donner, A.W. 1981. "The New Energy Agreement Prolongs Canada's Inflation Agony." Research Securities of Canada Ltd.
Lessard, D., and F. Modigliani 1975. "Inflation and the Housing Market: Problems and Solutions." In *New Mortgage Designs for Stable Housing in an Inflationary Environment,* edited by F. Modigliani and D. Lessard. Boston: Federal Reserve Bank of Boston.

7 HOUSING REPAIR AND HOUSING STOCKS

Peter Chinloy

This chapter examines the various effects of repair and maintenance policies on the existing stock of houses. Such an examination is needed because repair and maintenance are becoming
important components of total housing expenditure. In addition,
innovative preservation measures may significantly reduce future
and costly construction requirements.

The problem of repair and maintenance in the housing market
is introduced with details about the institutions and programs
relevant to the Canadian housing market. A model is then derived that provides for the estimation of net depreciation and
maintenance rates, which are used to estimate the capital stock
in housing. The construction of supply and demand estimates
for housing units is described. Finally, a simulation is performed
to determine the degree to which new construction requirements
can be reduced if repair and maintenance policies are followed in
Canada.

I am grateful to the editors of this volume, George Gau and Michael Goldberg, for
their helpful comments. Also comments by participants in the symposium, particularly
Ray Struyk, Bob Adamson, Larry Smith, and Jack Lowry assisted in developing the problem. Able research assistance has been performed by David Low. Research funding has
been provided by the Social Sciences and Humanities Research Council of Canada under
grant 410-79-0343-R1.

The issue of repair and maintenance on existing houses is assuming greater importance, in part because of financing and mobility rigidities arising in the housing market. For example, there are two areas where the locked-in nature of financing leads to increased maintenance effort, particularly in U.S. housing markets. First, suppose property tax assessments are frozen for existing owners, but market value assessments apply on resales. Tenure length increases, creating a greater incentive to repair. Second, if existing financing is available at low interest rates, but upon resale higher market rates are required, the same incentive applies to retain and maintain the existing dwelling. These conditions are not as prevalent in Canada, suggesting the effects of maintenance may be more substantial in the United States.

REPAIR AND MAINTENANCE IN THE CANADIAN CONTEXT

The continuing urbanization and increasing relative price of fuel and commuting suggests that the time is appropriate to examine rehabilitation of older homes. There has been an increasing influx of people from rural Canada and other countries to the urban areas. In some areas natural barriers such as waterways or mountains impede the expansion of low-cost developable land. Adding to the pressure are regulations to maintain agricultural land near urban areas. Repair and maintenance policies may preserve agricultural land. Moreover, since older housing in need of maintenance is typically located close to the central core, savings in travel time and fuel may also be affected. If repair and maintenance on existing houses are increased, the demand for new houses would fall. This reduction in demand may ultimately lead to reduction in the price of houses at a given supply level, and reduction in the demand for new construction.

Another method of increasing supply is new construction. The construction of living units, single and multiple, could be initiated, increasing the supply in urban areas. This construction, however, may occur at a marginal cost unit of given quality greater than that for the existing stock. Geographical constraints and zoning or density restrictions may render it difficult for this type of construction to take place.

The alternative is to upgrade the existing stock of houses by encouraging repair and maintenance. This alternative has several advantages. It will save on demolition and reduce depreciation and the need for new construction, especially in urban areas. This chapter examines this alternative as a method for reducing the demand for new houses and, ultimately, reducing construction costs through a process of repair and maintenance. The objective is to determine the savings that can be accomplished by undertaking such a program.

One of the principal government institutions established to deal with housing is the Canada Mortgage and Housing Corporation (CMHC). The principal administrator of repair and maintenance programs in Canada, CMHC has the responsibility of rehabilitating and conserving the existing housing stock. The only program that directly encourages this conservation is the Residential Rehabilitation Assistance Program (RRAP), initially instituted to assist municipalities where houses were deteriorating at a more rapid rate than average. Since then, the responsibility of RRAP has shifted to CMHC, although the program is still administered by municipalities. CMHC acts as the mortgage guarantor. The loan used to finance repair may be obtained from any chartered bank, credit union, or approved lender. Since RRAP is the only Canadian government-sponsored maintenance program, some time will be spent examining its administration, its beneficiaries, the amount of assistance it offers, and the qualification requirements for those who apply.

The objective of RRAP is to improve the housing conditions of low- and moderate-income people through assistance in the repair and conservation of existing residential buildings. Policy statements at the inception of the program indicated that the purposes of RRAP were to encourage and assist in the stabilization and preservation of older residential neighborhoods, to facilitate the conservation of existing housing stock, and to improve the living conditions of low- and moderate-income people living in substandard housing conditions. The objective was that houses, after repair, would have an incremental life span of at least fifteen years. In addition to the general goal of rehabilitating substandard housing, the program has five other specific objectives (CMHC 1981b). These are

1. To improve substandard housing to an agreed level of health and safety;

2. To assist low- and moderate-income people living in substandard housing;
3. To help prevent the spread of urban blight;
4. To promote an acceptable level of maintenance of the existing housing stock; and
5. To test the potential of creating additional family housing units and dormitory and hostel units.

The program is designed to provide a maximum loan of $10,000 for each family unit regardless of size and type. In the case of rental property, for example, five units would mean a total eligibility of $50,000. A nonprofit corporation may borrow up to $10,000 per unit or $1,000 per bed. Of the funds borrowed, the amount forgiven is $3,750 per family housing unit and $500 per hostel or dormitory. The repayable portion of the loan is amortized over a period not exceeding the life span of the house, up to twenty years. Monthly payments of principal and interest are paid directly to CMHC. The loan rate is set quarterly and is based on the rate at which CMHC can borrow plus an administrative cost. Up to $5,000 of the loan is secured by a promissory note. Above $5,000 it is secured by a registered mortgage.

Loans and grants under the RRAP assisted in the improvements of 39,647 dwelling units in 1980, an increase from 32,860 units in 1979 (CMHC 1980:20). A total of $157 million was set aside to assist homeowners. Of that, $133 million was awarded. Many of the RRAP commitments were made under the Rural and Native Housing Program. RRAP is the only program that is specifically geared toward the rehabilitation and repair of existing houses in federal, provincial, or municipal policy.[1]

The assistance given to the homeowner to upgrade or at least maintain a home is small compared to that spent on new construction programs. Most of the federal programs are geared toward new construction. The National Housing Act of 1944 clearly states that one of its two major objectives is to assist the private market in producing enough housing to meet the needs of most Canadians. The emphasis is on construction of new housing units. Although the government is concerned about the replacement factor in housing, a proportional amount of attention is not being given to rehabilitate the existing housing stock. New construction demand could be reduced by appropriate repair and maintenance policies.

Research on the repair and maintenance of the existing housing stock in Canada is very limited. Even in the United States, research is scarce. Some work has been specifically on repair and maintenance of houses, however, or in other areas where an analogy may be drawn with respect to housing. One of the more direct studies is by Mendelsohn (1977), which examines the incidence, timing, and distribution of home improvements. He provides evidence on the behavior of owner-occupants as consumers and investors in single-family housing. Four hypotheses are tested: (1) People with more income spend more on housing repairs; (2) owners who expect to stay longer spend more on repairs; (3) owners who are skillful in repair spend more time working on their houses; and (4) the higher the wage rate or income of the owner, the less time spent repairing the home, and the greater the expenditure on contracted services.

These four hypotheses are analyzed under very restricted assumptions. Mendelsohn blames the restriction on the lack of suitable data. From the results of the tests, he concludes that the first two hypotheses are plausible. In the third test it is only true for younger people who were skilled at home repair. He finds that the older a person, the more apt he is to bring in help. The fourth test is inconclusive because of the lack of data.

Feldstein and Foot (1971), in a more general context, document the relation between gross investment and replacement and modernization expenditures. The model is based on assumptions from the neoclassical tradition and flexible accelerator model. A principal assumption is that replacement investment is proportional to the capital stock. Also, a crucial assumption is that the ratio of replacement investment to the capital stock is constant. Their study measures replacement expenditures on planned manufacturing investment between 1949 and 1968. Results of their test indicate that there is a substantial variation from year to year in the ratio of planned replacement investment to the capital stock. The variables that are found to be significant are the internal availability of funds, the level of expansion investment, and the utilization rate of the capital stock.

A study similar to that of Feldstein and Foot was carried out by Eisner (1977). To explain the relation between replacement and modernization versus expansion, Eisner used data based on capital expenditures for replacement and modernization and for expansion as ratios of previous gross fixed assests from 1954 to 1955 and 1957 to 1968. He found the following: Expenditures planned for replacement and modernization vary over time and are not a constant proportion; replacement and modernization are not substitutes for expansion expenditure but move up and down with the latter; expenditure for expansion is closely related to past and expected sales; and replacement and modernization expenditures are positively related to previous depreciation charges and profits rather than to depreciation reserve as a possible proxy for the age of capital.

More research has been done on the practical side of repair and maintenance of the existing housing stock. It deals with the importance of revitalizing older neighborhoods in urban areas. One such work is a collection of articles edited by McKee (1977). This research stresses the importance of preservation and regeneration of older homes to avoid rundown neighborhoods. Whittle, Milgram, and Barber (1977) provide insight into housing code enforcement, repair and upgrading programs, financing, zoning and other urban planning processes. The effect of these regulations on the willingness of people to carry out repair on their houses is put to question. Given this background, we turn to a model of housing repair and maintenance.

CAPITAL STOCK

The purpose of this section is to construct the capital stock for a housing repair and maintenance model and to suggest factors that might change the existing stock of houses. The capital stock is constructed using a perpetual inventory method. Given an opening and closing stock benchmark, an investment series, and also a specification that depreciation is geometric, the capital stock at any point in time can be derived. The problem is to find the depreciation rate δ satisfying:

$$K_T = (1 - \delta)^T K_0 + \sum_{J=0}^{T} (1 - \delta)I_{T-j-1}, \qquad (7\text{-}1)$$

where K_0 and K_T are the initial and terminal stock benchmarks, respectively, and I_j is the investment series where $j = 0, \ldots, T$.

The model, described in Appendix 7A, permits testing of the hypothesis that there are different depreciation rates depending on the age of the house. These depreciation rates differ on a net and gross basis, depending on the rate of maintenance (which also appears to vary with age). Estimates from this research suggest that these rates increase with the age of the house. This conclusion is true for both maintenance and gross depreciation, the latter occurring if there is no repair.

If depreciation and maintenance rates are shown to vary with age, it is possible to target repair programs. The result indicates that these rates increase with age, particularly for units constructed prior to 1940 (see Chinloy 1980: table 3). This implies that repair policies may reduce the relatively large depreciation on older homes. For targeting purposes, other characteristics than age have been included in both the depreciation and maintenance functions. The results suggest that personal characteristics do not alter either rate.

The consequence of the separate rates, not constant with age, implies that capital stocks must be constructed using these rates. The procedure is to develop capital stocks in each age or date of construction category. Assuming capital is aggregable, then the total housing capital can be developed. Given that the age of the house is correlated with the depreciation rate, it follows that a change in the depreciation rate would affect the life span of a house. If the depreciation rate on a house is reduced, its life span could be longer. The reverse is true if the depreciation rates are increased.

The issue of whether depreciation can be reduced by an appropriate maintenance strategy is examined by comparing observed depreciation among houses with positive and zero maintenance. Other variables include the number of children and income, but these tend to be statistically insignificant (Chinloy 1980). The quantity of maintenance performed, however, does reduce the amount of observed depreciation.

DEMAND AND SUPPLY

The net new requirements for construction are developed in this section. These projections involve capital stock series based on varied depreciation rates for housing supply. By subtracting existing supply (given a depreciation series) from housing demand, new construction is estimated. These estimates are developed annually for Canada to the year 2000.

The total housing requirement for Canada is based on projections of CMHC in *Housing Requirements Model: Projection to 2000* (1978). To arrive at the total housing requirements, the model is divided into three submodels: (1) a demographic submodel, (2) a housing stock submodel, and (3) a housing requirement submodel.

Demographic factors, according to the CMHC model, are the major determinants of the long-term demand for housing. The demographic submodel is projected by analyzing the components of population through changes in fertility, mortality, marriage and marital status, including marriage and divorce rates by age and sex. The variables in the model are classified under stock, flow, or rate variables. The stock variable represents the cumulated stock at any point in time. Flow variables are used to generate stock variables in subsequent periods. The actual dynamic process is divided into six components: aging, fertility, mortality, marriage, divorce, and migration. Each aspect is reduced to a predictable equation and the sum total of the six can be used to obtain a projection of the demographic nature of the population. The demographic submodel can then be used to produce population projection inputs for the housing requirement submodel.

The housing stock submodel has a twofold purpose. First, it acts as a complement to the demographic submodel by supplying the major inputs for estimating house requirements. Second, as a by-product of that function, it produces the age profile of the housing stock, which can be used as a final output or as an input to studies on housing conditions. The model is based on two inputs, net housing replacements and allowance for vacancies. The housing stock is obtained by adding the completions and by subtracting the demolitions.

Using information obtained from the previous two submodels, it is possible to estimate the number of new household formations and future housing requirements using the housing requirement submodel. This submodel employs variable headship rates to estimate future household formation. The housing requirement submodel is thus made up of three components: the new household formation, the allowances for vacancies, and the demand for housing replacement. The projected total requirements are then calculated based on heads of household, demolitions, and allowance for vacancy. The report gives the projected housing requirements from 1977 to 2000 based on these calculations and models.

The construction of the age-specific capital stocks requires an initial inventory of the housing stocks and the relevant depreciation rates. There are five age groups within the 1971 Canadian census providing the benchmarks. The supply of houses without depreciation can be given as

$$S = S_1 + S_2 + S_3 + S_4 + S_5, \tag{7-2}$$

where S_1 = houses built before 1940;
S_2 = houses built 1941–1950;
S_3 = houses built 1951–1960;
S_4 = houses built 1961–1970;
S_5 = houses built after 1970.

To take into account depreciation, $(1 - \delta)$ 10 is added to each ten-year time period. The resulting equation is

$$S = S_1 (1 - \delta)^{10} + S_2 (1 - \delta)^{10} + S_3 (1 - \delta)^{10} + S_4 (1 - \delta)^{10} + S_5 (1 - \delta)^{10} \tag{7-3}$$

Because not all the houses in the last period are depreciating at the same rate, an extra term has to be included to recognize the lower depreciation rate during the last decade. The term to be added to the last construction period S_5 is

$$\sum_{j=0}^{10} I_t (1 - \delta)^{t-} \tag{7-4}$$

where I_t is the completions in year t with the available data. The total supply of houses S in a given year is thus the number that have been constructed in the previous years less the depreciation.

$$S = S_1 (1 - \delta)^{10} + S_2 (1 - \delta)^{10} + S_3 (1 - \delta)^{10} + S_4 (1 - \delta)^{10} + S_5 (1 - \delta)^{10} + \sum_{S=0}^{10} I_t (1 - \delta)^{t-s} \tag{7-5}$$

PRIMARY DATA

Table 7–1 shows the initial housing stock by age for Canada. The figures are taken from Statistics Canada based on the 1971 census survey. The period of construction in the survey was not appropriate for this study, however. To make the figures more suitable for this study, the numbers of houses are regrouped from seven to four categories. Adjustments are needed for the first two categories in Eq. (7-5) since they did not coincide with the period of construction in the Statistics Canada data. It is assumed that between 1941 and 1945, 70,781 houses were built. That number is added to those built between 1946 and 1950 to derive the second category. All other houses, as defined in the Statistics Canada grouping "1921–1940 construction," are placed in the pre-1940 category.

The completions presented in Table 7–2 are from CMHC. This table gives completions for each year from 1971 to 1980. The completions include single-detached, semi-detached, row, and apartment dwellings for Canada. Table 7–3 shows the demand for houses as projected by CMHC from 1981 to 2000. Because it is not possible to find a starting total projection, it is assumed that in 1977 the demand for housing equaled the supply. In that way, it is possible to take the total housing stock in that year and add on the projection in each succeeding year. To make the data more suitable, the demolitions each year are subtracted from the initial projected housing requirements.

SIMULATIONS

The first step in the simulation is to calculate the stock of houses that would be left after each time period based on the actual number of houses in 1980. By using the formula in Eq. (7-5), it is possible to calculate the stock of houses remaining after each period. The results are given in Table 7–4.

Next, using projected figures for the housing requirements in column 6, the additional housing required each year is calculated. The figures obtained are the total requirements minus the demolitions based on CMHC projections. The estimations are also reduced by 16 percent. This reduction is performed because it was found that when the projections from 1977 to 1980 are compared to the actual number of completions, the projections are higher by an average of 16 percent. The revised projections are shown in column 1. By adding the fixed housing stock to the required housing for each year after 1981, it is possible to calculate the total housing requirements from 1981 to 2000. The total housing requirement is given in column 8.

From Table 7–4 the number of houses that have been lost through depreciation can also be calculated. Column 2 gives the number of houses lost each year as the difference between the previous year and the year in question. These figures are the number of houses that have to be replaced because of inadequate repair and maintenance in each year. The number of additional

Table 7–1.   Initial Housing Stock by Age for Canada

Period of Construction	Housing Stock
Pre 1940	2,220,924
1941–1950	686,976
1951–1960	1,383,445
1961–1970	1,697,220

Source: Statistics Canada 1971.

Table 7–2.   Completions by Year

Period	Completions
1971	201,232
1972	232,227
1973	246,581
1974	251,243
1975	216,964
1976	236,249
1977	251,789
1978	246,533
1979	266,489
1980	176,168

Source: CMHC 1981c.

houses required each year can be calculated by adding the number of houses lost each year through depreciation in column 2, to the revised projections (column 7). The yearly requirements (columns 2 plus 7) are given in column 3.

If no maintenance is performed on a house, it has been estimated that the depreciation rate increases by 2 percent. This conclusion is derived from Chinloy (1980), where separate subsamples with no maintenance were compared. It was found that the total housing stock decreases by 2 percent each year without maintenance.

The additional number of houses needed each year is given in Table 7–4, column 4. Alternately, if maintenance performed is equal to the depreciation, the amount of housing required yearly would be those needed because of net household formation.

Table 7–3.   Projections of Housing Demand in Canada, 1981–2000

Year	Projected Demand
1981	8,486,152
1982	8,718,920
1983	8,945,623
1984	9,163,591
1985	9,370,278
1986	9,564,002
1987	9,744,882
1988	9,912,921
1989	10,069,401
1990	10,215,940
1991	10,355,245
1992	10,488,771
1993	10,616,898
1994	10,739,579
1995	10,858,604
1996	10,975,636
1997	11,091,874
1998	11,208,267
1999	11,325,513
2000	11,444,312

Source: CMHC (1978:105 and 118.

Table 7-4. Housing Model Projections

	(1) Housing Stock with Depreciation	(2) Number of Houses Lost Through Depreciation	(3) 'Normal' Additional Requirements	(4) 2 Percent Added Depreciation	(5) 0 Percent No Depreciation	(6) CMHC Projections – Demolitions	(7) Revised Projections (× .84)	(8) Total Housing Requirements
1981	7,497,325	79,546	278,349	348,752	198,803	236,671	198,803	7,696,128
1982	7,413,451	83,874	279,399	342,473	195,525	232,768	195,525	7,807,779
1983	7,327,475	85,976	276,406	334,439	190,430	226,703	190,430	7,912,233
1984	7,334,944	92,531	275,624	324,222	183,093	217,968	183,093	8,003,176
1985	7,161,719	73,225	246,842	311,923	173,617	206,687	173,617	8,103,602
1986	7,080,446	81,273	244,085	298,352	162,812	193,824	162,812	8,185,217
1987	6,999,803	80,643	232,498	284,684	151,855	180,780	151,855	8,256,444
1988	6,920,256	79,547	220,699	271,324	141,152	168,039	141,152	8,318,139
1989	6,841,367	78,889	210,332	259,012	131,443	156,480	131,443	8,370,692
1990	6,763,405	77,962	201,054	248,110	123,092	146,539	123,092	8,415,853
1991	6,685,409	77,995	195,011	239,533	117,016	139,305	117,016	8,454,959
1992	6,610,315	75,094	187,256	232,229	112,162	133,526	112,162	8,492,098
1993	6,536,895	73,420	181,047	225,292	107,627	128,127	107,627	8,526,357
1994	6,460,749	76,146	179,198	218,365	103,052	122,681	103,052	8,553,315
1995	6,387,407	73,343	173,324	212,987	99,981	119,025	99,981	8,580,045
1996	6,314,627	72,780	171,087	209,053	98,307	117,032	98,307	8,605,611
1997	6,242,768	71,859	170,339	207,012	98,480	116,238	98,480	8,631,416
1998	6,171,762	71,006	168,776	204,131	97,770	116,293	97,770	8,658,207
1999	6,101,726	70,036	168,523	202,720	98,487	117,246	98,487	8,686,703
2000	6,032,286	69,440	169,231	201,939	99,791	118,799	99,791	8,717,130

Source: CMHC 1978.

Under such a specification, the number of houses needed each
year is presented in column 5 and is the same as the revised projections in column 7.

To facilitate a calculation of the optimal quantity of repair to
be undertaken, a series of estimations are carried out over two
subsamples. People who performed any repairs on their houses
during the survey period are placed in one group, while those who
did not are assigned to another. Separate depreciation functions
are estimated for each subsample, and the results are reported in
Table 7–5.

Table 7–5.   Repair, Maintenance, and Depreciation Estimates

	Repair > 0		
	Net Depreciation Rate	Repair	Total
Pre 1940	−.0069	−.0171	−.0240
1941–1950	−.0070	−.0100	−.0170
1951–1960	−.0029	−.0090	−.0119
1961–1970	−.001	−.0011	.007

	Repair = 0		
	Net Depreciation Rate	Repair	Total
Pre 1940	−.0104	0	−.0104
1941–1950	−.0104	0	−.0104
1951–1960	−.0094	0	−.0094
1961–1970	−.0132	0	−.0132

	Complete Sample		
	Net Depreciation Rate	Repair	Total
Pre 1940	−.0101	−.0098	−.0199
1941–1950	−.0104	−.0062	−.0166
1951–1960	−.0095	−.0060	−.0155
1961–1970	−.0128	−.0022	−.0150

Source: Chinloy 1980: London, Ontario, subsample.

The first block of results indicates the net depreciation rate among those who repaired. In the first period, for relatively new houses, actual appreciation with age is observed. For 1961–1970, an unrepaired house depreciates at 1.32 percent annually (the −0.0132 entry in the second block of Table 7–5), while a repaired one appreciates by 0.07 percent (the 0.0007 entry in the first block), a difference of 1.39 percent. The direct repair costs amounted to 0.11 percent, indicating that repair is a profitable activity.

An estimate of saving is derived by subtracting the depreciation rate on repaired houses from that on unrepaired houses and comparing it to the average repair rate. The corresponding figures for 1951–1960 are −0.25 percent, −0.66 percent for 1951–1950, and −1.36 percent for pre-1940. This result suggests in general that repair at the margin may be unprofitable, at least in augmenting the price of the house. Given the consumptive aspects of home repair, other factors than mere investment are involved. Hence the results tend to understate the benefits from home repair.

CONCLUDING REMARKS

Further work on the issue of repair and maintenance for housing is needed to determine the profitability of this activity. Repair tends to be a diffused activity, performed by a number of small contractors. If owners are also carrying out the repairs as a hobby, partly for consumption, calculating returns to repair becomes even more complicated.

The results do suggest the need for comparison of returns at the margin between upgrading and new construction. Such comparison is required to derive appropriate measures of the return to housing investment.

As for housing policy implications, any tendency to lock households into their existing homes will increase the demand for maintenance. If there is a trend toward low property tax assessments to remain with the original owner or for mortgages not to be assumable, then there will be a greater emphasis on maintenance. Further, with high transaction and moving costs in housing markets, repair often becomes preferable to new purchase.

Appendix 7A
Model of Depreciation and Maintenance on Structures

The homeowner solves a model of housing demand. At time t, a house is owned aged τ, with an expected life T. It is possible for there to be a probability distribution on this life. Over the period $t = 0, T - \tau$, by household optimization, a sequence of demands for housing services in value terms $A_{t+s,\ \tau+s}$ is obtained. The homeowner also makes investment decisions on additions and repair, valued at $M_{t+s,\ \tau+s}$, $s = 0, \ldots, T - \tau$. The borrowing and lending mortgage rate is $R_j{}^t$, for investment in housing in year j $\geq t$, where expectations are formed at current time t.

This implies that the present value of the house at time t, aged τ as of this date, is

$$P_{t,\tau} = \sum_{s=0}^{T-\tau} \frac{A_{t+s,\omega+s} - M_{t+s,\omega+s}}{\prod\limits_{j=0}^{s} (1 + R_j^t)} \qquad (7A\text{-}1)$$

where $P_{t,\tau}$ is the expected selling price of the house. The value of housing services is the product of a rental price per unit of housing services and the number of housing services consumed. Thus $A_{t,\tau} = \bar{r}_t g_{t,\tau}$ where $\bar{r}_t$ is the rental price per unit of housing services at time t and $g_{t,\tau}$ the number of efficiency units aged τ consumed at t.

Maintenance services are the product of the rental price $\bar{r}_t$ and the quantity of housing efficiency units $y_{t,\tau}$ aged τ added in t. So $M_{t,\tau} = \bar{r}_t y_{t,\tau}$ is the maintenance relation.

At the end of the previous period, the house contains efficiency units indexed by $q_{t-1,\tau-1}$. Maintenance units added during t are $y_{t,\tau}$, while $g_{t,\tau}$ are consumed, all in homogeneous efficiency units. Hence

$$q_{t,\tau} = q_{t-1,\tau-1} + y_{t,\tau} - g_{t,\tau} \qquad (7A\text{-}2)$$

is the undepreciated balance of housing at the end of period t. In cross-sectional data, comparing houses of identical characteristics, t is fixed, so $q_{t,\tau-1} - q_{t,\tau} = g_{t,\tau} - y_{t,\tau}$. The measure $q_{t,\tau-1} - q_{t,\tau}$ is the absolute change in housing consumed, and $1 - (q_{t,\tau}/q_{t,\tau-1})$ the relative change, or depreciation rate. This rate is net depreciation only, being the difference between gross services consumed as a ratio of initial stock $g_{t,\tau}/q_{t,\tau-1}$ and maintenance added $y_{t,\tau}/q_{t,\tau-1}$ relative to the stock. These values are the gross depreciation and maintenance rates, respectively.

It is possible to observe $y_{t,\tau}$ from actual maintenance performed during t. Under appropriate restrictions, such as cross-sectional data, $q_{t,\tau-1}$ and $q_{t,\tau}$ can be observed for similar houses aged $\tau - 1$ and τ. Once the repair is performed, the stock of housing available for consumption is $q_{t,\tau-1} + y_{t,\tau}$. The owner allocates this stock by consuming $g_{t,\tau}$ on the housing market. Consequently, the repair capital $y_{t,\tau}$ need not be consumed entirely in the period. As an example, suppose the units of housing services consumed $g_{t,\tau}$ are proportional to the stock available, at fixed rate λ. Then $g_{t,\tau} = \lambda[q_{t,\tau-1} + y_{t,\tau}]$ and $q_{t,\tau} = (1 - \lambda) [q_{t,\tau-1} + y_{t,\tau}]$.

Given observations on maintenance and the change in housing stock, gross units of services consumed can be inferred, as they must satisfy Eq. (7A-4). In conventional depreciation studies, only comparisons of $q_{t,\tau-1}$ and $q_{t,\tau}$ are made, and repair is neglected. This approach is valid only if it is possible to introduce variables to correct for repair activity.

Suppose net depreciation $n_{t,\tau}$ is defined as $g_{t,\tau} - y_{t,\tau}$. Then

$$n_{t,\tau} = p_t a_\tau b_{t-\tau}, \tag{7A-3}$$

where p_t is an index of disembodied technical change at time t, augmenting all capital identically. The embodied techniques in capital as of the year the house was built are summarized by $b_{t-\tau}$, an index dependent on house characteristics, and a_τ, a deterioration index representing physical decay and obsolescence. This deterioration index is normalized at unity for new units. If there is no deterioration, then $a_\tau = 1$ for all ages.

Assuming static expectations on p_t and $b_{t-\tau}$ the house price becomes

$$P_{t,\tau} = b_{t-\tau} \sum_{s=0}^{T-\tau} \frac{a_{\tau+s}}{\prod_{j=0}^{s} (1 + R_j^t)} \tag{7A-4}$$

where

$$r_t = \bar{r}_t p_t, \tag{7A-5}$$

since the effect of disembodied technical change cannot be identified from that of inflation.

Let

$$r_t^* = r_t \sum_{s=0}^{T} \frac{a_s}{\prod_{j=0}^{s} (1 + R_j^t)} \tag{7A-6}$$

be the rental price of new housing correcting for quality change. Then

$$d_\rho \quad \frac{\displaystyle\sum_{s=0}^{T-\tau} \prod_{j=0}^{s} (1 + R_j^t)^{-1} a_{\tau+s}}{\displaystyle\sum_{s=0}^{T} \prod_{j=0}^{s} (1 + R_j^t)^{-1} a_s} \tag{7A-7}$$

can be defined as a depreciation index, or the present value of deterioration on an aged $-\tau$ house relative to a new one. This yields

$$\ln P_{t,\tau} = \ln r_t^* + \ln b_{t-\tau} + \ln d_\tau \tag{7A-8}$$

given the net consumption $n_{t,\tau}$ at time t, so the net depreciation rate can be obtained by examining the $\ln d_\tau$ sequence. This figure applies to house prices at time t if no future maintenance is contemplated.

Depreciation is the sum of net consumption of original capital and maintenance. If maintenance is zero then (7A-8) is sufficient to determine the depreciation rate, but this need not be the case.

Maintenance may be expressed $y_{t,\tau} = p_t F_{t-\tau} Z_\tau$, where p_t is the measure of disembodied technical change, $F_{t-\tau}$ an index of techniques embodied in the production of repair, and Z_τ the effect of deterioration on maintenance. The rate of embodied technical change in maintenance need not be identical to that on the basic house. Deterioration may require additional maintenance with age, accounting for the use of Z_τ. This form permits a nonconstant rate of maintenance with the aging of the house.

The rental price of capital is identical for maintenance, since it is measured in efficiency units, so $M_{t,\tau} = r_t^* F_{t-\tau} Z^*_\tau$ with

$$Z^*_\tau = \cfrac{Z_\tau}{\displaystyle\sum_{s=0}^{T} \prod_{j=0}^{s} (1 + R_t^j)_{-1} a_s} \tag{7A-9}$$

being the maintenance of a τ-aged house relative to the present value of deterioration on a new house. This equation indicates the relative services produced by maintenance as opposed to replacement by purchase of a new house.

The maintenance ratio is $m_{t,\tau} = M_{t,\tau} P_{t,\tau}$. If maintenance of a given vintage is relatively more efficient than new construction of that vintage, then the ratio exceeds unity. Finally

$$Z_\tau = \cfrac{Z_\tau}{\displaystyle\sum_{s=0}^{T-\theta} \prod_{j=0}^{s} (1 + R_j^t)^{-1} a_{\tau+s}} \tag{7A-10}$$

is the maintenance index. This is the repair on an aged-τ house relative to the present value of its future deterioration. As τ increases, the present value of deterioration declines, and even if Z_τ is constant, the relative maintenance index rises with age.

The total depreciation rate is the sum of the net depreciation rate and the amount of maintenance, so

$$\delta_{t,\tau} = \delta \ln P_{t,\tau}/\delta\tau + m_{t,\tau} \tag{7A-11}$$

The model thus derives separate gross estimates of depreciation and net rates that include the effects of maintenance.

NOTES

1. The only other program that subsidizes repairs for owners of older homes is the Canadian Homeowners Insulation Program (CHIP), known as the Home Insulation Program (HIP) in Prince Edward Island and Nova Scotia. The primary objective of CHIP and HIP is to conserve energy. The resulting upgrading of the house is only a secondary aspect. Funds are given out in the form of a grant in

amounts up to $500. The maximum grant received varies according to the type of dwelling. For example, a single-detached, semidetached or row unit is eligible for up to $350 for materials and $150 for labor incurred. In the case of an apartment building of three storeys or less containing more than six units, the maximum grant is $150 for materials and $65 for labor. In 1980, 467,000 people applied for CHIP grants, an increase of 45 percent over 1979. The primary reason for this large increase was that the eligibility requirements were changed making the program more accessible. CHIP gave out $206 million while HIP assisted 18,000 homeowners with $8 million.

REFERENCES

Canada Mortgage and Housing Corporation. 1978. *Housing Requirements Model: Projection to 2000.* Ottawa: CMHC.
_____. 1980. *Annual Report.* Ottawa: CMHC.
_____. 1981a. *CMHC and the National Housing Act.* Ottawa: CMHC.
_____. 1981b. *Residential Rehabilitation Assistance Program Manual.* Ottawa: CMHC.
_____. 1981c. *Dwelling Starts and Completion in Canada.* Ottawa: CMHC.
Chinloy, P. 1980. "The Effect of Maintenance Expenditures on the Measurement of Depreciation in Housing." *Journal of Urban Economics* 6:107–25.
Eisner, R. 1977. "Components of Capital Expenditures: Replacement and Modernization Versus Expansion." *Review of Economics and Statistics* 59:297–304.
Feldstein, M.S., and D.K. Foot. 1971. "The Other Half of Gross Investment: Replacement and Modernization Expenditure." *Review of Economics and Statistics* 53:49–58.
McKee, C., ed. 1977. *Innovative Strategies for the Renewal of Older Neighbourhoods.* Winnipeg: University of Winnipeg Press.
Mendelsohn, R. 1977. "Empirical Evidence on Home Improvements." *Journal of Urban Economics* 4:459–68.
Statistics Canada. 1971. *Census of Canada. Housing: Period of Construction and Length of Occupancy.* Cat. 93-731, Vol. 2, Part 3.
Trinh, A. 1978. "Housing Requirements Model: Projections to 2000." Canada Mortgage and Housing Corporation Program and Market Requirement Division.
Whittle, A., G. Milgram, and C. Barber. eds. 1977. *Analysis and Assessment of Present Policies and Programs.* Winnipeg: Institute of Urban Studies.

8 MANAGING THE EXISTING HOUSING STOCK: PROSPECTS AND PROBLEMS

Ira S. Lowry

In 1980 the housing inventory of the United States included about 86.7 million year-round habitable dwellings with an aggregate market value in excess of $3 trillion. Dwellings that now exist will house over three-fourths of all Americans at the end of this century. Indeed, if the past is any guide, half of these dwellings will still be in service in the year 2050. How well this inventory is managed will have much more effect on housing quality over the next twenty years than will new residential construction, which annually averages only about 2 percent of the inventory.

In the United States management of the existing inventory is highly decentralized. About two-thirds of the stock consists of owner-occupied homes whose maintenance is governed almost wholly by the occupants' decisions. Depending on their resources and expectations for the future, they may improve their dwellings, maintain the status quo, or consume capital by undermaintenance. The remaining third are rental dwellings, whose owners must cater to the market. Their maintenance policies are driven by their interpretations of consumer preferences and estimates of consumer purchasing power now and in the future. In most jurisdictions both homeowners and landlords are subject to housing maintenance codes, but these are rarely enforced except against egregious violations of health or safety conditions.

159

Decentralized decisions need not yield socially optimal outcomes. Many people regard housing deterioration as a societal mistake that could be remedied by public intervention. Some believe that elderly homeowners occupy, through inertia, dwellings better suited for and needed by younger households with children. The configuration of dwellings in space, often reflecting decades of parcel-by-parcel development decisions, rarely seems to us as good as the results that could be obtained by starting over with large blocks of raw land and coherent plans for its development.

These problems have a common origin in the technology of producing housing services. That technology is capital-intensive, and the capital is fixed as to location as well as being transgenerationally durable. Over time, housing preferences change as households change in size, composition, wealth, and life-styles. Aggregate demand for housing shifts both locally (within metropolitan areas, for example) and nationally (between regions) as people move and local populations grow unevenly. Each generation must either adapt an inherited capital stock to new conditions or abandon the portions of that stock that are least suitable. Housing shortages in one community commonly coexist with surpluses in others.

Most public intervention in response to these problems has operated at the margin of new construction, sometimes on raw land, sometimes demolishing existing dwellings and redeveloping their sites. The primary tools of such intervention have been land acquisition through the power of eminent domain, capital subsidies for development or redevelopment, and regulation of land use and structural characteristics by local authorities. Since the early 1950s, the federal government in the United States has provided small sums for selective rehabilitation of existing dwellings and to assist local governments with housing code enforcement, but these programs have never been large enough to have widespread effects. In recent years a number of local governments, perceiving a rental housing shortage, have regulated rents and restricted the conversion of multiple dwellings to condominiums. With these exceptions, managing the existing inventory has been left to its owners.

Would more or different kinds of public intervention improve the performance of the existing inventory? Looking ahead at the likely changes in housing demand between 1980 and 2000, assessing the technical adaptablity of the existing inventory to these changes, and considering the institutional barriers to technically efficient adaptations, this chapter concludes that decentralized decisionmaking serves us well in markets where aggregate demand for housing is growing, even when tastes have changed, but that they serve us poorly in markets where aggregate demand is shrinking. Some specific suggestions are made for intervention policies in both cases.

PROSPECTIVE DEMAND SHIFTS, 1980–2000

Patterns of life and work are changing in the United States in ways that were not anticipated twenty years ago, and there is little reason to believe that in 1980 we are better at predicting the future than we were in 1960. Nonetheless, recent trends remain the best guide to the future, so they are worth consulting. In any case, those trends have generated as-yet-unresolved stresses on housing markets that will engage policy attention over the next few years at least.

Six demand trends are especially pertinent to the utilization of the existing inventory: (1) interregional population redistribution, (2) intraregional dispersion of residence, (3) racial succession within urban areas, (4) declining household size and related shifts in the age distribution and marital statuses of household heads, (5) increased labor-force participation among females generally and married women specifically, and (6) changes in tenure preferences that have resulted from a decade of rapid general price inflation. Many of these trends are fully analyzed in other chapters of this volume; the present discussion comments on the trends' implications for housing supply and inventory management.

Interregional Population Redistribution

Since the 1950s population growth has been shifting from the northeast and north central regions of the United States to the south and west, following the locational preferences of new manufacturing and service industries that find the earlier industrial regions of the northeast and north central states unattractive for a variety of reasons. The Bureau of Economic Analysis (BEA) of the U.S. Department of Commerce expects this shift to continue, albeit abating as economic activity becomes more evenly distributed over the national landscape (see Chapter 4).

These population shifts imply rapidly growing housing demand in some regions and states, if not actual decline, in others. Thus the BEA expects the Rocky Mountain states to double their populations by the year 2000, while the eastern seaboard states, from New York south to Maryland, is expected to grow by only 1 percent. Taking these extremes as illustrative at least of possibilities, it is apparent that social efficiency in the growing regions implies both intensive utilization of the existing stock and rapid development of new housing. On the other hand, the existing inventory of a slow-growth region contains nearly enough capital to produce all the housing services that will be demanded over the next twenty years.

Intraregional Dispersion

Some of the forces that have caused interregional redistribution of population operate also at the intraregional scale, and they have been inadvertently reinforced by federal policies with respect to local transportation, housing finance, and racial segregation. Until about 1950 metropolitan central cities were the fastest growing class of jurisdictions in the nation. By 1970 they were the slowest in growth, and about one-half (nearly all of those unable to annex suburban territory) lost population between 1970 and 1980. During that decade population losses were also reported for twenty-nine entire metropolitan areas, all but one in the northeast or north central regions. The jurisdictions that grew most rapidly as a group were nonmetropolitan cities and counties (U.S. Bureau of the Census 1981).

The housing inventory management problems posed by intraregional population dispersion are similar to those created by interregional population shifts. One plausible policy response is changing the balance of intraregional locational incentives—getting suburbanites and exurbanites to move back to the central city where the surplus housing is located or at least channeling regional growth back to these central areas. The likelihood of reconcentration depends in turn on other trends, discussed below.

Racial Succession within Urban Areas

A major cause of central-city population losses has been the influx to those cities of racial minorities, principally black and Hispanic, leading to "white flight." During the 1960s metropolitan central cities as a group annually gained 100,000–150,000 blacks, Latins and orientals due to net migration, and annually lost about 500,000 whites. During the 1970s the minority inflow tapered off, but the white exodus grew to more than 1 million persons annually (Lowry 1980). Scholars do not entirely agree on the motivations for white flight, but the fact and the consequences for housing markets are clear. Nearly all central cities that have been through this process (some in the north central states have escaped it) have been left with a large surplus of unmarketable housing, which through neglect and vandalism soon becomes uninhabitable.

Although net migration by minorities to central cities is no longer substantial and for some locations is negative, the rate of natural increase of minorities is comparatively high and will doubtless continue at such levels for the rest of the century. By the end of the century it is likely that the erstwhile white majority will be a numerical minority in central cities. Already Gary, Cleveland, Newark, Detroit, Atlanta, Los Angeles, New Orleans, and Oakland have elected black mayors. As other cities lose white residents and their minority populations grow, the balance of political power will shift there as well.

Declining Household Size

Throughout the United States, in both metropolitan and nonmetropolitan areas, household sizes continue their long-term shrinkage. In 1980 over one-fifth of all households consisted of only one person, and over one-half consisted of no more than two persons. Yet two-thirds of the national housing inventory consists of single-family houses, nearly all of which have two or more bedrooms. Including multiple dwellings, the nation has available 420 million rooms to house 220 million people in households, or about 1.9 rooms per person. Put another way, the existing inventory could accommodate nearly twice as many people without violating current notions of unhealthful overcrowding.

Household sizes have shrunk for several reasons. One is that married couples now have fewer children than those of preceding generations. Another is that life spans have lengthened and more of the population is elderly; furthermore, social security benefits enable more of the elderly to maintain separate households rather than moving in with their adult children. Finally, children now usually leave their parental homes before marrying, living alone or with friends.

The evidence is clear that both the young and the elderly usually prefer to live apart from their parents in the first case and from their children in the second. Increasing prosperity has enabled them to afford separate dwellings, and housekeeping has been greatly simplified by mechanization (washing machines, refrigerators, automatic heating systems) and commercially preprocessed foods (frozen dinners, instant coffee). But some observers believe that housing tenure arrangements impede efficient reshuffling of people and dwellings as household circumstances change. They point especially to "empty-nesters," elderly household heads who continue to live in the large homes they bought while they were raising children, and to the complaints of younger parents that they are unable to find rental accommodations that are suitable for raising children.

Female Labor-Force Participation

Since World War II married women have entered the labor force in rapidly increasing numbers. By 1976 married couples in which both husband and wife worked outnumbered those in which only the husband worked, and 46 percent of all children had parents who both worked (Alonso 1980). The mechanization of domestic chores clearly eased the way for this transition. Nevertheless, it remains a surprise to me that in 1978 44 percent of all mothers with children under six years of age were employed.

When all adults in a household are employed outside the home, housekeeping and home maintenance are likely to be regarded as burdensome chores rather than opportunities to exhibit domestic skills and good taste. Although systematic evidence is lacking, many observers infer that dwelling preferences have or will shift in favor of smaller homes and apartments that require less attention from the occupants and more centrally located dwellings that reduce commuting time.

Tenure Preferences

Whatever the effect of growing female labor-force participation on housing preferences, it has not visibly altered tenure preferences: The United States is becoming a nation of homeowners. In 1950 about one-half of all households owned their homes. Today the proportion approaches two-thirds. Between 1970 and 1980 the incidence of homeownership rose at every level of real income above $10,000 (1978 purchasing power) (Lowry 1982).

Homeownership offers some practical advantages over renting, in that homeowners have more control over (but also more responsibility for) property maintenance and operating policies. But the national shift in housing tenure is also driven by financial considerations. A homeowner's mortgage interest payments and real estate taxes are deductible from taxable income in the United States, and the housing services yielded by equity investment are likewise untaxed. Even more important during the 1970s was the general expectation of capital gains in a rising real estate market.

The market for homeownership was further broadened in the 1970s by the perfection of legal instruments for the ownership of apartments in multiple dwellings. Owning a home no longer necessarily entails a commitment to mow the lawn or arrange for deliveries of heating fuel. Those who prefer apartment living in urban environments can also have the financial benefits of ownership tenure. Because of these events, households that previously were inclined to rent have entered the homeownership market in large numbers. A national study of new conventional mortgages reports that single people accounted for 0.5 percent of all homebuyers in 1970, but 24 percent in 1980. Whereas only 6 percent of all homebuyers were childless in 1970, 78 percent of the 1980 home purchasers had no children.[1]

Meanwhile, the rental market has floundered. The more prosperous tenants bought homes, and the others split into smaller households, each with fewer wage earners. Between 1970 and 1980 the median income for renters fell by about 20 percent in real terms. The rents they were willing and able to pay have lagged far behind the costs of supplying rental housing services. I estimate that the average revenue from a fixed bundle of rental housing services increased by 87 percent during the decade, but operating expenses rose by 141 percent. Net operating return fell by 37 percent in constant dollars (Lowry 1982). When feasible, landlords have converted rental dwellings to condominiums, often reaping large capital gains in the process. Others whose properties were poorly designed for conversion or located in unpromising neighborhoods have been less fortunate. They have responded to the tenure shift by undermaintenance and, in some cases, outright abandonment of their properties.

MANAGING THE EXISTING INVENTORY, 1980–2000

If recent trends continue, there is every reason to anticipate a poor fit between the existing inventory of dwellings and the preferences of consumers in the year 2000. The inventory is badly located with respect to the emerging spatial configuration of demand, is designed for larger households and more home-centered life-styles than are likely in the future, and has too many rental dwellings in it. Some of the trends that lead to these conclusions could moderate or even reverse, but it is nonetheless useful to ponder the inventory management policies that would best cope with the most probable future.

I suggest a basic division in inventory management problems between markets experiencing rapid population growth and those experiencing decline. In the former the problem is to get more housing service out of the existing inventory while augmenting that inventory as demand grows. In the latter the problem is to manage housing surpluses so that excess dwellings do not injure the financial prospects of the part of the inventory that should be retained. In both cases one might say that the market, un-hampered by public intervention, is capable of finding a solution. However, I think that the social costs of the market solution differ for growth and decline.

Inventory Management in Growing Regions

Where population is growing rapidly through net in-migration, the demand for housing should increase commensurately. Except at the beginning of a growth episode when vacancies are abundant, the existing inventory cannot absorb the extra demand without price increases that impel individual consumers to economize on housing (as by doubling up to form larger households occupying less space per person). In a market economy those price increases (higher rents and property values) are the signals that encourage developers to build additional housing.

Given a responsive building industry, the price increases would be self-limiting except for the near absolute scarcity of building sites in desirable locations. The characteristic American experience in growing regions has been a speculative increase in land prices greater than the market will sustain over the long run and a development "rush" that often gets ahead of the rate of growth in aggregate housing demand. Casual observation suggests roughly a three-year cycle of frantic development alternating with pauses during which excess supply is absorbed by further growth in aggregate demand.

It seems unlikely that inventory growth could be better managed by central planning of its pace. The reason for overbuilding is not that builders are unaware of other builders' activity, but that they collectively overestimate the pace of demand growth. Such overestimates are also characteristic of city and county planning agencies. In any case the social costs of fluctuations in construction activity are not large. The industry does not carry a heavy burden of fixed capital that stands idle in slack times, and building tradesmen are versatile as to alternative employment, for example, repairing or remodeling existing homes.[2]

A much better case can be made for regulating the location and design of subdivisions, because these aspects of development quite directly affect the cost of public services and congestion in the use of public facilities such as streets. Economies of scale in site assembly and development characteristically cause developers to prefer fairly large tracts of raw land, leading to leapfrog peripheral development. To city planners it often seems more desirable to redirect growth from external locations to the infill of unused sites within the built-up area or to the redevelopment of obsolete neighborhoods at higher densities.

One of the advantages of growth is the opportunity it offers for restructuring the composition of the housing inventory to achieve a better match between what consumers want and what is available. If small apartments or large single-family houses are in short supply, builders will concentrate on dwellings of that type, which will then become a larger share of the total inventory. During the remainder of this century it seems likely that small dwellings configured so as to be suitable for owner-occupancy will be the most readily marketable. These could be either single-family houses or apartments in multiple dwellings.

Cities in growing regions often have a substantial supply of older single-family houses on small lots that might accommodate the prospective demand for small owner-occupancy dwellings if problems of neighborhood quality could be resolved. Some are now occupied by elderly persons and will come on the market irregularly as their owners die or move into nursing homes. Others have already passed from owner-occupancy into the low-income rental market. Most of these dwellings need more maintenance than they get, simply to continue in service. Nearly all would need redecorating as well as substantial remodeling of kitchens and baths to appeal to prosperous working couples or single persons.

Such rehabilitation has occurred in some places (James 1980). Called "gentrification," it is greeted with mixed emotions by public officials and civic leaders. On the one hand, it seems to realize their fond hopes of attracting the middle class back to central cities overburdened with poor residents. On the other hand, it displaces those poor residents from some of the best housing that is available to them.

A key ingredient of gentrification during the 1970s was amateur real estate speculation. Although quality-controlled comparisons are difficult, single-family homes in central cities were selling for substantially less than their suburban counterparts, but property values generally were rising. Both young couples and single persons with good jobs saw home purchases as highly leveraged investments for their savings, with rates of return that far exceeded those of savings accounts, stocks, or bonds (Brueggeman and Peiser 1979). Without children they were unconcerned about school quality and, being young and vigorous, were less concerned about street crime than were older persons. Small, centrally located dwellings were therefore appealing to the young even in uncomfortable neighborhoods.

In growing regions the stimulus of rising property values should continue to encourage such central-city investments, with the result that the supply of rental housing will shrink. Restricting peripheral development by growth control ordinances, moratoria on sewer connections, and the like, would reinforce incentives for increased utilization of central-city housing and redevelopment of central-city sites.

The other side of gentrification is a narrowing of the rental market for lower income households, especially those with children. From a landlord's perspective, families with children are not preferred tenants. By and large, children are physically more active, noisier, and more destructive of property than are adults. Because of the noise problem and the absence of outdoor play space, owners of multiple dwellings often refuse to rent to families with children. However, in default of better prospects, small single-family houses in marginal neighborhoods are commonly rented to such families. Gentrification removes these homes from the rental market.

The competition for such dwellings could be eased by bringing more of them on the market. If urban empty-nesters could be persuaded to give up their single-family homes sooner, more dwellings would be available for both the "gentry" and the blue-collar and single-parent families. One promising scheme is to construct small apartment buildings on scattered sites in these same neighborhoods and trade them to elderly couples for their single-family houses, which could then be rented or sold to families. Such transactions would probably not be financially feasible without subsidy. The urban elderly may have enough equity in their homes to trade it for a life-interest in newer albeit smaller apartments with more services.

To sum up, unfettered market forces in a growing region will respond quickly to increases in the demand for housing, by a combination of sprawling peripheral development and selective improvement or redevelopment in central areas. Outcomes could perhaps be improved by public intervention to force more compact development and to facilitate recycling urban single-family houses, now occupied by elderly persons, into family use. Overall growth in the inventory will help it adapt to current preferences.

Inventory Management in Static and Declining Regions

Some regions of the United States now have enough dwellings to accommodate their foreseeable populations without significantly increasing the density of occupancy. Within these static and declining regions, the older urban centers have already lost substantial shares of their peak populations and presently have more dwelling space than their residents are able and willing to pay for. Although the recent intraregional dispersive movement will probably taper off, no one expects reconcentration within declining regions. Through the 1980s at least, an increasing number of central cities in the northeast and north central states and a few elsewhere will find themselves with an embarrassing surplus of housing, while residential construction continues in their suburbs and exurbs.

What should be done with all those empty dwellings? Conceptually, there are several options. One is to seal them up and hold them as potentially valuable capital resources to be reused in the event of unexpected population growth. Another is to keep them on the market as a price-depressing surplus. A third is to convert them to offices or other commerical use. Finally, we could demolish them and grow vegetables or play baseball on their sites.

Arguments for stockpiling vacant dwellings seem thin in the face of the persistent shrinkage of housing demand in declining regions and the technical difficulties of maintaining empty dwellings. In most neighborhoods where surplus housing is concentrated, draining the pipes and boarding up the windows is not enough. Armed guards on twenty-four-hour duty would be needed to prevent break-ins, vandalism, and arson. In any event, the stockpiling strategy lacks an effective constituency. The current generation would bear the storage costs for the benefit of a future generation.

While keeping vacant dwellings on the market may offer advantages to homebuyers by keeping prices low, the advantages to renters are less clear. A case in point is South Bend, Indiana, which has been losing population since about 1960. In 1974, the inner-city vacancy rate for homeowner dwellings was 4.2 percent and the average vacancy duration was 26 weeks. A two-bedroom house in reasonably good repair could readily be purchased for $10,000, far below replacement cost. However, commercial banks and thrift institutions could rarely be persuaded to finance such a transaction; either the seller financed the purchase on a land contract, or the buyer raised money from unconventional sources.[3]

Homes that are hard to sell drift into the rental market, where they also prove to be hard to rent. In the same part of South Bend, the rental vacancy rate in 1974 was 12.3 percent, and the average vacancy duration was nearly 11 weeks. With so much rent loss, it is not surprising that rental property values were also far below replacement cost. It was surprising to discover, however, that contract rents were only about 2 percent below those commanded by comparable suburban dwellings. Renters benefited from the housing surplus only in having more choices, and even that benefit is largely an illusion.[4]

Whatever the immediate benefit to tenants, a local surplus of rental housing is hard on landlords. Because of turnover, vacancies occur throughout the stock and in loose markets they last longer, reducing revenue even if rent levels are maintained. Property values are depressed, and long-term investment yields look bleak. A common response is disinvesting by undermaintaining rental properties. In extreme cases, such as New York City or St. Louis during the 1960s, buildings are abandoned by their owners or burned down for the insurance money.

On balance a local housing surplus is a public nuisance, and the market's devices for disposing of it are slow, messy, and even dangerous. There is much to be said for quick, surgical removal of redundant dwellings by public action. Vacant dwellings that are unfit for habitation are obvious candidates for prompt condemnation and demolition. Those in arrears on taxes can also be seized and removed from the inventory. Finally, the power of eminent domain can be invoked for land clearance and redevelopment in neighborhoods where the incidence of vacant dwellings is high. Whatever the method, the removal of the surplus will improve the financial prospects of the rest of the inventory and probably lead to better maintenance of it.

Both spot and neighborhood clearance generate relocation problems. Not all buildings that are obvious candidates for spot demolition are vacant, and their remaining occupants are usually poorly equipped, because of poverty or age or household circum-stances, to find other housing even when vacancies are abundant. Neighborhood clearance broadens the relocation problem by de-molishing many occupied dwellings. Yet by closing down an entire neighborhood (instead of every fourth house), neighborhood clear-ance reduces the need for territorially allocated public services (street cleaning, trash collection, police protection) and broadens the alternatives for reusing the site.

These considerations suggest that, where housing is abundant, the humane policy would be to select some declining neighbor-hoods for improvement and others for demolition and to schedule these operations so that an inventory of refurbished dwellings was always ready for those displaced by demolition. The idea is not new but has seldom been smoothly executed. In the massive clearance programs of the 1950s, the displaced usually just van-ished into the general milieu.

Aggressive demolition could remove the embarrassing surplus of housing in declining cities but would leave them with another embarrassment: parcels or tracts of unused land. Mamy of us can remember the vast and dreary expanses of urban land cleared in the 1950s for redevelopment, some of which lay idle for a decade or more. No one is anxious to repeat that experience unless the alternatives are worse. Eventually, most of those sites were redeveloped and now sport convention centers, industrial parks, luxury apartment blocks, and even some middle - or lower income housing. Redevelopment was slow because it was attempted in the context of a massive exodus of population and because the slow pace of redevelopment was not usually anticipated. No plans were made for the interim use of vacant land in ways that would make it a public amenity rather than an eyesore.

That problem could be avoided by deliberate land-banking. No one expects older central cities to flourish in the 1980s. Instead of following the bulldozers with anxious negotiators seeking to en-tice a consortium of developers with land-write-downs and tax breaks, city governments should landscape such sites and install recreational facilities that require minimal capital investment, such as playing fields and picnic grounds. The cleared land might be firmly dedicated to public use for a decade or even twenty years, whereupon the city fathers would be free to sell it off to developers. Although even those simple improvements to vacant land would cost money that strapped city governments cannot easily afford, it would be interesting to calculate how much they would save in public services as a consequence of demolishing redundant dwellings. Probably, the savings would not pay for a first-class park but might well pay for a pleasant playground.

Removing surplus housing would concentrate the urban population in the remainder of the inventory, thereby improving landlords' revenues by reducing their vacancy losses. In central South Bend, for example, reducing the vacancy rate from 12.3 to 5 percent would increase revenues by 8.3 percent. Unfortunately, that would not be enough to make rental housing an attractive investment.

As noted earlier, rental revenues have been lagging behind the cost of supplying rental housing services at least since 1970. Because of both an excess supply of rental housing and the declining real incomes of renters, landlords have been unable to pass their cost increases on to their tenants. Although some investors are misled by nominal increases in property values as all prices rise, the investment performance of rental housing has been dismal for at least a decade. To make rental property a generally attractive investment, most industry sources believe that rents would have to rise by 25 to 30 percent in real terms—that is, in addition to any annual increases needed to offset inflation. Low-income renters in urban areas typically spend 35 to 50 percent of their gross incomes for housing (contract rent plus utilities), and are unlikely to spend more voluntarily. Absent public intervention in the market, the rental inventory is likely to shrink and standards of rental property maintenance to fall.

Aside from a demolition program, what forms of public intervention would ameliorate this bleak prospect? The conventional remedy for low-income housing problems is subsidies for new construction, which would be irrelevant in markets that already have too much housing for their populations. The most likely intervention, rent control to protect tenants from rent increases, would only encourage the decline of the rental industry. Rent increases on the scale needed to cure a sick industry are likely to be achieved only by a general entitlement program of rent subsidies for low-income families.

During the 1970s the Section 8 Existing Housing Program of the U.S. Housing and Community Development Act at 1974 served that function on a limited scale. By 1981 over 600,000 rental dwellings were occupied by participants who paid a specified fraction of their incomes for rent, while the U.S. Department of Housing and Urban Development (HUD) contributed the balance under a contract with the landlord. An evaluation of this program conducted by HUD in 1976 (Drury et al. 1978), revealed that when dwellings entered the program, their rents rose sharply. For dwellings that did not change tenants and did not need repairs in order to qualify for the program, the average rent increase upon entry was 26 percent. That increase was borne entirely by HUD and resulted in an annual transfer (at 1979 program levels) of $218.5 million to landlords over and above the market rents of their dwellings (Rydell, Mulford, and Helpers 1980).

In October 1981 the President's Commission on Housing recommended that "consumer housing assistance grants," also known as "housing allowances" or "housing vouchers" be substituted for future commitments to subsidize the construction of rental housing (President's Commission on Housing 1981). It also suggested that continuing subsidies to existing projects, including both public housing and the Section & program described, might eventually be transformed into an allowance program. The present HUD secretary, Samuel R. Pierce, Jr., has indicated his general agreement with the commission's recommendations, and is preparing a legislative proposal for an allowance program.

If large enough, such a program could considerably improve the prospects of the rental housing industry for the rest of this century.[5] The main problem, aside from the cost of an allowance program, is finding the appropriate balance between desirable rent increases, needed to improve the yield of rental property investments, and desirable decreases in the rent burdens of participating households. In short, how should a federal subsidy be split between landlords and tenants?

To summarize, the main foreseeable housing problem of declining regions is a general surplus of housing that will be most conspicuous in their older urban centers. Single-family homes that cannot be sold to owner-occupants will drift into the rental market, adding to the excess supply of rental dwellings that already exists. The rental population, minus upper income families who can shift to homeownership, may decline numerically and will certainly have lower average incomes than in the past. For all these reasons, the revenues from rental properties are unlikely to rise to levels that would encourage investment in or even maintenance of the existing inventory. Two kinds of public intervention would help these housing markets adjust to their prospects: demolishing the redundant stock and subsidizing rents for low-income households.

NOTES

1. Information supplied by Max Rogel, Investors Mortgage Insurance Company, April 29, 1981.
2. The housing slump of 1980–81, for example, seems to be having that result. A survey of member firms conducted by the National Association of Home Builders early in 1982 found that "more than two out of three residential building firms are either diversifying to non-residential construction or have plans to do so within the next 12 months. . . . About one-third of the respondents indicated that they have switched or plan to do so to the rehabilitation and remodeling business. Another 48% are going into the non-residential construction business" (*Los Angeles Times,* February 7, 1982).
3. These data are from the Housing Assistance Supply Experiment, conducted by the RAND Corporation in Green Bay, Wisconsin, and South Bend, Indiana, from 1974 to 1979. See Rydell 1979 and Shanley and Hotchkiss 1979.
4. According to the conventional wisdom, renters have more choices in a market with a high vacancy rate because there are more vacant dwellings at any given time from which to choose. The proposition is true as far as it goes but assumes that an apartment hunter spends just one day at that task. A much better measure of the availability of alternatives is the turnover rate—the fraction of all dwellings that become vacant during a specified period of time. In central South Bend, where the rental vacancy rate was 12.3 percent, the annual turnover rate was 60 per 100 dwellings; in Green Bay, with a rental vacancy rate of only 5.1 percent, annual turnover was 65 per 100 dwellings. The national average rental turnover rate is about 60 per 100 dwellings annually (Rydell 1979).
5. Khadduri and Struyk estimate that "an open enrollment program using existing units exclusively would cost about $1,701 per subsi-

dized household in 1979 dollars, or about $4.4 billion per year, for the 2.5 million additional households [renter households not now receiving assistance] that would join the program. . . . By the seventh year of the entitlement program, outlays [would] be lower than they would have been if current program were continued." (1980:19 and 23.)

REFERENCES

Alonoso, William. 1980. "The Population Factor and Urban Structure." In *The Prospective City,* edited by Arthur P. Solomon. Cambridge, Mass.: MIT Press.

Brueggeman, William B., and Richard B. Peiser. 1979. "Housing Choice and Relative Tenure Prices." *Journal of Finance and Quantitative Analysis* 14 (November):735–51.

Drury, Margaret, Olson Lee, Michael Springer, and Lorene Yap. 1978. *Lower Income Housing Assistance Program (Section 8): National Evaluation of the Existing Housing Program.* Washington, D.C.: U.S. Department of Housing and Urban Development.

James, Franklin J. 1980. "The Revitalization of Older Urban Housing and Neighborhoods." In *The Prospective City,* edited by Arthur P. Solomon. Cambridge, Mass. MIT Press.

Khadduri, Jill, and Raymond J. Struyk. 1980. "Housing Vouchers: From Here to Entitlement." Working Paper 1536–01, The Urban Institute.

Lowry, Ira S. 1980. "The Dismal Future of Central Cities." In *The Prospective City,* edited by Arthur P. Solomon. Cambridge, Mass.: MIT Press.

_____. 1982. *Rental Housing in the 1970s: Searching for the Crisis.* Santa Monica, Calif.: The RAND Corporation.

President's Commission on Housing. 1981. *Interim Report.* Washington, D.C.: U.S. Government Printing Office.

Rydell, C. Peter. 1979. *Vacancy Duration and Housing Market Condition.* Santa Monica, Calif.: The RAND Corporation.

Rydell, C. Peter, John E. Mulford, and Lawrence Helbers. 1980. *Price Increases Caused by Housing Assistance Programs.* Santa Monica, Calif.: The RAND Corporation.

Shanley, Michael G., and Charles M. Horchkiss. 1979. *How Low-Income Renters Buy Homes.* Santa Monica, Calif.: The RAND Corporation.

U.S. Bureau of the Census. 1981. "Standard Metropolian Statistical Areas and Standard Consolidated Statistical Areas: 1980." Supplementary Report PC80-S1-5. *1980 Census of Population.* Washington, D.C.: U.S. Government Printing Office.

III HOUSING FINANCE

The 1970s and early 1980s have been a relatively turbulent period for the housing finance systems in both the United States and Canada. Recent experiences with historically high interest rates on residential mortgages have raised widespread concern over the affordability of homeownership for most households. In addition, in an environment of rapidly changing interest rates, the risks created by volatile market rates cause problems for mortgage lenders in their management of assets and liabilities and for borrowers facing uncertain mortgage payments. In the United States these pressures on lenders have generated extremely serious questions concerning the financial viability of the savings and loan industry.

The suggested affordability problem is created by high inflation rates when mortgage contracts are written with level payments determined by the nominal interest rate. Under inflationary conditions borrowers are forced by rising interest rates to pay higher initial mortgage payments to offset the reduced real value of their subsequent payments; in other words, there is a tilt of the real payment stream toward the beginning of the loan. The severity of the tilt is directly related to the level of anticipated inflation rates.

Historically in both countries the standard mortgage instruments have been level-payment loans with nominal interest rates. Under such a design the affordability constraint is greatest during the early years of the mortgage and eases as time progresses. That is, inflating incomes and constant mortgage payments result in a falling ratio of payment to income over time. To alleviate this perceived problem a number of alternative, non-level-payment instruments have been suggested for the mortgage market, including the graduated-payment mortgage (GPM), the price-level-adjusted mortgage (PLAM), and the shared-appreciation mortgage (SAM). The purpose of each of these alternative designs is to reduce the tilt effect imposed by the standard mortgage instrument.

Conflicting with the concerns raised with respect to affordability, the 1970s have been a time of generally high demand for homeownership and declining age of new home purchasers. It is now widely recognized that higher mortgage interest rates resulting from inflation do not necessarily increase the overall cost of homeownership. The total cost of ownership consists of the outlays necessary to purchase and maintain the dwelling, less the value of the house when sold. If the market value of the house rises with the price level, the inflation premium paid to finance the housing investment can be recaptured through the subsequent capital gain. Also, with the tax shelters provided homeowners in both countries, inflation may generally lower the real cost of ownership when recognition is given to the after-tax investment return from the asset. The outstanding question is whether these superior returns from housing investment can be expected to continue in the future.

The second basic concern for housing finance in an inflationary environment is that interest-rate volatility can increase the inherent risks of any financial contract where the income (for lenders) and the costs (to borrowers) are a function of fluctuating market rates. Until recently the traditional mortgage instrument in the United States has been a long-term, fixed-rate mortgage. Under such a design the risks created by volatile interest rates are assumed by the mortgage lender. To the extent that the institution does not have matching long-term, fixed-rate deposits, the intermediary does bear a high level of interest-rate risk. With the rollover instrument presently dominating Canadian mortgage markets, interest-rate risk is split between the lender and borrower. The financial institution absorbs the risk during the term of the mortgage (one to five years), while the borrower bears the risk of uncertain mortgage payments upon the renewal of the mortgage at the end of the term. In both countries, however, the amplification of interest-rate volatility and a shortening of deposit maturities has led to the introduction of a wave of new adjustable-rate instruments, such as variable-rate mortgages (VRMs), which require borrowers to assume a greater portion of the interest-rate risk.

Inflation, interest-rate volatility, and the introduction of alternative mortgage instruments have combined to force changes that can be characterized as revolutionary, in the basic tenents of housing finance systems in North America. The following four chapters address these changes and the issues related to the expected characteristics of housing finance in the future. Chapter 9 by Patric Hendershott and Kevin Villani, "Housing Finance in America in the Year 2001," provides a perceptive view of the probable future form of the U.S. financial system as well as the institutions and instruments likely to operate in the housing finance sectors. Starting with an analysis of the essential elements of a financial system, Hendershott and Villani describe how government regulations have historically inhibited the evolution of the housing finance structure in the United States and how the present economic forces of high and volatile interest rates alone with technological change are overwhelming the existing constraints. Interestingly, the ultimate financial system they forsee has many of the characteristics of the current Canadian housing finance system, which evolved in a less regulated setting.

The next two chapters, on mortgage instruments, take different perspectives in their analysis of the twin problems of affordability and interest-rate volatility. "Inflation, Uncertainty and Future Mortgage Instruments" Jack Carr and Lawrence Smith first give a useful historical analysis of the monetary developments that have contributed to the present environment of high and variable interest rates. They then present a thorough discussion of the characteristics and issues surrounding the alternative designs that have been proposed for residential mortgage markets. Chapter 11 "Optimal Mortgage Instrument Designs," examines alternative mortgage instruments through the development of expected utility-maximizing models for mortgage borrowers and lenders under conditions of uncertain interest rates. Dennis Capozza ad George Gau argue that, given the likely savings and risk preferences of most households, the preferred mortgage instrument is generally a level-payment, fixed-rate mortgage. They then consider alternatives for financial intermediaries to adjustable-rate mortgages as approaches to hedging interest-rate risk, mechanisms such as futures and options markets.

The final chapter in this part, "Inflation, House Prices, and Investment: A U.S. Perspective," is by John Tuccillo. He provides a comprehensive analysis of the interactions between inflation and housing as an investment, including the bias introduced into the asset acquisition decisions of households by government taxation prices. Based on this analysis Tuccillo assesses the probable future directions of housing prices and homeownership as an investment.

9 HOUSING FINANCE IN AMERICA IN THE YEAR 2001*

Patric H. Hendershott and Kevin E. Villani

The U.S. financial system is currently undergoing revolutionary changes. Lines of demarcation between banks, thrifts, other financial intermediaries, and industry are rapidly eroding. Existing firms are expanding beyond traditional functions, and new firms are performing nontraditional functions as innovation renders regulatory boundaries obsolete. New financial institutions and instruments are developing in response to fundamental economic, regulatory, and institutional forces. Identification of these forces and of the logical end to which they will lead is necessary to understand both current developments and the likely evolution of the housing finance system into the twenty-first century.

It is generally held that the housing finance system of the United States in the 1970s was the result of regulations and that these regulations are being phased out. It is also realized, although far less widely, that nonneutral taxes have influenced the housing finance system and that changes in tax laws are likely to reduce the nonneutralities. Thus the future housing finance system will probably approach what would have developed in the absence of regulations and nonneutral taxes.

This study was supported by the Center for Real Estate Education and Research, The Ohio State University, from funds supplied by the Ohio Real Estate Education and Research Fund.

This view of the future has led us to structure this chapter in the following way: First we identify the essential services provided by a financial system and then derive the characteristics of the system that would exist in a technologically advanced society unfettered by nonneutral taxes and regulations. Next we consider how taxes and regulations have shaped the existing American financial structure. Finally, we posit likely tax and regulatory changes and conjecture as to how technological innovation will further interact with these changes to alter the American financial system.

THE ESSENTIAL ELEMENTS OF FINANCE

The first step in understanding the financial structure and in distinguishing between regulatory and economic induced innovation is to identify these elements of finance that are essential to household portfolio optimization.[1] From this, the characteristics of a minimal financial sector (utilizing current technology) follow in a straightforward manner.

Essential Financial Services

Four essential financial services would be provided in some form in any well-developed financial system: (1) a medium of exchange, (2) security underwriting, (3) security brokerage, and (4) denomination intermediation. Each of these services is discussed briefly in the remainder of this section.

Medium of exchange. The first and most important financial service is the provision of a medium of exchange. Bruner and Meltzer (1971) have shown that the costs of exchanging goods in an uncertain world can be reduced if one good serves as a medium of exchange. This medium, generally labeled money, must exhibit two characteristics. First, it should be generally acceptable. To accomplish this, it must convey information regarding its ability to be converted into real goods. Second, it should be portable. The more portable it is, the greater are the efficiency gains it generates. As will be discussed later, technology is the limiting factor in conveying information and transporting money.

Security underwriting. The second most important financial service is the provision of a financial claim that allows the transfer of income from surplus to deficit units (Gurley and Shaw 1956). This transfer reallocates real resources from less useful or less productive activities to more productive activities. The key characteristic of the transfer is the information embodied in the financial claim regarding the probability the deficit unit will repay the surplus unit. The primary function of security underwriting is to identify the parameters affecting *ex post* nominal returns and to provide information to surplus units to allow them to form reasonable subjective probability distributions regarding the future value of these parameters, and thus the probability that the terms of the contract will be met. Because a given value of a parameter may increase the *ex post* nominal return on some instruments and decrease the return on others, diversification reduces the variability of portfolio returns.

Security brokerage. The need for brokerage stems from the desire by households either to reallocate their portfolios or to change their net worth. The reallocation-induced demand for brokerage services arises primarily from differing expectations of future outcomes affecting portfolio returns. Households reducing net worth (deficit units) need a mechanism to transfer assets to households increasing net worth (surplus units). Again, the essential characteristic of brokerage is the transfer of information between surplus and deficit households to facilitate the exchange.

Denomination intermediation. Deficit units issue financial instruments that presumably reflect their needs and available collateral. A major benefit of finance is its contribution to superior allocation of risk-bearing in the economy (Arrow 1964). This derives from the ability of economic units to diversify risks associated with multiple securities. The optimal portfolio for a household may include the obligations of many issuers but in smaller amounts than are efficient for the issuer to supply. The major role of financial intermediaries is to provide these smaller denominations.

Denomination intermediation also allows diversification of inflation risk through maturity intermediation. In a tax-neutral world, the real value of capital should be unaffected by inflation, anticipated or unanticipated. Thus, to the extent that financial contracts finance real assets, inflation does not affect real wealth. Human capital may be considered a real asset, but households cannot issue equity shares. Insofar as households issue debt contracts (which provide a claim on future nominal income) to increase current consumption above current income, the real value of those contracts will fall in response to an increase in inflation. To the extent that the inflation is unanticipated—not built into the contract interest rate—the real wealth of deficit units increases at the expense of surplus units. Theoretically, individual households can hedge their debt porfolios against uncertain inflation rates by either selling financial assets short or writing options contracts. But as long as some households issue claims on future nominal income, unanticipated inflation will have distributional consequences.

In summary, only a few financial services are essential. Deficit units would issue instruments reflecting the collateral; either the market value of the asset or, in the case of unsecured debt, the income stream the unit produces. Some form of banking would be created to provide a medium of exchange, and some form of underwriting would develop to convey appropriate information regarding the return parameters of the instruments. Brokers would arise to facilitate the transfer of assets, and denomination intermediaries would be created to facilitate diversification of nominal and real risk.

Characteristics of an Unfettered Financial System

Before turning to the existing financial structure, we speculate on the characteristics of a financial structure utilizing existing technology but unfettered by taxes, regulation or fixed institutional capital (hereafter called institutional memory). A subsequent section contrasts this unfettered system with the existing structure, identifying the consequences of taxes, regulations, and institutional memory.

Consider a simple world in which the private capital stock consists of residential and industrial capital. Producers of housing services and other goods and services would issue both ownership shares in individual units (or collections of units) of capital and debt instruments collateralized by individual units or collections of these units. We denote the demand for shares of the *j*th unit of capital by

$$c_j = f(P_j,\ d_j \pi j)$$

where P_j, the anticipated productivity of the *j*th unit (or collection of units) of capital, P_j, the anticipated depreciation rate, and π_j, the anticipated rate of price increase, are subjective probability distributions. Note that productivity is defined as the rents accruing to capital.

An interesting question is, Are there any reasons why households would want to corner the market on an individual housing unit? That is, would full homeownership exist in a well-developed financial system without tax preferences? Households desire management control to allow them to make all decisions regarding the use of this capital, just as some shareholders of industrial capital desire to maintain a majority interest; but, given the current management prerogatives of shareholders, this explains a 51 percent ownership share, not a 100 percent share. In fact, homeownership is most prevalent in very primitive societies without financial systems. Rental markets exist in more developed societies and require a more developed financial system to sell equity shares. *Ex post* returns on equity shares in different houses will vary for the same reason as they do on equity shares in different industrial plants and companies. That is, the actual returns will depend on the *ex post* value of the parameters. Portfolio optimization implies diversification among shares in residential as well as industrial capital.

What does all this imply for security supplies? Thus far, our analysis suggests the existence of equity shares financing residential and industrial capital and of debt collateralized by residential and industrial capital. Intermediaries will offer these four instruments in smaller denominations. Whether or not there are a sufficient number of instruments for all households to optimize their portfolios—that is, to reduce the benefits from further diversification to zero—depends on the characteristic of the debt instruments. This leads to a more fundamental question: What information does the debt collateral convey?

Two of the three parameters in the demand functions for shares, P_j and d_j, reflect the physical characteristics of the capital and are independent of the third parameter, inflation. This information is most fully utilized if the instruments offer a fixed real interest rate and the principal is repaid at the depreciation rate. The difference between debt and equity is that the risks embodied in p_j and d_j are borne mostly by the equity-holders. A specific example may be useful here. Assume capital markets are efficient and there exists a security (government?) of maturity k with a "certain" real rate of interest r. In risk-neutral markets, the most likely or mean expected real return on a capital good with a life k and no physical depreciation is also r. Suppose further that the capital good is one-half equity-financed and one-half bond-financed. The bondholders' *ex post* yield is r plus a small default premium δ so long as the equity share has positive value. The return on equity reflects the actual productivity and depreciation rates of this particular piece of capital and the extent of bond leveraging. In this case, if *ex post* earnings were twice those expected (r), then the return to equity would be almost three times $(3r\text{-}\delta)$ that expected.

The bone instrument described contracts for the "most likely" real return on existing capital plus δ. How does this differ from a perfectly diversified equity portfolio? The expected real return on the latter would reflect the mean value of the subjective probability distributions of the parameters P_j and d_j, in other words, the variance of these parameters for a perfectly diversified equity portfolio is zero. But suppose that subjective probabilities turn out to be wrong in all cases, resulting in a lower (or higher) *ex post* return on capital generally. This result will be reflected in the return on the perfectly diversified equity portfolio but not the bond return (unless the return on capital was markedly lower). The same certain return could be achieved with a diversified equity portfolio and options contracts.[2] That is, debt instruments are not an essential instrument of finance! Thus the primary effect of bonds is on the distributional impact of the actual real earnings generated by existing capital.

We have thus far ignored instruments to finance consumption in excess of income. These unsecured instruments are collateralized by the productivity or earnings potential of human capital. Conceptually at least, there could exist equity and debt instruments with characteristics similar to those financing nonhuman capital.

If all households shared the same expectations and were risk-neutral, then no other nonmoney financial instruments would exist.[3] If expectations regarding inflation differed, then some households would write options to other households reflecting these differences and an options market could develop.

THE CURRENT HOUSING FINANCE SYSTEM

The foregoing discussion has conjectured that in an unfettered system residential capital would be financed with equity shares and mortgage debt, mortgage underwriters would originate real-denominated housing finance instruments, and financial institutions would develop as pooling arrangements to facilitate diversification by lowering minimum denominations. The existing housing finance system differs in important respects from this hypothetical model. Equity shares in residential capital are scarce, mortgage instruments pay nominal returns; and housing finance intermediaries have undiversified portfolios. In this section we attempt to explain the roles that taxes, regulation, and institutional memory have played in the formation of the current system.

Tax Preferences and Regulations

The most important consequences of the current tax law stem from the failure to tax imputed rent on owner-occupied housing and the preferential treatment of capital gains for homeowners. These tax preferences explain why almost two-thirds of all households in the United States own their own homes and why the ownership rate is greater for higher income households.[4] These preferences, in turn, give rise to mortgage instruments collateralized by individual units and to many households having real housing assets far in excess of their net worth. As a consequence, the total stock of financial debt is dramatically increased, and most household balance sheets are extremely undiversified and leveraged. Because of the latter, the return to household net worth varies far more than proportionately with the returns on individual houses for these homeowners.

The ultimate constraint on arbitrage between owner-occupied housing and financial markets is the diminishing marginal utility of housing services. In equilibrium, wealthier households (and those lower income households for whom homeownership does not pay) ultimately finance the owner-occupied housing of middle-income households. There is a general loss to society in that benefits of diversification are foregone. In addition, the portfolios of wealthier households are tilted toward more debt and less equity. There are thus distributional consequences to other than the most likely outcomes of P_j, d_j and, particularly, Π_j.

The second major tax policy affecting the housing financial system is the preferential tax treatment of income from mortgages held in thrift institution portfolios. Currently, U.S. savings and loan institutions are allowed to put up to 40 percent of their earnings into a "bad debt" reserve without paying federal tax on the income so long as at least 82 percent of their assets are invested in residential mortgages.[5] Virtually all institutions have been induced to meet this requirement. This tax preference, combined with regulatory prohibitions (or threats of the same) against variable-rate loans, has resulted in an industry with a substantially undiversified portfolio of fixed-rate mortgage investments. From the depositor's perspective, this policy is counterproductive to the essential financial service of thrifts: issuing small denomination shares of diversified portfolios paying market interest rates.

These tax preferences have provided rationales for federal regulation. One tax policy, the tax preference on owner-occupied housing, results in "excess" mortgage debt issues by middle-income households, justifying protective consumer regulation. A second tax preference results in this debt being financed by, in part, even lower income depositors who are less able to diversify and thus are in need of protective deposit regulation. For many years virtually all consumer protections and safeguards focused on the types of liabilities households were allowed to issue and basically prohibited all but fixed nominal rate instruments. Lenders were subjected to numerous regulations affecting who got credit and at what risk, for example, the Truth in Lending Act in the United States. Depositors, in contrast, were prohibited from diversifying out of this long-term, fixed-rate mortgage portfolio by limits imposed on the minimum denomination of alternative investments. Although thrift deposits are essentially equivalent to mutual fund pools in Treasury bills, the yields on Treasury bills were not made generally available to depositors, who thus paid the price for the years of protective mortgage regulation.[6]

Debt Instruments and Returns

In the previous section, it was argued that debt instruments were not essential elements of finance and that, if issued, would reflect the real value of the underlying collateral. There are thus two issues regarding the use of debt instruments in the current system. The first is why they exist at all. The second is why they are denominated in nominal terms. Of course, these issues pertain to the entire financial system, not simply housing finance. We have several observations but no definite answers to the questions.

As already explained, households issue mortgage debt because their tax-induced demand for owner-occupied housing generally exceeds net worth. Selling shares in owner-occupied residential capital has not developed as an alternative and would probably result in a loss of the tax preference for the owners. Of course this tax preference cannot explain corporate bond issues. In fact, whereas owner-occupied residential capital is tax-favored, industrial capital is tax-penalized. Returns to shareholders are taxed twice, at the corporate and individual levels. It is somewhat anomalous that double taxation of corporate income leads to the same result with respect to corporate debt as no taxation regarding household debt. Because returns to bondholders are taxed only once, the substitution of bond financing for equity-financing reduces the tax burden on industrial capital generally.

A second reason for the existence of bonds is that it may be more efficient for households to hold bond portfolios than the alternative of fully diversified equity portfolios with options contracts. Diversification is obtained at some costs. Because these are fixed costs of obtaining information, diversification costs are large for households with small asset portfolios.

The payment of nominal, rather than real, returns on mortgages can possibly be attributed to regulations. As noted before, federally chartered thrift institutions have long faced prohibitions (or threats of the same) against variable-rate and negative-amortization loans. Mortgage banking too, has been constrained. Because there are economies of scale to mortgage originations, a significant volume of issues of any specific type of mortgage is necessary to make the process profitable. Thus the willingness of the ultimate investors in the originations of mortgage bankers to accept mortgages with real returns is key. And the primary purchasers of these originations—the Federal National Mortgage Association (FNMA) and the Federal Home Loan Mortgage Corporation (FHLMC)—did not buy variable-rate or negative-amortization loans prior to 1979. Because the Government National Mortgage Association (GNMA) has purchased graduated-payment mortgages, an FHA-VA graduated-payment loan has developed. Nonetheless, the regulatory explanation is not totally satisfactory.

Several general reasons, which apply to mortgage as well as corporate debt, have been offered for the absence of indexed debt. One explanation may be innovation lag. Existing instruments were designed in a noninflationary environment, and tax and accounting procedures developed around these instruments. Other factors may be the difficulties involved in choosing the appropriate index or appraising the value of residential and industrial capital. Finally, Fisher (1979) has suggested (with little enthusiasm) that lenders as a group are more optimistic about inflation than borrowers.

Underwriting, Brokerage, and Exchange

The preferred tax treatment of mortgages in thrift portfolios and regulations limiting asset selection also help explain the structure of the mortgage underwriting industry. Mortgage underwriting conceptually involves the same tasks as bond underwriting. What distinguishes mortgage banking from investment banking is the greater need for local verification of loans collateralized with residential as opposed to industrial capital. The production function for mortgage loan underwriting is thus quite similar to the production function for denomination intermediation. The thrift industry has, in fact, become increasingly cognizant of the value of the existing plant in producing mortgages as deposit flows have slowed. The development of mortgage "brokerage" services by the FHLMC simply reflects the comparative advantage of thrifts in mortgage banking given their existing physical deposit-taking capacity.

Much significance has been imputed to the various secondary mortgage market institutions: FNMA, GNMA, AND FHLMC. Actually, these institutions act largely as demanders in the primary market for new mortgage securities; they provide little brokerage. In essence their role is to provide denomination intermediation (to facilitate diversification), as well as to diversify risks of holding mortgages. They also provide ultimate investors an essential element of underwriting, additional information (Van Order and Villani 1981). Mortgage bankers provide investors with information pertaining to the quality of the collateral. Federal and quasi-federal institutions provide information on the quality of the underwriters. There are obvious scale economies to producing and providing this information, which is why, for example, GNMA is actually quite profitable.

Where then, are existing mortgages brokered? The secondary market for these mortgages is made up mostly of private dealers who seek out private placements. Trades are relatively infrequent because little is to be gained from them. The perceived gains from trade reflect either the different expectations of the buyer and seller or the need for liquidity. Expectatious regarding existing mortgages are homogeneous, and few institutions typically need to sell mortgages for liquidity (the early 1980s environment is an exception).

The story is somewhat different for owner-occupied residential capital. People move for a variety of reasons, some financial. When an owner-occupant moves, ownership must change hands.[7] Movement gives rise to repeated trades during the lifetime of a house. The real estate brokerage industry is not publicly regulated but subject only to the self-policing of appropriate industry practices established by a representative trade organization.

By definition, the accepted mediums of exchange are currency and demand deposits at commercial banks. The McFadden Act and Douglas Amendment prevent bank mergers and branching across state lines, resulting in a fragmented industry. Thrift institutions have been prohibited by law from offering demand deposits, resulting in a duplicity of physical capacity to provide a payment mechanism. But the barriers to entry for transactions mechanisms are already crumbling. The implications of this change are explained more fully in the next section.

EVOLUTION OF THE HOUSING FINANCE STRUCTURE

In this section the basic economic and regulatory forces of change in the existing financial structure are first considered and then the implications for housing finance derived. The forces are viewed as driving the system toward the hypothetical unfettered model developed in the first section.[8]

The Forces for Change

Inflation has been the most powerful economic force behind changes in the financial structure. It has resulted in windfall gains to existing homeowners, increased the demand for owner-occupied housing, and resulted in an explosion in the supply of home mortgage debt (Hendershott and Hsieh 1980). Simultaneously, it significantly raised nominal interest rates and now threatens the viability of thrift institutions. These developments have temporarily abated the regulatory and legislative sympathies for borrowers, created empathy for depositors, and heightened concern for the federal insurance funds. The deregulation of deposit rate ceilings, which began in March 1980 with enactment of the Depository Institutions Deregulation and Monetary Control Act,[9] is being accelerated.[10] A decade of debate over the appropriate consumer safeguards in variable-rate mortgage contracts ended with the virtual total deregulation of these contracts.[11] The economic forces in this case simply overwhelmed the existing regulations.

Concern with the viability of the federal insurance funds, namely, the Federal Deposit Insurance Corporation and especially the Federal Savings and Loan Insurance Corporation, is providing additional impetus for reform. The first step will be a provision to allow commercial banks to purchase "troubled" thrifts across state lines. This provision is essentially a device to test the waters for repeal of the McFadden Act and the Douglas Amendment. The ultimate step is the elimination of prohibitions on branching mergers and acquisitions.

A major distinction between thrifts and commercial banks has been the prohibition of the former from issuing demand deposit liabilities. (This law is particularly capricious because the physical capital of the two types of institutions is virtually identical.) Both disintermediation and the rising costs of existing deposits enhanced the attractiveness of demand deposits at thrifts. The law was ultimately circumvented first by marketing innovation (for example, a deposit is not a demand deposit if you do not call it one) and then by technological innovation such as bill-paying by phone. Demand deposits for thrift institutions were legitimized in the NOW (Negotiated Order of Withdrawal) account provisions of the Depository Institutions Act.

Further evidence of the belated regulatory response to innovation with the payments mechanism and the ultimate inability of regulators to prevail is provided by the experience with international banking. Foreign deposits easily evaded American regulations by flowing to other countries. Domestic banks responded by establishing Caribbean subsidiaries to handle these funds. In June 1981 the Federal Reserve issued regulations approving the establishment of international banking facilities in the United States, thus ending the prohibition and the flow.

Technological innovation is providing an additional powerful economic force; computer technology will ultimately facilitate a revolution of the transactions mechanism. In May 1981 the Federal Home Loan Bank Board (FHLBB) eliminated existing geographic restrictions on "remote service unit" operations. The rationale for this first step into interstate banking by thrift institutions is parity with commercial banks.

With this blurring of the distinction between thrifts and commercial banks came a similar obscuring of the distinction between deposit and nondeposit financial intermediaries and between financial and industrial firms. Merrill Lynch's cash management account may be the closest substitute to currency as a nationally recognized medium of exchange. Moreover, as existing financial firms are moving into banking, industrial firms are moving into finance.

Existing tax preferences favoring housing will also be of declining significance, contributing to the transition of thrifts into banks. The immediate impetus for the removal of the bad debt allowance is provided, paradoxically, by the current earnings squeeze of thrifts. This earnings squeeze is attributable to low rates on past mortgage loans, the existence of which are attributable to the bad debt allowance, limited asset powers and restrictions against variable-rate mortgages. Thrifts have already been granted expanded asset powers; these powers will be enlarged further and the mortgage tax preference will be reduced when thrift earnings make doing so feasible.

The Ultimate Financial Structure

The point is that economic and technological forces will render most existing regulations obsolete within the next twenty years.[12] This movement has three major implications for the financial structure and, in particular, housing finance institutions in the United States. First, various types of firms will offer a medium of exchange. Money transfers will for the most part be electronic. Banks and thrifts will still exist (although the two will not be readily distinguishable), but in far fewer numbers and with significantly less physical capital. The primary purposes of most remaining branches will be to convert small deposits to currency (and vice versa) and to produce mortgages. Federal deposit insurance will contract commensurate with the reduced role of deposit (or denomination) intermediaries, and the two insurers will be merged into one.

Second, mortgage banking subsidiaries will be formed by commercial bank holding companies, savings and loan service corporations, and investment bankers. For the most part, mortgage origination and mortgage finance will be carried out by separate entities. Mortgages will be financed by various pooling arrangements developed by the institutions just described. The federal role in pooling mortgages will likely decline in response both to the improved transfer of underwriting information in the private sector and the political backlash to the expanding use of federal guarantees. Private mortgage insurance will play a larger role in the formation of these pools.

Third, the real estate brokerage industry will be agglomerated. There are currently 600,000 firms, 63 percent of which only have one office (U.S. Department of Housing and Urban Development 1980: II.20 and II.22). Merrill Lynch's entry into the real estate brokerage industry on a national scale will be followed by the entry of other firms as the ability to readily transmit information expands. The distinction between trading in homes and other assets will diminish proportionately with the falling price of conveying specific characteristics through computer technology. In this regard, long-distance sales via telecommunication are envisaged. In addition, larger firms with sufficient net worth will become dealers in houses, following the lead of the Merrill Lynch and Sears executive relocation services. Small firms will still dominate in less populated areas where volume is insufficient to achieve the economies of scale necessary for telecommunication and the necessary dealer inventory turnover. Home brokerage services will thus begin to resemble stock and bond brokerage services.

The previous discussion indicated that the housing finance institutions are unlikely to exist in their current form by the beginning of the next century. The key issue is what this implies for the financing of owner-occupied housing in the year 2001. The quantity of housing, as opposed to the quantity of housing credit, will depend on the real user cost or rental price of housing capital.[13] The absolute tax advantage to owner-occupied housing will remain, due to politically insurmountable obstacles, but the relative advantage will be reduced by successive reductions in the corporate income tax and increases in accelerated depreciation and investment tax credits.[14] The result will be a general rise in before-tax interest rates and a fall in the demand for housing services. The disappearance of housing finance institutions will have a negligible effect on the quantity of mortgage credit available. We have argued previously (Hendershott and Villani 1980) that by the end of the 1970s housing finance had been substantially integrated with the capital markets and thus that mortgage markets cleared at capital market interest rates. Further, empirical forecasts of housing demand in 1979 and the first half of 1980 suggested that the most recent housing collapse in the United States can be fully explained without appeal to rationing effects (Hendershott 1980). The expected gradual disappearance of institutions identifiable as housing finance institutions is consistent with this integration of markets.

The Mortgage Instrument

The most important concern regarding housing finance in the year 2001 is the design of the mortgage instrument. This concern arises from the fact that, for many homeowners, mortgage debt will continue to far exceed net worth. The tax advantage will continue to provide incentives to issue mortgage debt, and many households will still not have the flexibility in the remainder of their portfolios to take actions offsetting undesirable mortgage characteristics. To put it another way, some households may have no alternative to accepting more cash-flow risk in a mortgage contract than their income and balance sheets warrant.

We are not advocating regulation of mortgage contracts. Our point is that, at least in the short run, mortgage instruments are designed by existing financial institutions and their regulators, thus reflecting existing problems facing the institutions and regulators (insurers). Our concern is that the pendulum may have swung too far in the direction of depositor and federal insurer interests to redress past grievances—this characterizes the FHLBB regulations issued during the spring of 1981. We assume the pendulum will reach balance by the year 2001 (and we hope much sooner), at which point the mortgage instrument will reflect the needs of issuers as well as capital market realities.

The principle change from the present is that mortgage contracts with fixed nominal interest rates will be rare. Most mortgages will contain various provisions for adjustment, as described more fully below. The rate flexibility in the contracts will remove the economic incentive for lenders to require "due on sale" clauses. The application of computer technology will likely result in an adjustable mortgage principal. Thus mortgages will be assumed with greater frequency simply to avoid the transactions costs of additional underwriting. Similarly, flexible mortgage rates and adjustable loan principal will remove the economic incentive for borrowers to refinance. Finally, the concepts of maturity and amortization will likely lose significance. That is, once the principal balance becomes flexible, a timetable for repaying debt will disappear. The mortgage instrument will resemble a line of credit in this regard, with the maximum balance moving with the current market value of the asset. Lenders and property tax appraisers may combine forces to produce current market appraisals.

A possible concern of borrowers with real mortgage contract rates is the cash-flow risks some instruments pose.[15] There are essentially two ways to convert nominal contract rates to real rates. The first indexes nominal yields to the actual real productivity of the house, in effect converting the mortgage to an equity share. An example is the shared-appreciation mortgage (SAM). Technically, the lender receives a share of the appreciation—either when the house is sold or at some of the appreciation—either when the house is sold or at some prescribed date—as an interest payment. The amount of this payment will reflect the real *ex post* productivity of the specific housing capital and is thus in essence an equity interest. Cash flows are certain until the prespecified date. The second way is to index nominal yields to market interest rates; this effectively ties the real yield on the mortgage to the *ex post* real yield on new capital generally. Examples of this method are variable-rate mortgage (VRM) where the index rate is not subject to dampeners. Flexible rate contracts that require full payment of nominal interest when it accrues, in addition to scheduled principal payments (due to amortization), immediately expose the borrower to substantial cash-flow risks.

The first type of index provides a complete hedge to the homebuyer. Lenders can diversify their implicit residential equity shares to earn the average *ex post* real rate on housing equity by investing in multiple SAMs, ideally in a wide geographical area. With the VRM the lender earns the actual real return on new capital in each future period; households thus bear both the risk of the return on an individual house being below average and the risk that future real returns will rise above returns on existing housing. The SAM is thus the preferred real-dominated mortgage contract from the borrower's perspective. Moreover, it may be preferred from society's viewpoint in that lenders are better able to diversify away the risk of returns on individual houses.

SUMMARY

The four essential services provided by a financial system—a medium of exchange, security underwriting, security brokerage, and denomination intermediation—avoid the costs of barter, increase the productivity of investment by separating the investment and saving decisions, reduce transaction costs by providing marketability or liquidity, and lower risk by permitting asset diversification. In a housing finance system unfettered by nonneutral taxes and regulations, residential capital would be financed by equity shares and (mortgage) debt; mortgage underwriters would organize real-dominated housing finance instruments (paying real returns indexed, at least roughly, to the nominal value of the underlying house asset); and financial institutions would facilitate portfolio diversification by holding a wide variety of assets, including mortgages, and by offering small-denomination liabilities.

The current housing finance system in the United States differs widely (at least until very recently) in all respects from this hypothetical model. The large part of residential capital that is owner-occupied is financed by a single equity share (100 percent ownership); mortgages have carried fixed nominal rates and negative amortization has been precluded; and housing finance institutions exist with undiversified portfolios. These differences can be attributed virtually entirely to the existence of nonneutral taxes and a myriad of government regulations. Because the tax subsidy to homeownership is available only to owner-occupiers, there are strong incentives against issuing multiple equity shares. Because tax preferences for thrift institutions are contingent upon a large percentage investment in mortgages, thrifts hold undiversified portfolios. Finally, regulations, or the threat of them, have prevented thrifts from originating variable-rate mortgages and investing in certain classes of assets.

The driving force for change of the housing finance system has been the acceleration of inflation. Increased nominal interest rates have threatened the viability of thrift institutions and created enormous cash-flow problems for homebuyers. As a result, regulators now favor variable-rate mortgages, and mortgages with negative amortization, such as graduated-payment mortgages, are being utilized. Moreover, because returns on shared-appreciation mortgages are tied to the movement in the price of the underlying house, this instrument is equivalent to an equity and allows diversification of part of the risk of the investment in individual houses. Such instruments will most likely become widespread in the future. The early disappearance of fixed-rate mortgages is obvious.

Other likely changes affecting housing finance include the following: The tax preferences of thrifts and relative tax advantage of owner-occupied housing will be reduced, the latter by cutting effective tax rates on other assets (reductions in the corporate and capital gains tax rates and increases in tax depreciation and investment tax credits). There will be fewer brokerage firms and financial institutions, and there will be few, if any, undiversified "housing finance" institutions. Mortgage origination and finance will be carried out almost entirely by different institutions. Finally, the federal role in housing finance and insurance will be contracts.

The reduction in the relative tax advantage for owner-occupied housing will obviously tilt households away from ownership and tend to reduce the quantity of housing desired, but the development of mortgages with negative amortization will act to raise housing demand. The projected demise of traditional housing finance institutions will have little impact on housing demand because the mortgage market is already generally integrated with capital markets.

NOTES

1. See Silber 1975 for an enlightening discussion of financial systems and innovations.
2. For example, suppose the holder of a perfectly diversified equity portfolio is extremely averse to actual productivity of capital generally falling short of *ex ante* expected productivity. A contract can be written, the value of which depends on the difference between actual and expected productivity. If f_e is the expected forward price and f_a the actual forward price, the difference will reflect the difference between expected and actual productivity. The options contract would simply give the writer the ability to "put" the equity shares into the portfolio of the holder of the option at f_e.

3. It takes time to produce capital, and the production period is uncertain. Consequently, optional delivery markets would develop for real and financial instruments.

4. See Hendershott and Shilling 1981 and Rosen and Rosen 1980 for analyses of the determination of tenure choice in the United States.

5. For more details on this tax preference and a discussion of its impact on the portfolio behavior of thrifts and the relation between mortgages and bond rates, see Hendershott and Villani (1980, 1981).

6. See Kane 1970 and Hendershott and Villani 1978: chap. 6 for discussions of the distributional impacts of minimum purchase requirements in conjunction with deposit interest-rate ceilings.

7. Simonson and Villani (1982) formally derive the demand for brokerage services resulting from the homeowner tax preference.

8. For an overview of the movement toward financial reform in the United States, see Hendershott and Villani 1978.

9. Deposit-rate deregulation provides another example of a belated regulatory response to an innovation, in this case the money market certificate introduced in June 1978 to circumvent existing regulations.

10. Thrift institutions perceived the Depository Institutions Deregulation Committee as proceeding too fast and sued in Federal District Court for slower deregulation in the summer of 1980. The Congress has criticized the committee only for moving too slowly, however, and the Reagan administration has accelerated the pace of deregulation.

11. In April 1981, several weeks after Richard Pratt became chairman, the Federal Home Loan Bank Board issued extremely flexible regulations for savings and loans regarding interest-rate adjustability.

12. For an expanded discussion of regulation-induced innovation in banking, see Kane 1981.

13. See Hendershott 1980 for a discussion of the real user cost concept and estimates of its empirical relevance.

14. Since this chapter was written, the Economic Recovery Tax Act of 1981 was passed. One analysis of the impact of this act suggests that it has eliminated the tax advantage for owner-occupied housing of low- to middle-income households (Hendershott and Shilling 1982).

15. Note that our focus on cash-flow risk differs from the usual problem associated with fixed-rate, level-payment mortgages during inflationary periods. With inflation, this mortgage causes too rapid a

build-up of real homeowner equity and consumes too large a share of homeowner income. Homeowners unable to issue other forms of debt and with little wealth are constrained to save more income and/or consume less housing than they desire (see Alm and Follain 1982).

REFERENCES

Alm, James, and James R. Follain, Jr. 1982. "Alternative Mortgage Instruments and Consumer Housing Choices in an Inflationary Environment." *Public Finance Quarterly* (April).

Arrow, Kenneth J. 1964. "The Role of Securities in the Optimal Allocation of Risk Bearing." *Review of Economic Studies* 31.

Brunner, Karl, and Allan H. Meltzer. 1971. "The Uses of Money: Money in a Theory of an Exchange Economy." *American Economic Review* (December).

Fisher, Stanley. 1979. "Corporate Supply of Index Bonds." NBER Working Paper 331, National Bureau of Economic Research.

Gurley, John G., and Edward Shaw. 1956. "Financial Intermediaries and the Savings-Investment Process." *Journal of Finance* 11 (May).

Hendershott, Patric H. 1980. "Real User Costs and the Demand for Single-Family Housing." *Brookings Papers on Economic Activity* 2:401–44.

Hendershott, Patric H., and Chang-Tseh Hsieh. 1980. "Inflation and the Growth in Home Mortgage Debt, 1964–78." *Journal of Financial Research* 3 (Fall): 189–202.

Hendershott, Patric H. and James D. Shilling. 1981. "The Economics of Tenure Choice, 1955—79." In *Research in Real Estate*, edited by C.F. Sirmans, vol. 1. Greenwich, Connecticut: JAI Press.

———. 1982. "The Impacts on Capital Allocation of Some Aspects of the Economic Recovery Act of 1981." *Public Finance Quarterly* (April).

Hendershott, Patric H., and Kevin E. Villani. 1978. *Regulation and Reform of the Housing Finance System.* Washington, D.C.: American Enterprise Institute.

———. 1980. "Secondary Residential Mortgage Markets and the Relative Cost of Mortgage Funds." *American Real Estate and Urban Economics Association Journal* 8 (Spring):50–76.

———. 1981. "Savings and Loan Usage of the Authority to Invest in Corporate Bonds." *Savings and Loan Asset Management under Deregulation.* San Francisco: Federal Home Loan Bank of San Francisco.

Kane, Edward J. 1970. "Shortchanging the Small Saver: Federal Government Discrimination Against Small Savers During the Vietnam War." *Journal of Money Credit and Banking* 2 (November).

———. 1981. "Accelerating Inflation, Technological Innovation, and the Decreasing Effectiveness of Banking Regulation." *Journal of Finance* 36 (May):355–67.

Rosen, Harvey S., and Kenneth T. Rosen. 1980 "Federal Taxes and Homeownership: Evidence from Time Series." *Journal of Political Economy* (February).

Silber, William B. 1975. "Towards a Theory of Financial Innovation." In *Financial Innovation*, edited by William B. Silber. Lexington, Mass.: D.C. Heath.

Simonson, John C., and Kevin E. Villani. 1982. "Real Estate Settlement Pricing: A Theoretical Framework." *American Real Estate and Urban Economics Association Journal* 10 (Summer).

U.S. Department of Housing and Urban Development. 1980. *DRAFT RESPA—Section 142: The Real Estate Settlement Procedures Act, Volume II: Settlement Performance Evaluation.* Washington, D. C.

Van Order, Robert, and Kevin E. Villani. 1981. "A Study of the GNMA Conventional Mortgage Pass-Through Security Program." *Occasional Papers in Housing and Community Affairs* 9. Washington, D.C.: U.S. Department of Housing and Urban Development.

10 INFLATION, UNCERTAINTY AND FUTURE MORTGAGE INSTRUMENTS

Jack L. Carr and Lawrence B. Smith

Since the early 1970s the rate of inflation in North America has been both high and variable and has begun to have a pronounced effect on capital and equity markets. Some of the most significant changes have occured in housing and mortgage markets, and to the extent that high and variable inflation continues throughout the balance of the century, these markets are likely to undergo further substantial changes. This chapter considers some of the changes that might be expected as a result of a continuation of these high and variable inflation rates.

INFLATION TRENDS OVER THE LAST HUNDRED YEARS IN CANADA

Crucial for the development of the mortgage instrument over the next twenty years will be the nature of the monetary standard during that time. To help understand what this standard might be and its importance, it is useful to look at the past and the relation between the monetary standard and inflation. Conse-

This research was partially funded by the Social Sciences and Humanities Research Council of Canada, Research award 451-81-2999 to the second author.

quently, we begin with an examination of the changes in monetary systems and their effects in Canada over the last 100 years, divided for analysis into three subperiods.

The Gold Standard Period, 1867–1913

From 1867 to 1913 Canada, like most other countries in the western world, was on the gold standard, which meant that currencies were convertible at fixed rates of exchange into gold. Episodes of inflation alternated with episodes of deflation such that the price level, as measured by the Wholesale Price Index (WPI), was approximately the same at the end as at the beginning of the period. Moreover, only once during these forty-six years did the annual price movement reach double digits. At the outbreak of World War I Canada temporarily suspended the gold standard, allowing increased government war expenditures to be financed by the printing of paper money without having to worry about having sufficient gold backing for the additional currency.[1]

The Transition Period, 1914–1953

The next forty years were a period in search of a new monetary standard, a period of political and economic instability, with three major wars and the Great Depression of 1929–1933. After World War I it took some time and a major deflation in 1921 to get back on the gold standard; Canada officially went back on gold in 1926. The return was brief, as for all practical purposes Canada went back off the gold standard in 1929 (although not officially until 1931). Nevertheless, many market participants felt Canada would return to the standard once the political and economic uncertainty was eliminated. Without the tie to gold a new monetary institution, the Bank of Canada, was established in 1935 to control the money in Canada. During this 1914–1953 period the price level moved quite erratically but with an upward trend such that at the end of the period the price level was almost triple that at the beginning of the period. During these forty years the annual movement in prices reached double digits eleven times.

The Pure Fiduciary Standard Period, 1954 to the Present

By the mid-1950s it was clear that gold would no longer play a strategic role in controlling the money supply and that the Bank of Canada virtually had unconstrained control since the money supply could now be increased whether or not the nation had sufficient gold reserves. Essentially, by the 1950s Canada had fully adopted a new monetary standard.[2]

What is the significance of the development of a new monetary standard? First of all it should be noted that the idea that the gold standard leads to a stable price level is just a myth since there was substantial year-to-year movement in the price index during the gold standard period of 1867–1913. The gold standard does not eliminate short-term variability in the price level. What it does eliminate to a large extent is long-term variability in the price level. The reason for this is the self-correcting nature of the gold standard. If a country overissues its currency and as a consequence has inflation, the self-correcting nature of the standard, via a balance-of-payments deficit and gold outflow, brings about a subsequent reduction in the money supply with a resulting deflation. Consequently, year to year the price level may vary, but over a longer period the price level will be relatively stable. The WPI was 4 percent higher in 1913 than in 1867, representing an annual average inflation rate of 0.08 percent. Hence under a gold standard there is relative stability in the long-term price level and the long-term price level is quite predictable.

This predictability stands in considerable contrast to the situation under the new fiduciary standard—substantial variability in the price level from year to year. Distinguishing the new fiduciary standard from the gold standard, even more importantly, is that the fiduciary standard lacks a self-correcting mechanism. Periods of inflation are not necessarily followed by periods of deflation to bring the price level back to some long-run equilibrium value. In fact, the striking aspect of the behavior of the WPI from 1954 to the present is that in no year did the value of the WPI decline from its value in the previous year. Unlike the gold standard, which had periods of deflation following inflation, the fiduciary standard, as Canadians have experienced it in the last three decades, has not led to one year of deflation. It is thus no wonder that a large part of the Canadian population thinks that inflation is an inevitable feature of a modern industrial economy.

Because inflation in one period is not followed by deflation in a subsequent period, the long-run price level is much more unpredictable under the fiduciary standard than under the gold standard. Not only is the long-run price level more unpredictable, but the degree of price level unpredictability has been increasing over time. One rather crude way to measure this unpredictability is to look at the variance of the inflation rate.[3] Table 10–1 shows what has been happening to the mean and standard deviation of the inflation rates. This table clearly shows that both the mean and standard deviation of inflation rates has been increasing since the Korean War and that consequently the price level has become more and more unpredictable.[4]

Thus Canada is suffering from both high and variable inflation rates and price-level unpredictability and variable inflation rates seem, unfortunately, to be an integral feature of its new monetary standard. Since any radical changes in the monetary standard are unlikely in the foreseeable future, Canadians will have to learn to live in the 1980s and 1990s with an unpredictable price level and high and variable inflation rates. Their monetary instruments will have to adapt to this situation.

EFFECTS OF PRICE-LEVEL UNPREDICTABILITY AND HIGH AND VARIABLE INFLATION RATES

Money has a number of uses, including being a standard of deferred payment. As such a standard, money is the unit of account

Table 10–1. Mean and Standard Deviation of Inflation Rate under Fiduciary Monetary Standard in Canada, 1954–1978

	Mean Inflation Rate (WPI)	Standard Deviation of Inflation Rate
1954–1954-65	1.05	1.24
1966–1978	7.14	5.00

Source: Bank of Canada Review, various issues.

in long-term contracts. When the price level is unpredictable, resulting in unexpected inflation or deflation, the usefulness of money in long-term contracts is decreased. Price-level uncertainty introduces additional variability in the real payoffs in long-term contracts. Hence this unpredictability discourages the formation of long-term contracts and, in formal models where market participants minimize the costs of being out of equilibrium, an increase in such uncertainty leads to a shortening in contract length.[5] Shortening in contract length can take place either explicitly or through an indexation scheme where the terms of the contract are automatically altered as some measure of the price-level changes.

Hence theory predicts that with price-level unpredictability contracts of all types will be shortened. Klein (1978), for example, found that the average maturity of new corporate debt in the United States declined as price-level uncertainty increased, and in Canada the practice of issuing bonds in perpetuity has now ceased. In wage contracts at the beginning of the 1970s a three-year contract was not all that unusual. Now one- or two-year wage contracts are the norm. In 1973 some form of indexation in wage contracts was relatively rare, existing in only about 15 percent of major collective agreements, but by 1980 some form of indexation was prevalent in about 35 percent of major collective agreements (Labour Canada 1980).

A similar evolution has occurred in the mortgage contract. The beginning of the transition period to a new monetary standard (the late 1910s and early 1920s) saw a fairly unstable price level. Consequently, one would expect relatively short-term mortgages, which was the case. In the late 1920s and early 1930s the standard mortgage in Canada had a five-year term requiring payment of a fixed principal amount plus interest.[6] Since the principal repayments were insufficient to pay the mortgage off in five years, the mortgage had a balloon payment, which either had to be paid off or renewed and renegotiated at the end of the original term. In the mid-1930s mortgage loans under the Dominion Housing Act of 1935 had an initial term to maturity of ten years (and could be returned for another ten years at terms negotiated at the initial maturity). Ignoring the Korean War period, the 1950s and early 1960s in Canada were a period of relatively stable and predictable prices as the WPI grew at an almost steady average rate of 1.2 percent per year between 1954 to 1964. During this period the twenty-five-year and thirty-year mortgage became relatively common. However, as described, price-level unpredictability increased dramatically in the late 1960s and throughout the 1970s. As this occurred, mortgage maturity decreased dramatically. By the early 1970s the five-year mortgage was standard, and by 1981 many mortgages were being negotiated with one-, two- or three-year terms (see Lessard 1975).

The evidence for contracts in general and mortgages in particular indicates that as price-level uncertainty has increased, the term of all contracts has shortened. If prices continue to be unpredictable, the term of mortgages will tend to be relatively short and, as in wage contracts, the mortgage market may implicitly shorten the effective contract length by the inclusion of indexing figures into the mortgage.

The continuation of the new monetary standard will have a number of other effects (either direct or indirect) on the mortgage market. First, the adoption of the new standard means that a period of inflation is no longer followed by a period of deflation. When inflation occurs, market participants will no longer expect it to end. As a consequence, current inflation will be more rapidly incorporated into expected inflation. This by itself will induce more interest-rate volatility. One of the reasons for the current increased volatility is the more rapid incorporation of current inflation into the formation of expectations.

Second, high and variable inflation rates induce individuals to reduce their holdings of money and to increase their holdings of real assets. In inflationary times, therefore, the demand for real assets such as land and houses will go up, causing the price of land and houses to increase and the demand for mortgage credit to increase.

Third, our present tax system is nonneutral with respect to price-level changes. If the price level increases and, as a consequence, the price of real assets rises, owners of most forms of assets will be liable for a capital gains tax imposed by our tax system on the nominal gains associated with most investments and real assets. Capital gains accruing to a principal residence are exempted from taxation, however. Consequently, inflation increases the attractiveness of homeownership vis-à-vis other assets and increases both the absolute and the relative price of houses. It also indirectly increases the demand for mortgage credit.

THE TILT AND UNCERTAINTY PROBLEMS IN THE MORTGAGE MARKET

Under the present international and domestic monetary systems, there is a very strong likelihood of a high and variable inflation rate and consequently of a high and widely fluctuating nominal rate of interest. These two phenomena have important implications for the mortgage market and the nature of the mortgage instrument via the tilt problem and increased risks for both lenders and borrowers under the traditional level-payment mortgage (LPM).

The Tilt Problem

The so-called tilt problem arises from an increase in the fully anticipated inflation rate, which alters the time profile of the stream of annual mortgage payments in real terms under the LPM, creating a considerable cash flow constraint on households during and immediately following an increase in the expected inflation rate. (See Lessard and Modigliani 1975:14–15 and Pesando 1977). An increase in the fully anticipated rate of inflation causes a rise in the nominal rate of interest such that the expectations of future inflation are fully incorporated in the level of the nominal interest rate (See Carr and Smith 1972, and Carr, Pesando, and Smith 1976). Ignoring tax and nonneutrality effects, an increase of one percentage point in the fully anticipated inflation rate increases the nominal interest rate by one percentage point.[7] An increase in the fully anticipated inflation rate also raises household incomes in nominal terms, but these incomes only increase by the change in the rate of inflation. Consequently, even if the nominal mortgage amount were fixed, the ratio of mortgage payments to income would increase substantially in the years immediately following an increase in the fully anticipated inflation rate under a LPM, because the increased inflation affects the level of interest rates but only at the rate of change of household income. This phenomenon is considered a tilt problem because inflation does not change the present value of future mortgage payments (which would be discounted at the higher nominal interest rate) but only changes the time profile of real mortgage payments, increasing them in the early years and reducing them in the later years.

Analytically there is also another way of considering the tilt problem. When inflation is expected, the interest payment on mortgages can be broken into two parts. One is the real interest rate payable on mortgages. The other is an inflationary premium to compensate the lending institution for the fact that it is being paid back in money that is worth less in terms of purchasing power than the original dollars lent. This premium compensates for the decline in the real value of the principal outstanding. As such this premium is really a repayment of capital.[8] The greater the expected inflation, the greater the premium and the greater the rate of capital repayment. Higher expected inflation with resulting higher interest rates therefore means a shorter duration of the mortgage.[9] The higher expected inflation is in essence a shortening of the amortization period of the loan (the average real dollar outstanding is paid back sooner). This shortening of the amortization results in higher annual payments (these are both higher nominal and real payments in the early years of the loan, but only higher nominal payments on the later years of the loan). Hence the tilt phenomenon for mortgages is analytically equivalent to the decrease in duration for bonds, with both occuring when expected inflation rates and interest rates increase.

The changing time profile of real mortgage payments arising from an increase in the expected inflation is set out in Table 10–2. This example shows that for LPMs the ratio of mortgage payments-to-income rises from 13.96 percent to 30.74 percent in the first year that the expected inflation increases from 0 to 10 percent. But, by the twenty-fifth year the mortgage payment-to-income ratio falls from 8.70 percent to only 2.03 percent. Consequently, an increase in the actual and expected inflation rate significantly increases real mortgage payments in the early years and reduces them in the later years.

This higher ratio of mortgage payments to income in the early years arises from the fact that in the inflationary situation a greater amount of principal (in real terms) is being paid off in the early years. For example, in the noninflationary situation $990 of

Table 10–2. Comparison of Level-Payment Mortgage (LPM) with Graduated-Payment Mortgage(GPM)

Year	Beginning Principal	Interest Amount — Real Component	Interest Amount — Inflation Component[b]	Annual Payment	Ending Principal	Borrower Income	Annual Mortgage Payment-to-Income Ratio (Current Dollars)
1. Level-Payment Mortgage (LPM)							
A. Zero inflation: 5 percent real interest, 5 percent nominal interest							
1	…	…	…	$3,490	…	$25,000	13.96%
5	…	…	…	3,490	…	27,061	12.90
10	…	…	…	3,490	…	29,877	11.68
15	…	…	…	3,490	…	32,987	10.58
20	…	…	…	3,490	…	36,420	9.58
25	…	…	…	3,490	…	40,211	8.70
B. 10 percent inflation: 5 percent real interest, 15 percent nominal interest							
1	$50,000	$7,465	…	$7,685	$49,800	$25,000	30.74%
5	48,900	7,285	…	7,685	48,500	39,338	19.54
10	46,300	6,885	…	7,685	45,500	69,327	11.09
15	40,900	6,085	…	7,685	39,300	122,178	6.29
20	29,800	4,335	…	7,685	26,450	215,319	3.57
25	6,900	785	…	7,685	0	379,466	2.03
2. Graduated-payment mortgage (GPM)							
10 percent inflation: 5 percent real interest, 15 percent nominal interest							
1	$50,000	$2,500	$5,000	$3,490	$54,010	$25,000	13.96%
5	67,478	3,374	6,748	5,173	72,427	39,338	13.15
10	93,636	4,682	9,364	8,483	99,198	69,327	12.24
15	119,570	5,979	11,957	14,119	123,387	122,178	11.56
20	124,059	6,203	12,406	24,440	118,228	215,319	11.35
25	41,513	1,038	2,0976	42,551	0	379,466	11.2

a. Calculation based upon a $50,000 mortgage, amortized over 25 years, assuming a 5 percent real rate of interest and initial borrower income of $25,000 assumed to increase at the rate of inflation plus 2 percent. If the initial payment was based on the amount necessary to amortize a 25-year mortgage at a 3 percent interest rate (5 percent real rate minus 2 percent real income in income), the annual mortgage payment-to-income ratio would remain constant over the 25-year term.

b. Inflation component based on the actual rate equaling the expected rate of 10 percent.

principal is paid in the first year, leaving an outstanding balance of $49,010. In the 10 percent inflation case $200 of principal is paid, leaving an outstanding balance of $49,800. However, the outstanding balance is in terms of year 1 dollars, not in terms of year 0 dollars, the dollars in which the loan was made. Because of the 10 percent inflation, the real value of the amount outstanding declines by 10 percent to $44,820. If the mortgagee were then to borrow an additional $4,190 in the inflationary case, the principal owing in real terms would again be $49,010, the same as in the noninflationary case. If this additional borrowing were used to defray the high annual payment in year 1, the net annual cash outflow in the inflationary case would be $3,475 in year 1, approximately the same as the $3,490 annual payment in the noninflationary case.[10] With a series of borrowings in the early years and repayments in the later years, the payment-to-income ratio in the inflationary case could be made to equal the ratio in the noninflationary case.

If this is the case, the question arises why tilting is a problem, since either the mortgagee can arrange for additional financing in the early years or the mortgagor can automatically arrange for it.[11] In either case the time path of the repayment of principal (in real terms) is similar to that in the noninflationary case and so the mortgagor would be virtually unaffected by the inflation.

The problem arises because such incremental borrowing arrangements are rare. The explanation usually offered for this rarity is that market imperfections such as high transaction costs in arranging additional financing, restrictions on financial intermediary loan-to-value ratios based on the market value of the security at the time of the origination of the loan, and the failure of market participants to understand the difference between nominal and real magnitudes inhibit such arrangements. However, although some of these market imperfections exist, the primary explanation centers on lenders' uncertainty, which is a function of the high variability in the future inflation.

If capital markets were perfect, lenders would still be reluctant in today's economic environment to increase fully the nominal value of the mortgage loans outstanding. If incremental lending arrangements were contracted at the origination of the loan, the nominal value of the annual net cash outlays for mortgage payments would increase at the expected inflation rate of 10 percent.

If lenders could be certain that 10 percent inflation would prevail over the twenty-five-year term of the mortgage, there would be no problems and lenders would be perfectly willing to increase nominal values of the outstanding balance.

Suppose, on the other hand, that 10 percent was the expected twenty-five year annual inflation rate, but there was a substantial variance of future inflation rates, leading lenders to hold some probability of a zero inflation rate. If this zero rate were realized, borrower income would not rise at 12 percent per year as assumed in Table 10–2, but would rise only at 2 percent. Mortgage payments, however, would still be rising at 10 percent per year, causing the mortgage payment-to-income ratio to rise. Analogously, the mortgage loan-to-value ratio would also rise in real terms during the early years of the mortgage. The risk of default and loss would therefore increase. Moreover, the risk of loss increases interactively from these ratio changes through the "moral hazard problem."[12] As the mortgage payment-to-income ratio rises and borrowers find it more difficult to make mortgage payments, the probability of foreclosure increases and borrowers have less incentive to maintain the usual standard of care of their property. When this happens, the lender's security is eroded and the probability of loss increases since taxes may go unpaid, repairs and maintenance may be ignored, and general deterioration may be allowed.[13]

It is clear that the more variable the inflation the greater the default and loss risk and hence the less likely the adoption of incremental loan schemes to offset the tilt problem. High and variable inflation, which create the tilt problem, thus adversely affect real housing demand in the early years of an inflation because of the cash-flow problems they create and the lender response they trigger. Furthermore, in the Canadian setting, the tilt effect can create major financing difficulties for households renewing rollover or variable-rate mortgages, since they can lie exposed to substantially higher real mortgage payments if there is an increase in expected inflation immediately prior to mortgage renewal. In an environment of potentially large and variable inflationary increases the negative implications of the traditional LPM on real housing demand for new home buyers and mortgage renewers are so substantial that alternative financing forms are inevitable.[14]

Increased Risk to Lenders and Borrowers

As indicated previously, high inflation rates have been consistent with greater variability in inflation, and the higher the inflation rate the greater the uncertainty as to the future rate of inflation. Borrowers gain from inflation higher than expected but lose from inflation lower than expected. From a "minimax" viewpoint, borrowers/risk-aversion is logical since failure to obtain an unanticipated gain has lower real costs than realizing an unanticipated loss (which could cause mortgage default, foreclosure, and substantial loss of equity). Therefore, as inflation rises, the risk to borrowers from long-term level-payment contracts rises and borrowers prefer short-term contracts. Short-term level-payment contracts, however, continually expose borrowers to the tilt problem, since accelerating inflation will increase their real payments and expose them to similar potential costs as under long-term contracts with decelerating inflation.[15]

Increased uncertainty also imposes additional problems for lenders if they are unable to match completely their asset and liability maturities. The majority of the mortgage finance for new single-detached home purchases in Canada is provided by the chartered banks (25 percent), trust companies (18 percent) and mortgage loan companies (13 percent).[16] These institutions obtain a substantial proportion of their funds in the form of demand or short-term deposits.[17] The banks have always been primarily short-term borrowers, but trust and mortgage loan company liabilities have shortened considerably in recent years in response to the accelerating inflation and higher interest-rate volatility. The shortening average maturity of their debt means that the risk exposure for financial institutions has increased with respect to an average loan maturity in excess of the original average debt maturity and, as the volatility of rates increases, the potential risks associated with this long-term debt increase. Lenders therefore have a significant incentive to shorten the average maturity of their mortgage loans to match their shorter and shortening liability structure or else to create alternative debt obligation forms to encourage longer term deposits. Given the public's risk-aversion and preference for shorter maturities, institutional pressures likely will be in the direction of shorter loan terms.[18]

Capital markets adjust to a high rate of inflation, but variable inflation rates impose costs on the capital market, one of which is the tilt problem. With high and *stable* inflation rates relatively easy solutions to the tilt problem are possible. With high and *variable* inflation, as is now the case, more complex solutions are needed, since the easy solutions involve increased risks of default and risk of loss to lenders and hence become unacceptable (or only acceptable after lenders are sufficiently compensated for the greater risks).

ALTERNATIVE MORTGAGE FORMS

The combination of the tilt problem and increased risk to lenders and borrowers arising from higher and increasingly volatile rates of inflation suggests that considerable change will occur in the mortgage instrument. Some of the possible evolutions are as follows.

Variable-Rate Mortgage (VRM)

In response to the increasing uncertainty associated with higher inflation and the greater risks of short-term borrowing by financial institutions, the average maturity term for mortgages has been declining in Canada. As mentioned earlier, during the 1960s and early 1970s, a steadily increasing proportion of conventional mortgages were written on a five-year rollover basis.[19] As inflation and volatility accelerated during the 1970s, the average term decreased and a significant proportion of loans became one-year rollover or variable-rate mortgages (VRM). (for a discussion of the variable-rate mortgage, see Lessard and Modigliani 1975:26–31 and Pesando 1981).

The advantages to the lender of short-term VRMs (one year or less) are obvious since they enable lenders: (1) to match their liability structures better; (2) to offer variable-rate obligations desired by the public, and (3) to avoid capital losses in the event of an unanticipated increase in inflation. VRMs also enable that segment of the borrowing public that expects a future inflation rate lower than the level incorporated in nominal interest rates to obtain a debt structure consistent with its expectations. Consequently, it would be reasonable to expect a higher proportion of rollover or variable-rate mortgages to be of the one-year or less variety (possibly even monthly), and for this instrument form to remain in wide use in the future.

On the other hand, as indicated earlier, level-payment VRMs do nothing to eliminate or lessen the tilt problem and, in fact, extend the problem to virtually all mortgage borrowers compared to only new borrowers under a fully amortized LPM. As a result, a variety of alternative mortgage forms are likely to increase in popularity and the use of VRMs is likely to decline though they will continue to exist.

An additional problem with VRMs is the likelihood that further government intervention will arise. One form of intervention could be pressure on institutions to limit their increase in mortgage rates at the adjustment date so as to prevent undue hardship on borrowers.[20] Such a limitation, of course, would undercut the entire concept of VRMs and destroy their usefulness to lending institutions. If it were carried to an extreme, thrift institutions could experience severe difficulties and generate pressure for government bail-out assistance. If such intervention were anticipated, the mortgage rate would increase on these types of loans to reflect the additional risk and the use of this form of loan would also decline. Another form of intervention could be government assistance to existing borrowers whose mortgage payment-to-income ratio rose above some predetermined level as a result of mortgage rate increases. Although less directly market-distorting than mortgage rate limitations, this assistance would be undesirable in most cases since it would remove virtually all the risks from borrowers and thereby excessively stimulate housing demand. It would also involve government in a potentially long-term, open-ended subsidy program. A variety of other tax, subsidy, and control responses are possible, the likelihood of which is greater if alternative mortgage forms do not evolve.[21]

Graduated-Payment Mortgages (GPM)

Graduated-payment mortgages, which have evolved in response to the tilt problem, involve a restructuring of the payments schedule in such a way that mortgage payments begin low and rise over time.[22] The present value of the payments stream is unaffected but the payments then better match the household's expected income stream. In principle any pattern of rising payments could be used in GPMs but the theoretically preferred form generates payments that increase over time at a rate equal to the expected rate of inflation. This pattern has the effect of creating a mortgage payment-to-income ratio similar to that which occurs with the LPM in the noninflationary case (for a discussion of GPM payment patterns, see Lessard and Modigliani 1975:31 and Pesando 1981:4). If inflation expectations are realized, the GPM will mitigate the tilt effect of an increase in inflation by reducing the mortgage payment-to-income ratio in the early years. This reduction is illustrated in Table 10–2. Under the conditions described in the table, the mortgage payment-to-income ratio with a GPM begins at 13.96 percent compared to 30.74 percent under the LPM, but falls much more slowly so that by year 9 the ratios are similar. By year 25 they are 11.21 percent under the GPM, compared to only 2.03 percent with the LPM.

Although the GPM does relieve the tilt problem, it does not fully insulate the borrower from the consequences of a high and variable inflation rate and may worsen the lender's position. GPMs commit the borrower to a payment stream that rises over time in proportion to the expected change in the price level. If the actual inflation rate is less than anticipated at the start of the loan or if a household's income fails to rise with inflation, the mortgage payment-to-income ratio will be higher than anticipated and borrowers may be unable to meet their commitments. This form of loan is therefore best suited for households who expect their income to at least keep pace with inflation.

The major problems, however, arise on the supply side. First, since the initial payments under a GPM are lower than under a LPM, the outstanding principal rises in the early years of the contract, reducing lender equity in these years. If inflation is lower than anticipated or if real housing prices fall, the loan-to-value ratio rises and lender security is not only lower than with a LPM but actually declines over time, which considerably increases lender risk. Second, the possibility of default increases because of the rising nominal payment schedule. Third, the lower payments in the early years create cash-flow problems for lenders whose contracted payments would not be reduced during these years. This cash-flow problem could be overcome if institutions could restructure their liabilities by introducing graduated-payment deposits, but such a restructuring is not likely to be widely embraced by the public without tax incentives. Fourth, GPMs do nothing to solve the problem of mismatching asset and liability maturities and hence to reduce the risks associated with borrowing short-term and lending long-term. Therefore, although GPMs do mitigate the tilt problem and are a useful borrowing instrument for selected borrowers, they are unlikely to become widely used without government support.

Government support for GPMs could come in a variety of forms. It could take the form of insuring lenders for the excess mortgage principal over the initial loan amount or over the amount that would arise under LPMs (so-called last-dollar insurance); it could take the form of a GPM bank to supply loans to institutions to cover cash-flow deficiencies arising from growing GPM portfolios as a result of early payments being below the equivalent level mortgage payments, with these loans to be repaid in the later years when mortgage payments have increased; or it could take the form of tax benefits to encourage the public to accept graduated-payment deposits. On the other hand, alternative forms of government intervention could pose a potential risk for lenders under widespread use of GPMs in the event that the actual inflation rate fell significantly below the anticipated inflation rate, since mortgage payment freezes or reductions could occur in the face of rising mortgage payment-to-income ratios (a similar risk was described for VRMs). Combining all these effects, it is unlikely that GPMs will become widely adopted in Canada, although with government support they might play a minor role.

Price-Level-Adjusted Mortgages (PLAMs)

In contrast to VRMs and GPMs, which assist either the lender or the borrower but at the expense of the other, the price-level-adjusted mortgage (PLAM) or indexed mortgage has the potential to improve both lender and borrower positions. The basic principle behind PLAMs is that a contractual real rate of interest is used to establish the basic mortgage payment, and the outstanding principal is periodically revalued in accordance with the change in the price-level index, to which it is tied. (PLAMs are described in Lessard and Modigliani 1975:33–41 and Pesando 1977:33–35). Each time the principal balance is revalued the mortgage payment is correspondingly adjusted; the originally determined contract real interest rate is applied to the new balance and new payments are determined based on amortizing the mortgage over the original term. As a result, the PLAM payment stream adjusts with changes in the price level.

A PLAM is illustrated in Table 10–3 and compared to a GPM under conditions of varying actual inflation. This table indicates that regardless of the unanticipated change (upward or downward) in the inflation rate, the PLAM mortgage payment-to-income ratio approximates that of the GPM when the expected rate under the GPM is realized. When the actual inflation rate exceeds the expected (years 3–5), the mortgage payment-to-income ratio under a GPM falls relative to the PLAM and relative to that anticipated. When the actual inflation rate is lower than expected (years 6–9), the mortgage payment-to-income ratio with a GPM rises relative to the PLAM and relative to that anticipated. Consequently, PLAMs stabilize the mortgage payment-to-income stream for borrowers regardless of the fluctuations in inflation and provide lenders with a constant *ex post* real interest return.

The table thus demonstrates that PLAMs combine many of the basic features of both the VRM and GPM. From the borrower's viewpoint PLAMs mitigate the tilt problem since the initial mortgage payments are based on a real (noninflationary) interest rate. The payments initially start low and rise as a result of incorporating the unpaid actual inflation component of the rate of interest into the outstanding principal. This procedure initially reduces the mortgage payment-to-income ratio and enables it to be maintained over the loan term. Moreover, since both income and mortgage payments rise in response to the actual inflation rate and not the expected rate, the borrower is protected from changes in the payment-to-income ratio resulting from an unexpected decline in inflation.

From the lender's viewpoint PLAMs enable an approximate matching of yields on longer term assets with shorter term liabilities. The effective mortgage yield is adjusted annually to reflect changes in the actual inflation rate and hence should approximate

Table 10-3. Comparison of Mortgage Payments and Payment-to-Income Ratios under a Graduated-Payment Mortgage (GPM) and Price-Level-Adjusted Mortgage (PLAM) with Variable Inflation[a]

Year	Inflation Rate	Beginning Principal	Interest Amount Real Component	Interest Amount Inflation Component	Annual Payment	Ending Principal	Borrower Income	Annual Mortgage Payment-to-Income Ratio (Current Dollars)
Price-Level-Adjusted Mortgage (PLAM)								
1	10	$50,000	$2,500	$5,000	$3,490	$54,010	$25,000	13.96%
2	10	54,010	2,700	5,400	3,850	58,260	28,000	13.75
3	15	58,260	2,915	8,739	4,247	64,667	31,360	13.54
4	15	65,667	3,283	9,849	4,905	73,894	36,691	13.37
5	15	73,894	3,695	11,084	5,665	83,008	42,929	13.20
6	3	83,008	4,150	2,490	6,546	83,102	50,227	13.03
7	3	83,102	4,115	2,493	6,756	83,210	52,378	12.81
8	3	82,210	4,161	2,496	6,993	82,884	55,375	12.63
9	3	82,884	4,114	2,487	7,221	82,294	58,144	12.41
Graduated-Payment Mortgage (GPM)								
1	10	$50,000	$2,500	$5,000	$3,490	$54,010	$25,000	13.96%
2	10	54,101	2,700	5,400	3,850	58,260	28,000	13.75
3	15	58,260	2,913	5,826	4,247	62,752	31,360	13.54
4	15	62,752	3,138	6,275	4,687	67,478	36,691	12.77
5	15	67,478	3,374	6,748	5,173	72,427	42,929	12.05
6	3	72,427	3,621	7,243	5,712	77,579	50,227	11.37
7	3	77,579	3,879	7,758	6,3007	82,909	52,738	11.96
8	3	82,090	4,145	8,290	6,967	88,378	55,375	12.58
9	3	88,378	4,419	8,838	7,699	93,636	58,144	13.24

a. Calculations based upon a $50,000 mortgage, amortized over 25 years, assuming a 5 percent real rate of interest, an expected inflation rate of 10 percent when the mortgages are contracted, an actual inflation rate of 10 percent for years 1 and 2, 15 percent for years 3 to 5 and 3 percent for years 6 to 8, and an initial nominal mortgage rate of 15 percent. Borrower income is initially $25,000 and assumed to increase at the rate of inflation of the previous year plus 2 percent. PLAM mortgage payment-to-income ratio approximately equals GPM ratio when actual inflation equals expected inflation (i.e., PLAM ratio in Table 10–3 approximates GPM ratio in Table 10–2.)

a capital market, institutional borrowing rate that incorporates current inflationary expectations. Institutions, however, are still faced with a cash-flow problem using their normal borrowing instruments because their payments on deposits incorporate both the real interest rate and the inflation component, whereas their current mortgage receipts reflect only the real rate (with inflation incorporated as a nonrealized component in the mortgage balance). Institutions also experience a decline in loan security compared to the LPM since the outstanding mortgage balance rises in nominal terms in the early years rather than declining as under LPMs. But since this increase is in response to actually experienced inflation, lender security remains unaffected in real terms. Nevertheless, the higher lender risk (in the event that a particular borrower's income or property value does not rise with inflation) suggests that lenders would require a risk premium and therefore the yield on PLAMs would exceed the yield on VRMs.

A consequence of the cash-flow problem associated with PLAMs is that lenders would be encouraged to develop matching obligations, or price-level-adjusted deposits (PLADs). If the public could be induced to accept such deposits, institutions could adjust their deposit payments to their mortgage payment inflows and avoid liquidity problems. However, since PLADs would mean a lower cash flow for depositors, they in turn would need to be induced by either tax concessions or higher deposit interest (which would reinforce the pressure for higher rates on PLAMs).

A further problem for lenders is the appropriate real rate of interest for PLAMs (see Cohn and Fisher 1975). For lenders to be fully matched, PLAMs and PLADs should be based on the same long- or short-term real rate. Yet, since nominal short-term rates have more volatility than long-term rates, if the PLAM rate is the long-term real rate, the nominal yield on PLADs may be insufficient at times to compete with alternative instruments, creating a break in the actual matching and periodically reducing the lender's yield spreads. This is a problem associated with variable inflation and interest rates implicit in all indexing arrangements and, although the problem cannot be fully overcome, PLAMs go a long way toward reducing it.

As with all indexed instruments, there is also the problem of selecting the appropriate index for PLAMs and PLADs. Indexing schemes arise when uncertainty as to the future value of money is great and it becomes costly to use money in its traditional role as a standard of deferred payment. Instead of utilizing money, the indexing schemes use a bundle of commodities that make up the chosen index. For example, if PLAMs are adjusted by changes in the CPI, the standard of deferred payment is essentially the bundle of commodities that enter the CPI, where the weights of the commodities are the percentage of the household's income spent on the specific commodities. Individual lenders (or shareholders of lending institutions) would like the weights of commodities used in the index to correspond to their individual consumption patterns, not to the consumption patterns in the economy as a whole. Hence, individual lenders would desire their own indexes. (see Fischer 1975 for a discussion of the index). In addition, indexes like the CPI give inadequate weight to the prices of existing capital goods making them rather poor measures of the purchasing power of money (see Alchian and Klein 1973 for elaboration of this point). These indexes become even poorer measures in time of wage and price controls. As a result, PLAMs and PLADs are most useful for reducing risk when the variability of future inflation rates is very high and the problems associated with index choice are relatively less important. Consequently, if price-level volatility increases in the future, one can expect more and more use of PLAMs since, in the absence of a stable monetary environment, an indexing scheme (although based on an imperfect index) is a second best solution.[23] Another general problem associated with PLAMs and PLADs is the tax treatment of the unreceived income arising in the form of mortgage or deposit write-ups. Unless taxes on these could be deferred, the relative rate differentials would have to widen between these and alternative standard investments.[24]

It is clear that the widespread adoption of PLAMs depends to some extent on the cooperation of government in the tax treatment of various items. Government could further facilitate their adoption by providing final dollar insurance for the additional mortgage principal over the initial or LPM balance outstanding at a time of default (as discussed under GPMs) or by acting as a temporary lender or "mortgage banker" for institutions whose PLAM portfolios are growing and thus experiencing cash-flow problems (as discussed under GPMs). In contrast to other mortgage forms, the likelihood of destabilizing government intervention is relatively low because mortgage payments adjust to actual rather than expected inflation, and thus real payments and the mortgage payment-to-income ratio will remain relatively constant over time and not increase in response to unexpected price changes.

Shared-Appreciation Mortgages (SAMs)

A variety of alternative mortgage designs also exist under which lenders would supply mortgage financing at a reduced interest rate to help overcome the initial high mortgage payment created by accelerating inflation in exchange for some form of equity participation in the property (see Pesando 1981:6 for a brief discussion of these mortgage forms). The equity participation could take the form of a share in any realized capital gains (with or without a deemed realization provision if the property were not sold after some time), a purchase by the lender and leasing arrangement of the land on which the improvements are built, or a variety of other arrangements. The nature of the interest and mortgage payment reductions could also take many forms, including readjustments after given time periods. The basic concept of these schemes is that financing costs could be reduced for borrowers to enable them more easily to acquire housing and to reduce the risks associated with high nominal rates. In exchange, the lender obtains the possibility of substantial future gains through capital appreciation.

The risks and relative merits for each participant vary according to the specifics of each plan and in theory there is sufficient latitude for both parties to benefit. Shared-appreciation schemes have the potential to become an increasingly common form of housing finance. SAMs have the additional advantage for the borrower of essentially tying the borrowing costs or lender return to the *ex post* gain on the specific property as opposed to a general or average index as under PLAMs. For the lender, however, SAMs have the same cash-flow problems as other new mortgage designs and usually will generate a realization of the appreciation after a substantial lag. SAMs are therefore best suited for growing institutions with relatively long-term liabilities, such as pension funds and life insurance companies.

Moreover, there is a major problem that has to be overcome in the SAM scheme (as in any form of equity financing), the well-known principal-agent problem. Under the SAM scheme an enterprise is set up to provide housing services. The real capital of this enterprise (the real improvements and the land) are owned jointly by the household receiving housing services and the institution providing the mortgage financing. The enterprise is managed by the household receiving the housing services. The problem facing the institution providing the mortgage financing is to design the SAM contract to insure that the manager (the agent, which would usually be the household) acts in the interest of *all* the owners (the principals, including the lender). Will the mortgagee (household) make the optimal level of repairs to the property given that it pays all the costs and gets only part of the benefits? Can a scheme be devised to reimburse it for its costs? Would such a scheme involve substantial monitoring costs? Could there be non-arms-length sales of properties to reduce the recorded capital appreciation of the properties?

These concerns are just some of the potential principal-agent problems that exist for the SAM schemes. If these problems with their resulting monitoring costs are large in relation to the potential benefits of the SAM schemes, these designs will not provide a significant form of housing finance. SAMs are most likely to arise for large-scale loans such as financing of commercial, industrial, or residential rental property where the lender can receive a percentage of the rent. The monitoring costs of a large rental property are not likely to exceed those for a residential property, but the potential benefits are much larger. Consequently, SAM schemes are most likely to be used for rental properties and are unlikely to be adopted for individual residential properties.

Reverse Mortgages or Reverse-Annuity Mortgages (RAMs)

In addition to the anticipated high and variable inflation rate, the changing age composition of the population will exert a significant influence upon the nature of housing finance and the mortgage instrument (for a study of changing demographics in Canada, see Chapter 1 by Philip Brown in this volume). The growing proportion of elderly and the declining number of net new households will have a substantial effect on the mortgage market at the end of the century. New housing will account for a significantly smaller proportion of the total mortgage demand; new housing requirements in the year 2000 are estimated to be less than 1.25 percent of the existing housing stock, compared to approximately 3.5 percent in the mid and late 1970s, while financing the needs of the elderly will become much more important (Canada Mortgage and Housing Corporation 1978:2). In 1977 under 10 percent of homeowners whose head was 65 or over had any mortgage debt compared to 85 percent of ages 25–34, 75 percent of ages 35–44, 54 percent of ages 45–54, and 54 percent overall (Statistics Canada 1979:table 3). A large and growing group of elderly homeowners exists with substantial home equity but sharply reduced cash-flow incomes. A debt instrument such as a reverse mortgage, which would enable them to dis-save systematically while retaining homeownership, should be in large demand.

Reverse mortgages or reverse-annuity mortgages (RAMs) basically entail utilizing previously accumulated wealth by the mortgaging of one's house to acquire a future stream of income. A variety of possible schemes exist, but are basically of a form similar to RAMs. (Much of the discussion of RAMs is based on Bartel and Daly 1980 and Daly 1980.) With a RAM, a mortgage loan is made to the borrower, who then uses the proceeds to acquire a lifetime annuity, with repayment of the loan deferred either until death or the disposition of the property. Under this design the borrower receives monthly annuity payments of principal and interest and makes monthly interest payments, basically receiving a net cash flow equal to the principal payments reduced by the interest differential between the loan and the annuity.

Rising inflation should increase the attractiveness of RAMs because the tax advantages of homeownership increase with inflation. RAMs enable elderly households to retain homeownership while improving their net cash flow. Some forms of RAMs, however, are more appropriate to an inflationary environment than others. Since the net cash flow is reduced with rising interest rates, a RAM that netted out the interest and provided payments consisting of the principal on the annuity, less the interest arising by applying the net rate differential (the loan rate minus the annuity rate) to the loan would be preferable. It would also greatly reduce the sensitivity of RAMs to the tax treatment. Regularly readjusting RAMs to increase the mortgage size and annuity as nominal equity through inflation is built up would essentially create an inflation-linked annuity and also increase the attractiveness of RAMs to borrowers.

Although RAMs would appear quite advantageous for elderly homeowners, they are not without complications for lenders. First, RAMs entail negative cash flows for institutions and hence are only suited for lenders with steady cash inflows and long-term obligations. Second, their annuity feature makes them most suited for life insurance companies. In Canada, only life insurance companies can presently offer life annuities. These companies, however, have been reducing their activities in the single-family housing market since they tend to have centralized operations and prefer larger size transactions. Third, in some schemes the loan amount increases over time, which increases the risk of reducing the lender security of the real property. On balance, these problems (which are similar to those that arise under PLAMs and SAMs) are manageable and if the appropriate tax regulations were introduced, reverse mortgages are likely to become a significant aspect of the mortgage market in the next few decades.

CONCLUSIONS

In the early 1950s Canada moved to a new monetary standard. The experience of the last fifteen years under this new monetary standard has been dominated by substantial price-level unpredictability. During this period both high and variable inflation rates have persisted, and it is likely that these rates will continue into the future. Monetary volatility is likely to have profound effects on the mortgage market as financial markets adjust to alleviate the effects of the increased uncertainty.

As is currently happening, long-term level-payment mortgages at fixed interest rates will probably disappear and be replaced by a variety of mortgage instruments, the most common of which are likely to be price-level-adjusted mortgages and shared-appreciation mortgages (primarily in the rental market), and, to a lesser extent, short-term variable-rate mortgages. Because of the interaction of changing demographics and price level uncertainty, reverse-annuity mortgages are also likely to become increasingly important.

NOTES

1. Some economists have argued that inflationary finance is an efficient way to fund temporary, once-and-for-all wartime expenditures. See Barro (1977).
2. This term was first used with respect to U.S monetary developments by Klein (1975).
3. For a discussion of how to measure price-level unpredictability, see Klein 1978.
4. This positive correlation between the mean and variance of inflation rates does not seem to be confined to Canada. For international evidence of this point, see Hendry 1980. Hendry found, using data for nineteen countries for the years 1961–1979, that the standard deviation of inflation equaled -1 to $+0.75$ times the mean inflation rate.
5. This argument was first raised by Fisher (1911) and has recently been made more explicit by Gray (1978) and Bordo (1980) in their formulation of contract theory.
6. For a history of mortgages in Canada, see Woodard 1959.
7. Since we assume the rate of inflation is fully anticipated, there are no time lags nor lock-in effects.
8. See Jump (1980) for a discussion of how inflation blurs the distinction between interest and principal.
9. For a discussion of the concept of duration, see Macaulay 1938 and Carr, Halpern, and McCallum 1974.
10. These two amounts are only approximately equal because of rounding error and different compounding periods.
11. One can imagine an incremental scheme where the mortgagor arranges for this financing at the time of the loan origination at a fixed rate in a manner similar to graduated-payment mortgages discussed later in the chapter.
12. The moral hazard argument simply says that, as the expected equity of the mortgagor in the property declines, the probability of inadequate maintenance increases.
13. There are also other lender costs of default such as loss of goodwill in the community.
14. If the tilt problem reduces the demand for housing, one may question why the 1970s have seen both an accelerating inflation that

aggravates the tilt problem and a sharp increase in real housing prices. The answer lies in the nonneutrality of the tax system. There is no taxation of realized capital gains on a principal residence and also the imputed rent is not taxed. The significance of these tax benefits increases with inflation since the expected nontaxable capital gain and the nontaxed imputed rent became greater, and hence the investment demand for homeownership increases with inflation. An increase in the real capital value of housing during a period of accelerating inflation thus simply implies that the positive tax effects outweigh the negative tilt effect, reducing real housing demand in the early years of an accelerating inflation. The negative tilt effects also diminish the longer a higher inflation rate remains stable. Other explanations for rising real prices include an actual inflation in excess of that expected throughout most of the period, providing unanticipated real gains for mortgage debtors in the form of rising house prices, and rising real demand with supply lags.

15. This description assumes the principal mortgage balance remains the same on renewal as at the end of the initial maturity.

16. Based on late 1970s figures (Canada Mortgage and Housing Corporation 1980:10–35). The balance of the funds are provided by life insurance companies 8 percent, government 4 percent, and other lenders 33 percent.

17. Trust and mortgage loan companies had 30 percent of their liabilities issued for one year or less, and the chartered banks had almost all their Canadian dollar liabilities for less than one year (with 56 percent payable on demand) (*Bank of Canada Review* 1981:S34, 81).

18. An alternative is to have variable or indexed deposit rates, which amount to the same thing.

19. There was nothing sacred about five years. However, under the Canadian Interest Act noncorporate homeowners had the statutory right to repay mortgages after five years on penalty of ninety days interest. Since a high proportion of trust and mortgage loan company obligations were five years, the five year rollover evolved to eliminate the asymmetrical interest risk for lenders and to provide a reasonable matching of asset and liability maturity terms.

20. This type of interest-rate limitation has occurred in Britain. See Cohen and Lessard 1975:193–5 and Cullingworth 1980 for discussions of such intervention.

21. An appropriate form of government intervention would be the encouragement of alternative mortgage forms such as price-level-adjusted mortgages (PLAMs).

22. This concept was introduced in Canada under the Assisted Home-ownership Program. For a discussion of this program and its difficulties, see Smith 1981.
23. The best solution is to have a stable monetary environment.
24. If mortgage interest were ever tax-deductible in Canada, a new problem would arise—namely, whether the increased principal should be treated as a deductible interest payment. For a discussion of tax problems, see Holland 1975.

REFERENCES

Alchian, A., and B. Klein. 1973. "On a Correct Measure of Inflation." *Journal of Money, Credit and Banking* 5 (February):173–91.

Bank of Canada Review 1981. (March).

Barro, P. J. 1977. "Unanticipated Money Growth and Unemployment in the United States." *American Economic Review* 67 (March):101–15.

Bartel, H., and M. Daly. 1980. "Reverse Annuity Mortgages as a Source of Retirement Income." *Canadian Public Policy* 6 (Autumn):584–90.

Bordo, M. 1980. "The Effects of Monetary Changes on Relative Commodity Prices and the Role of Long-Term Contracts." *Journal of Political Economy* 88 (December):1088–1109.

Canada Mortgage and Housing Corporation. 1978. "Projecting Long-Term Housing Requirements and Assessing Current Housing Needs: The Canadian Experience." Ottawa. Mimeo.

———. 1980. *Canadian Housing Statistics*. Ottawa: CMHC.

Carr, J. L., P. J. Halpern, and J. S. McCallum. 1974. "Correcting the Yield Curve: A Re-Interpretation of the Duration Problem." *Journal of Finance* 29 (September):1287–1294.

Carr, J. L., J. E. Pesando, and L. B. Smith. 1976. "Tax Effects, Price Expectations and the Nominal Rate of Interest." *Economic Inquiry* 14 (June):259–69.

Carr, J. L., and L. B. Smith. 1972. "Money Supply, Interest Rates and the Yield Curve." *Journal of Money, Credit and Banking* 4 (August):582–94.

Cohen, D., and D. Lessard. 1975. "Experience with Variable Rate Mortgages: The Case of the United Kingdom." In *New Mortgage Designs for Stable Housing in an Inflationary Environment*, edited by F. Modigliani and D. Lessard. Boston: Federal Reserve Bank of Boston.

Cohn, R., and S. Fischer. 1975. "Alternative Mortgage Designs." In *New Mortgage Designs for Stable Housing in an Inflationary Environment*, edited by F. Modigliani and D. Lessard. Boston: Federal Reserve Bank of Boston.

Cullingworth, J. B. 1980. "New Mortgage Instruments: U.K. Experience." Paper presented to the Canadian Council of Social Development National Symposium on the Future of Home Ownership in Canada, Calgary, September.

Daly, M. J. 1980. "Reverse Mortgages as a Means of Unlocking Equity for Elderly Homeowners." Paper presented to the Canadian Council on Social Development National Symposium on the Future of Home Ownership in Canada, Calgary, September.

Fischer, S. 1975. "The Demand for Index Bonds." *Journal of Political Economy* 83 (June):509–34.

Fisher, I. 1911. *Purchasing Power of Money.* New York: Augustus M. Kelley.

Gray, Jo Anna. 1978. "On Indexation and Contract Length." *Journal of Political Economy* 86 (February:1–18.

Hendry, D. F. 1980. "Econometric Evidence in the Appraisal of Monetary Policy." In Appendices to the Minutes of Evidence Taken Before the Treasury and Civil Service Committee, Parliament of the United Kingdom.

Holland, D. 1975. "Tax and Regulatory Problems Posed by Alternative Nonstandard Mortgages." In New Mortgage Designs for Stable Housing in an Inflationary Environment, edited by D. Lessard and F. Modigliani. Boston: Federal Reserve Bank of Boston.

Jump, G. V. 1980. "Interest Rates, Inflation Expectations and Spurious Elements in Measured Real Income and Saving." *American Economic Review* 70 (December):990–1004.

Klein, B. 1975. "Our New Monetary Standard: The Measurement and Effects of Price Uncertainty, 1800–1971." *Economic Inquiry* 13 (December):461–84.

———. 1978. "The Measurement of Long- and Short-term Price Uncertainty: A Moving Regression Time Series Analysis." Mimeo.

Labour Canada. 1980. *Annual Review.* Ottawa: Labour Canada.

Lessard, D. 1975. "Roll-Over Mortgages in Canada." In *New Mortgage Designs for Stable Housing in an Inflationary Environment,* edited by F. Modigliani and D. Lessard. Boston: Federal Reserve Bank of Boston.

Lessard, D., and F. Modigliani. 1975. "Inflation and the Housing Market: Problems and Solutions." In *New Mortgage Designs for Stable Housing in an Inflationary Environment,* edited by F. Modigliani and D. Lessard. Boston: Federal Reserve Bank of Boston.

Macaulay, F. R. 1938. *The Movements of Interest Rates, Bond Yields and Stock Yields in the United States since 1856.* New York: National Bureau of Economic Research.

Pesando, J. E. 1977. *The Impact of Inflation on Financial Markets in Canada.* Montreal: C. D. Howe Research Institute.

————. 1981. "Possible Initiatives in the Design of Mortgage Instruments to Facilitate Housing Purchases in an Inflationary Environment." Paper presented at the Canadian Real Estate Association National Housing Conference, Ottawa, March.

Smith, L. B. 1981. "Canadian Housing Policy in the Seventies." *Land Economics* 57 (August):338–52.

Statistics Canada, Consumer Income and Statistics Division. 1979. "Home Ownership and Mortgage Debt in Canada, 1977." Ottawa. Mimeo.

Woodard, H. 1959. *Canadian Mortgages.* Toronto: Collins.

11 OPTIMAL MORTGAGE INSTRUMENT DESIGNS

Dennis R. Capozza and George W. Gau

Recent experiences in Canadian and U.S. mortgage have raised concerns over the viability of the current housing finance systems in both countries. As shown in Tables 11–1 and 11–2, recent years in Canada and the United States have been a time of not only historically high but also quite volatile mortgage interest rates. For the years of 1976–1980, the variance of conventional mortgage rates on a monthly basis in Canada is 2.59 percent, more than double the variance of 1.15 percent during the 1971–1975 period. Similarly in the United States, the variance jumps from 0.41 percent (1971 to 1975) to 2.06 percent (1976 to 1980).

The prime source of the instability in financial markets has been inflation with its attendant active monetary policies. Changes in the consumer price index in Canada and the United States over the past decade are presented in Tables 11–3 and 11–4. With nominal interest rates reflecting the real rate plus an inflation premium, fluctuations of inflationary expectations have a direct impact on interest-rate volatility. Assuming the present inflationary environment does not subside, high and unstable interest rates will remain a fundamental characteristic of financial markets.

The instability in residential mortgage markets has generated concern about the affordability of homeownership in periods of

Table 11–1. Canadian Residential Mortgage Interest Rates (end of Quarter)

Year and Quarter	Conventional[a] (%)	NHA[b] (%)	Year and Quarter	Conventional (%)	NHA (%)
1971			1976		
I	9.28	8.98	I	11.90	11.56
II	9.34	8.80	III	11.93	11.91
III	9.55	9.05	III	11.76	11.75
IV	9.10	8.91	IV	11.27	11.18
1972			1977		
I	8.97	8.79	I	10.25	10.21
II	9.37	8.98	II	10.35	10.25
III	9.38	9.06	III	10.32	10.21
IV	9.22	9.00	IV	10.33	10.16
1973			1978		
I	9.07	9.02	I	10.33	10.15
II	9.52	9.25	III	10.32	10.16
III	10.13	9.72	III	10.67	10.19
1974			1979		
I	10.04	10.05	I	11.11	10.97
II	11.37	10.69	III	11.16	10.92
III	12.05	11.77	III	12.25	11.51
IV	11.88	11.75	IV	13.58	12.93
1975			1980		
I	10.65	11.04	I	14.69	13.70
II	11.23	10.68	II	12.92	13.09
III	11.94	11.32	III	14.50	13.38
IV	11.89	11.89	IV	15.60	14.66

Source: Canadian Housing Statistics, CMHC. Various years.
a. Conventional lending institution mortgage rate.
b. National Housing Act (NHA) insured mortgage rate.

high interest rates as well as about the risk inherent in the standard mortgage instruments with interest-rate volatility. To alleviate the perceived affordability problem, a number of alternative, non-level-payment instruments have been suggested, including the graduated-payment mortgage (GPM), the price-level-adjusted mortgage (PLAM), and the shared-appreciation mortgage (SAM).[1] The purpose of these alternative designs is to reduce the tilt

Table 11–2.   U.S. Residential Mortgage Interest Rates (End of Quarter)

Year and Quarter	Rate (%)	Year and Quarter	Rate (%)
1971		1976	
I	7.66	I	8.93
II	7.50	II	8.89
III	7.83	III	9.08
IV	7.77	IV	9.10
1972		1977	
I	7.52	I	8.95
II	7.55	II	8.98
III	7.57	III	9.04
IV	7.66	IV	9.09
1973		1978	
I	7.68	I	9.26
II	7.79	II	9.46
III	8.17	III	9.73
IV	8.49	IV	10.02
1974		1979	
I	8.64	I	10.307
II	8.85	II	10.66
III	9.19	III	10.02
IV	9.3	IV	11.64
1975		1980	
I	9.06	I	12.62
II	8.96	II	12.66
III	8.94	III	12.34
IV	9.01	IV	13.28

Source: Federal Reserve Bulletin. Various Years.

effect imposed by the standard level-payment instrument. Similarly, in both countries the amplification of interest-rate volatility has led to the introduction of a wave of new adjustable-rate instruments, such as variable-rate mortgages (VRM), which require mortgage borrowers to assume a greater portion of the interest-rate risk.

With the creation of new mechanisms for housing finance and the continued presence of interest-rate volatility in both coun-

Table 11–3. Canadian Consumer Price Index Percentage Change in Annual Rates (End of Quarter)

Year and Quarter	Rate (%)	Year and Quarter	Rate (%)
1976		1976	
I	4.6	I	5.3
II	5.2	II	6.8
III	5.1	III	5.4
IV	4.8	IV	5.3
1972		1977	
I	3.2	I	11.3
II	3.2	II	8.4
III	9.5	III	7.7
IV	4.2	IV	9.3
1973		1978	
I	6.7	I	8.6
II	11.0	II	10.1
III	11.2	III	5.5
IV	6.5	IV	8.6
1974		1979	
I	11.3	I	11.7
II	14.7	II	8.6
III	9.4	III	8.2
IV	12.0	IV	9.3
1975		1980	
I	7.3	I	10.1
II	11.3	II	11.6
III	10.4	III	10.5
IV	7.9	IV	11.0

Source: Bank of Canada Review. Various years.

tries, an important question becomes how best to allocate interest-rate risk among the parties to the mortgage contract. Are instruments that shift a greater proportion of the risk to borrowers Pareto optimal in the mortgage market? If borrowers are compensated for assuming the interest-rate risk through lower initial mortgage rates, under what conditions are adjustable-rate mortgages their preferred instrument design? Alternatively, should the risk be shifted to other outside parties through hedging vehicles such as futures markets?

Table 11–4.   U.S. Consumer Price Index Percentage Change in Annual Rates (End of Quarter)

Year and Quarter	Rate %	Year and Quarter	Rate %
1971		1976	
I	4.0	I	2.9
II	7.0	II	6.4
III	2.0	III	4.0
IV	4.9	IV	3.5
1972		1977	
I	1.9	I	7.5
II	2.9	II	8.0
III	4.8	III	4.6
IV	3.8	IV	4.5
1973		1978	
I	11.2	I	8.9
II	8.2	II	12.4
III	3.5	III	9.6
IV	7.8	IV	5.3
1974		1979	
I	13.6	I	11.6
II	11.5	II	14.0
III	14.4	III	12.5
IV	8.6	IV	12.7
1975		1980	
I	4.6	I	17.3
II	9.8	II	13.2
III	5.9	III	11.1
IV	5.1	IV	10.3

Source: Federal Reserve Bulletin. Various years.

Although many forms of non-level-payment mortgages have been proposed to correct the affordability problem of level-payment instruments, none of these mortgage designs have been widely adopted in either Canada or the United States. Although partial explanations for their absence may be regulatory constraints or institutional inertia, an area that has not been adequately explored is the conditions under which alternative mortgage instruments are the optimal designs for borrowers. In

other words, how do savings, investment, and tax-shelter preferences enter into borrowers' instrument choices?

This chapter addresses these risk-allocation and optimal-design
questions by developing expected-utility-maximizing models for
mortgage borrowers and lenders under conditions of uncertain interest rates.[2] For borrowers, the basic idea is that they prefer
mortgage designs that maximize the utility of their expected consumption. In the lender's model, institutions seek to maximize
their expected income derived from the differences between their
earnings on mortgages and their costs of funds. The implications
of this theoretical analysis for the mortgage markets in Canada
and the United States are discussed and the prospective role in
housing finance of alternative hedging mechanisms considered.

MORTGAGE BORROWER'S FRAMEWORK

The typical consumer purchasing a house is making the largest
single consumption decision of a lifetime. Not widely recognized
is the fact that the financing of the purchase is also a major savings, investment, and tax-shelter decision. These three elements
of the borrower's mortgage choice are strongly influenced by the
form of the instrument employed in the financing of the housing
consumption.

Savings

One characteristic of mortgage that has changed radically as interest rates have increased is the real savings component of the
loan. In a period of stable prices this component is simply the
amortization schedule. For the level-payment, fully amortized
mortgage (the FRM, or fixed-rate mortgage), savings are low early in the mortgage and increase with time, as shown in Figure 10–
1. Conversely, when anticipated inflation is high and impounded
into the interest rate, the savings pattern under an FRM is downward sloping over time in real terms, as in Figure 10–2. The additional savings in the early periods arises from the falling real
value of the mortgage debt and an increasing real housing equity
(assuming constant real values of the house).[3] This phenomenon

Figure 11–1.   Real Savings Pattern: Fixed-Rate Mortgage without Inflation

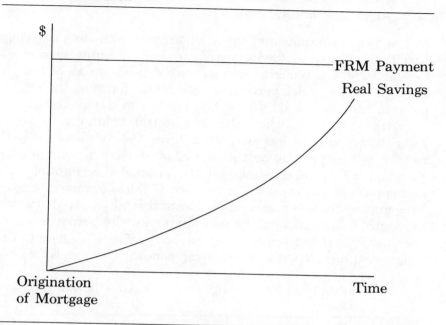

is another type of inflation tilt. The GPM or PLAM can return the savings schedule to the original FRM pattern by suitably adjusting for inflation. The adjustable-rate mortgage (ARM) does not change the schedule with respect to anticipated inflation from the FRM.

The two savings schedules are quite different, but which is preferred for most borrowers? The answer is not obvious. In general, consumers are assumed to maximize the discounted utility of consumption subject to certain income or wealth constraints. A standard analytical formulation (for example, see Samuelson 1969) would be

$$\text{Max } H = \int_0^T e^{-\delta t} \, U(c(t)) dt$$

$$\text{subject to } W = \int_0^T y(t) e^{-rt} \qquad (11\text{–}1)$$

where δ = the degree of time bias (borrower's rate of discount);
$U(\ )$ = a utility function;

$$
\begin{aligned}
c(t) &= \text{consumption at time } t; \\
y(t) &= \text{income at time } t; \\
r &= \text{the interest rate.}
\end{aligned}
$$

In this type of formulation the solution involves finding a savings path that will convert the income stream into the optimal consumption pattern. The preferred savings path depends on all of the parameters of the model, particularly the utility function, the income pattern, and the degree of time bias relative to the interest rate.

In the special case where the time horizon is infinite, utility is logarithmic, and the income path is level, the consumption path rises or falls depending on the sign of $(\delta - r)$. With diminishing marginal utility of consumption the optimal consumption and saving path can be expected to be smooth unless income is erratic. This implies that mortgage instruments that allow rapid changes in monthly payments will be undesirable for the borrower unless the fluctuations in payments can be easily offset elsewhere in the consumer's budget without upsetting consumption levels.

Figure 11–2.   Real Savings Pattern: Fixed-Rate Mortgage with Inflation

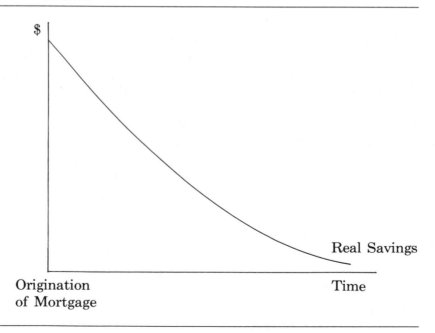

In cases where the income stream begins after and ends before the consumption stream over the life cycle, a hump-shaped savings pattern is likely. Young mortgage borrowers purchasing a house would be in the early portion of the hump where incomes are low and savings requirements are also quite low. A non-level-payment design with a small initial savings component could offer a preferred savings pattern for middle portion of the hump, where earnings are high and where savings for future retirement would be greatest. An instrument with a large savings component in the initial years, such as an FRM in an inflationary environment, might be highly compatible with the desired savings rate for these borrowers.[4]

Table 11–5 shows a representative age profile of Canadian mortgage borrowers during the 1970s.[5] The average age of borrowers fell over the decade; nonetheless, approximately one-half of all Canadian borrowers are over thirty years old. With the continued shift of the population distribution to older age groups, the proportion of mortgage borrowers over thirty should increase in the future. These middle-aged borrowers are likely to prefer mortgage designs that offer substantial levels of real savings in periods of inflation.[5]

When nominal interest rates were much lower, the savings component of FRMs for many borrowers may have been lower

Table 11–5.   Age Profile: Canadian Mortgage Borrowers

Age of Borrower	Percentage of NHA Borrowers for New Housing					
	1970	1972	1974	1976	1978	1979
0-24	9.3	12.3	13.6	15.3	19.8	19.0
25-29	31.1	32.9	36.0	37.5	33.9	33.2
30-34	23.7	23.3	23.4	23.7	22.7	23.2
35-39	16.6	14.5	13.1	11.3	11.4	10.9
40-44	9.5	8.5	7.0	6.0	5.6	6.3
45-49	5.6	4.6	3.8	3.3	3.2	3.3
50+	4.2	3.9	3.1	2.9	3.4	4.0
Average age (years)	33.1	32.2	31.4	31.0	30.7	31.0

Source: Canadian Housing Statistics, CMHC. Various years.

than desired based on this model. Other methods of savings would have been necessary to supplement the amortization schedule. These alternatives might include choosing mortgages with shorter maturities, buying whole-life insurance, and investing in common stock or mutual funds. Higher interest and inflation rates have, in essence, reduced the need for forms of savings. Preliminary evidence of this proposition in the United States appears in Table 11–6. The increase in the maturity of mortgages and net the sales of mutual funds shares during the 1970s suggest a savings reduction elsewhere in the consumer's balance sheet, perhaps to offset the inflation tilt.

Investment

A second important aspect of the mortgage decision is its effect on the consumer's level of risk. In general consumers vary in willingness to bear risk. Moreover, individuals all constantly adjust their personal and financial habits to maintain an optimal balance. Affecting this balance are the choice of a career path, the decision to marry, the purchase and sale of various assets, and many other choices.

Table 11–6.   U.S. Savings Data

Year	Average Maturity Conventional Mortgages (Years)	Net Purchase Mutual Fund Shares ($ Billions)
1971	26.2	+1.1
1972	27.2	−.7
1973	26.3	−1.6
1974	26.3	−.7
1975	26.8	−.1
1976	27.2	−1.0
1977	27.9	−.9
1978	28.0	−1.0
1979	28.5	−1.0
1980	28.2	−2.0

Source: Federal Reserve Bulletin. Various years.

In the context of the earlier analysis, the borrower must choose not only a consumption or savings path but also a portfolio mix with the portfolio containing risky assets. The decision model now becomes

$$\text{Max } H = \int_0^T e^{-\delta t} U(c(t)) dt$$

$$\text{subject to } c(t) = W(t) = W(t)\Sigma r_i \Theta_i - W(t), \qquad (11\text{--}2)$$

where Θ_i = portfolio proportions such that $\Sigma_i = 1$;

r_i = returns on the assets with some rates being stochastic variables.

At least some of the Θ_i must be under the control of the consumer and one of the returns can be the return on human capital. The individual must choose both a consumption path $[c(t)]$ and the portfolio mix (Θ_i).

A number of authors have studied problems of this kind (see Hakansson 1970, for example). As might be expected, the choice of portfolio proportions depends on the risky and riskless returns r_i and the utility function. Interestingly, the portfolio weights are not affected by the level of wealth or the rate of time preference δ. The consumer is expected to increase the proportion of risky assets as the returns on these assets increase relative to the riskless returns.

If the mortgage is viewed as one of the risky assets, two factors must be recognized. First, a mortgage instrument riskyiness does not make it undesirable. Most consumers are willing to bear risk to some degree. The essential issue is whether a particular mortgage instrument is so risky that few borrowers would be willing or able to carry the risk. As with the level of savings embodied in a mortgage design, one must consider what alternative methods the borrower can utilize to adjust his level of risk. Risk can be reduced in numerous ways elsewhere in a portfolio if the level of risk in the mortgage increases, as by holding smaller proportions of other risky assets, buying more insurance against possible losses, using more equity in the housing purchase, or choosing a less risky career path. Some of these adjustments may be second best, but they do provide the borrower with considerable flexibility.

The second factor concerns the borrower's portfolio risk and the real rate, inflation rate, and cash-flow components of the interest-rate risk of different mortgage instruments. Since a mortgage is a liability within a consumer's portfolio, it tends to reduce net risk if the consumer's assets have similar characteristics to the mortgage. Typical mortgage borrowers have two principal portfolio assets; their individual stock of human capital or labor income and the real estate asset securing the loan. Both of these assets carry little inflation risk and react to price changes with about a unitary elasticity (Fama and Schwert 1977). Both carry substantial real rate risk, however movements of the real rate change the value of human capital and real estate, because the flow of future income or services is discounted at different rates.[7]

As shown in Table 11–7, none of the mortgage instruments perfectly matches the risk pattern of the consumer's two principal portfolio assets. In choosing a mortgage design borrowers in effect must select the type of risk they are willing to bear. For example, if the real estate asset is financed with an ARM, the borrower is carrying on balance real rate and cash-flow risk. With a PLAM any portfolio risk results from changes in the real rate, and with a GPM there is primarily net inflation risk.

The standard level-payment mortgage with a prepayment option (identified as a SLPM) tends to be an intermediate case where the mortgage borrower bears some of each type of risk. The portfolio risk is mainly one-sided because of the prepayment op-

Table 11–7   Risk Relations

	Real Rate Cov (x, r)	Inflation Cov (x, π)	Cash Flow Var (dc/dp)
Human capital	Large	Small	Varies with employment
Real estate	Large	Small	Small
FRM (no prepayment option)	Large	Large	Small
SLPM	Some (one-sided)	Some (one-sided)	Small
GPM	Large	Large	Small
ARM	Small	Small	Large
OPLAM	Large	None	None
SAM	Some	Some	Small

tion. That is, the borrower gains if rates rise but is protected if rates fall low enough to justify paying the penalties to refinance. Survey results have suggested that this type of one-sided contract is the preferred mortgage instrument of most borrowers (Colton et al. 1977). It is consistent with the well-known tendency of consumers to both buy insurance against losses and gamble at less than fair odds. Thus, while the SLPM has become riskier in recent years because of the greater volatility of interest rates and inflation, the risk being borne by the borrower is the one-sided kind that consumers show a willingness to bear.

Taxes

Homeownership in the past decade has been attractive partially because of the tax laws. There are three primary ways that homeownership affects the tax situation of the consumer:

1. Implicit rents are not taxed (both Canada and United States).
2. Nominal interest payments are deductible (United States, but generally not in Canada).[8]
3. Capital gains are either not taxed (Canada) or the tax is deferred (United States).

The first tax effect is the major difference between homeownership and other investment. As a number of authors have pointed out, it is not the deductability of interest that makes home investment unique, it is the tax-free income (implicit rent). Yet this element of homeownership has always existed and is not affected by high or volatile interest rates.

The second item is not unique to homeownership but is greatly influenced by the level of interest rates. It is also the only item affected by the form of the mortgage instrument and therefore will receive the most attention here. As nominal rates rise borrowers are allowed to deduct a phantom expense: the inflation premium in the interest rate. This expense is offset by the increase in the nominal value of the property; but the price increase is not counted as current income. Thus contemporary tax-accounting principles are ill-suited to the current period of high inflation rates. It should be remembered that all real assets are subject to this same tax benefit.

The third item complements the second. For interest deductibility to provide a tax shelter, capital gains must either be untaxed or taxed only on realization. If capital gains were taxed on accrual, mortgage interest deductibility would be largely tax-neutral.

The tax-shelter element of a mortgage depends primarily on the level of interest rates rather than their volatility and on whether the taxpayer uses a cash or accrual accounting basis. United States tax law permits both individuals and corporations to choose their method of accounting (see Peat, Marwick, and Mitchell and Company 1977). As a practical matter, however, most individuals are on a cash basis. In Canada, corporations report on an accrual basis and individuals on a cash basis.

An important consideration for the alternative mortgage design is the treatment of the deferred interest in a GPM, PLAM, or SAM. Borrowers want to deduct interest as it accrues, whereas lenders prefer deferring the interest income at least until receipt. If the individual is on a cash basis, the deferment of interest reduces the tax shelter received by the borrower. If the lender is on an accrual basis, the institution must pay tax on the accrued interest even though it has not been received. Therefore both parties to these alternative designs may be adversely influenced by the tax implications.

One possible strategy for the mortgage lender would be to switch to a cash basis where possible. This still leaves the borrower in a less desirable tax position. One solution that has been suggested is for the lender to lend the deferred interest to the borrower each year. This would solve the borrower's tax problem but would return the institution to the position of paying tax on unrealized income.

INTERMEDIARY MODEL

In this section a mean-variance model of financial intermediation is employed to analyze interest-rate risk from the mortgage lender's perspective.[9] It is assumed that the risk-averse lender selects a portfolio of securities, assets, and liabilities, on the basis of a quadratic utility function that has as its parameters the mean and variance of the lender's wealth (shareholder's equity). The lender buys or sells securities at the start of a period with the holding-period yield per dollar of security j equal to r_j, the sum of the current income received or paid over the period plus any price change of the security during the period divided by the market value of the security at the beginning of the period.

The analysis starts with an intermediary choosing between two types of securities, one asset (mortgages) and one liability (deposits). Let X_0 be the number of dollars of deposits sold by the lender at the start of the period and X_1 be the amount of mortgages purchased by the intermediary. The r_j's for these securities are stochastic variables that are uncertain at the start of the period, but they are assumed to have known probability distributions with means $\mu(r_0)$ and $\mu(r_1)$ as well as variances $\sigma^2(r_0)$ and $\sigma^2(r_1)$[10] The expected value of the lenders's wealth at the end of the period is therefore

$$E(W) = E(r_1)X_1 + E(r_0)X_0, \qquad (11\text{--}3)$$

having a variance

$$\sigma^2(W) = X_1^2\sigma^2(r_1) + X_0^2\sigma^2(r_1, r_0\sigma(r_1)\sigma(r_0)), \qquad (11\text{--}4)$$

with $\rho(r_1,r_0)$ = the correlation between the yields of X_1 and X_0.

As indicated in Eq. (11–4), the level of risk for the lender is a function not only of the variances of the yields of the asset and liability, but also of the degree of dependence between these yields. Taking the derivative of $\sigma^2(W)$ with respect to $\rho(r_1,r_0)$,

$$\frac{\partial\sigma^2(W)}{\partial\rho(r_1 r_0)}2X_1X_0\sigma(r_1)\sigma(r_0). \qquad (11\text{--}5)$$

Assuming $X_1 > 0$ (no short asset positions) and $X_0 < 0$ (no long liability positions), Eq. (11–5) < 0. The greater the correlation between X_1 and X_0, the lower the variance of the intermediary's terminal wealth. Therefore, one method for the mortgage lender to reduce its risk is by trying to match the maturities of its mortgages and deposits and thereby increasing $\rho(r_1,r_0)$.

Ignoring for the moment any cash-flow constraints on intermediaries, the choice of x_1 such that $\rho(r_1,r_0) = 1$ may not be the optimal portfolio for the intermediary. A mortgage lender with a quadratic utility function displaying diminishing marginal utility can maximize its expected utility by selecting portfolios with the maximum return for a given level of risk. Letting ϕ represent the intermediary's preference for return relative to risk, the mortgage lender's objective function can be written as

$$\text{Max } Z = \phi E(W) - \sigma^2(W) \tag{11-6}$$

and finding the derivative of Z with respect to X_1

$$\frac{\partial Z}{\partial X_1} = \phi E(r_1) - 2X_1\sigma^2\,(r_1) - 2X_0\rho\,(r_1,\,r_0)\sigma(r_1)\sigma(r_0) \tag{11-7}$$

Even with $\sigma\,(r_1,\,r_0) = 1$, the sign of Eq. (11–7) is ambiguous. Since $\phi > 0$ (assuming a risk-averse lender), the sign of (11–7) is dependent on the expected return sacrificed (lower $E(r_1)$) by reducing the maturity of the mortgage compared to the expected utility gained from the lower portfolio risk. If, as indicated in the previous section, the risk premium for most mortgage borrowers is quite high, the reduction in the expected yield on a adjustable-rate instrument with a short maturity may be substantial and could actually cause Eq. (11–7) to be less than zero for this mortgage design.

Also, for mortgage lenders whose shareholder's equity is traded in capital markets, risk-minimization at the intermediary level is not necessarily optimizing shareholder's wealth. As noted by Baesel and Biger (1980) in the context of inflation risk, capital market theory argues that the risk characteristics of the mortgage lender's portfolio should pass through to the market and be reflected in the market equilibrium values of the common stock of the intermediary. In a world of perfectly competitive, efficient capital markets, the reduction of interest-rate risk by mortgage lenders through the shifting of this risk to borrowers does not necessarily increase the expected utility of lenders' shareholders, since this risk could be diversified by shareholders through their investment portfolios.

Defining ε_k to be the single-period return of the stock intermediary k, capital market theory implies that

$$E(\varepsilon_k) = r_f + \beta_k[E\,(\varepsilon_m) - r_f], \tag{11-8}$$

where r_f = rate of return on the risk-free asset;

ε_m = rate of return on the market portfolio;

$$\beta_k = \frac{\text{Cov}(\varepsilon_k, \varepsilon_m)}{\sigma^2(\varepsilon_m)}.$$

Equation (11–8) expresses the equilibrium relation between the expected return to the shareholders and the level of interest-rate risk of the intermediary, β_k . The expected shareholder's return exceeds the risk-free rate by a risk premium, $\beta_k [E(\varepsilon_m) - r_f]$. The size of the risk premium depends on β_k, which itself is a function of the residual interest-rate risk of the lender that has not been hedged within the firm's portfolio. Under equilibrium conditions the risk premium is the market price of interest-rate risk.

Yet for an intermediary subject to cash-flow constraints, the analysis thus far is not sufficient. Mortgage lenders may attempt to match perfectly the maturity characteristics of their assets and liabilities to ensure that their mortgage income and deposit expense flows coincide every period. Regulatory restrictions often limit the capability of financial intermediaries to weather short-term losses. Mortgage lenders with liquid deposits facing such constraints must either purchase mortgages of short maturities (and thus shift a greater portion of interest-rate risk to borrowers) or utilize other methods of diversification to satisfy cash-flow requirements.

To examine alternative approaches to diversification for mortgage lenders, the intermediation model can be expanded to consider portfolio decisions with three securities, the original mortgage asset and deposit liability plus a second diversification asset. Let X_2 be the number of dollars of the second asset purchased at the start of the period. Similar to the other securities, the holding-period yield for this asset, r_2, is a random variable with a known probability distribution. The expected value of the lender's terminal wealth is now

$$E(W) = E(r_2)X_2 + E(r_1)X_1 + E(r_0)X_0 \tag{11–9}$$

and the variance becomes

$$\sigma^2(W) = {}_2^2\sigma^2(r_2) + X_1^2\sigma^2(r_1) + X_0^2\sigma^2(r_0) + 2X_2X_1\rho(r_2,r_1)$$
$$\sigma(r_2)\sigma(r_1) + 2X_2X_0\rho(r_2,r_0)\sigma(r_0) + 2X_1X_0\rho(r_1,r_2)\sigma(r_1)\sigma(r_0). \tag{11–10}$$

With the addition of a second asset to the model, the optimal characteristics of alternative instruments for interest-rate hedging/diversification can be analyzed for mortgage lenders. Taking the derivative of (11-10) with respect to $\rho(r_2,r_1)$ and $\rho(r_2,r_0)$,

$$\frac{\partial \sigma^2(W)}{\partial \rho(r_2, r_1)} = 2X_2X_1\sigma(r_2)\sigma(r_1); \tag{11–11}$$

$$\frac{\partial^2(W)}{\partial \rho(r_2, r_0)} = 2X_2X_0\sigma(r_2)\sigma(r_0). \tag{11–12}$$

In the case of Eq. (11–11) with $X_2 > 0$ (acquire long positions in other securities), the sign of (11–11) is positive. The higher the correlation between the yields on mortgages and the returns on the diversification asset, the smaller the reduction of interest-rate risk for the lender. For Eq. (11–12) with $X_2 > 0$, the sign is negative ($X_0 < 0$) and assets whose returns are highly correlated with deposits provide diversification.

These results suggest two alternative methods open to mortgage lenders for hedging interest-rate risk. First, the lender can acquire short-term, interest-bearing assets with maturities similar to the characteristics of their deposits. Note, however, that in so doing, the lender not only reduces risk but also loses return by surrendering the maturity premium existing in the "borrow short and lend long" intermediation position. Alternatively, if $X_2 < 0$, the signs of both equations reverse and instruments with high positive correlations with mortgages and low correlations with deposits provide the most effective hedging approaches. In other words, taking short positions in mortgagelike instruments offers an alternative method of diversifying interest-rate risk for mortgage lenders without shifting the risk to borrowers through short-term mortgage instruments.

ALTERNATIVE HEDGING VEHICLES

Based on the results in the first section of this chapter, a form of fixed-rate instruments can be an optimal design for many mortgage borrowers. Yet as shown in the second section, these instruments can cause financial intermediaries to absorb a significant level of residual interest-rate risk if their liabilities are predominately short-term deposits. These results suggest the need for alternative methods for financial institutions to hedge the risk of fixed-rate mortgages. This section of the study describes two alternative hedging vehicles: futures markets and options.

Futures Markets

A recent innovation in the financial sector has been the creation of futures markets for financial instruments. Participants in these markets can speculate on the future movements of interest rates or hedge against the impact of adverse rate changes on the value of a financial position. The development of these markets in financial instruments is a new phenomenon, especially in Canada. The first futures contract in a debt security was offered in the United States by the Chicago Board of Trade in October 1975 in Government National Mortgage Association (GNMA) pass-through certificates—a marketable security representing shares in pools of residential mortgages guaranteed with respect to default by the U.S. government.[11] Since that time futures contracts have been created in a wide variety of instruments by a total of four U.S. commodity and stock exchanges. In Canada the Toronto and Montreal Stock Exchanges in September 1980 and the Winnipeg Commodity Exchange in February 1981 opened futures markets in short-term Canadian Treasury bills and long-term Canadian Treasury bonds.

Basically, a futures transaction is an agreement to buy or sell a contract for a standardized amount of a commodity with subsequent delivery during a specific future month at a price determined at the time of the transaction. Futures trades are technically three-party agreements with the futures exchange acting as an intermediary between the buying and selling traders. The role of the exchange is important in a futures market since it acts as a guarantor of all transactions and it allows participants to fulfill their agreements without actually making or taking delivery. A futures position can thus be closed at any time before the delivery date by reversing the original transaction in the same exchange contract.

For the hedger with a financial position subject to interest-rate risk, futures trading can be employed to shift risk to another party. To cover the potential losses in the value of a financial position due to increases in interest rates, the trader undertakes a "short" hedge by selling futures contracts at a specified price. Then if interest rates rise, with the market prices of financial instruments and futures contracts falling, the hedger can close the futures trade by buying the contracts at a lower price than the first futures transaction. The futures gain offsets the losses suffered by the hedger from declining market values of the financial position. Of course, if interest rates fall and the values of debt securities rise, the hedger must close the futures position by purchasing now higher priced contracts, thereby losing on the futures trade and relinquishing gains experienced in the underlying financial position.

For the mortgage lender and borrower, the futures markets could be utilized to hedge interest-rate risk in the mortgage markets. For instance, the financial institution can hedge through a diversification asset. With the GNMA futures market it could offer a fixed-rate mortgage to the borrower and then undertake a short position in GNMA futures contracts. If mortgage and GNMA rates rise, any decline in the market value of the fixed-rate mortgage is offset by increases in the value of the GNMA futures.[12] By timing the hedge terms of their GNMA futures position to coincide with the average maturities of their deposits, intermediaries can fix their interest margins for the terms of the mortgages. Alternatively, mortgage lenders could lock in the future cost of their deposits by acquiring a short position in Treasury bills or certificates of deposit (CD) futures contracts for time periods beyond the maturity of their deposits. This deposit alternative, however, requires futures contracts with hedge terms equivalent in length to the mortgage maturities and therefore would limit intermediaries to FRM designs with rates fixed for up to only two years, currently the longest term of any outstanding Treasury bill or CD futures contract.

Options

An option contract as written on the options exchanges gives the purchaser for the price of the option the right to buy (the call option) or sell (the put option) a specified amount of an asset at a fixed price (the exercise or striking price) for a specific length of time. The owner of the option can exercise only at maturity (the European option) or at any time up to the maturity date (the American option). Similar to the futures markets, the option exchange acts as an intermediary and guarantor of all transactions. By selling put options in mortgages or mortgagelike instruments, a financial institution could hedge against the impact of rising interest rates on the market value of a fixed-rate mortgage.

An example of an options contract in mortgages that has been available for many years in the United States is the purchase commitment offered by the Federal National Mortgage Association (FNMA). The FNMA commitment gives the purchaser (mortgage lender) for a fee the right to sell a set quantity of mortgages to FNMA at a fixed price at any point during a four-month period. Thus the commitment is essentially an American put.[13] If interest rates rise during the commitment period, the lender/option buyer can exercise the commitment and is thereby protected from drops in the market value of the mortgages. Conversely, if interest rates fall, the lender does not sell the mortgages to FNMA and its only loss is the commitment fee.

Recently in the United States the Chicago Board Options Exchange announced plans to offer contracts in GNMA securities ("SEC Move . . . ," *Wall Street Journal* 1981). With the introduction of this option market, mortgage lenders and borrowers would be able to acquire both put and call GNMA options and hedge against rising and falling market interest rates over a range of exercise periods. An important difference between interest-rate hedging in futures and options markets is that with options, the hedge is not symmetric. The downside loss is limited to the option price. For example, in a short futures hedge, the gain or loss on the futures position is unlimited if interest rates fluctuate during the hedge. With a put option the loss on the option position if interest rates fall is restricted to the cost of the option, but if they rise, the option gain is unlimited.

SUMMARY AND CONCLUSIONS

This chapter has developed an analytical framework for the analysis of the optimal instrument design from the perspective of both mortgage borrowers and mortgage lenders. Borrowers' instrument choices are dependent upon their savings, investment, and tax-shelter preferences. Given the present and expected future age profile of mortgage borrowers, a high savings level in the early years of a mortgage may be the preferred path for most borrowers. This savings choice would encourage nominal-rate mortgages like the SLPM and ARM. For these borrowers the non-level-payment designs, such as GPM and PLAM, might not conform to their savings preferences, even though these designs may very well meet the needs of younger borrowers.

The risky investment aspects are quite complicated. The optimal instrument for offsetting the risk of the real estate asset is probably the PLAM. Most consumers show a willingness to bear some portfolio risk, however, particularly a one-sided risk where losses are insured. This preference tends to encourage the SLPM where the prepayment option provides protection. Tax aspects also favor nominal-rate loans over non-level-payment designs with deferred interest payments.

On balance, optimal savings, investment, and taxation aspects of mortgage designs appear to encourage nominal-rate mortgages and particularly SLPMs as a desirable mortgage form for many borrowers. For middle-aged borrowers (thirty to fifty years of age) concerns over the tilt effect and the affordability of the standard mortgage instrument may have been greatly exaggerated. For these consumers the real concern is which design best meets their savings preferences. In the recent environment of modest inflation, the standard level-payment mortgage may be quite well matched to consumer desires.

For financial intermediaries in an unregulated environment, their choice of mortgage instrument among the various forms of fixed-rate and adjustable-rate designs is dependent upon the maturity characteristics of their deposits and the intermediary's risk/return preferences. For thrift institutions whose assets historically have consisted primarily of mortgages, portfolio risk has been a function of the correlation of the costs of their deposits and the interest on their mortgage investments, while their return has basically been determined by the slope of the yield curve. Under conditions of interest-rate volatility and shortening deposit maturities, these intermediaries can reduce their risk by shortening the maturities of their mortgages through ARM designs, although this policy entails a sacrificing of return in the form of lower interest margins. In an unregulated setting the choice of an optimal mortgage instrument, FRM or ARM, would be determined by the comparative risk premiums sought by lenders and borrowers to assume interest-rate risk.

In regulated financial markets, where risk levels assumed by intermediaries are constrained, institutions may be required to further lower their portfolio risk below the utility-maximizing level. To satisfy regulatory constraints in periods of interest-rate volatility, mortgage lenders can invest in ARMs or alternatively retain some form of FRMs and reduce their risk through diversification or hedging. Because of their high negative correlations with the returns on FRMs, futures and options markets in mortgagelike instruments offer viable mechanisms for portfolio diversification. Both of these markets allow for the effective hedging of interest-rate risk by financial intermediaries.

Clearly no one mortgage instrument is likely to be optimal for all borrowers. From the borrowers' perspective the best possible instrument is one where the savings, investment, and tax components could be tailored to borrower preferences and which retain the tax benefits of nominal rate loans. Lenders, on the other hand, should be indifferent to the savings and investment components if financial markets price these components properly and if markets are sufficiently complete to allow lenders to readjust net positions via hedging or other methods. Lenders will not be indifferent to the tax implications. Given that the variety and liquidity of hedging vehicles for mortgages is constantly improving, the primary impediment to an efficient mortgage instrument that will satisfy both borrowers and lenders may be the tax laws.

NOTES

1. For a description of the general forms of the alternative mortgage instruments that have been proposed and in some cases adopted in the United States and Canada, see Modigliani and Lessard 1975, Federal Home Loan Bank Board 1977, Findlay and Capozza 1977, and Gau 1981.
2. This type of approach to the analysis of alternative mortgage instruments was first suggested in Edelstein 1978.

3. The increase in the mortgage borrower's rate of savings under conditions of anticipated inflation is discussed in Kearl 1979.

4. This framework could also be applied to the case of the optimal mortgage design for elderly households. Being in the latter portion of the hump in the savings pattern, these borrowers would prefer a mortgage form that would allow for negative or dis-savings, an instrument such as a reverse-annuity mortgage (RAM). RAMs are mortgages under which elderly homeowners can convert the equity in their homes into a stream of income while retaining the right to live in the house. For a further discussion of RAMs, consult Guttentag 1977.

5. It should be noted that the age profile in Table 11–5 is a biased approximation of the age distribution of Canadian mortgage borrowers. This profile is based solely on NHA borrowers for recently constructed housing. These borrowers would tend to be younger than borrowers with conventional mortgages, as well as purchasers of existing houses. Therefore the distribution in Table 11–5 is generally skewed toward the younger age groups.

6. This view is supported by a national survey performed in the United States to determine borrowers' attitudes toward alternative mortgage instruments (Colton et al. 1977). The survey found that about two-thirds of all middle-age households prefer the standard level-payment design over a non-level-payment form.

7. The questions of whether the real rate is constant over time and whether it is influenced by inflationary expectations have been the subject of considerable debate since the 1975 article by Fama. Recent evidence supports the conclusion that the real rate does fluctuate in a manner not independent of anticipated inflation. For instance, see Levi and Makin 1979.

8. In Canada interest on home mortgages is generally not deductible for income tax purposes. However, a strategy of liquidating investment assets to pay off the mortgage and then remortgaging to purchase the assets will make the interest deductible as an investment expense. A second strategy is simply to use more equity in a housing purchase and less mortgage debt. The money that is not borrowed in effect then earns tax free the mortgage interest rate. As a result, low loan-to-value mortgages and early repayment of mortgage loans are common in Canada.

9. The framework of the mortgage lender's model is similar to the development in Pyle 1971.

10. It is assumed in the model that each of these securities has no default risk and the only sources of variability for their yields are changes in market interest rates.

11. For an introduction to futures markets for financial instruments, consult Ederington 1979 as well as Capozza and Cornell 1979.
12. A rigorous testing of the effectiveness of futures markets to hedge the interest-rate risk inherent in mortgage positions in both the United States and Canada is provided in Gau and Goldberg 1981.
13. For an application of option pricing theory to FNMA commitments, see Asay and Capozza 1981.

REFERENCES

Asay, M.R., and D.R. Capozza. 1981. "The FNMA Free Market System Auction: Valuation, Bidding Rules, and Hedging Choices." *Occasional Papers in Housing and Community Affairs* 9. Washington, D.C.: U.S. Department of Housing and Urban Development.

Baesel, J.B., and N. Biger. 1980. "The Allocation of Risk: Some Implications of Fixed Versus Index-Linked Mortgages." *Journal of Financial and Quantitative Analysis* 15, 2 (June): 457–68.

Capozza, D.R., and B. Cornell. 1979. "Treasury Bill Pricing in the Spot and Futures Markets." *Review of Economics and Statistics* (November): 513–20.

Colton, K.W., D.R. Lessard, D.M. Modest, and A.P. Solomon. 1977. "The National Borrower Study." *Alternative Mortgage Instruments Research Study* I. Washington, D.C.: Federal Home Loan Bank Board.

Edelstein, R.H. 1978. "The Alternative Mortgage Instruments Research Study: What Is Omitted." Invited Research Working Paper, Federal Home Loan Bank Board.

Ederington, L.H. 1979. "The Hedging Performance of the New Futures Markets." *Journal of Finance* 34, 1 (March): 157–70.

Fama, E.F. 1975. "Short-Term Interest Rates as Predictors of Inflation." *American Economic Review* (June): 269–82.

Fama, E.F., and G.W. Schwert. 1977. "Asset Returns and Inflation." *Journal of Financial Economics* 4 (November): 115–46.

Federal Home Loan Bank Board. 1977. *Alternative Mortgage Instruments Research Study* I–III. Washington, D.C.

Findlay, M.C., and D.R. Capozza. 1977. "The Variable Rate Mortgage and Risk in the Mortgage Market." *Journal of Money, Credit and Banking* 9 (May): 356–64.

Gau, G.W. 1981. "An Examination of Alternatives to the Rollover Mortgage." Discussion Paper, Canada Mortgage and Housing Corporation.

Gau, G.W., and M.A. Goldberg. 1981. "Cross-Hedging among Mortgage and Futures Markets." Urban Land Economics Working Paper, University of British Columbia.

Guttentag, J. 1977. "Reverse Annuity Mortgages." *Alternative Mortgage Instruments Research Study* III. Washington, D.C.: Federal Home Loan Bank Board.

Hakansson, N.H. 1970. "Optimal Investment and Consumption Strategies under Risk for a Class of Utility Functions." *Econometrica* (September): 587–607.

Kearl, J.R. 1979. "Inflation, Mortgages, and Housing." *Journal of Political Economy* (October): 1115–38.

Levi, M.D., and J.H. Makin. 1979. "Fisher, Phillips, Friedman and Measured Impact of Inflation on Interest." *Journal of Finance* 34, 1 (March): 35–52.

Modigliani, F., and D.R. Lessard, eds. 1975. *New Mortgage Designs for Stable Housing in an Inflationary Environment.* Boston: Federal Reserve Bank of Boston.

Peat, Marwick, and Mitchell and Company. 1977. "Accounting, Taxation, Origination, and Servicing Implications of AMI's." *Alternative Mortgage Instruments Research Study* II. Washington, D.C.: Federal Home Loan Bank Board.

Pyle, D.H. 1971. "On the Theory of Financial Intermediation." *Journal of Finance* 26, 3 (June): 737–47.

Samuelson, P.A. 1969. "Lifetime Portfolio Selection by Dynamic Stochastic Programming." *Review of Economics and Statistics* (August): 239–46.

"SEC Move to Regulate Options Trading Is Blow to Commodity Futures Industry." 1981. *Wall Street Journal* (February 26):8.

12 INFLATION, HOUSE PRICES, AND INVESTMENT: A U.S. PERSPECTIVE

John A. Tuccillo

High rates of inflation have induced an atmosphere of pessimism and uncertainty that has reduced the growth rate of the capital stock and is in danger of generating a significant slowdown of all economic activity. The impacts of inflation have been especially obvious in the housing sector of the economy. Although the general rate of inflation during the 1970s is remarkable by U.S. historical standards, the increase in the price of houses has been nothing short of spectacular. While the Consumer Price Index (CPI) has more than doubled since 1967 (it is currently about 121 percent above its 1967 base), housing costs have increased to nearly 2.5 times their 1967 levels (U.S. Department of Labor 1980). Currently, the housing market is the source of an interesting paradox: Larger and larger house price increases have been associated with rising numbers of home sales.[1] The reason for this paradox is that the rapid escalation of prices makes housing very attractive relative to other investments. Briefly, inflation, through its impact on housing, has distorted investment patterns in the economy. By giving housing the position in the 1970s held

The views expressed in this chapter are my own and are not meant to represent The Urban Institute or any of its sponsors. Doug Diamond, Jack Goodman, Larry Ozanne, Ray Struyk, and John Weicher provided valuable suggestions during the preparation of this chapter.

by the stock market in the 1920s, persistent inflation has drawn funds away from plant and equipment investment and has had a deleterious effect on economic growth.

Because housing becomes so attractive when inflation rates are high, a larger percentage of household wealth is lodged in this asset. A general decline in the rate of inflation causes a drop in the demand for houses and thus a decrease in their price. Policymakers might find it hard to deal with constituents whose wealth positions have been severely damaged, and thus they may be biased against vigorous pursuit of a stable price goal.[2]

This chapter deals with many of these issues. It synthesizes a number of analyses as an aid to the understanding of the housing sector's role in the economy as a whole, how that role changes in a period of high, chronic inflation, and the importance of those changes for public policy formation. It is of interest to survey what is known of the interactions present among housing, inflation, and investment and the questions that need to be answered in order to guide effectively the future course of housing policy, together with the variations that will occur in major factors affecting these relationships.

The next section examines the rise in house prices over the past fifteen years relative to the general level of prices, the validity of the way that rise is measured, and the causes for the rise. The question of affordability of housing is examined along with the evidence on both sides of the affordability debate. The second section looks at the dual impact of inflation and taxes on interest rates and the relative attractiveness of different assets. Of particular importance is the relation between housing and other capital assets: The combination of inflation and the tax system makes corporate investment an inferior alternative to residential investment. The third section deals with the impact of inflation on the household's decision to save and the second-order decision as to the allocation of that saving among competing assets. The chapter's view is expanded there to include financial as well as real assets. One striking aspect of this investigation is the systematic bias introduced by government policy into the asset-acquisition behavior of households. While general economic policy pushes interest rates up, selective policies such as interest-rate ceilings block households from profiting from high rates. The overall result has been the weakening of the traditional channels of monetary policies as markets adjust to regulatory constraint. The final section projects the trends of the past into the future and assesses the probable changes in the relation of housing investment to inflation over the coming two decades.

ASPECTS OF HOUSING INFLATION

Housing is viewed here as primarily an investment good in light of its ramifications for the allocation of economic activity and the distribution of income and wealth. In part this reflects the general change in the concern of housing analysts about the impact of inflation on the housing sector. Early treatments of the relation between inflation and housing consumption stressed the linkage between escalating house prices and reduced consumption opportunities (see for example, Solomon and Frieden 1975 and Gough and Stoddard 1979). Using an arbitrary rule of thumb for the ratio of either house price or mortgage payment-to-income ratios, these papers documented the declining percentage of families able to afford the median- (or average-) priced house. This view, however, assumes away the impact of inflation and expectations on consumption *and* investment behavior. The more recent literature considers these aspects in examining the behavior of housing markets (a good example is Grebler and Mittelbach 1979).[5] The degree to which funds flow into the housing sector relative to other sectors becomes a predominant concern.

It is useful to clarify some definitional problems at the beginning. The term *housing* is used here to mean owner-occupied housing. The primary benefits of inflation accrue to that form more than to rental housing (which will be referred to explicitly). In any discussion of housing and inflation, the difference between nominal and relative prices is crucial, a distinction that is made carefully throughout the chapter. Finally, except in those cases when taxation is explicitly discussed, all references are to before-tax magnitudes.

The Magnitude and Pattern of Price Increases

Since 1965 the rate of increase in the general price level has been extraordinarily high by historical standards in the United

States. At the end of 1980 the CPI stood about 137 percent above its 1967 base, an average annual growth rate of more than 7.2 percent. This increase has not been steady, moreover, but marked by accelerating annual rates of inflation. Between 1965 and 1969 the annual average percentage change in the CPI was 3.4 percent; for the period 1970–1974, it was 6.1 percent; for the period 1975–1980, it was about 9.0 percent (U.S. Department of Labor, 1980). This time of sustained high inflation has generated a number of distortions in the American economy. Financial markets have witnessed the introduction of many new, inflation-indexed instruments that have reduced the importance of traditional instruments and institutions. Reacting to the uncertainty that has accompanied the surge in prices, firms have reduced their rate of investment, preferring to recycle profits by acquiring used capital through merger and takeovers.[3] Inflation-induced mandated increases in social security benefits have reduced the system to a shoestring existence. (For a summary of recent thinking on the general problem of inflation, see Frisch 1977.)

During the last few years the most noticeable aspect of the general increase in prices has been the surge in the relative price of housing. No single measure captures all the complexities of the housing bundle, but in fact all measures of housing costs and the relative price of houses have been rising.

1. The costs of materials used in the housing sector have risen relative to the general price level.
2. The homeownership component of the CPI, which reflects both house prices and mortgage rates, has risen faster than the overall CPI.[4]
3. The price of both the standard quality house and the median house sold have risen relative to the CPI.[5]
4. House prices have risen relative to median household income. (U.S. Department of Labor 1980, and U.S. Department of Commerce 1980.)

The increases in the price of housing have varied across regions in the United States. During the 1970s for example, the average new house price rose much faster (on an annual basis) in the

South and West than it did in the Northeast and Midwest. Furthermore, within each region, house price increases have varied greatly among Standard Metropolitan Statistical Areas (SMSAs). Tables 12–1 and 12–2 indicate these regional disparities. This relative change in house prices across regions partially reflects the demand for housing and mirrors the changing geographical pattern of economic activity.

The price of rental housing has not kept pace with the price of homeownership. Since 1967 the price of rental housing has increased by 87.1 percent, less than both the homeownership index and the general level of prices (U.S. Department of Labor 1980). Although part of this difference is due to the pure flow aspects of the rental index (as opposed to the asset component of owner-occupied housing), it is curious in that rental and owner-occupied housing represent substitute goods and so their prices ought to remain in constant relation.

Having looked at the general increase in prices and the particular pattern of price changes in the housing market, it would be fruitful to address the question of the origin of the price increases in the housing sector. Table 12–3 shows the pattern of costs of maintaining homeownership[6] Note that while the cost of land has been rising most rapidly, all components of construction costs from 1967 to 1980 exceeded the 137 percent rise in the general CPI over the same period.[7] The major increases in the cost of homeownership have occurred in utility costs (most since 1974), property taxes, and maintenance.

Table 12–1 Annualized Percentage Change in Average Sale Price of New and Existing Houses, 1973–1978

	Existing	New
Northeast	8.68	9.48
South	8.69	7.68
North Central	10.30	11.65
West	13.99	13.76

Source: Sulvetta and Smolin 1979: table 2.

Relative Price Changes and Affordability

The change in the relative price of housing has generated a great deal of public debate. On one side of the question, it is argued that the declining portion of households that can afford the median-priced house constitutes a public policy problem of significant dimension.[8] Generally, this line of argument compares the price index for various components of homeownership costs (house

Table 12–2 Annual Percentage Change in Home Prices, by SMSA, 1973–1978

SMSA	New Homes 1973–1978	1977–1978	Existing Homes 1973–1978	1977–1978
Altanta	6.97	7.73	7.10	2.25
Dallas	10.34	20.59	8.91	14.91
Houston	8.61	9.80	11.62	13.62
Miami–Fort Lauderdale	4.78	6.18	7.31	8.02
South	7.68	11.08	8.69	9.70
Boston	6.46	24.21	4.95	8.60
Baltimore	11.77	15.80	10.29	7.91
New York City	9.96	13.27	7.32	9.22
Philadelphia	7.50	8.74	8.76	9.41
Washington, D.C.	11.69	17.50	12.08	16.55
Northeast	9.48	15.90	8.68	10.34
Cleveland–Akron	13.378	14.65	9.14	13.12
Chicago–Gary	13.17	21.82	11.13	10.84
Detroit	10.42	19.56	7.99	14.17
Minneapolis–St. Paul	12.53	26.74	11.24	13.04
St. Louis	8.80	8.62	12.02	9.31
North Central	11.65	18.29	10.30	12.10
Denver	12.89	5.03	14.43	18.07
Los Angeles–Long Beach	16.71	22.48	15.84	16.95
San Francisco–Oakland	15.59	22.11	14.80	18.80
Seattle–Tacoma	9.84	11.23	10.90	24.03
West	1376	15.21	13.99	19.46

Source: Sulvetta and Smolkin 1979: table 3.

Table 12–3 Comparative Increases in Housing Cost Factors: CP1 for Selected Items, 1967–1980 (Second Quarter)

Year	Rent	Home ownership	Mortgage Interest Rates	Property Taxes	Property Insurance Rates	Maintenance and Repair	Fuel and Utilities		
							Fuel Oil and Coal	Gas	Electricity
1967	100.0	100.0	100.0	100.0	100.0	100.0	100.0	100.0	100.0
1968	102.4	105.7	106.7	105.6	104.7	106.1	103.1	101.0	100.9
1969	105.7	116.0	120.0	120.0	111.9	109.3	115.0	105.6	102.8
1970	110.0	128.5	132.1	121.0	113.4	124.0	110.1	108.5	106.2
1971	115.2	113.7	120.4	131.1	119.9	133.7	116.5	116.2	113.2
1972	119.2	140.1	117.5	145.6	123.2	140.7	118.5	122.3	118.9
1973	124.3	146.7	123.2	152.3	124.4	151.0	136.0	127.9	124.9
1974	130.6	163.2	140.2	151.2	124.2	171.6	214.6	143.9	147.5
1975	137.3	181.7	142.1	158.8	131.4	187.6	235.3	172.5	167.0
1976	144.7	191.7	140.9	167.6	144.3	199.6	250.8	201.2	177.6
1977	151.5	201.7	137.3	180.2	152.1	211.4	280.4	234.5	186.5
1978	169.5	239.5	153.6	179.3	163.2	243.3	311.8	236.2	202.0
1979	182.9	286.9	178.3	186.0	323.1	268.3	488.0	270.8	224.7
1980	199.6	334.2	205.1	194.5	365.8	321.5	585.3	313.9	262.3

Source: U.S. Department of Labor, *Consumer Price Index.* 1967–80.

price, mortgage payments, utilities, property tax, and maintenance) to the index for household income and comes to a pessimistic conclusion: Using an arbitrary expenditure rule, fewer and
fewer families can afford housing. If housing expenditures are restricted to 25 percent of household income, this is in fact true.
Table 12–4 illustrates this trend (note that the numbers in Table
12–4 do not show the actual percentage of income households
devote to homeownership). Households have increasingly been
absorbing mortgage payment-to-income ratios in excess of 25 percent. For those moving during 1978, payment-to-income ratios exceeded 25 percent for all households with incomes below $13,000
per year (U.S. Department of Commerce 1978).

Current figures are less reliable, but the increase of interest
rates and house prices since 1978 suggests that if households are
still buying houses in the same proportions, payment-to-income
ratios exceed 25 percent for a much wider range of household income. The fact that households are sustaining these ratios is a
market test of the demand for housing that gives the lie to the 25
percent rule of thumb. Finally, several analysts offer alternative

Table 12–4 Percentage of Families Able to Afford New Homes, 1967–1976

	HUD Series[a]	Census Series[b]
1967	41.2	34.7
1968	37.6	28.7
1969	38.3	32.3
1970	45.2	31.7
1971	44.0	32.4
1972	42.8	33.0
1973	36.8	31.3
1974	31.4	25.7
1975	31.5	23.7
1976	27.2	22.7
1977	34.4	...
1978	29.1	...

a. Calculated from HUD Statistical Yearbook.
b. Calculated from Construction Reports C27 series, "Prices of New One-Family Homes Sold."
Source: Weicher 1978: exhibit I, p. 398

interpretations of the data, pointing out the relative stability of shelter expenditure-to-income ratios and the impact of federal housing subsidy programs as factors reducing the magnitude of the problem. (For the alternative view, see Feins 1977; Follain and Struyk 1979; Sulvetta and Smolkin 1979; U.S. league of Savings Associations 1978; and Weicher 1977.)

HOUSING AND ALTERNATIVE INVESTMENTS IN AN INFLATIONARY ENVIRONMENT

Even though both owner-occupied and rental housing has generally performed better than other long-term assets in this period of inflation, it is not inflation alone that generates the increased demand for housing. Rather, it is the preferential tax treatment for housing that causes its rate of return to respond so favorably to persistent inflation. As the rate of inflation rises, the value of the tax benefits attached to the ownership of housing rises at an increasing rate. On the other hand, the tax preferences alone are insufficient to explain the performance of housing as an asset. Just as market rates between taxable and tax-exempt securities adjust to take notice of differences in tax treatment, the rate of return to the ownership of housing relative to that of alternative assets would also adjust in a world of constant prices. The relatively greater return to housing is a product of the interaction of inflation with the operation of the tax system. The purpose of this section is to look at how that interaction affects housing as well as how it affects other capital assets. The major conclusion is that the rise in the demand for housing can be traced to the fact that, in an inflationary environment, the tax system favors investment in housing while it discourages investment in other assets.

The Fisher effect suggests that the rate of inflation ought to affect the returns to all assets equally; besides requiring a constant real rate of interest, however, this also requires a uniform effect of taxes (see Darby 1975; Feldstein 1976; and Feidstein, Green, and Sheshinski 1978). The U.S. income tax subsidizes owner-occupied housing, mainly through the exemption from income of the service flow received by the homeowner from the house.[9] This subsidy amounts to about 3 percent of the value of the housing stock, in 1980 about $35 billion. Additionally, the homeowner is allowed to deduct from taxable income the amount paid for interest on home financing and the amount paid in property taxes. It was estimated that this subsidy would amount to about $29 billion in fiscal 1981 (U.S. Office of Management and Budget 1981).[10] This latter subsidy depends on the degree to which the housing investment is leveraged (itself a function of other variables) and is being reduced in value by tax changes that have increased the standard deduction.[11] Both rental and owner-occupied housing share the preferential treatment of capital gains, but the capital gains on owner-occupied housing can, in effect, be deferred indefinitely as long as one remains the owner of any house of value equal to that owned previously.[12]

For the individual homeowner the impact of these tax preferences can be fairly substantial. Since these preferences take the form of deductions, they increase with income and tax bracket. For the taxpayer in the 50 percent bracket, the subsidy has a present value of 50 percent of the house price, in a world of constant prices. Put another way, because of the mortgage interest and property tax deductibility and the deferral of capital gains, the cost of acquiring and maintaining housing capital for the 50 percent bracket taxpayer is reduced by about 38 percent (see Villani 1979; 34-35)

These gains occur in the absence of inflation. With inflation the benefits to housing increase for two reasons. First, the higher the rate of inflation, the faster are individuals pushed into higher brackets, increasing the value of the deduction provisions under the tax law.[13] At a rate of inflation of 9 percent, the present value of the tax subsidy to homeowners in the 50 percent tax bracket rises to 162.5 percent of house price (compared to the 50 percent of price without inflation). This pattern is repeated for owners in other brackets.

Second, to the extent that the purchase of the home is financed by a fixed-rate mortgage, the owner benefits from a decline in the real value of indebtedness over time. This reduction occurs because the mortgage is repaid in a constant pretax amount of nominal dollars and the rising value of the tax deduction implies a falling posttax nominal payment. Both of these effects imply a falling real cost of mortgage debt.[14] It has been estimated that the mortgage effect is responsible for the bulk of the extraordinary real return to housing in the recent past (see Hendershott and Hu 1979:4). This effect disappears if mortgage rates adjust completely to the rate of inflation. However, it has been the pattern that mortgage rates adjust imperfectly to the rate of inflation, opening up the possibility of extraordinary gain during transition periods.[15]

While the tax system favors investment in housing, it has the opposite impact on competing assets, specifically corporate equities. This occurs because the corporate tax system contains far fewer preferences than those offered the homeowner. In periods of rising prices, the higher level of taxation reduces the return on corporate equities, channels savings flows away from corporations and pushes up the marginal cost of undertaking new investment.

The key channel through which inflation affects relative rates of return is expectations.[16] Two problems are encountered when one analyzes the impact of inflationary expectations on housing and other investments. The first deals with the input used by firms and households in forming expectations: How should expectations be measured? The second is the question of whether expectations about inflation are stable or whether they vary more with higher levels of inflation. This last problem is significant in that an increase in the variance of expectations with an increase in the rate of inflation will destroy the capacity of traditional financial arrangements to fulfill their role in economic life. For example, increasing uncertainty about the future course of prices will lead to either an incomplete adjustment of mortgage rates, generating extraordinary capital gains for home buyers, or an overreaction by mortgage lenders and a breakdown in the housing finance system. It is necessary to understand not only the manner in which current inflation affects forecasts of future inflation but also the manner in which that level affects the distribution of forecasts.

Let us consider the latter question first. A strong body of evidence indicates that as the rate of inflation increases, prices will react differently[17] Unanticipated inflation will generate different supply responses in different sectors, causing relative prices to change the distribution of income and thus the distribution of economic activity. Added to this are the differences in the real costs of supplying different goods at different times, which intensifies the trends in relative prices.[18] This change in relative prices is reflected in the differences in rates of return.[19] Although the seasonal components of price changes appear to be ignored in the setting of interest rates, some evidence exists that high rates of inflation introduce differentials in market interest rates.

The correct measurement of inflationary expectations is quite a different matter, however. Conventionally, expectations are modeled as a distributed lag on past price changes. The lag structure will differ depending on the level of previous rates of inflation and on the regressive or extrapolative nature of the assumptions regarding expectations. An added degree of precision for these estimates of expectations is achieved through the use of rational-expectations models in which expectations are considered as if produced from the optimization an economic model. The problem with these approaches, however, is that they fail to recognize abrupt and perhaps short-live changes. This failure can be illustrated by reference to recent behavior in the housing sector. Based on the conventional generation of inflationary expectations, housing activity forecasts are issued each year.[20] In 1979 the abrupt surge of prices generated a change in expectations that led to a strong housing sector. Consequently, the forecasts for housing activity in 1979 (issued in 1978) appear to be low by a margin of 3 to 14 percent. Forecasts for 1980, on the other hand, were from 7 to 15 percent high, suggesting an excessive error learning process.

There appears to be a systematic bias in the tax system that promotes residential investment over plant and equipment investment during periods of high inflation. This bias occurs not only because of the tax incentives to housing built into the tax structure but also because of the disincentives to other investment that arise from the interaction of inflation with the corporate tax. Furthermore, the occurrence of high rates of inflation increases uncertainty regarding both future rates of inflation and the future course of economic activity. This uncertainty will itself affect various forms of investment differently. The household finds that with a fixed-rate mortgage, its costs of capital has little risk of rising rates. With inflation the cost of capital fails, while if prices go down the housing investment can be refinanced at lower interest rates. On the other hand, the firm is in quite the opposite situation. In order to finance investment through equity, the firm will need to assure investors of a larger real cash flow in the future. With inflation and the increase in uncertainty, this is not possible. The firm is therefore forced to rely on increasingly costly debt and internal finance, and investment is discouraged.

Although a considerable literature deals with these concerns, several gaps remain. The whole question of how uncertainty affects the allocation of investment needs to be analyzed empirically and related to the development of the economy. The trend toward housing investment has implications both for the general level of productivity and for the manner in which factors are employed in the housing sector. Alternatively, it is conceivable that the extraordinary gains to housing that lead to a bias in investment may be a function solely of the transition to a new set of inflationary expectations. In that case, the future may well be characterized by a return to patterns of investment exhibited in periods of relative price stability. These questions need to be addressed in order to understand the future relation of the housing sector to other forms of investment.

INFLATION AND CONSUMER BEHAVIOR

Let us turn now to the impact of inflation on the decisions made by the household. It is of interest to examine the effect of inflation, either anticipated or unanticipated, on the decisions made by the household to allocate income between consumption and savings, and the subsequent decision as to the distribution of that saving among available assets. This two-stage decision process is related to housing in three ways. First, to the extent that the house purchase is financed through a mortgage, a portion of the household's income (that used to pay off the mortgage principal) is automatically earmarked as savings. Moreover, since lenders add a premium to interest rates to offset inflation, savings through this mechanism are automatically higher for households who finance house purchases in periods of rapidly rising prices. Second, as we have seen, housing itself is an asset that competes with other assets available to the household portfolio. In addition, a number of housing-related financial assets are available to the household. As the demand for housing increases, for reasons discussed earlier, these assets bear more and more attractive rates and thus influence both the decision to save and the form taken by savings. Finally, in order to protect traditional housing lenders (and thus secure the flow of funds into housing), government regulatory agencies have systematically interfered in financial markets to adjust the rates available to households on certain classes of assets.[21] This market intervention creates artificial disincentives that bias the allocation of household savings.

If households wish to reorder their inflation-distorted consumption–savings mix, they can issue a mortgage against all or part of the accumulated equity in the housing asset. This provides a straightforward test for the impact of inflation on savings through housing. If homeowners increase their borrowing against home equity in inflationary periods, it is safe to conclude that inflation is either neutral or has a negative impact on savings. If households do not increase borrowings against inflation-generated equity, then inflation has a positive impact on savings.

Evidence exists that the recent inflationary increases in accumulated home equity have been partially liquidated through increased borrowings on the part of households.[22] Though small relative to the value of the housing stock, the increase in borrowing is nonetheless significant in light of the ambiguity surrounding the relation of inflation to savings. The problem is that data do not exist that would allow for the analysis of the uses of these borrowed funds. If the borrowings are used to acquire other assets, in an effort to diversify portfolios, then the results of the test are not completely straightforward. What is needed is a more thorough look at how inflation has affected the wealth of households through its impact on housing and how households have reacted to this change.

The second stage of the household decision process is the allocation of savings among a number of competing assets. This allocation is determined by a variety of factors, reflecting both the economic environment (such as interest rates) and the institutional setting (denomination constraints, for example). We assume the household attempts to maximize a portfolio return while minimizing risk. Thus, the degree of risk and the return on assets are the household's decision parameters. In a world in which prices change and taxes exist, the portfolio formation process is contingent on the real, after-tax returns offered by different assets. Inflation affects this process by altering the after-tax returns from different assets in different ways. Taxable assets that yield a return in the form of money are inferior in a period of inflation to inflation-adjusted, tax-exempt assets. If capital markets are efficient, however, this impact will be diffused over time as rates adjust to the new rate of inflation.[23] Housing has become much more attractive with inflation. Prospective capital gains and relatively low transactions costs have made the house an ideal investment vehicle for the average household[35] (see, for example, Lusht 1978; Seelig and Freund 1979; and Villani 1979. For the Canadian case, see McFayden and Hobart 1978). Moreover, the risk involved in the housing asset is low relative to corporate equities. Given the traditional fixed-rate mortgage, the cost of the housing asset reaches its peak at the point of acquisition. Increases in the rate of inflation can benefit the homeowner only by increasing the expected capital gain and thus the rate of return to the asset. A decline in the rate of inflation reduces not only the return to housing but also mortgage rates, enabling the refinancing of the asset at a lower nominal rate and thus a lower cost. If the rate of inflation remains constant, neither cost nor benefit changes.[24] Thus the housing asset is perfectly hedged against the future course prices. The conclusion is that using a risk-return criterion, inflation has introduced a bias into household portfolios away from corporate equities and toward housing.

The situation is much the same with respect to financial assets. By definition, any asset whose return is denominated in fixed money terms must lose value when prices rise. The current inflation has pushed up the rate of interest on most fixed-income securities as issuers attempt to compensate buyers for the erosion of their capital. Existing securities, issued at lower rates in less inflationary times, sell at deep discounts in order to bring their yields into line with current issues. Tax-exempt bonds tend to sell at rates closer to taxable bonds than those found in the absence of inflation. Yet all these adjustments are what is to be expected in the transition to a higher rate of inflation. Rate alternations would be expected to leave financial assets in the same position relative to real assets. In other words, the risk-return tradeoff for financial assets relative to real assets will be the same at a higher steady state rate of inflation as it was at a lower rate. The two will differ during the transition period because uncertainty affects financial assets to a greater extent.

This is not true, however, for all financial assets. For those assets whose rates are regulated by administrative decision rather than by the mechanism of the market, the transition stage may never end. For assets governed by interest-rate ceilings, there is no mechanism to ensure that the risk-return tradeoff will eventually adjust to the new rate of inflation. Indeed, given the rationale for the existence of ceilings (the provision of a steady flow of funds into housing and the maintenance of the financial viability of traditional housing lenders), the ceilings can be expected to remain below the market.[25] The dominance of housing as an investment good in an inflationary environment appears to have been recognized by consumers. This recognition takes the form of an increasing reliance on the single-family house as a savings vehicle to the detriment of other, more traditional savings channels. Besides becoming more important in household wealth portfolios, housing appears also to have affected the general consumption/saving tradeoff to the point where the overall savings rate has increased, if the equity accumulation in the house is considered. A number of studies have looked at the impact of inflation on both the consumption/savings decision and the allocation of transactable savings. The next step in the development of the literature is to focus on the role of the housing sector in this process and, conversely, on how inflation has affected the manner in which the housing finance system operates.

Significant to policy is the question of how the financial system operates, particularly the subsector that deals with housing. Since the early seventies debate has occurred in the United States over the advisability of homogenizing the financial system through a gradual deregulation. That debate was brought to a conclusion of sorts with the passage of legislation in 1980 that will eventually decontrol interest rates on savings instruments and increase the control of the Federal Reserve over the credit system. Yet this action presents further problems. If the operation of the tax system in an inflationary era has made homeownership the fastest route to wealth for most households, it is possible to argue that specialized intermediaries are no longer needed to deal with the financing of housing. Rather, a case exists for general decontrol and the creation of a single form of depository intermediary. The question that has been the center of the financial policy debate is thus resolved. On the other hand, if inflation is reduced and the tax system reformed, then housing needs a specialized intermediary. The answer to the question of the financial system is then the

opposite: more regulation and the maintenance of a special, federally supported intermediary. Any investigation along the lines
suggested in this section must address this policy issue.

TRENDS FOR THE FUTURE

From both the data on the 1970s and the weight of analysis, it
appears safe to conclude that the past decade was one extremely
favorable to the growth of homeownership. Unexpectedly high
and variable inflation combined with a beneficial tax system provided a negative cost of capital for owned housing. Households
switched their portfolios to include more housing and less
financial assets by adjusting their savings flows. The remarkably
low rates of aggregate savings during the late seventies reflected
in part this behavior. As a result, investment in plant and equipment languished below the levels necessary to maintain historical
growth rates. By the end of the decade, more and more suggestions were heard that housing was receiving an excessive share of
capital.

In a sense this question is irrelevant. In an efficient capital
market each form of investment will command its proper share of
funds. In another sense, however, it is quite probable that the
deck has been stacked in favor of housing. If housing did not receive an excessive amount of capital, then certainly homeowners
received significant windfall gains.

In the future the factors benefiting housing will change so as
to increase the cost of capital to the homeowner and reduce the
desirability of owning the housing asset. Changes in the housing
finance system will increase the nominal rate of mortgage
financing relative to other rates, and new instruments tied to
movements in interest rates will increase the duration of the
mortgage. Inflation rates will level off and perhaps fall, causing
the rate of return to owner-occupied housing to decrease relative
to the returns to other assets. Revisions of tax laws will remove
some of the incentives to own a house for investment purposes.
In addition, demographic movements (as discussed in other
chapters in this volume) are occurring that will alter the aggregate demand for housing as well as the demand for specific housing types.

Changes in the Housing Finance System

The featured actors in the mortgage market have changed since the 1960s, with mortgage bankers and government pools and agencies replacing mutual savings and banks and life insurance companies as mortgage originators. Additionally, the cast of characters has grown as pension funds and other investors become the ultimate owners of the mortgages originated by mortgage bankers and pooled through the Government National Mortgage Asociation (GNMA). During this change, savings and loan associations remained the single largest intermediary in the market, and in fact increased their share of total mortgages held over the decade. These patterns can be seen in Table 12–5, which compares mortgage holdings for 1970 and 1980.

Besides this transformation in the sources of mortgage credit, the instruments through which the credit is extended have altered in response to the general financial reform of the decade. The inflation and variable interest rates of the seventies have caused both borrowers and lenders to become dissatisfied with the standard mortgage instrument. Lenders have discovered that their predictions for interest rates have been woefully low, making the fixed-rate mortgage an inferior investment and placing them in a revenue squeeze. Borrowers have found that increasing house prices have raised the downpayment necessary for home-ownership. For those with accumulated equity, this was a bothersome but not insurmountable obstacle. For the first-time

Table 12–5.   Home Mortgage Holdings, 1970 and 1980 (Percentage of Total Home Mortgages)

	1970	1980
Life insurance companies' pension funds	10.5	2.1
Agencies and mortgage pools	6.2	19.1
Commercial banks	14.2	16.4
Mutual savings banks	14.2	7.4
Savings and loans	41.8	44.0
Other	13.1	11.0

Source: Federal Reserve System, Flow of Funds Accounts.

homebuyer, ownership required an increasingly larger capital out-
lay in absolute terms. From both sides of the market came demands for change. Although the fixed-rate mortgage instrument
has remained the dominant vehicle for mortgage lending in the
United States in the 1980s, it exists merely as the most common
of a number of different types of designs, rather than as the only
available contract.

What are the prospects for continued changes in the sources of
mortgage credit and the innovation of new mortgage instruments? Those changes depend directly on the course of inflation
over the decade. Should variable inflation with its attendant uncertainty become a permanent feature of the economy, mortgage
lenders will seek ways of shortening the maturity of their assets
both to index them to the rate of price movement and to match
them more closely with their liabilities. In part they will exploit
the new powers granted institutions under recent legislation; in
part they will modify the way they invest in mortgages.

The mortgage-backed securities developed by GNMA and the
Federal Home Loan Mortgage Coporation have proven popular
vehicles for mortgage investment during an inflationary period.
The popularity stems at least in part from the ability of mortgage lenders to use these instruments to recycle funds at market
rates, reducing the average maturity of their portfolios and tying
them closely to market rates. The fact the GNMA securities are
now regularly traded on futures and options markets makes them
an even more flexible vehicle for asset portfolio adjustment.
Moreover, the GNMA experience has served as an example to the
private sector. By absorbing the enterpreneurial costs associated
with these securities, GNMA has given individual commercial
banks and savings and loans the opportunity to issue their own
securities under favorable conditions.

Continued high and variable inflation will also push lenders toward the use of alternative mortgage instruments. Additionally,
borrowers (especially first-time homebuyers) will be attracted to
those instruments that reduce the investment hurdle. The preference of lenders will push them toward more use of the newly authorized forms of adjustable-rate instruments such as variable-
rate mortgages(VRMs), since these instruments will allow them
to track market interest rates as closely as possible.[26] Borrowers
will opt for graduated-payment mortgages (GPM) but will tend

to shy away from VRMs. This suggests an impasse that may result in neither alternative achieving wide spread use.

This impasse is unlikely to be easily broken. Shocked by volatile interest rates, lenders are less likely now (or in the future) to commit to a long-term, fixed-rate contract. Increasingly, lender groups are requesting the authority to lend through what are essentially "cost-plus" mortages: variable-rate instruments tied as directly as possible to the cost of the funds to the individual association. The Federal Home Loan Bank Board actions in the early 1980s are in part a response to those requests. Consumer groups recognized that these instruments would shift the interest-rate risk of the mortgage to the borrower, who (they argue) is less able than the institution to absorb it. From the borrower's viewpoint, the fixed-rate mortgage is most preferred, with the GPM a close second and certain forms of adjustable-rate mortgage acceptable with strict limitations. In equity terms, risk ought to be shared between borrower and lender as long as high housing inflation rates accompany high interest rates. In efficiency terms, it is unclear where risk should be borne, since the housing sector need not rely on a single source of funds.[27]

Regardless of the dominant instrument of the future, there now exists a menu of mortgage instruments sufficient to suit the needs of households in various life-cycle stages and economic circumstances. The GPM will be the province of the younger household with good income growth prospects; the shared-appreciation mortgage (SAM) may appeal to high-wealth, low-income households who desire to trade off future gain for current income; elderly households may opt for a modified SMA in which they sell portions of their accumulated equity for an income flow. The future issue of the mortgage market is thus not what kind of instument will be present but, rather, to what degree the standard instrument will be used. In the presence of inflationary experience similar to that of the seventies, the eighties will see the end of the standard mortgage instrument as the dominant mortgage vehicle. If inflation subsides or exhibits less variability, the standard mortgage instrument will remain the norm in mortgage markets and alternatives will be available to those households whose particular circumstances warrant their use.[28]

The upshot of the increased use of alternative mortgage instruments is the removal of the windfall gains accruing to the homeowner with a fixed-rate mortgage in times of unanticipated inflation. The risk of interest rate movements that had been borne previously by lenders will be shifted to borrowers. In financial terms the duration of the mortgage will have increased, since a mortgage tied to movements in market rates will be freed from the inflation-induced tilt built into the fixed-rate mortgage. The mortgage principal will be paid off later and the equity build-up for the owner will be slower. The increase in the duration of a mortgage will decrease the demand for housing. Accordingly, any substantial movement to adjustable-rate mortgages will cause a decline in the demand for housing by increasing the user cost of capital.

The Path of Inflation

Recent experience with inflitation leads to the expectation that the future will be characterized by continued volatility of prices and high rates of price increase. This view ignores both the cyclical and secular forces that are acting on the rate of inflation, however. Essentially, the inflation of the seventies can be broken down into a relatively stable but increasing core rate and a number of high volatile marginal factors. The pattern of these factors, chiefly the price of oil, has formed the fluctutations that have been observed in the general rate of inflation and that have provided much of the windfall gain for homeowners during the decade. Additionally, the second half of the seventies was characterized by strong economic expansion, with the concomitant increases in the rate of inflation.

It appears that in the near future the rate of inflation in the United States will be declining. The nation is in the early stages of recovery from a recession, a period in the economic cycle typically marked by a reduction in price increases. Sufficient slack exists in the economy to accommodate expansion without placing pressure on existing resources. The more volatile economic forces of the seventies appear to be stabilizing. The worldwide excess supply of oil, together with political pressures, have operated to eliminate the drastic increases in oil prices that consumers have come to expect. High interest rates, largely the result of inflation, have dampened the volume of housing purchases to the point where house prices have begun to moderate. The net result has been a general downward revision in the forecasted rates of inflation by the keepers of the major models. Currently, the consensus forecast for the changes in the CPI for 1983 is 7.5 percent, with some optimism that the rate of price change may fall as low as 6 percent by then.

In the longer run, this trend may continue. Although the downward revisions of inflation forecasts are based largely on the moderation of the transitory components of inflation, it appears that the core rate is dropping as well. This drop stems from current and projected increases in industrial productivity that will decrease the excess demand for goods driving the current inflation. Moreover, cyclical declines in the rate of prices increase will cause households to revise downward their own expectations about the future course of inflation. This in turn will moderate wage demands and add to the declining trend in inflation rates. Finally, moderation in oil and house prices will cause the CPI to decline even more than it should. The work of Douherty and Van Order (1979) indicated that during the seventies, when house prices were rising more quickly than the price of other goods, the CPI in the United States overstated the rate of inflation. On the downside, the opposite occurs. As house prices level off, the CPI will consistently understate the real actual rate of inflation. Those contracts and income adjustments tied to the CPI will provide a counterinflationary impulse, just as they provided a proinflationary impulse in the late seventies.

In terms of housing, the decline in the rate of inflation will generate a shift away from housing as an investment and toward housing as a consumption good. One of the prime engines in the housing boom of the past decade has been the inflationary expectation held by households. The expectation of extraordinary capital gain has prompted households to stretch their income as far as possible and acquire as large a house as possible. With a moderation of inflation, the gains promised by owner-occupied units will fall. Preferences for smaller units and for rental housing will emerge, and the pattern of housing activity will change.

Reinforcing all this will be modifications of the tax laws. It is virtually inconceivable that the tax preferences attached to owner-occupied housing will be altered by the current administration or any other. However, these preferences are contingent on the level of the overall tax rate and grow in value as tax rates increase. The proposed tax rate cuts now being considered by the U.S. Congress will reduce the value of the deductions associated with homeowners. The combination of lower inflation and decreased tax brackets is considerable. Work done by Villani (1979) indicates that a drop in the inflation rate from 11 to 7 percent combined with a 10-percentage-point decrease in marginal tax rates will reduce the tax subsidy to homeowners by over 41 percent. The decrease in subsidy is equivalent to an increase in the cost of capital and will lead to a decline in the demand for owner-occupied housing.

Conclusions

A changing financial system, moderating inflation and lower tax rates, as well as demographic trends, will combine to shape the pattern of housing investment in the United States into the next century. Their interaction will produce differential rates of return and different rates of activity in housing for different parts of the country. Overall, the rate of return to housing investment will fall over the next two decades and with it the demand for housing as an investment. During the 1970s owner-occupied housing carried with it a relativwly low cost of capital. This meant that investment funds became misallocated; those who invested in housing received extraordinary profits, and those who financed housing through fixed-rate instruments suffered extraordinary losses. In a world in which capital markets approach efficiency, these conditions cannot continue. In the housing market they are being and will continue to be reversed as traditional lenders will lend only through vehicles that shadow market rates or will abdicate the housing finance market.

In the future housing will cost more in relative terms and will yield less as an investment. The stock of housing currently extant will become less and less able to meet the particular demands of the type of households that will make up the U.S. population. The bottom line is the decline in housing as an investment over the next two decades. Housing will still be demanded, but households will desire smaller rental units. This demand will be markedly different from that of the 1970s and the household wealth that we have seen rise so remarkably during that decade may melt away in the next two.

NOTES

1. The Canadian experience is quite similar (see Scheffman 1978). For a partial explanation of this paradox, see Gillogly 1975.
2. The magnitude of this effect is not easily estimated. However, Downs 1977 presents an analysis of who has won and who has lost in the run up of housing values. Basically, the experience of a large body of middle-class homeowners tells them that the housing market is their path to wealth. While they may oppose inflation in principle, concretely they build their investment strategy on the expectation of its continuation.
3. A recent survey reported in the *Washington Post* indicates that 60.3 percent of corporate investment financing comes from retained earnings, as against 33.4 percent in 1970.
4. Since 1967 the homeownership component of the CPI has increased by about 236 percent and the price of a standard quality home has increased by 154 percent, as opposed to a 137 percent increase in the entire index (U.S. Department of Labor 1980).
5. Since 1967 the price of a standard-quality home has increased by 154 percent, while the price of the average home purchased increased by 138 percent (U.S. Department of Commerce 1980).
6. Weicher and Simonson (1975) emphasize the view that these increases in homeownership costs are a result of demand increases rather than supply problems.
7. On top of these must be factored the impact of macroeconomic cycles on the homebuilding industry. The tendency toward cyclicity has prevented builders from adopting a more efficient technology, since the amplitude of the swings in housing activity mandates the use of a production process that minimizes fixed costs. This means relying on the periodic absorption and release of labor resources as the demand for housing shifts. Combined with unionization in the building trades, this factor generates higher unit labor costs, as labor attempts to offset periodic unemployment through high wage rates. See Solomon 1977: 20–22 for elaboration of this point.
8. The "affordability crisis" position can be found most clearly in Solomon and Frieden 1975. See also Farb 1975; Frieden and Solomon 1977; Congressional Budget Office 1977; and U.S. Department of Housing and Urban Development 1978.

9.   This feature has been discussed in an extensive literature. For a recent restatement, see de Leeuw and Ozanne 1979. For a description of the full tax preferences for housing, see Surrey 1973. The exclusion of the service flow from housing from taxable income is really no different from the tax treatment for all consumer durable goods. However, housing is the largest single consumer durable purchase. What is said concerning housing in this section can also be applied to a greater or lesser extent to all durable goods.

10. Note that households without mortgages do not benefit from this feature. Additionally, the value of this deduction increases with the degree to which the housing investment is levered.

11. For an extensive discussion of this point, see Diamond 1979. deLeeuw and Ozanne (1979) also discuss the changes that have occurred in the tax code and their impact in housing investment.

12. Rental housing is favored to a lesser extent, with the major preferences centering about the allowances for accelerated depreciation. The differences between the tax treatment of rental housing and that of owner-occupied housing will also affect tenure choice, albeit indirectly, through the supply of owner and rental housing. For a discussion of the direct tax impacts on tenure choice, see Diamond 1978.

13. For the impact of inflation on after-tax income and the distribution of income, see Arak 1976 and Budd and Seiders 1971.

14. It is entirely possible that mortgage lenders have built into mortgage rates inflation premiums that adequately preserve the value of their capital. This would tilt the real stream of payments in the manner described in Lessard and Modigliani 1975. However, this would require perfect foresight and instantaneous adjustment of mortgage rates to inflation, neither of which have been in evidence in mortgage markets. A 1979 article by Kearl suggests that these adjustments are the source of long-run distortions in housing sector real activity.

15. This point is discussed in deLeeuw and Ozanne 1979:26–29. The less than complete adjustment of mortgage rates intensifies the tax difference between owner-occupied and rental housing.

16. High rates of inflation will generate expectations as to the future course of prices, either regressive (generating pessimistic investment behavior by firms and households), extrapolative (firms and households will act in such manner as to perpetuate the high rate of inflation), or neither (in which case firms and households will adopt risk-minimizing behavior).

17. Parks (1978) uses a rational-expectations framework to examine the behavior of relative prices in the United States and the Nether-

lands. He finds that the level of unanticipated inflation is positively and significantly related to changes in relative prices. Cukierman and Wachtel (1979) provide the basis to extend this work to cases in which expectations are heterogeneous.

18. Fama and Schwert (1979) measure this seasonal component. They decompose price changes for different commodity groups into common and seasonal components and relate these components to Treasury bill rates, finding that the bill market responds only to the common component of price change.

19. Brenner (1977) provides an initial approach to the manner in which rates of interest respond differently to the degree of uncertainty generated by high rates of inflation. Modigliani and Cohn (1979) incorporate this uncertainty into their discussion of stock prices and valuation.

20. The largest assemblage of these forecasts is found at the annual conference held by the Federal Home Loan Bank Board in December of each year. At the conference three to six forecasts are presented for the next year. These forecasts are usually the products of large econometric models utilizing the approach described in the text. For 1979 the forecasts ranged from 1.5 to 1.7 million housing starts. The actual figure appears to be about 1.75 million. This is a significant underprediction.

21. The March 1980 legislation deregulating interest rates has little impact here as full decontrol will not take place until 1986.

22. Seiders (1978a, b) has produced the most detailed analysis of the growing importance of inflated home equity values as a source to consumer spending. Unfortunately, his data are not sufficient to determine the extent to which borrowings against equity are suporting consumption as opposed to the acquisition of other forms of assets, including reinvestment in housing.

23. Efficiency as used here assumes perfect knowledge, no transactions costs, and no institutional constraints. Since decisions by investors are made on the basis of expected return and the variance of that return, if inflation affects the variance of return for different assets differently, variable rates of inflation will distort market behavior.

24. This relation of course poses a problem for the speculative buyer. However, the deductibility of interest payments and the tax exempt nature of the service flow should yield a positive return.

25. The case against the ceilings is, by now, a well-rehearsed tale. For a review see the papers by Kane and Tuccillo in U.S. House of Representatives 1979.

26. A harbinger of this role for adjustable-rate mortgages is the fact that in winter 1980–81, as mortgage interest rates began to climb

higher than had been anticipated, the largest California savings and loan associations were lending only in the form of the variable-rate mortgage.

27. Consumer groups argue that institutions enjoy economies of scale in risk-bearing. To the extent that the market for mortgages is efficient (mortgage features are priced properly) and there are no barriers to entry (such as tax preferences and insurance subsidies given certain investors), the inability of thrifts institutions to absorb risk will not diminish the supply of funds to the market. Rather, other investors, able to absorb risk at prevailing yields, will take the place of thrifts. This is, of course, the reverse of the situation that induced life insurance companies to leave the mortgage market.

28. Note that, with the abatement of inflation the variable-rate mortgage becomes quite similar to the standard mortgage. Thus the VRM may be the dominant instrument because it resembles the standard mortgage with no inflation but affords lenders a hedge against the occurrence of unanticipated inflation.

REFERENCES

Arak, Marcelle. 1976. "The Effect of Federal Individual Income Tax on Real After-Tax Incomes during Inflation." *Southern Economic Journal* 46 (April):720–24.

Brenner, Menachem. 1977. "Inflation, Uncertainty and Rates of Return on Marketable Securities: First Tests." In *Understanding Capital Markets,* vol. II, edited by A.W. Sametz and P. Wachtel. Lexington, Mass.: D.C. Heath.

Budd, E. C., and D. F. Seiders. 1971. "The Impact of Inflation on the Distribution of Income and Wealth." *American Economic Review* 61 (May):128–38.

Congressional Budget Office. 1979. *Homeownership: The Changing Relationship of Costs and Incomes, and Possible Federal Roles.* Washington, D.C.: U.S. Government Printing Office.

Cukierman, A., and P. Wachtel. 1979. "Differential Inflationary Expectations and the Variability of the Rate of Inflation: Theory and Evidence." *American Economic Review* 69 (September):595–609.

Darby, Michael R. 1975. "The Financial and Tax Effects of Monetary Policy on Interest Rates." *Economic Inquiry* 8 (June): 266–76.

deLeeuw, F., and L. Ozanne. 1979. "Investment in Housing and the Federal Income Tax." Paper delivered at a Brookings Institution Conference on the Economic Impact of Taxation, October 19.

Diamond, Douglas B., Jr. 1978. "A Note on Inflation and Relative Tenure Prices." *American Real Estate and Urban Economics Association Journal* 6 (Winter):438–50.

————. 1979. "Taxes, Inflation, Speculation and the Cost of Homeownership: 1963–78." Paper presented at Mid-Year Meetings of the American Real Estate and Urban Economics Association, May.

Dougherty, A. J., and R. Van Order. 1979. "Inflation and Housing Costs." U.S. Department of Housing and Urban Development. Mimeo.

Downs, Anthony. 1977. "The Rising Cost of Housing and What Should Be Done about It." Paper presented at The Urban Institute, October.

Fama, E. F., and G.W. Schwert. 1979. "Inflation, Interest and Relative Price." *The Journal of Business* 52 (April):183–210.

Farb, Warren E. 1975. "Availability of Homes for Middle Income Families." Library of Congress, Congressional Research Service, May.

Feins, Judith D. 1977. "Historical Trends in the Ratio of Shelter Expenditures for Income." Paper presented at the Meeting of the Southern Economic Association, November.

Feldstein, M. 1976. "Inflation, Income Taxes and the Rate of Interest: A Theoretical Analysis." *American Economic Review* 66 (December):809–20.

Feldstein, M., J. Green, E. Sheskinski, with A. Auerbach. 1978. "Inflation and Taxes in a Growing Economy with Debt and Equity Finance." *Journal of Political Economy* 86, 2 (April):S53–S70.

Follain, J. R., Jr., and R. J. Struyk. 1979. "Is the American Dream Really Threatened?" *Real Estate Review* 8 (Winter):65–70.

Frieden, B. J., and A. P. Solomon. 1977. "The Controversy over Homeownership Affordability." *American Real Estate and Urban Economics Association Journal* 5 (Fall):355–59.

Frisch, Helmut. 1977. "Inflation Theory 1963–1975: "A 'Second Generation' Survey." *Journal of Economic Literature* 15 (December):1289–1317.

Gillogly, David K. 1975. "Housing & Inflation—Victim or Villain?" *Business Economics* 11 (January):23–30.

Gough, Robert, and Stoddard, Anne. 1979. "Housing after Volcker." *Data Resources Review* (November): I.11–I.19.

Grebler, L., and F. Mittelbach. 1979. *The Inflation of House Prices.* Lexington, Mass.: D.C. Heath.

Hendershott, P. H., and S.C. Hu. 1979. "Inflation, Taxes, and the Mortgage Contract and the Benefits from Owner-Occupied Housing." Paper delivered at the Mid-Year Meetings of the American Real Estate and Urban Economics Association, Washington, D.C., May.

Kearl, James. 1979. "Inflation, Mortgages and Housing." *Journal of Political Economy* 87, Part I (October):I 1115–1138.

Lessard, D. R., and F. Modigliani. 1975. "Inflation and the Housing Market: Problems and Potential Solutions." In *New Mortgage Designs for Stable Housing in an Inflationary Environment,* edited by F. Modigliani and D. Lessard. Boston: Federal Reserve Bank of Boston.

Lusht, K. 1978. "Inflation and Real Estate Investment Values." *American Real Estate and Urban Economics Association Journal* 6 (Spring):37–49.

McFayden, S.M., and R.J. Hobart. 1978. "Inflation and Urban Homeownership." In *Urban Housing Markets: Recent Directions in Policy and Research,* edited by L.S. Bourne and J.R. Hitchcock. Toronto: University of Toronto Press.

Modigliani, F., and R. A. Cohn. 1979. "Inflation, Rational Valuation and the Market." *Financial Analysts Journal* 31 (March/April):24–44.

Parks, Richard W. 1978. "Inflation and Relative Price Variability." *Journal of Political Economy* 86 (January):79–95.

Scheffman, David T. 1978. "Some Evidence on the Recent Boom in Land and Housing." In *Urban Housing Markets: Recent Directions in Policy and Research,* edited by L.S. Bourne and J. R. Hitchcock. Toronto: University of Toronto Press.

Seelig, S. A., and J. L. Freund. 1979. "The Single Family Home as an Investment Good." Paper presented at the Annual Conference of the Western Economics Association, June.

Seiders, David F. 1978a. "Mortgage Borrowing against Equity in Existing Homes: Measurement, Generation and Implications for Economic Activity." Board of Governors, Federal Reserve System, Staff Study 96.

———. 1978b. "Junior Mortgage Financing and Other Borrowing against Inflated Housing Equity." Credit Research Center, Purdue University, Working Paper 25.

Solomon, Arthur P. 1977. "The Cost of Housing: An Analysis of Trends, Incidence and Causes." In *The Cost of Housing,* Proceedings of the Third Annual Conference of the Federal Home Loan Bank of San Francisco.

Solomon, A., and B. Frieden. 1975. *The Nation's Housing Needs 1975–1985.* Cambridge, Mass.: Joint Center for Urban Studies.

Sulvetta, A.J., and H.M. Smolkin. 1979. "Housing Affordability in an Inflationary Environment." U.S. Office of Management and Budget.

Surrey, Stanley S. 1973. *Tax Inventives for Housing.* U.S. Department of Housing and Urban Development.

U.S. Department of Commerce. 1978. *Annual Housing Survey.* Washington, D.C.: U.S. Government Printing Office.

———. 1980a. *Business Conditions Digest.* Washington, D.C.: U.S. Government Printing Office.

_____. 1980b. *Construction Reports*. Washington, D.C.: U.S. Government Printing Office.

U.S. Department of Housing and Urban Development. 1978. *Final Report of the Task Force on Housing Costs*.

_____. Various years. *HUD Statistical Yearbook,* Washington, D.C.: U.S. Government Printing Office.

U.S. Department of Labor. 1980. *CPI Detailed Report*. Washington, D.C.: U.S. Government Printing Office.

U.S. House of Representatives, Committee on Government Operations. 1979. *Interest Rate Regulation on Small Savings Accounts*. Washington, D.C.: U.S. Government Printing Office.

U.S. League of Savings Associations. 1978. *Homeownership: Realizing the American Dream*. Chicago.

U.S. Office of Management and Budget. 1981. *Special Analyses*. Washington, D.C.: U.S. Government Printing Office.

Villani, K.E. 1979. "The Tax Subsidy to Housing in an Inflationary Environment: Implications for After Tax Housing Costs." Working Paper, U.S. Department of Housing and Urban Development.

Weicher, John C. 1977. "The Affordability of New Homes." *American Real Estate and Urban Economics Association Journal* 5 (Summer):209–26.

_____. 1978. "New Home Affordability, Equity and Housing Market Behavior." *American Real Estate and Urban Economics Association Journal* 6 (Winter): 395–416.

Weicher, John C., and J. C. Simonson. 1975. "Recent Trends in Housing Costs." *Journal of Economics and Business* 27 (Winter):1–185.

IV GOVERNMENT HOUSING POLICIES

Studying issues in the area of the housing finance system gives an inkling of the importance of government policy in the housing sector. The final section of this volume explicitly addresses questions regarding the appropriate government housing policy. Perhaps more than in any of the other sections, the virtue of the comparative approach will be obvious. The United States and Canada have faced very similar housing problems in the post-World War II era. Governments in both countries have responded with a broad array of policies, many closely parallel though often with important institutional differences underlying the apparent similarities.

Among the leading issues facing government policymakers in housing are the following: Which level(s) of government are the appropriate purveyors of housing policy? What are the preferred roles and relations of each level of government in the housing delivery system? Is there likely to be less, rather than more, federal involvement in housing? Or, somewhat differently, will the federal governments of both countries continue to withdraw from the housing sector, leaving it to the state or provinces and to the private market? What is the nature of public/private interface in housing policy? Who will provide for low-income households, who by virtue of their low levels of spending power are precluded from market housing? Is affordability an issue and, if so, to whom and what should governments do about it?

There is a growing sympathy in both countries for governmental retreat from expensive programs. Housing is such a program when all relevant subsidies are considered. Will this retreat continue? Whether it does or not, how can the appropriateness and effectiveness of government housing policies be judged? Who should make this kind of evaluation, and what sorts of methods are available for evaluating housing policies and programs? Chapters 13 and 14 consider these and related issues in Canadian and U.S. contexts. The various emphases of the respective papers are instructive in their own right and illustrative of the diverse perceptions that exist among housing researchers doing work within different cultural and institutional settings such as those found in North America.

George Fallis, in his chapter on Canadian housing policy, "The Normative Basis of Housing Policy," forcefully argues that coherent government policies follow from consistently applied normative criteria and that this approach has not been followed by economists or policymakers in the area of housing policy. Fallis uses a tenet of economic theory—government intervention is justified if it raises social welfare—to rationalize government housing policies. He reviews Canadian housing policy and discusses future policy problems. The second chapter in this part, by William Grigsby, Morton Baratz, and Duncan Maclennan, "Toward Coherent U.S. Housing Policy," provides a thoughtful overview of U.S. policies and programs that affect housing. After carefully defining the dimensions of housing policy, they identify the foundations of U.S. housing policy and its apparent incoherence historically. The chapter concludes with a review of the current and probable future trends of U.S. housing policy into the twenty-first century.

The panel discussion on government housing policy at the end of the symposium brought together a broad cross-section of expertise from both countries. Several themes emerged; they are reviewed briefly here, and Chapter 15 presents short statements prepared by the chairman of the panel discussion, John Weicher, and three members of the panel, Kevin Villani, Larry Smith, and Dick Muth.

There was general agreement that the thrust and direction of housing policy (including government policies in the area of housing finance) was away from direct involvement by federal governments. In times of budget deficits and sluggish economic growth the capacity of governments to mount expensive housing or mortgage subsidy programs is severely diminished. This lack of capacity when combined with the questionable effectiveness of many previous housing policies in both Canada and the United States calls into serious question further or continued government involvement.

Many of the panelists believe there is little role for governments in the housing area over the coming decades. Some members of the audience disagreed with this position, however, arguing for a continued role for governments in certain aspects of the housing market. In particular, strong views were expressed about the ongoing need for the removal of any remaining racial barriers in U.S. markets. In a Canadian context some speakers thought that there are classes of households (such as the elderly, handicapped, and poor) that are unable to compete for privately developed housing, and that governments have a responsibility to provide access to adequate housing for these groups. It was also observed that responding to such needs could be extremely expensive, and the cost effectiveness must be carefully weighed before embarking on ambitious housing interventions in times of budgetary stringency.

Many thought there are significant roles in housing policy to be played in the two countries by levels of government other than the federal. State or provincial, regional, and local governments all can fulfill potentially important functions in the housing delivery system. A more highly articulated and coordinated governmental effort needs to be explored to ensure the efficient production of new housing and the maintenance of existing units. Of particular concern is the potential redistributive role to be played by states or provinces to supplement federal efforts and the potential for trimming costs and easing supply restrictions at the regional and local levels.

13 THE NORMATIVE BASIS OF HOUSING POLICY

George Fallis

The development of a housing policy involves, at least implicitly, three steps: identifying the desired state of the world, analyzing the way the world operates, and selecting an instrument that will move a society from the existing to the desired state of the world (given the way the world operates). Together these constitute the normative basis of housing policy or indeed, any government policy[1] They justify the intervention of government.

Each step demands careful thought and analysis, without which contradictory or ineffective programs are likely to result. If it has not been decided whether the goal of policy is to increase the housing consumption or welfare of low-income households; or if it has not been recognized that the financing of public mortgage loans reduces private mortgage lending; or if the differences between public sector loans at reduced interest rates and publicly subsidized insurance on private loans has not been explored, it should not be surprising when sound programs do not emerge.

The development of coherent housing policies in Canada into the twenty-first century requires that the normative basis of policy be more fully developed. Most of the chapters thus far have dealt with positive analysis, which in this context is part of the second step of analyzing the way housing policy operates. This

293

chapter focuses on instead the first step, identifying the desirable state of the world, and the third step, choosing the optimal instrument for intervention.

Some would contend that economists as scientists have no role to play in selecting the norms that justify housing programs. They assert that values cannot be discovered scientifically; that is, they cannot be verified by an appeal to the facts. However, this does not deny scientists a role. Economists can contribute to examining the logic and implications of alternative norms as part of the selection process. Often problems are defined using economic concepts or data that are misunderstood.

The current discussions in Canada about the need for housing assistance focus on housing affordability problems. The next section of this chapter examines the concept of an affordability problem, the norm implicit within it, the techniques of measuring its extent, and concludes that affordability should not be used as a basis for housing policy. The following section examines how economic theory chooses the optimal instrument for intervention. The familiar framework of applied welfare economics is reviewed, outlining the necessary conditions for government intervention to achieve a social welfare maximum. It is argued that economists have to go a step farther to identify and quantify the optimal intervention. The argument is illustrated by examining how economists have dealt with the design of housing assistance for the poor.

The policymaking process is often portrayed as purely an intellectual exercise, without acknowledging the role of politics, as if government implements the product of rational thought. Of course, this is nonsense, In society, it is the political process that generates a collective expression of what is a desirable state of the world and produces programs to change things. Cabinet members, backbenchers, the media, interest groups, voters, academics, and civil servants interact in the creation of policy. Policy changes result from changes in behavior of these participants, perhaps following alteration of the incentives facing them and the rules under which they interact. Academic economists can create change by altering their policy advice or by criticizing the logic of other actors, which may change behavior. Both sorts of activity are engaged in this chapter.

THE AFFORDABILITY PROBLEM

In Canada the civil service analyses of social housing issues refer frequently to two sorts of housing problems: adequacy problems and affordability problems, reflecting the norms that housing must be "adequate" and "affordable" (for example see Canada Housing and Mortage Corporation 1981).[2] In 1973 the minister of the federal government responsible for Canada Mortgage and Housing Corporation (CMHC) stated that the federal government has "adopted the basic principle that (says) it is a fundamental right of Canadians, regardless of their economic circumstances, to enjoy adequate shelter at reasonable cost" (*Hansard* 1973: 186).

An adequacy problem exists if a household consumes too little housing. Presumably society somehow decides a minimum acceptable consumption of housing services. The extent of the problem is measured by the number of households living in overcrowded dwelling units or in units without basic services such as central heating or hot water or in units in poor condition, for example, with sagging roofs or cracks in the foundation or broken windows. Table 13–1 illustrates that a relatively small percentage of households in Canada suffer adequacy problems, if defined as crowding or lack of services. Less than 5 percent of households have

Table 13–1. Housing Conditions in Canada

	Percentage of Total Dwellings				
	1951	*1961*	*1971*	*1974*	*1978*
Crowding					
More than one person per room	18.8	16.5	9.4	6.0	3.5
Families not maintaining own household	9.4	5.2	2.9	n.a.	n.a.
Physical Attributes					
No central or electric heating	52.0	32.5	18.9	10.9	n.a.
No piped hot and cold water	43.1	19.9	7.3	4.2	1.9
No exclusive use of flush toilet	35.9	21.0	6.9	3.0	17

Source: CMHC :1981:13).

problems; a dramatic improvement over the last thirty years. Table 13–2 presents data derived from a special survey of dwelling units in census metropolitan areas. This survey permitted measurement of inadequate housing using the broad definition (dwellings that are crowded, lack basic services, or are in poor condition). The table shows only about 11 percent of renters suffered adequacy problems. If both renters and owners from both urban and rural areas were included, the figure for the nation would likely be less than 10 percent of households. Clearly, most Canadians are adequately housed.

Since the middle of the 1960s, housing policy in Canada has focused increasingly on affordability problems and will likely continue to do so.[3] Unfortunately, careful consideration of the definition and measurement of the affordability problem reveals ambiguity about the concept and examples of faulty reasoning.

Consider first the problem defined as a household spending more than 30 percent of their income on housing. Presumably, society does not have some percentage distribution of household expenditure as a norm. Rather, the 30 percent figure is used as a proxy for a fuller argument. This argument would be stated as follows: If a household spends more than 30 percent of its income on housing *and it has a low income, then it will not have the money left to acquire the socially acceptable minimum of other commodities and therefore* there is a social problem.[4] The italicized portions is usually omitted, however.

Table 13–2. Distribution of Renters, by Type of Shelter Problem, Canada 1979[a]

Problem	Number (Thousands)	Percentage
Affordability only	318	$ 4.4
Adequacy only	66	3.0
Affordability and adequacy	183	8.3
No problem	1640	74.3
Total renters	2207	100.0

a. The affordability problem was defined as spending more than 25 percent of income on rent.
Source: CMHC 1981:15.

The argument is logical, assuming society has norms about the minimum acceptable consumption of many commodities. And the approach of using a housing expenditure-to-income ratio as a proxy may have some appeal if housing expenditure and income are the easiest variables to measure. The approach has not been correctly applied, however.

The percentage of income spent on housing that indicates inadequate consumption of other things should vary with income. Suppose at given prices the social minimum of housing for a family could be obtained for $2,500, and other essentials (perhaps food, clothing, education, health care and transportation) for $5,000. If a family with an income of $7,500 spends more than 33 percent of its income on housing, they have a problem. If a family with a $7,000 income spends more than 28 percent ($2,000) there is a social problem; and so on until if a household with an income of $5,000 spends anything on housing, it will have inadequate consumption of some other commodity. However, this alteration by income class is seldom made. The proxy must also change as income rises, otherwise households with high incomes spending more than 30 percent of their income on housing are said to have a problem. The conclusion is clearly absurd, although it is often drawn (CMHC 1981). The measure must also be adjusted over time for changes in relative prices.

More important, this approach is very misleading. It labels the inadequate consumption of nonhousing items as a housing problem. It diverts attention from the fundamental fact that household incomes are inadequate to purchase the social minimum of *all* commodities. The approach leads to both bad housing policy and bad social policy. It implies public policies that reduce the relative price of housing in order to increase nonhousing consumption, surely a most indirect and ineffective method of proceeding. It does not suggest the more direct response of income redistribution.

The development of housing policy in Canada would be well served by abandoning the affordability problem measured by a shelter expenditure-to-income ratio. The focus should be exclusively on the adequacy of housing consumed by Canadians. This would no doubt reveal that relatively few suffer housing problems and they fall into identifiable groups such as native peoples, those in certain rural areas, the elderly, and perhaps mother-led single-parent families. The inadequate consumption of other commodities should not be a housing problem.

Changes in affordability over time have also been documented by comparing changes in housing costs and incomes, which also entails a number of problems. The comparisons of income and housing costs typically have used an inappropriate index of housing costs. For the computation of such an index, it is the cost of consuming the flow of shelter services provided by a house that should be measured. This cost can be measured either as the rental equivalence or the user cost (which are the same in perfect markets with no uncertainty). The user cost approach is more appropriate in the case of housing because the rental market for detached housing is undeveloped. At time t, user cost of a given house C_t may be specified as in Eq. (13-1), where $r^e{}_t$ is the opportunity cost of equity, E_t the amount of equity, $r_t{}^m$ the mortgage interest rate, M^t the amount of mortgage, A^t the change in the house price over the period, and R_t, I_t, and P_t the expenditures on repairs, insurance, and property taxes, respectively.

$$C_t = r_t^e\, E_t + r_t^m M_t - A_t + R_t + I_t + -P_t \qquad (13\text{-}1)$$

This user cost method was used to compute the index of ownership costs in Table 13-3, which was then utilized to derive a homeowners' consumer price index. For a more complete discussion of the problems of measuring housing costs in a consumer price index, see Fallis 1980, Gillingham 1980, Loyns 1972, and McFadyen and Hobart 1978.

Despite public perception to the contrary, it is clear that neither those who have rented over the period or those who have owned have become worse off. This should be obvious without exploring the intricacies of index numbers. Real incomes have been rising, so it is highly unlikely that any enormous group such as owners or renters would have become worse off. Public outcries may partly be the pleadings of special interests and partly the result of the false idea that everyone gets worse off with inflation. Owners as a group have done somewhat better than renters at some points, but the reverse has been true at other points.[5]

Another affordability problem attracting much attention is that of young families seeking to buy their first home. Here the comparison is not of the same household at two points in time

Table 13–3. Indexes of Housing Costs and Incomes, 1962–1980 (1961 = 100)

Year	Rent Index	Ownership Index	Renters CPI	Owners CPI	Per Capita Disposable Income
1962	100.3	96.1	101.5	100 2	107.1
1967	107.1	27.9	114.3	97.4	140.3
1072	124.3	74.2	134.4	123.2	207.5
1977	157.0	315.8	204.8	234.7	406.6
1980	181.6	202.0	269.4	269.5	572.7

Source: The rent index is that used in the CPI (CMHC, various years). The ownership index was computed by creating an index from actual user costs using Eq. (13-1). Both the return on equity and the mortgage rate of interest were assumed to be the mortgage rate for that year (CMHC, various years). The Multiple Listing Service average residential transaction for Canada was used to measure house prices (correspondence with MLS). Expenditures on all other items were created using the actual 1967 expenditure of the CIP target group (correspondence, Statistics Canda) and the CIP price indices of the various components (CMHC, various years). The renters' CPI used a weight of 0.178 for housing, the owners' CPI used 0.204. Personal disposable income per capita was derived from the *Economic Review 1979.* 1980 was estimated using third-quarter data.

but, rather, of a type of household at two times. The question becomes: Is it more difficult for the young family today to buy a house than for the young family twenty years ago? As before, the relevant measure is the user cost of consuming the flow of shelter through owning a home as in Eq. (13-1.) The cost of buying the bundle of all commodities, including owned housing, purchased by a young family has not risen as much as income (Table 13–3). Today's young family is better off than its counterpart of twenty years ago.[6] Again, this is not the perception of the public. Public concern follows from comparing incomes with the mortgage payments to carry the average house. The index of mortgage carrying costs stands at a level far in excess of income gains.

The data in Table 13–3 reveal a further interesting point. The user cost of owned housing displays enormous volatility. A purchaser faces great uncertainty about the cost of acquiring shelter through ownership. At today's high house prices and high mortgage interest rates, housing will be extremely costly if house prices remain stable. If prices rise the cost falls and can even be negative. However, this cost reduction is achieved through capital gains, usually unrealized, while the mortgage must still be met. Many a prospective purchaser has said, "I cannot afford to buy a house, but then again I cannot afford not to."

This examination of affordability problems measured by comparing incomes and costs confirms the previous conclusion. The affordability problem is not a sound basis for developing housing policy. Index numbers have been misused, leading to false claims and advocacy of subsidies for homeowners and purchasers of a first home. Attention has been diverted from the real need for adjustment of the mortgage instrument. Many of the so-called affordability problems would disappear with mortgage innovation.

If society cares about the housing consumption of people, the social housing problem is an adequacy problem. If society cares about the consumption of other commodities as well as housing, this should be addressed directly, not through housing affordability measures—perhaps even so directly as to recognize that the fundamental reason for inadequate consumption of necessities is inadequate income.

THE OPTIMAL INSTRUMENTS OF HOUSING POLICY

The three steps in developing a policy described earlier are taken somewhat differently by various people and the various social sciences. The previous section discussed how policy writings of the civil service had chosen to define a housing problem. In economics, the three steps are called welfare economics. The purpose of this section is to review briefly welfare economics as it applies to housing policy and to suggest that considerable work remains before economics can offer coherent, concrete policy recommendations. The problem of an optimal housing assistance program will be discussed as an example of where such work is needed.

The analysis of welfare economics begins by identifying the conditions that hold when there is an ideal allocation of resources in a society, given some criterion for judgment.[8] Usually this criterion is specified by a social welfare function whose only arguments are the utility levels of individuals. The function embodies society's values about the fair distribution of utilities among people. Frequently, economists specify the ideal resource allocation given the Pareto optimality criterion, which does not require interpersonal utility judgments. Perhaps this is because the source of the social welfare function is unclear and because economic science cannot verify which social welfare function is correct.

Regardless of the criterion, the ideal allocation is derived without regard to the societal organization that would achieve it. Given the criterion, as well as factor endowments and technology, the necessary conditions for a maximum are derived. Then it is shown, using Adam Smith's theorem of the invisible hand, that a freely functioning market economy will yield the ideal resource allocation, provided all markets are competitive and equilibraint, there are no merit goods, there are no technological external effects, there is no uncertainty, and the distribution of factor ownership is appropriate for the social welfare maximum.[8] If even one of these conditions does not hold, private markets will not generate the social optimum and hence government action might yield an improvement. However, violation of one condition is a necessary but not sufficient condition for government intervention. The level of social welfare achieved must be shown to be higher under a given instrument of intervention than under all other instruments and higher than the situation without government. It is certainly possible that the optimal instrument will be to do nothing at all.

Welfare economics provides the normative basis for policy recommendations by economists, although interestingly, only relatively recently have economists used it as the organizing structure of their housing policy discussions.[9] This may be because there has been much public debate about the appropriate role for government after the breakdown of the consensus that existed in the 1950s and 1960s. Discussions of housing programs now are often conducted in terms of capital market failures, housing consumption externalities, or the prisoner's dilemma facing homeowners considering renovation—rather than in terms of encouraging homeownership, clearing slums, or meeting targets for annual housing production. This change has undoubtedly improved the analysis of housing policy, as evidenced in a recent major housing policy review in Canada (CMHC 1979). However, while housing economists have set out the criterion of judgment and the necessary conditions for intervention in general terms and made considerable advances in the positive analysis of markets and programs, the optimal instrument of intervention has not been carefully analyzed.[10]

As an example of how an optimal instrument should be chosen, consider the problem of housing assistance to low-income households. Numerous other issues could have served equally well. To begin, the social welfare function and necessary conditions for intervention must be set out. Welfare economics suggests three justifications for offering housing assistance. The first concerns income distribution. The social welfare function (13–2), where there are m goods, including leisure, and n households with utility functions $U_i (X_{i1}, X_{i2}, \ldots X_{im})$ where X_{ij} is consumption by the i th household of the jth good,

$$W = W [U_1(U_1(X_{11}, \ldots X_{1m}), U_2(X_{21}, \ldots X_{2m}), \ldots U_n(X_{n1}, \ldots X_{nm})]$$

$$\frac{\partial W}{\partial U_i} > 0 \qquad\qquad (13\text{–}2)$$

might indicate that reducing the utility of high-income households and raising the utility of low-income households through housing assistance yields a gain in social welfare.

The second relates to merit goods. The social welfare function (13–3) indicates that society cares not only about the utility levels achieved by households but also about the consumption by each household of the kth good, housing[11]

$$W = W [U_1(X_{11},\ldots X_{1m}), U_2(X_{21},\ldots X_{2m}),\ldots U_n(X_{n1},\ldots X_{nm},) \; X_{1k}, X_{2k},\ldots X_{nk}]$$

$$\frac{\partial W}{\partial U_1} > 0 \; ; \qquad \frac{\partial W}{\partial X_{iK}} \left\{ \begin{array}{l} = \dfrac{\partial W}{\partial U_1} \cdot \dfrac{\partial U_i}{\partial X_{iK}} \quad \text{if } X_{ik} \geq X \\[2mm] > \dfrac{\partial W}{\partial U_1} \cdot \dfrac{\partial U_i}{\partial X_{iK}} \quad \text{if } X_{ik} < X \end{array} \right. \qquad (13\text{–}3)$$

The specific functional form of the social welfare function might value, apart from the gain in utility to the consuming household, housing consumption by households up to some minimum acceptable level X.

The third justification follows from interdependent utility functions.[12] The utility of one household is influenced by the housing consumption of another household as in (13–4). This interdependence might be

$$W = W\,[U_1(X_{11},\ \ldots,\ X_{1m},\ X_{2k},\ X_{3k},\ \ldots X_{nk}),$$
$$\ldots U_n(X_{n1},\ \ldots X_{1k},\ X_{2k},\ \ldots X_{n-1k})]$$

$$\frac{\partial W}{\partial U_i} > 0\ ; \qquad \frac{\partial U_i}{\partial X_{hk}} \begin{array}{l} > 0 \quad \text{if } X_{hk} < \overline{X} \\ = 0 \quad \text{if } X_{hk} > \overline{X} \end{array} \quad \text{h} \neq \text{i} \qquad (13\text{--}4)$$

from a feeling of charity sometimes referred to as donor preferences or from any housing consumption externality. In 13-4 it has
been assumed that this interdependence does not include envy
and ceases once housing consumption has reached the acceptable
minimum.

In each case government intervention potentially may increase
the level of social welfare. A shelter allowance that taxes the rich
and provides housing at less than marginal cost to the poor might
be suggested. The reduction in the income of the rich reduces
their utility and social welfare. But this may be more than offset
by the gain in social welfare resulting either from the increase in
the utility of the poor caused by increased consumption of housing (and likely other commodities); or from this increase in the
poor's utility plus the social welfare gain from increased consumption of the merit good housing; or from this increase in the poor's
utility plus the social welfare gain because the utility of the rich
increases as the poor consume more housing.

This qualitative argument for a shelter allowance may be valid,
but it does not constitute a sufficient condition for intervention.
The optimal instrument must be chosen. Only if a shelter allowance yields higher social welfare than any alternative should it be
implemented. It is here that much work remains before producing
policy recommendations.

The notion of an optimal instrument has been used by economists when discusing shelter allowances justified by income distribution concerns. Using a simple model of consumer choice
between housing and other goods, the recipient achieves a higher
level of utility from a lump-sum cash transfer than from an
equal-cost shelter allowance. Therefore, it is argued, shelter allowances are an inefficient instrument for redistributing income;
the optimal instrument is a cash-transfer system. Unfortunately,
while the logic of the consumer choice model is correct, the policy
conclusion is wrong.

Consumers choose not only between housing and other commodities, but also between present and future consumption and between income and leisure. Furthermore, households differ in their ability to earn income (also conceivably in the utility derived from consumption), and, because this cannot be observed directly, cash transfers are provided on the basis of labor market outcomes. The amount of the cash transfer is contingent upon the income of the household. Actual cash-transfer systems are therefore not lump-sum transfers but are contingent on decisions by the household. A shelter allowance distorts choices among commodities, and a cash—transfer system distorts choices between income and leisure. Theory does not reveal one or the other as the optimal instrument, with no constraints on the social welfare function or the utility functions.

Choice of the optimal instrument requires the solution of a complex problem that cannot be presented in a two-dimentional diagram. Suppose the only rationale for intervention is income redistribution. The government seeks to maximize social welfare, Eq. (13-2), with respect to either a shelter allowance or a cash transfer. The shelter allowance sets the price of housing to the consumer, $\bar{P}_k$, below the market price P_k. A linear cash-transfer system sets the transfer to the ith household equal to a $- bp_{i1}$ $(24 - X_{i1})$ where p_{i1} is the wage rate and X_{i1} the hours of leisure of the ith household.[13] The redistribution must also be financed.

If for simplicity the financing of the system is ignored and it is assumed that there is a given amount of money R to be distributed to the designated first g households, the problem becomes as in (13-5). The government maximizes the social welfare function defined on the recipient households:

$$\text{Max } W = W\left[U_1(X_{11},...X_{1m}),...U_g(X_{g1},...X_{gm})\right] \qquad (13\text{--}5)$$

w.r.t. $\bar{p}_k, a, b$

subject to

$$\sum_{i=1}^{g} (p_k - \bar{p}_k)\, X_{ik} + \sum_{i=1}^{g} \left[a - bp_{i1}\, (24 - X_{i1})\right] \leq R.$$

$$\frac{\partial U_i}{\partial X_{i1}} = \lambda_i p_{i1}(1 - b); \quad \frac{\partial U_i}{\partial X_{ik}} = \lambda_i \bar{p}_k; \quad \frac{\partial U_i}{\partial X_{ij}} = \lambda_i p_j \text{ for all } j \neq 1, k$$

$$\bar{p}_k \, X_{ik} - p_k \, X_{ik} + \sum_{j=2}^{m} p_j x_{ij} = a + (1 - b) \, p_{i_1}(24 - b_{i_1}),$$

$$\bar{p}_k < p_k, \quad a - bp_{i_1}(24 - X_{i_1}) \geq 0.$$

The function is maximized by choosing the parameters of the transfer system subject to the available revenue constraint, the maximizing behavior of households (λ_i is the marginal utility of income of the ith household), the budget constraint of each household, and the constraint that all transfers be positive. The optimal system in general will involve both the shelter allowance and a cash-transfer system. Under certain restrictions on the social welfare and utility functions, the optimal solution can be a shelter allowance, under other restrictions a cash transfer.[14] Similiar formulations could be made of the problem with merit goods or interdependence among households.

The foregoing problem is also simplified by assuming that all producer prices P_j are unchanged by the transfer systems. This is equivalent to assuming that the supply curves of all commodities are perfectly elastic. In this world, the impact of a subsidy is the same as the incidence and there is no need to look beyond the beneficiaries to determine the change in real incomes from government action. However, supply curves are not perfectly elastic. In the short run, prices will change, some factors will enjoy quasi-rents, and others be paid less than before. In long-run general equilibrium there would be a new set of factor prices and commodity prices. The actual government problem is to maximize social welfare recognizing the changes in individual utilities caused by the long-run response to an intervention.

The intent of specifying the model in (13-5) is not to provide a solution and recommend the solution as public policy.[15] The model is mathematically complex and cumbersome despite simplification—almost to the point of unreality. Rather, the purpose is to suggest a way of thinking and the sort of research that should be part of the development of housing policy. Economists have used welfare economics to identify the rationale for intervention but have not followed its logic in choosing the instrument of intervention. A shelter allowance cannot be designed without a clear specification of the social welfare function. Different specifications, each of which could imply a housing assistance program, will yield different optimal designs. Policy anlaysis of housing assistance must recognize that actual cash—transfer systems also have welfare costs compared to a lump-sum transfer. Unfortunately most economic analysis has been devoted to a positive analysis of alternative instruments. Work on shelter allowances has sought to discover their effects on housing consumption, tenure choice, housing prices, housing rehabilitation, and so on. There has not been the parallel work on optimal policies, which in conjunction with the positive analysis permits the formulation of policy recommendations.

CONCLUDING COMMENTS

It is now a time of decision in Canadian housing policy. After a long period of increasing government intervention, an interval of restraint has begun. The programs to be adopted by governments over the next twenty years are being discussed but have not been decided. In thinking about future housing policy, two approaches are possible: one normative, which specifies what housing policy ought to be, and the other positive, which predicts what housing policy will be. This chapter's orientation is normative. It has been argued that the specification of the objective function and the design of the optimal intervention must be further developed if coherent policy is to emerge. This is true of social housing policy, as illustrated in examining the definition and measurement affordability problems and the economic analysis of housing assistance options. It is also true of two other issues that are likely to be very important in Canada over the next twenty years, the allocation of housing responsibilities and revenue-raising capabilities among the three levels of government and housing programs in times of restrictive monetary policy.

Until the middle of the 1960s, the federal government was almost alone in housing policy. During the next ten years provincial involvement grew. Provinces participated in the expanding shared-cost programs, established special-purpose housing agencies or ministries of housing, and mounted programs independently. The federal government at first resisted the change but now has tried to shift responsibilities to the provincial level. And some provinces have tried to shift them to the local level. This seems to be a political game of pass-the-deficit rather than reform based on housing priorities. A clearer assignment of responsibilities is needed, based on an optimal instruments approach. That allocation of responsibilities should be chosen that will bring Canada closest to the social welfare maximum. It is a problem of optimal government.

The Government of Canada is currently pursuing a moderately restrictive monetary policy. This is likely to continue over the next few years. The higher interest rates significantly curtail new residential construction, redistribute income away from those assuming new mortgages, and often lead to recommendations for sheltering the mortgage market. Economists have supported and rejected these suggestions but without arguments based on normative economic theory. What is required is an analysis of an optimal housing policy in the face of given monetary policy (or an optimal monetary policy). The analysis would judge monetary decisions not on the basis of their impact on inflation but rather of their impact on social welfare, including all the effects of inflation. Only then can decisions be made about sectorally specific adjustments to macroeconomic policy.

A complete study of housing issues using the normative approach of welfare economics would likely reccommend a very limited role for governments. The output markets and most markets for inputs into housing, including the mortgage market, are completitive: Both real and financial resources are efficiently allocated. Governments might provide mortgage insurance and lend to a small number of unserviced mortgage borrowers. There are undoubtedly externalities from housing consumption and interdependent utility functions in the form of donor preferences. However, these are not likely to be operative when there is an optimal distribution of income. The focus should therefore be on the redistribution of income, not on raising housing consumption. Reductions in the long-run average price of housing services might be obtainable from stabilizing construction fluctuations, and mortgage lending by governments might be part of an optimal fiscal or monetary policy.

These recommendations of what government policy should be, of course, are not a prediction of what policy will be over the next twenty years. A prediction would require a positive analysis of the process of policymaking, using public choice analysis. It is interesting to note that the federal government in Canada has dramatically curtailed its mortgage lending activities and has not extended new housing assistance, with the result that current policy is approaching the recommendations of welfare economics. This is not because of a change in attitude about the role of government in housing matters, however, but because of the need to reduce government expenditure and borrowing as part of macroeconomic policy. It proves relatively easy to restrain new housing initiatives. If Canada's macroeconomic problems were solved, government housing interventions would likely emerge again.

To change policy in the long run requires change in the behavior of the principal agents in the policy process—voters, politicians, and civil servants. Policy recommendations by economists are no doubt of influence, but significant change requires alterations in the incentives facing agents. Therefore, coherent housing policy into the twenty-first century will need both the development of the normative basis of housing policy and reform of the incentive structure in the policy process.

NOTES

1. Of course, the second step involves pure positive analysis, which could be undertaken apart from developing policy.
2. The term *social housing* is used in government documents to refer to the problems of "those households who lack the means to buy or rent housing that provides them with a reasonable standard of space and quality" (CMHC 1981).
3. Considerable difference exists between cities and between regions in the emphasis on this problem.
4. The fuller argument is clearly implicit in the initial discussion of the social housing problem in CMHC's *Background Paper on Social Housing* (1981:2) but is forgotten as the analysis proceeds.
5. A complete analysis would also include an index of returns on all assets held by owners and renters. It is unlikely to reverse the conclusion, however.
6. This analysis does not consider the problem of saving a downpayment. This has probably become more difficult because house prices have risen more than incomes. The conclusion that homeownership

has become easier that results from the user cost concept is confirmed by data showing the average age of the NHA (National Housing Act) home purchasers has fallen and showing the incidence of homeownership among households aged 25–35 has risen. Many affordability measures produce conclusions that are not consistent with market outcomes.

7. There are numerous excellent presentations of welfare economics. Layard and Walters 1978 is particularly concise and lucid.

8. This discussion assumes the criterion to be the social welfare function rather than Pareto optimality. The latter could be accommodated with few alterations.

9. For example, the welfare economic rationale for government intervention is the starting point in Smith 1978 but not in Smith 1974, and in Grigsby et. al. 1977 but not in Grigsby 1963.

10. Other fields of economics have gone from necessary conditions to optimal instrument. For example, given the technological externalities of collective consumption goods, public investment may be called for and cost/benefit analysis selects the optimal instrument. Or, given that income is to be redistributed and therefore taxes are to be levied, the optimal tax problem has been specified and solved, at least under certain conditions.

11. This formulation of a social welfare function with merit goods is discussed in Pazner 1972 and Hillman 1980. Interdependent utility functions are considered to be a type of merit good by Hillman (1980).

12. Interdependent utility functions can imply housing assistance even without using a social welfare function (Olsen 1980). The Pareto optimality criterion can require such programs. The formulation (13-4) combining interpersonal utility comparisons and interdependent utility functions seems very close to the actual situation in Canadian society.

13. The form of the shelter allowance and cash-transfer system have been arbitrarily restricted in this specification. This was done for simplicity but limits the generality of the results. The optimal tax literature shows solutions are sensitive to the array of instruments available to governments.

14. In a slightly more general model permitting transfers in kind on all commodities except leisure and a linear cash-transfer system (Fallis 1981), both in-kind and in-cash transfers were part of the optimal system.

15. Solutions to models of this sort have been derived, although not specifically in a housing context; for example see Fallis 1981, Hillman 1980, and Sandmo 1976.

REFERENCES

Canada Mortgage and Housing Corporation. 1979. *Report on Canada Mortgage and Housing Corporation*. Ottawa: CMHC.
_____. 1981. *Background Document on Social Housing*. Ottawa: CMHC.
_____. Various years. *Canadian Housing Statistics*. Housing Corporation. Ottawa: CMHC.
Fallis, G. 1980. *Housing Programs and Income Distribution in Ontario*. Toronto: University of Toronto Press for the Ontario Economic Council.
_____. 1981. "Optimal Distribution." Department of Economics Working Paper, York University, Toronto.
Gillingham, R. 1980. "Estimating the User Cost of Owner Occupied Housing." *Monthly Labour Review* 103 (February):31–35.
Grigsby, W.G. 1963. *Housing Markets and Public Policy*. Philadelphia: University of Pennsylvania Press.
Grigsby, W.G., S.B. White, D.U. Levine, R.M. Kelly, M.R. Perelman, and G.L. Claflen, Jr. 1977. *Rethinking Housing and Community Development Policy*. Philadelphia: Department of City and Regional Planning, University of Pennsylvania.
Hansard. 1973 (January 11). Ottawa: Government of Canada.
Hillman, A.L. 1980. "Notions of Merit Want." *Public Finance/Finances Publique* 35,2:213–25.
Layard, P.R.G, and A.A. Walters. 1978. *Microeconomic Theory*. New York: McGraw-Hill.
Loyns, R.M.A. 1972. *CPI and IPI as Measures of Recent Price Change*. Ottawa: Prices and Incomes Commission, Information Canada.
McFadyen, S., and R. Hobart. 1978. "An Alternative Measure of Housing Costs and the Consumer Price Index." *Canadian Journal of Economics* 11 (February):105–11.
Olsen, E.O. 1980. "Pareto-Desirable Redistribution in Kind: Comment." *American Economic Review* 70 (December):1028–30.
Pazner, E.A. 1972. "Merit Wants and the Theory of Taxation." *Public Finance/Finances Publique* 24,4:460–72.
Sandmo, A. 1976. "Optimal Taxation." *Journal of Public Economics* 6 (July-August):37–54.
Smith, L.B. 1974. *The Postwar Canadian Housing and Residential Mortgage Markets and the Role of Government*. Toronto: University of Toronto Press.
_____. 1978. "Federal Housing Programs and the Allocation of Credit and Resources." In *Government in Canada Capital Markets*. Montreal. C.D. Howe Research Institute.

14 TOWARD COHERENT U. S. HOUSING POLICIES

William Grigsby, Morton Baratz, and Duncan Maclennan

In examining housing policy, analysts usually focus on discrete, narrowly defined problems of immediate rather than longer run concern, for example, housing abandonment and the decline of unsubsidized rental construction. Such an approach to policy analysis is not only necessary, it is desirable. Since large portions of policy are quite stable, with change occurring only in small increments at the margin, frequent comprehensive policy reviews are not needed. Periodically, however, it is productive to try to review the broad sweep of policy, as did the administrations of Presidents Johnson, Nixon, and Carter. This is what the authors of the present volume have tried to do, except with resources much more limited and a focus much further into the future. Both advantages and disadvantages accrue to adopting such a long-term horizon. One advantage is that twenty years from now no one is likely to check the reasonableness of our views. A possible disadvantage is that no one today may be very interested in what we have to say, unless our forecasts depart drastically from commonly held views.

This chapter was begun with the objective of surveying the entire policy forest. As the number and variegated character of policy issues became increasingly apparent, the goal became correspondingly more realistic. The result of several attempts to

311

treat housing policy comprehensively is, therefore, more of an organization of the subject matter than a review and analysis. We now appreciate more fully why most books on housing policies, while competently done, seem so superficial.

The next three sections attempt simply to create a common ground for discussion, defining the word *policy*, taking one general meaning of the word to specify the determinants, boundaries, and content of housing policy, and outlining the foundations of U.S. housing policy to describe its characteristics today. Although these three tasks should all be straightforward, not everyone will be satisfied with all portions of the treatment. Perhaps this is to be preferred to consensus, since disagreement often leads to valuable further inquiry.

The apparent incoherence of housing policy is discussed next and questions presented that must be considered in developing a decisionmaking structure that might produce a more comprehensible set of policies and programs. Finally, current and likely future trends in several major substantive areas of policy are reviewed.

WHAT IS POLICY?

A major impediment to a comprehensive overview of U.S. housing policy is the difficulty entailed in specifying what that policy actually is. This difficulty stems in turn from different meanings assigned to *housing policy* and to *policy* itself. To avoid confusion here, we shall try to define them more precisely, even though it is not always necessary to assign a word a single meaning and a definition that is useless or misleading in one context may be very serviceable in another.

Broadly speaking, *policy* is the product of certain important decisions that set a course of action for an individual, group, or organization, thereby establishing the framework for subsequent decisions. In other words, policy decisions are high level and give general direction toward some implied or expressed objective. Various types of decisions are of a policy nature. Some policy decisions express a general posture ("benign neglect"): others specify a particular goal (elimination of substandard housing). Some create and fund organizations and institutional arrangements in furtherance of various goals. Still others prescribe fundamental rules for the conduct of personal or organizational affairs (constitutional provisions with respect to private property ownership). Finally, some are in the nature of broad strategies (neighborhood stabilization).

Program decisions, by contrast, have to do with specific ways of implementing policy. An example is the Section 312 low-interest loan program for rehabilitation, which is one programmatic way of implementing the policy of housing preservation. Most explicit decisions with regard to housing are made at the program level, the specifics of implementation. Collectively and incrementally, these specifics are often transformed into policy as well as deriving therefrom. Thus, national housing policy is the accretive product of a multitude of laws, administrative regulations, and actual administrative practices. This composite of choices may deviate rather significantly from what the U.S. Congress or the executive branch conceives policy to be. Equally, policy may emerge out of a history of nondecisions about critical issues, although some analysts prefer to view a situation in which certain courses of action are consciously or unconsciously avoided as the absence of policy. So, for example, the complaint is sometimes made that the United States has no land development policy. It is also true that not all high-level decisions are of a policy nature, in that they fail directly or indirectly to set the framework for future decisions. Still further, simply stating a goal or adopting a posture on paper is not necessarily an act of policymaking. In the words of Raymond Bauer, such pronouncements may only be "moralizing." Policy not implemented is not policy. Resources must be committed, rules enforced, and behavior changed.

This view of policy, although useful here, may not be entirely satisfactory for at least two reasons. First, some may find its scope too limited. Several analysts, for example, have conceptualized policy to include not only the kinds of choice just illustrated, but also the exercise of influence by individuals and groups, as well as societal values and customs that lie beneath and shape formal public postures toward specific conditions.

Second, because there is a goals/means/goals/means continuum running from the highest level decisions to the lowest and because policies may take the form of both goals and means, actions at a number of levels could be viewed as having a policy component. So, at the upper end of the continuum, it is not clear whether to regard certain sections of the U.S. Constitution as an integral part of housing policy or as a shaper of policy; for, by our definition, a shaper of policy is an ingredient of policy itself. Equally, at the lower end of the continuum, the dividing line between policy and programs is difficult to draw because many programs have implicit policy content.

There is no easy way around these complexities. Any single definition of policy is likely to appeal to very few, seeming too all-encompassing for some and too narrow for others. Rather than risk getting bogged down in definitional questions at the outset, it is better to leave somewhat undefined the conceptual boundaries of the term *policy* and to start instead with the embracing view described before, reducing its scope as the occasion requires.

WHAT IS HOUSING POLICY?

The boundaries, if not the substance, of housing policy can be described by reference to: (1) the purposes of public intervention in housing; (2) the housing variables that are affected by public intervention; (3) the instruments of policy (the way in which policy is made); and (4) the participants in formulation of housing policy. The objectives, variables, instruments, and responsible groups collectively constitute a rather imposing number of items to consider in trying to review housing policy as a whole (Tables 14–1 to 14–4).

Although the purpose of housing intervention is usually to affect some aspect of housing itself, the intended and actual *nonhousing* effects are frequently more central to policy discussions. Thus, housing policy decisions are commonly made with the view of preserving the natural environment, maintaining a low tax rate, equalizing access to employment and educational opportunities, redistributing income and wealth, and helping to stabilize the economy. It is rare that the pursuit of one objective is not at the expense of another.

Equally, while virtually all public intervention in housing will, by accident or design, shape policy, not all housing policy takes the form of housing interventions (Table 14–3). Just as employment objectives, for example, may be approached through housing strategies, so housing objectives may be furthered by employment and other nonhousing programs. Commitment of monies to job training, income guarantees, crime prevention, or any of a number of other social programs may, in effect, be part of housing policy. Indeed, it has often been argued that some of the most significant effects on housing have been produced as the inadvertent consequence of policies and programs aimed at quite differ-

Table 14-1.   The Purposes of Public Intervention in Housing

Ready imperfections or frictions in the functioning of housing markets—that is, improve allocative efficiency

Counteract negative spillovers (external diseconomies) engendered by individual market participants or encourage positive spillovers

Promote minimal consumptions of housing services

Produce housing-related goods and services that the private market cannot provide at a profit

Promote attainment of various nonhousing objectives, such as economic and social stability, urban fiscal health, equality of opportunity

Establish legal rights and responsibilities of buyers, sellers, and intermediaries

Table 14-2.   Housing Variables Affected by Public Intervention

Volume of new construction
Quality of existing stock and new construction
Cost, price, and quality of housing services
Type of tenure
Density
Building type, style, and size
Type of rate of occupancy
Level of upkeep
Location of housing and households
Neighborhood environment
Rights and responsibilities of consumers, suppliers, and market intermediaries

ent problems. The U.S. highway program is probably the most commonly cited example.

With so much of housing policy implicit and indirect, there is a natural tendency to center attention on only its most visible features. This leads in turn to greater emphasis in most policy discussions (at least in academia) on immediate questions having to do with *what* should be done and how—that is, policy and program effectiveness—rather than on the longer term issue of *who* should decide *what* to do—that is, the distribution of responsibilities for setting courses of action (Table 14–4). Yet historically, the hottest housing policy debates in the United States have

Table 14–3.   How Housing Policy Is Made

Creation of organizations and agencies to deal with various housing problems

Commitment of resources to various housing problems

Legislative and judicial decisions specifying rights and responsibilities of housing actors

Land-use decisions

Commitment of resources to the resolution of housing-related problems

Commitment of resources to programs that encourage private investment of housing

Program design

Cumulative effect of administrative decisions

Income tax and real estate tax legislation

Inaction

Table 14–4.   Participants in Formulation of Housing Policy

Legislative branches of the several levels of government

Administrative agencies at each level of government

Judiciary

Private groups with quasi-public powers

Private sector, through its direct and indirect influence on public officials and through its acceptance or rejection of policy initiatives

---

stemmed from sharply conflicting views over the appropriate housing roles for the federal, state, and local governments and private business. Political philosophy has permeated most housing policy proposals, and the contours of policy in nearly every major country have been shaped by the relative permanence of much of the structure of power.

THE FOUNDATION AND SPECIFICS OF U.S. HOUSING POLICY

Social systems and individual persons alike are in a genuine sense prisoners of their heritage—which is to say, of the established norms, values, beliefs, myths, institutions, and procedures that characterize the environment into which they are born and grow up. To be sure, all these elements of a culture can and do change over time, but except in rare circumstances, the rate of change is slow at most. In part that is because most human beings cling to the known until it seems intolerable to persons and groups who benefit most (or think they benefit most) from things as they are and go to great lengths to preserve and promote the predominant ideology, institutions, and rules of the game. In order to understand U.S. housing policy, therefore, we must look first to its foundations—the fundamental values that are widely, if not universally, shared in the United States and that are systematically promoted through indoctrination of all persons from an early age. To catalogue fully the predominant value system would require much more space than can be spared here. A few examples particularly germane to housing policy must suffice:

1. The primary responsibility for each family's social and economic well-being resides with that family.
2. Every American should enjoy relatively equal opportunity in education and employment, but there can be no guarantee of relatively equal outcomes for all. To the contrary, that result is ruled out on the principle that merit (somehow defined) ought to be rewarded appropriately.
3. Although unequal outcomes among individuals are condoned in principle as well as in practice, and although none is owed a living, neither should any American be permitted to live in

utter squalor. Some minimal standard of decency in material condition of life should be assured to all, both as a matter of elemental justice and to negate the adverse "third-party" or "spillover" effects of individuals' poverty.

4. Although all who are in dire need must be helped, some deserve less help than others. The distinction between the deserving and undeserving is drawn primarily by reference to the seeming cause or causes for their plight. The aged, the disabled, the displaced are seen as deserving because their plight stems from circumstances beyond their own control. Those considered to be lazy or depraved, by contrast, have little or no legitimate claim upon society's largesse.

One need not be an expert in federal housing policy to recognize how fully these and associated propositions are reflected in housing legislation. They also go far to explain why certain policies in effect elsewhere in the world have not even reached the political agenda in the United States, let alone become coursesetting choices.

In addition to growing out of the values of the kind just listed, housing policy is built on a set of institutions that significantly determine which latent or actual demands for change in the established distribution of benefits and privileges will become political issues and which will not; which will or will not enter the decisionmaking arena; which will be agreed to and which rejected; and which of those agreed to will be implemented fully, partially, or not at all. Two such institutions, the market economy and private-property ownership, particularly fit this description in the United States. Their presence establishes a powerful presumption in favor of private, rather than governmental supply of housing services. With few exceptions, federal housing policy in the United States is carried out not by supplanting the market system but by changing the market conduct of private entrepreneurs through a system of incentives and disincentives. Similarly, policies that would reduce the rights of property owners to use or dispose of their real property are strongly resisted even in circumstances where the preponderance of those immediately affected would much prefer otherwise.

In addition to growing out of the values of the kind just listed, housing policy is built on a set of institutions that significantly determine which latent or actual demands for change in the established distribution of benefits and privileges will become political issues and which will not; which will or will not enter the decisionmaking arena; which will be agreed to and which rejected; and which of those agreed to will be implemented fully, partially, or not at all. Two such institutions, the market economy and private-property ownership, particularly fit this description in the United States. Their presence establishes a powerful presumption in favor of private, rather than governmental supply of housing services. With few exceptions, federal housing policy in the United States is carried out not by supplanting the market system but by changing the market conduct of private entrepreneurs through a system of incentives and disincentives. Similarly, policies that would reduce the rights of property owners to use or dispose of their real property are strongly resisted even in circumstances where the preponderance of those immediately affected would much prefer otherwise.

The relation between public policy and the key institutions can be seen from a slightly different perspective. In the American setting, government's role is to remedy the deficiencies generated by the market system and private ownership of property, to correct its specific errors of commission or omission. It does not set the pace; rather, it countervails. For instance, it provides subsidies to low-income households because the market mechanism inherently generates an unequal distribution of income. Government also provides stimuli to new construction if the volume of private construction falls below the level at which housing resources are fully employed. Equally, it subsidizes urban redevelopment only in the absence of private initiative in that direction.

Interwoven into the institutional framework is a set of procedures, rules of the game, some of them merely established practices, others embodied in statutes or case law. Included are such things as the mutual obligations of landlords and tenants, brokers and customers, lenders and borrowers, and so on. These rules, too, help to shape or determine federal housing policy. For many years, as a notorious example, the Federal Housing Administration condoned racial segregation of housing markets and "red lining" of certain districts by financial intermediaries. Similarly, housing policy is affected by the expressed and tacit rules of federalism, rules that set limits upon what the federal government may and may not do, in contradistinction to states and municipal governments. To illustrate, while it is within the ken of the federal government to pursue a strategy of stimulating and maintaining a continually high level of new construction, the law carefully leaves to lower levels the formulation and enforcement of zoning, building, and health codes.

Although these values and institutions set the perimeter within which housing and other policies must be confined, the boundaries are far from permanently fixed. Values and institutions do change through time. Moreover, within the boundaries there is typically much room for choice among competing courses of action. There tends to be inconsistencies or conflicts among and between predominant values, beliefs, institutions, and rules, as well as gaps between what is believed and what is practiced. When these disjunctures are forcefully pointed up, as was the case with respect to the civil rights of racial minorities and women during the 1960s and 1970s, policy may change materially.

Turning from the foundations of U.S. housing policy to the specifics, we are faced with a descriptive task of some enormity. So many different parts of the public sector have become involved with various aspects of housing, and such a large amount of policy is implicit and can only be inferred from a myriad of laws, regulations, and programs, it seems doubtful if any two persons could describe U.S. housing policy in exactly the same way. Each would emphasize different aspects and levels of policy, and their respective interpretations would often not coincide. To bring some order to the discussion, it is useful to distinguish between the distribution of responsibility for making policy and the policies themselves.

Decision Structure of Policy

The housing production and distribution "system" in the United States can be viewed as a huge decentralized organization with various rights and responsibilities for making housing decisions, spread broadly among builders, developers, owner-occupants, landlords, tenants, real estate brokers, lenders, borrowers, various federal, state, local, and regional agencies, and most parts of the judiciary.

The extent of decentralization is not uniform across the system. Decisions concerning housing finance and civil rights, for example, are much more centralized than are matters involving building codes and land subdivision. Moreover, there is a constant tension between the forces of centralization and decentralization, resulting in continual movement of decisionmaking powers up, down, and across the organizational hierarchy. Nevertheless, the particular federal system of government in the United States and the ineluctable local nature of housing markets provide some limits to the amount of centralization or decentralization that can occur.

One virtually inevitable consequence of decentralization is much greater complexity, contradiction, and apparent incoherence among programs and policies than is likely in a command economy. An attempt to capture some of the flavor of this complexity is Table 14–5, which lists the various ways in which federal, state, and local governments are involved in different aspects of housing. Extensive as the list is, it excludes a number of important forms of indirect involvement and omits the activities of regional agencies, quasi-public organizations, and the judiciary. Most important, it does not speak directly to the decision structure of policy, since the precise nature of the listed activities is not described and the distribution of responsibility for their design is not indicated.

Many of the policy and program contradictions arise from conflicting objectives within and among the several levels of government. The conflicts among levels of government are especially apparent. The federal government has tried to perform functions that state and local governments have largely ignored, and it does not trust the lower levels of government to pursue national objectives. The lower levels meanwhile share a belief that the federal bureaucracy is a heavy-handed intruder that uses the largesse of federal grants to change local behavior from an otherwise preferred pattern. These sources of latent or actual conflict often place the federal government in an almost adversarial relationship with state and local governments. Federal housing policy is shaped to a considerable extent, therefore, by the clear recognition that its full implementation is considerably dependent upon the collaboration of the other levels of government. A prime example of the effects of noncollaboration is the public housing pro-

Table 14–5. Ways in Which the Public Sector Is Involved Directly in Housing

Type of Involvement	Local	Sector of Government	
		State	National
Regulatory	Housing codes	All powers granted to local government: e.g., zoning, subdivision	Supervision of some classes of mortgage lender
	Building codes	Mortgage law and supervision of lenders	Labor laws
	Zoning and subdivision regulations	Usury laws	Interstate land sales act
	Landlord/tenant law	Real estate brokerage law and supervision	Civil rights laws and regulations
	Civil rights law	Civil rights law	Environmental protection laws
	Environmental laws	Agricultural protection laws	Laws governing all cases of lenders, e.g., truth-in-lending
	Rent control (some localities)	Building codes (a few states)	Housing codes (as these relate to federal programs)
	Nuisance laws	Environmental protection laws	OSHA
		Title insurance law (some states)	Building code for manufactured homes
		Landlord/tenant laws	Energy code for building
		Other laws concerning contracts and real property	
		Supervision of public utilities	

Taxation and eminent domain	Real estate tax Sew charges Eminent domain Tax exemption on new construction (some localities) Nuisance taxes	Real estate transfer tax Laws governing real estate tax (e.g. homestead exemptions, ad valorem, etc.) Housing treatment in state income tax law Eminent domain	Treatment of housing and land in internal revenue code Eminent domain (rarely used in housing)
Housing and housing related services provided directly	Power and light (some localities) Water, garbage collection (sometimes provided privately) Street, sewer, fire, police	Research and planning Direct loan programs at market interest rates New towns Mortgage insurance programs	Research on building technology, market conditions, etc. Mortgage insurance and guarantee Secondary market for mortgage loans Advances to mortgage lenders Home construction in special situations
Housing and Housing Related Subsidy Programs	Public housing Direct loan programs Neighborhood redevelopment and renewal Homesteading	Enabling legislation for federal programs Direct loan programs Neighborhood development subsidies Rent component of public assistance	Public housing Section 8, 235 Community development block grants Aid for elderly and handicapped Planning grants

gram, which two decades after its inception had still not been able to reach into every state and was anathema in a large number of communities. The Carter administration tried to eliminate the adversarial relationship by creating an "urban partnership." While laudable, the attempt served only to highlight the fundamental nature of the conflicting positions, for the proposed partnership agreement placed state and local government in a clearly subordinate position.

The Substance of U.S. Housing Policy

Analysts seem to find it far easier to prescribe what the substance of U.S. housing policy should be than to describe what it actually is. Why this is so is not clear. It may be because, as mentioned before, prescriptions usually apply at the margin while description must explore the interior as well. Also, although it is comparatively easy to present in great detail what different parts of the public sector do in the area of housing, synthesizing these details into policy statements that are precise, accurate, and sufficiently descriptive requires some imagination.

The reader is asked to participate in a simple exercise illustrating the problem. The following paragraphs describe in outline what appear to be key features of U.S. housing policy with respect to six major housing goals. Before reading our description, jot down your own and note the lack of correspondence between yours and ours. After reading the entire list of key features presented here, also ask yourself whether you might have organized a description of U.S. housing policy in a quite different fashion. This is not exactly a fair test of our point, since it is conceivable that after everyone's preferred descriptions had been compared, it would be possible to move toward consensus around a composite picture. Even the fact that such an exercise would probably be required, however, is indicative of the difficulties involved in agreeing on what should be called housing policy and then ferreting it out.

1. *A decent home and suitable living environment for every American family at an affordable price.* This objective has been pursued through a variety of housing programs at all levels of government (subsidies, code enforcement, etc.) and it is these pro-

grams that are usually described in policy analyses relating to the objective. Discussions emphasize cost-effectiveness of various approaches, the gradual shift from supply- to demand-side programs, the increasing importance given to neighborhood improvement, and the changing standards of affordability and decency, among other things. But at a different level, policy with respect to the stated objective can be described quite differently, stressing that despite the plethora of subsidy programs created over the years to further the objective, only about one-seventh of all lower income households receive housing subsidies to obtain decent shelter. This fact suggests that the implicit policy being applied to achieve the objective is general economic growth, that is, promotion of rising living levels for all Americans. The federal government has assumed the major responsibility in this area, a few state governments have also made major efforts, and a large proportion of local governments are either indifferent to the objective or positively opposed to it. This opposition, in fact, is a major influence shaping the federal effort.

2. *Choice of tenure.* Although some policy analyses stress the promotion of owner-*occupancy* in federal housing programs and the federal tax structure, it could be argued that, in effect, it is owner-*occupants* who are favored, not owner-occupancy, since the vast majority of households who purchase a home would do so even in the absence of the federal incentives, and since the incentives themselves are least attractive to the income groups at the margin between owner-occupancy and renting. Regardless of whether this is true, it raises an interesting question as to how to describe policy when its purposes and consequences are in conflict with each other. If government announces objective A and genuinely tries to achieve it with program X but instead achieves result B, should policy be described with respect to the actual or intended result?

3. *Lower housing costs through greater market efficiency.* Policy in this area is rather complex. At the federal level, the general presumption has been that housing costs are higher than they should be because of various types of market inefficiency. Federal intervention, however, has been quite selective, focusing primarily on housing finance. The efficiency of the homebuilding industry has been left largely to others. Nevertheless, as early as the 1920s, under the leadership of then Secretary of Commerce Herbert

Hoover, the federal government took an interest in modernizing building codes, and through sponsorship of research in building technology, it has continued to do so to this day. More recently the federal government has focused on counteracting market inefficiencies in the purchase and sale of homes and in land development.

At the local level, concern over housing costs and market efficiency has, if anything, been quite the opposite. Local regulations with respect to homebuilding, zoning, and subdivision have introduced inefficiencies that appear to have no offsetting social benefits. To describe policy accurately in this area the offsetting federal and local postures have somehow to be blended and policy's effects, such as the steady intrusion of manufactured homes into the picture, have to be taken into account.

4. *Broader locational choice for lower income households.* Although this objective has been explicitly recognized in federal legislation since 1974 and although rhetoric about the objective's importance may lead to the belief that it enjoys broad support, actual policy, as measured by resource commitment and related indicators of effort, reflects minimal enthusiasm at any level of government. This is in part because large subsidies per family are required in order to create locational opportunities for households in neighborhoods outside traditional low-income areas. Additionally, questions regarding scale of dispersal of various types of low-income households for the purpose of achieving different societal objectives have never been more than casually addressed, thus leaving great uncertainty about what priority the objective will or should be given.

5. *Maintaining an adequate volume of residential construction.* For several decades an assumption of U.S. housing policy has been that the residential construction industry has a chronic tendency to produce fewer dwellings than the nation requires to house an expanding population. Various devices to stimulate homebuilding have been used to compensate for this tendency, and at times the volume of subsidized construction has been quite large. There has never been an agreement, however, about how to measure the amount of "needed" construction. As a result, there also has never been agreement about when a fundamental (as opposed to a cyclical) shortfall in production exists. Further, there is disagreement about the relative efficiency and equity of differ-

ent devices designed to cause an expansion in the number of dwelling units constructed. For example, because new construction subsidies for moderate- and middle-income households may be comparatively shallow, they can be spread over a larger number of recipients than new-construction subsidies to low-income households. However, they help families who need no assistance to be decently housed and have been shown to add inappreciably to the amount of construction that would occur anyway. By contrast, new construction subsidies for low-income households are faulted for failing, because of the depth of the subsidy per recipient, to expand construction significantly at modest public cost and for providing just a few lucky households with vastly more assistance than is necessary to raise their housing welfare to acceptable standards. In view of the disagreement about the required annual volume of production and because of inherent deficiencies in any type of subsidy that could be used to expand construction, federal policy with respect to the extent and kind of support to be given the homebuilding industry has understandably vacillated considerably over the years. Barring some dramatic resolution of the sources of dispute, it will probably continue to do so, even though it seems unlikely that direct or indirect subsidy support will be withdrawn entirely.

6. *Reducing racial discrimination and de facto segregation.* Policy in this area is quite contradictory. Two very different objectives are being pursued simultaneously. The Civil Rights Act of 1968 and related Supreme Court decisions have addressed *discrimination.* Although this kind of behavior persists in housing markets, the federal government has been serious in its efforts to give meaning to the law, so considerable progress toward color-blind housing markets has been made. The federal judiciary, however, has ruled that the absence of discriminatory practices is not enough and that *de facto segregation* is also undesirable (Shannon v. U.S. Department of Housing and Urban Development 436F. 2nd 809 (3rd Cir. 1970)). Some of the school busing decisions handed down by federal courts also seem implicitly to take this view. Pursuant to the Shannon decision, the Department of Housing and Urban Development (HUD) expended much effort to promote racial mixture among beneficiaries of programs under its control. Currently, however, this thrust has weakened perceptibly because of doubts about the conclusions in Shannon that de

facto residential segregation is necessarily undesirable and that it is a condition that the federal government is obliged to address.

Can U.S. Housing Policy Be Understood?

Although the preceding descriptions serve a useful purpose, they provide no historical perspective and leave too many unanswered questions about U.S. housing policy. Why, for example, does the federal government involve itself in certain housing problems much more extensively than in others the same in character or severity? To illustrate, why has it created a national energy code for homebuilders and a national building code for manufactured homes, while steadfastly refusing to develop a national health and safety code for existing housing? Similarly, why was Congress ready to tackle all of the housing problems of lower income households in 1968 but not in 1978? And why does Congress authorize housing subsidies for moderate-income households when it has barely touched the low-income sector? In the Section 8 rental-assistance program, which is a response in part to concern over horizontal equity, why does it resist universal entitlement? Each of these questions and others in a similar vein can, of course, be answered by reference to some valid and familiar hypothesis such as budgetary constraints, the separation of powers among levels of government, or the prevailing political climate. Nevertheless, we harbor the suspicion that the particularities conceal as much as they reveal, that there is some overarching framework into which the individual explanations and the several policies themselves may be integrated.

Two models of political behavior deserve serious consideration in this connection. The first one, already mentioned earlier, devolves around the established norms, institutions, and procedures—backed where thought necessary by nondecisions—conspire to preclude action upon certain proposed policy charges or, at the least, to limit the extent of change. Almost certainly, for example, congressional resistance to the universal entitlement of low-income households to direct housing subsidies is grounded upon and therefore primarily explained by reference to the established social beliefs that only some in the low-income cohort are "deserving." The second model of political behavior is "disjointed incrementalism"—muddling through. Disjointed incrementalism in housing policy formulation is exemplified in the frequent modification of policy in discrete and ill-connected steps at the margin rather than in one fell swoop. The policymaking process through time is characterized by trial and error (and still further trial) of one approach after another.

These two models are complementary, not competing explanations. Values and institutions combined to circumscribe the kinds of change that may be applied incrementally; for example, the conventions that preclude universal entitlement to housing subsidies dictate that the form of the subsidies may be altered, but not their scope or coverage. Conversely, however, through the process of disjointed incrementalism, institutions may be gradually modified and the way thereby opened to the adoption of policies or programs hitherto out of the question. As an illustration, demand-side subsidies in housing were almost unthinkable in the early 1930s, but forty years later became socially acceptable in light of the perceived failure of various supply-side interventions that were attempted sequentially.

DESIGNING A DECISION STRUCTURE FOR HOUSING POLICY

Speculating either normatively or positively about housing policies for the twenty-first century might appear at first glance to be a fruitless exercise. Who in 1929, '39, '49, '59, or '69 could have accurately predicted conditions in the subsequent decade to which the public sector would have to respond? Or if able to predict correctly, who would have been listened to? On the other hand, recognition of the inability to predict accurately is helpful in thinking about policies for the future. As mentioned earlier, there are several layers of policy, among which the less visible layers often are the most basic and least subject to manipulation, the ones that give the necessary continuity and stability to policy generally. Most policy discussions, because they are concerned with immediate problems, focus on the most variable aspects of policy. The farther we project into the future, however, the more aspects that can be considered amenable to change. Looking into the twenty-first century, therefore, we need assume only that the fundamental policy structure set by the key institutions—chiefly, the private-property system and the market economy—will remain intact.

The first layer of policy below that dealing with substantive housing issues is the decisionmaking apparatus. The key question with respect to this machinery is whether in light of the present distribution of rights and responsibilities for making important housing decisions it is likely or unlikely that the public sector will respond quickly, appropriately, and effectively to changing, largely unanticipated conditions over time. It is somewhat artificial, of course, to suggest by reference to layers of policy that policy substance is entirely derivative, and not at all a determinant, of the decision structure. Individually and cumulatively, decisions regarding substance affect the shape of the policy apparatus. Nevertheless, different organizational arrangements yield different outcomes. Hence with a time horizon of twenty years to work with, it is reasonable to ask if and how present organizational arrangements should be changed in order to produce more efficient and equitable housing policies and programs. We address these two questions, considering first whether it is accurate to characterize present policy as incoherent and, if so, to attribute incoherence to the policymaking apparatus; and second, what issues must be confronted when modifying or redesigning the apparatus.

The Inevitability of Incoherence

A major criticism of the present public decisionmaking machinery in housing is that it produces policies and programs that collectively are so numerous, overlapping, conflicting, and complex as to be incomprehensible; and that the incomprehensibility increases each year as more and more public agencies discover new problems in housing to which they wish to give their attention. In the area of neighborhood revitalization alone there were twelve different federal assistance programs in early 1981, all financed at a very low level but all requiring separate bureacracies with which city and neighborhood groups must deal.

If the present structure has indeed resulted in policies and programs that are poorly understood by thoses who instated them, many of the policies and programs are probably seriously misdirected. For although coherent policy can also be misguided, it seems almost impossible for incoherent policy to produce admirable results. There is a question, though, about how one can verify that contradictions and incomprehensibility are indeed present in serious proportions. Policy may appear to be unintelligible only to those who are not close enough to the policy apparatus to understand the intricacies of policy formation. There may be hidden logic to apparent contradiction. Beyond that, terms like incoherence and incomprehensibility do nothing to clarify assessments of whether policies and programs are deficient because collectively they are beyond understanding or because individually they fail to address adequately the problems they are intended to resolve. In both cases bad policy may be said to stem from something wrong in the policymaking apparatus, but if policies are individually deficient the fault may lie instead with poor analysis of the problem being addressed.

Regardless of the coherence or incoherence of U.S. housing policies and programs, the present decisionmaking process at the federal level does seem to have mired Congress and the executive branch in an inordinate amount of program detail, making it virtually impossible for adequate attention to be given to policy and programs design and assessment. The problem is compounded, as others have noted, by the fact that elected officials receive more political points for legislating new programs than for monitoring existing ones.

The opportunity costs of the present system seem especially high. Beyond the direct administrative burden of perhaps 15 percent or so for every program, there is an additional cost of exercising supervision in general. HUD, other housing agencies, the Office of Management and Budget, the General Accounting Office, the Congressional Budget Office, the Library of Congress, and congressmen and their staffs are all engulfed in this process. Beyond these costs are those incured by local and state government and nonprofit groups implementing federal programs, interest groups who prepare informational material and testify at congressional hearings, contestants in law suits developing out of housing legislation, those engaged in independent scholarly evaluations of programs, and ordinary citizens who attend countless neighborhood meetings at their own expense in order that their communites may receive a small bundle of federal cash. Perhaps the greatest opportunity cost of all, however, is the consequences, whatever they are, that flow from the inability of members of congress, their staff, and high-level persons in the executive branch to focus the bulk of their time on issues of greatest national and international importance.

The appropriate response to such a situation seems to be for the federal government to get out of as much of the housing business as possible and to "streamline" the programs it retains. Essentially, this is the posture of those who are in the philosophical camp of Milton Friedman, and certainly this has been the objective of both the Nixon and Reagan administrations. The essential objective would be to cease using housing policy for income redistribution and have it concentrate on increasing market efficiency.

The barriers to achievement of coherence through this or any other approach are, however, formidable. The most significant ones merit mention:

1. With respect to many housing matters, the federal government is all too often in a adversary situation with local government. To cite one example, since localities can to a considerable degree influence the location, structural characteristics, price, and quantity of dwelling units built in their jurisdictions, the federal government cannot unthinkingly presume that the private market will produce the optimum amount and mix of dwellings. Chronic underdevelopment in some local housing markets is a theoretical possibility. Worded more broadly, even though a free housing market, somehow defined, may be in some respects superior to a guided one, reducing the amount of federal involvement in housing will not necessarily increase market freedom and might easily reduce it.

2. Housing policy is profoundly affected by other kinds of national policy—monetary and fiscal, welfare, transportation, civil rights — so it is impossible for federal agencies to ignore the fact that the housing sector is constantly being buffeted by actions taken throughout almost all parts of the public sector.

3. Continuously changing conditions and problems require the passage of time to be understood and dealt with; hence at any one time policies and programs are often out of tune with

prevailing conditions, and new approaches often conflict with old ones that are still in place.

4. For long periods of time views may conflict about the nature of the problem being observed, frequently causing policy to ride two horses at once. This was true of British housing policy during most of the nineteenth century.

5. The public sector commonly tries to achieve multiple housing objectives for diverse interest groups. Although simultaneous pursuit of these objectives may be possible without the emergence of contradiction and conflict, that result seems unlikely if only because competition among objectives and among groups with sharply divergent political philosophies must at some point produce compromises that are neither fish nor fowl.

6. Since legislators are inclined to deal with emerging problems on a somewhat ad hoc basis, and since they cannot avoid problems brought to their attention, and since the greater the public involvement the more time must be spent correcting mistakes resulting from this public involvement, there is an almost natural tendency for complexity to increase. To paraphrase a popular organizational principle, the federal government extends its activities until it reaches or exceeds its own perimeter of incompetence.

Because policy is made at three levels of government and in three branches of government and in several different places within each level and each branch; and because policy is also made in the private sector; and because people at all of these various locations in the system have different perceptions of housing problems, different responsibilities, different objectives, and different constituencies—because of all of this, there is bound to be incoherence and contradiction. It is reasonable to believe that the decentralization that is sought in order to simplify things at the federal level would be helpful in certain respects but also might introduce greater complexity and contradiction in the system as a whole.

Toward a New Decision Structure for Policy

Because of these serious organizational obstacles to a more cogent and manageable corpus of housing policy, a focus on the decisionmaking structure of policy seems especially worthwhile. Here, it is possible only to outline a few of the questions that deserve to be explored. Admittedly, this is the easy part, but specifying the questions may help to illustrate the nature of the task.

First of all, what are the housing issues and problems of truly compelling national concern with which Congress and the executive branch should exclusively or at least primarily concern themselves? For instance, the overriding of the federal interest in civil rights is beyond question, but may the same be said about inclusion of neighborhood revitalization on the national agenda? In the same general vein, under what circumstances should the federal government concern itself with the proportion of gross national product going into housing, with the effect of the volume of housing production on the rest of the economy, with the distribution of housing investment and consumption among various population subgroups, with the effect of fluctuations in the volume of construction on the housing industry, with the first-time homebuyer, and so on? Could widely accepted criteria be developed that would help the federal government decide whether and how to accept responsibility for housing problems that are thrust upon it by various interest groups?

Second, what is the likelihood of obtaining a "responsible" decision, with respect to particular types of problems at various levels of government, in the judiciary, and in the private sector? Local land-use controls are a frequently cited example of irresponsibility, in the sense that they poorly reflect the wishes of those whom they affect. Even though recommendations to eliminate these controls in their present form have surfaced off and on for over twenty years, state governments have been loath to override local powers and preferences. So the federal government can only work around the controls. The upshot often is that public, private and intergovernmental disputes end up in the courts, which means much of the nation's housing policy is determined by the judiciary. Can the decisionmaking structure be altered so as to make the interests of lower level units more nearly consonant with those at upper levels? Are there or can there be created appropriate institutional mechanisms at each level to deal with various aspects of housing problems?

Third, what is the likelihood of obtaining a *competent* decision in various parts of the U.S. federal system? The judiciary is usually responsible, but many of its decisions (such as Shannon v. HUD), are poorly grounded in the real world's verities. In the bureaucratic sphere, part of housing policy at the federal level under both Democratic and Republican administrations has been designed for the purpose of "capacity building" at the local level, that is, enlarging the pool of technical expertise, in order that more responsibilities can be decentralized. In this regard what sorts of technical support are best kept centralized at the state or federal level and what functions should be assigned to a growing corp of experts in local governments?

Fourth , going a little beyond the decision structure itself, what signals does the federal government need to determine if certain housing conditions, say, a decline in unsubsidized rental production or housing abandonment or decline of inner-city neighborhoods, should be viewed negatively, positively, or neutrally? What mechanisms are required to assure that the signals are received and interpreted more quickly? To cite a case in point, HUD is currently engaged in a pilot effort to obtain greater detail about housing characteristics so Congress and others will know more precisely the ways in which dwelling-unit quality is changing over time. Since these data bear no necessary relation to the problems presumed to stem from poor housing quality and in which Congress is primarily interested, they are likely to result in a flood of signals not relevant to policy.

Finally, to abridge the discussion, what sorts of organizational arrangements are likely to foster innovation and adaptation, pride in one's residential surroundings, various types of efficiency and equity, and specific housing and housing-related objectives such as broader locational choice, income/class integration, and, yes, coherence?

FUTURE TRENDS IN THE SUBSTANCE OF POLICY

It is extremely difficult to forecast what policy will or should be twenty years hence, because prediction of conditions so far into the future is virtually impossible. That statement must now be qualified. Parts of housing policy, particularly in the area of housing finance and civil rights, have evolved in a somewhat predictable way. Many other parts have been predictable to those who were closely associated with the problems involved.

So perhaps one or two guesses, however venturesome, are worth attempting. One way of doing so is by trying to relate emerging and already popular policy ideas to the conditions they address in order to see if the policies are still relevant. That kind of approach anticipated the decline of public housing many years before the decline occurred. It might have predicted the sudden disappearance of housing production goals after the zenith of their popularity in late 1960s and early 1970s. It has no magic properties but perhaps is as good a way to proceed as any.

The major policy idea in good currency today, though it is still controversial, is housing allowances. Will it become the center-piece of low-income housing policy in the twenty-first century, as the President's Commission on Housing and others think it should, or by then will it have given way to something else?

Numerous questions have been raised with respect to al-lowances—whether there should be universal or limited entitle-ment; why assistance should be tied to occupancy of a standard unit; whether tying a program of upgrading and maintenance to the real estate tax system would be more or less efficacious; what the effect of allowances is on rents, residential mobility, and new construction—to name a few. Allowances do appear to have one major advantage over other subsidy approaches, however; they lead housing policy toward greater simplicity and coherance. Nev-ertheless, by the year 2001 or so, allowances are likely to have become a part of history.

The basis for this belief can perhaps be most clearly summa-rized by reference to an imaginary spectrum of possible housing conditions ranging from one extreme, in which all low-income households live in seriously substandard dwelling units, to the op-posite extreme, in which all such households reside in acceptable accommodations. In the former situation, allowances have gener-ally been presumed to be inappropriate because movement of a large number of allowance recipients out of these units would cre-ate undue pressure on rents and prices. In the latter situation—absence of substandard housing—allowances would be unneces-sary, thus also inappropriate, unless housing objectives other than universal occupancy and decent shelter were being sought.

Housing allowances may have a place somewhere along the spectrum, but where? Where, relative to the "optimal" place, are the present housing situations of various metropolitan areas around the country? And how would combinations of allowances and other programs differ at different points on the spectrum? We have no clear idea. It appears, though, that allowances are at most an interim solution. As substandard housing is gradually eliminated through economic progress, normal losses of dwellings from the standing stock, and the contribution of housing programs themselves, the decent-housing requirements of the allowance will become ever more superfluous. As this happens, federal government should be able to shift the responsibility for maintenance of housing standards to the local level, permitting the gradual transformation of the housing allowance into a more general income supplement. And as the argument for tying receipt of an income subsidy to occupancy of standard housing becomes less and less compelling, the argument for truly universal entitlement becomes more so. This situation may already have been reached in many communities. The disappearance of housing allowances will not mean the disappearance of housing assistance. Special situations and particular groups will be attended to through targeted efforts redolent of the now unpopular categorical grant approach.

Turning to other trends, possibly more out of hope than reason, we expect race to become a much less important market variable. The year 2001 may not seem far enough away to permit significant racial progress to be achieved. Looking backward an equal number of years, however, one can recall that those arguing at the time for equal housing rights for blacks were a small minority and expected a much longer battle than actually ensued. What will keep race from disappearing almost entirely from the housing picture is the concentration of poverty among minorities, a much more intractable problem. Because of this concentration, neighborhood issues will continue to remain conspicuous and will shape policy accordingly.

Policy trends in two other current areas of concern—limited locational choice for lower income households living in large metropolitan areas and perceived chronic underproduction of dwelling units by homebuilding industry—seem totally beyond prediction. It is not unlikely that stable policy postures in these two areas will have emerged by the turn of the century, but we can only guess at what they might be.

Policy predictions could be couched more generally with reference to the two broad goals of efficiency and equality. Taking this approach, it seems fair to say that from roughly 1933 to 1969 various forms of equality were more dominant concerns in housing than was efficiency. This dominance was, of course, not complete. Promotion of greater efficiency in housing finance markets, for example, was a continuing theme. But efficiency was of second-order policy importance. Since about 1969 efficiency (and productivity) have moved to the top of the agenda, to no small extent because the worst aspects of inequality in housing are being eradicated. Some forecasters anticipate that another twenty to twenty-five years will elapse before the efficiency emphasis begins to subside. If so, relatively limited attention might be expected to the residul housing problems that still remain. Were this to be the case it would be most unfortunate. For although it is true that the United States has achieved an enviable record of housing progress over the last fifty years, the size of the residual is depressingly large. There is no country with a similar level and distribution of income that has a comparable proportion of its population living in bad physical environments. The contrast between the United States and Canada is especially instructive in this regard. And even several poorer countries lack the slums characteristic of parts of urban America. A truly coherent policy addressing all of the dimensions and causes of housing problems is likely not to permit this fact to be submerged by other pressing issues even in the coming age of austerity.

15 PANEL DISCUSSION ON GOVERNMENT HOUSING POLICY

JOHN C. WEICHER, CHAIRMAN

Some years ago I represented the United States at a housing conference sponsored by the U.N. Economic Commission for Europe. At the end of the conference, a Swiss delegate, who had spent some time studying American housing, asked me if there was any country represented whose housing problems were close enough to ours so that we had a common frame of reference for policy discussions. He expected that I would have to say no. But in the course of the conference, a different answer had gradually become clear: There was *one* delegation — the Canadians.

We seem to have very similar policy concerns on both sides of the forty-ninth parallel. Moreover, we recommend very similar solutions as well. Before I discuss these similarities, it is only fair to point out that the "we" in those two sentences is not the same: "We with similar policy concerns" refers to policymakers, "we with similar solutions" to academic and other independent analysts. Both groups are represented in this volume, and some of the authors have worn both hats, but the points of view of analyst and policymaker are often quite different.

Since I am an American, with much more knowledge of American than Canadian housing policy, I am most impressed by the extent to which Canadian discussions of housing policy remind me of home. Accordingly I will center my remarks on this topic on George Fallis's paper, leaving to Canadian readers the question of whether and to what extent Bill Grigsby's survey of American housing policy issues is applicable to Canada as well.

Fallis's discussion of housing adequacy and affordability in Canada could be transferred to the United States merely by changing the numbers in the tables. In many if not most instances, even the numbers would not be very different. For example, he reports crowding has declined from 19 to 3.5 percent of all households between 1951 and 1978; U.S. figures show a decline from 16 to 4.5 percent from 1950 to 1978. In both countries the data appear to indicate that affordability is now a more frequent problem for low-income households than is physical or structural housing adequacy, and policy discussions are beginning to reflect that perception. In both countries the trend in the incidence of apparent affordability problems is upward over the same period that the trend in physical adequacy problems is downward. Unfortunately, it is also true in both countries that the affordability problem is measured inappropriately as a ratio of housing expense to income, rather than as the cost of constant-quality housing. Fallis presents data to show that both rents and owner-accupant costs have increased less rapidly than income. The same is clearly true in the United States, as a number of calculations have shown in recent years (Weicher 1980; Hendershott and Hu 1981). Finally, there is a remarkable symmetry in the perceived affordability problem of the first-time homebuyer and the reality that in both countries younger and younger families are in fact buying homes from year to your; perception and reality are steadily diverging (Weicher 1978).

The similarity in problems is matched by a remarkable coincidence of policies. We continually seem to be learning from each other; often we learn the wrong things. Sometimes Canada appears to be copying American housing policies and sometimes the reverse is true. Thus in the late 1960s the United States created two subsidy programs for low-income households: Section 235 for homebuyers and Section 236 for renters. These programs provided interest rate subsidies to reduce the mortgage payment, or the rent, to 26 percent of the household's income. Both programs also involved Federal Housing Administration (FHA) insurance of the mortgages. By the early 1970s defaults in both programs were widespread, the insurance funds were verging on being actuarially unsound, and the budget outlays were mounting unacceptably. In 1973 President Nixon suspended the programs and set up a task force to recommend alternatives. At that moment Canada was establishing the Assisted Home Ownership Program (AHOP), which provided subsidies for low-income households to reduce the mortgage payment to 25 percent of the household's income. The loans were insured by Canada Mortage and Housing Corporation (CMHC). In 1975 a companion program, the Assisted Rental Program (ARP), was created for rental housing. By the late 1970s defaults in the AHOP program were increasing, depleting the Federal Mortgage Insurance Fund, and the programs were ended in 1979. The U.S. and Canadian programs were not identical, but they were so close that the main difference appears to be that we used numbers to identify ours, and you used acronyms. (For a discussion of AHOP and ARP, consult Smith 1981.) Otherwise the Canadian experience almost appears to be a tape-delayed replay of the American.

An example in which American policy has followed Canadian is the case of the rollover mortgage, which in only now becoming common in the United States; indeed, there have been frequent appeals to the Canadian experience in the American policy discussions surrounding the adoption of variable-rate mortgages and other alternative mortgage instruments (Lessard 1975). A potential example is the Registered Home Owners Savings Plan, providing tax incentives to save for the downpayment on a house; this has been receiving policy attention in the United States almost since Canada adopted it, but has not yet become law (Rosen 1977; Buckly 1978).

The following commentaries reveal the basic similarity in policy prescriptions among analysts on both sides of the border. The general agreement on housing policy among academic economists in the United States (Weicher 1979:501) extends to the rest of the continent as well. Agreement appears general that the housing problems of the poor are best treated as problems of poverty, not housing market failure, and that income tranfers are a more appropriate mechanism for dealing with these problems than is the production of new subsidized housing, which has been the favored policy in both countries. Sharing in this consensus are individuals who disagreed substantially on professional issues and broad political issues such as racial discrimination in housing markets after the panel presentation. Even though academicians on the panel and in the audience had quite divergent views about the importance of housing market discrimination (at least in the United States) and about the efficiency of markets in providing housing to minority groups, they tended to agree on the principle that income transfers are the preferred way of improving housing conditions for the poor. This uniformity may merely reflect the fact that most participants in the conference were economists; analysts with other disciplinary backgrounds might not share this consensus. But it seems remarkable that in a profession rife with jokes about our disagreements, we find so little to debate in housing policy.

Does this professional uniformity have implications for North American housing policy during the rest of this century? It would be nice to think so, but I am doubtful if not pessimistic. In the United States, at least, academic criticism of housing subsidy programs has been widespread for more than a decade, while policy has moved back and forth, shifting toward income transfers from about 1971 to 1975, then reversing itself toward subsidized production until the present. Now policy may be reversing again, but it is too soon to be sure. Canada appears to be now about where the United States was in 1975 on this issue, which does not necessarily imply that there will be a new subsidized production program emanating from Ottawa; but on the other hand, it suggests caution about whether Canada has fully learned the lessons of AHOP and ARP any sooner than the United States has come to grips with the implications of Sections 235 and 236. It will be interesting to see how much the policy issues and the policies have changed in another five years or so on both sides of the border.

9320   342-5

KEVIN E. VILLANI*

The fact that the Unites States and Canada have—and should have—national housing ministries is rarely questioned: such ministries are characteristic of all developed and most developing nations. Nevertheless, although economic rationalizations abound, the activities (and perhaps the very existence) of these ministries appear basically inconsistent with the free-market underpinnings of the United States and Canadian economic systems.

Lofty public policy pronouncements notwithstanding, most of the direct federal involvement in the production of housing reflects narrow political rather than broad public policy judgments. Often these political judgments are provided with an economic rationale, for example, that housing subsidies redistribute income appropriately; occasionally they are given an empirical basis, for example, that housing "needs" require the production of x units in housing per year. Such rationales and empiricisms do not explain why legislators vote for housing subsidies. If they did, then housing programs would presumably reflect the designs of economists. In fact programs often reflect the designs of the many special interest groups with substantial political influence. To illustrate, housing construction trade organizations continually draft legislation oriented toward housing production, with substantial incentives to the producers.

It is time to reaffirm the economic rationale for government intervention in housing markets consistent with the free-market economies. But we must go beyond providing a list of potential economic rationales that may be used to justify inappropriate political actions; we must reexamine the applicability of these various rationales and the implications of various empiricisms for North American housing markets. Economists should be more sensitive to the inappropriate use of partial economic analysis by policymakers to justify policy and should make clear where they stand on the economics of housing policy.

The economic rationales for government intervention in housing markets are to improve economic efficiency or to redistribute income. Sources of economic inefficiency are external effects, economies of scale, and barriers to entry. What follows are some observations on these rationales as justifications for North American housing policies.

The existence of external effects in the consumption of housing underlies many federal housing programs. Physically inadequate or overcrowed housing is said to cause disease, depression, and deviant behavior affecting both the occupants and innocent observers. This "rationalizes" housing production programs, the homeownership tax subsidy, rental subsidy programs with minimum housing quality standards, zoning codes, and so on. The fact is that the proportion of the North American housing stock that could seriously be thought to generate substantial negative external effects has declined precipitously since World War II—primarily due to rising real incomes and, consequently, the demand for higher quality housing—and currently amounts to less than 5 percent of the housing stock. Moreover, much of this stock is in rural areas where, presumably, the external effects are diminished. Assuming that existing subsidy and regulation policies could significantly reduce the magnitude of these externalities, although there is no clear evidence that they have thus far, it is unlikely that the magnitude of the social costs of these negative externalities is sufficiently great and visible to generate widespread political support for these policies.

Economies of scale may provide an economic rationale for actuarially sound national housing finance policies, although these policies are rarely thought of in this perspective. If, for example, one views federal guarantees of pools of heterogeneous mortgage instruments as, essentially, the sale of information to secondary market investors, the production of which exhibits economies of scale, then this activity could be justified as improving market efficiency. Federal innovation in mortgage designs may be similarly justified. Despite much debate over the full economic costs of these programs, the minimal (in most cases nonexistent) direct costs would seem to require less empirical justification than other expenditure programs.

Barriers to entry provide the original economic rationale for public housing, justifying the direct participation of government in the production process. It was argued that supply would not be forthcoming without the essentially entrepreneurial role of government. By implication, a barrier to entry existed to private developers. To my knowledge, no firm empirical evidence exists in support of this hypothesis.

The second major economic rationale for government intervention, to redistribute income, has been much in vogue in both Canada and the United States since the early seventies. The popular perspective is the increasing lack of affordability of housing. The emergence of income redistribution as the primary rational for federal intervention (most households in need in both the United States and Canada suffer only from affordability problems) stems from the eroding empirical base of other rationales, a misinterpretation of the affordability data and misinterpretation of the rationale. First, the data. As the price of rental housing fell, households consumed more. Failure to distinguish price from total expenditures and the changing statistical base resulted in an inappropriate conclusion of declining affordability for rental housing. Similarly, homeownership expenditures rose, but the price of housing services—after taking into account tax and inflation effects—fell. Second, the rationale. Great significance has been imputed to the fraction of income devoted to housing expense, however measured. By implication, when the housing is of sufficient quality to minimize external effects, the problem is presumably the inability to consume a sufficient quantity of other goods. Yet this does not justify housing subsidies.

Housing voucher programs have a dual justification: external effects and income redistribution or affordability. Thus, the income supplement is tied to a requirement for a minimal level of housing consumption. However, the magnitude of these externalities, as already noted, is not clear. Moreover, in existing programs there is little relation between the magnitude and distribution of the subsidy and the resulting reduction in externalities.

What does this analysis imply for future economic analysis and housing policy? First, the theoretical rationales must be precisely defined. Second, the magnitude of the effects must be quantified. Third, judgments must be made about the efficacy of existing or potential federal policy responses.

345-8

9320
Canada

LAWRENCE B. SMITH

The topic of projecting housing policy in the twenty-first century is fraught with many complications. In addition to the usual difficulties of forecasting, a major complication arises in anticipating the differences between the set of policies that would appear to be ideal or appropriate and the set of policies that will actually be implemented. Although it is to be hoped that the actual and the appropriate policies would coincide, based upon housing policy performance in Canada in the 1970s, this hope is probably unduly optimistic. Nevertheless, let us assume that, political considerations aside, the economically appropriate policies will be followed.

In his excellent chapter on the "Normative Basic of Housing Policy," George Fallis enunciated an approach to policymaking that I support, namely that politics should be formulated on a normative basis both with respect to the objective functions that are to be maximized and the design of the optimal form of intervention. Although the full theoretical and empirical apparatus does not yet exist to specify policy precisely using this approach, especially in the area of policy design, sufficient knowledge does exist to determine the rationale for intervention. The usual economic grounds for intervention in the housing market include (1) the removal of or compensation for market imperfections: (2) the existence of externalities: (3) the reduction of cyclical instability (either in the housing sector or in the economy in general, although these objectives may conflict): and (4) income redistribution.

During the 1940s, 1950s, and the first half of the 1960s housing policy in Canada was based upon the first three of these grounds and contributed significantly to the very high quality of Canadian housing. During the late 1960s and most of the 1970s the emphasis of policy shifted to income distribution. This shift contributed to an overstimulation of housing demand and, although it facilitated the continued improvement of housing standards, it did so at an excessive price in terms of resource allocation. The shift also introduced considerable distortions in the market (such as rent control, AHOP, and ARP) and set the stage for greater instability in the housing industry.

A review of the policy performance of the past together with the normative analytical approach offered by Fallis suggests that the appropriate role for government in the future is a return to improving the efficiency of the market mechanism and to limiting direct intervention to situations when efficiency is not obtainable through market processes. This approach suggests a greatly reduced federal government intervention in the future for the following reasons:

1. The quality of Canadian housing is sufficiently high that, except for isolated areas such as housing for native peoples, the handicapped, and in some cases the elderly, there are likely to be few externalities associated with increased housing consumption.

2. The issue of affordability is really not an issue since prices simply reflect market preferences unless they are distorted by market imperfections. Some groups with so-called affordability problems will have legitimate income problems (which will justify direct income distribution policies).

3 Most market imperfections have been largely eliminated in Canada except for those generated by specific government policy, such as rent control. Here the appropriate economic response is dismantling of the policies creating the imperfections (rather than layering additional programs under the guise of a second best solution).

4. The private sector has demonstrated a resilience to market fluctuations, which indicates that except in extreme cases, probably generated by government actions with respect to other policy targets such as the exchange rate, the benefits from intervention to reduce cyclical fluctuations in housing are likely to be relatively small. Moreover, the largest single source of cyclical instability in housing is in the adoption and termination of various government housing programs. A scaling down of these interventions should reduce market volatility.

5. Finally, there is hope that income distribution objectives will be pursued more directly through social welfare policies and that the reliance on the housing sector to accomplish income redistribution will be reduced. Consequently, although the housing policy actually implemented in the twenty-first century may differ considerably from that which now appears to be theoretically appropriate, the most dramatic aspect of housing policy should be a recognition again that housing is a good like any other good and that its production and consumption can best be encouraged by removing imperfections in the market place rather than trying to specify and control housing variables directly. As a result, the involvement of government in housing should decline considerably in the twenty-first century. The involvement that does occur should increasingly be local or provincial in recognition of the increasingly localized nature of housing problems, and the sub-

stance of federal housing policy should shift to counter newly emerging market imperfections that arise in the future.

9320
US

348-51

RICHARD F. MUTH

A common failing of normative economic analysis is the following: Having concluded that the workings of the private market are less than ideal in some particular sphere, it prescribes immediate government intervention to correct the shortcoming. The likely consequences of each intervention are rarely explored, however. Thus, the results of governmental action are often quite different than contemplated. Indeed, the empirical evidence on the effects of government intervention into the determination of relative prices and outputs in the United States shows that matters have almost invariably been made worse rather than better. Nowhere is this more strongly the case than in the field of housing.

Numerous examples of government intervention into housing support the contention I have just made. Let me cite just three. Repeatedly in different countries and at different times, various units of government have set ceilings on the rents private landlords are allowed to charge. Such controls are invariably justified as necessary to keep housing affordable. Yet where rents have been controlled for any substantial period of time, the effect is to reduce the stock of rental housing and thus make housing more, not less expensive.

Even when the rental stock is unchanged, by holding rentals below freemarket levels, a shortage of rental housing is created. Moreover, since the maintenance and upkeep of rental units is less profitable to its owners under rent controls, less of it is done. Owners also have the incentive to shift dwellings from the rental to the owner-occupied segment of the housing market. The decline over the long run in the rental stock means that the maximum rents that could be charged in the absence of controls increase. There are a wide variety of ways by which those seeking to find rental accommodation and those seeking to increase their returns from it can arrange to pay the higher rental in ways not readily discerned by those administering controls. Inevitably, then, rent controls not only produce a housing shortage and lead to a decline in the rental housing stock but increase rent levels actually paid as well.

As a second example, consider the personal tax treatment of the implicit income from owner-occupied housing. Under the United States tax system, such income need not be included as taxable income but mortgage interest and property tax payments may be deducted. The net effect is that homeowners receive a tax subsidy equal to their marginal tax rate multiplied by the sum of interest (whether on their equity or on borrowed funds) and property tax costs associated with their home. Though not necessarily the reason why the income from owner-occupied housing is treated in this way by our tax laws, such treatment is often justified by the alleged benefits to society of promoting homeownership. But according to one recent estimate, the effect of this tax treatment in the United States has been to increase the proportion of owner-occupied units only from about 60 to 64 percent (Rosen and Rosen 1980).

At the same time the tax treatment of owner-occupied housing has probably shifted about 5 percent of the United States capital stock from the nonhousing to the housing sector of the economy. Currently, the revenue losses to the U.S. Treasury resulting from the tax treatment of owner-occupied housing are estimated at about $35 billion per year, roughly seven times the amount the federal government spends on lower income housing programs. Since homeowners tend to have higher income than renters, the current subsidy to homeownership is a highly regressive one. Moreover, since marginal tax rates rise with income and the fraction of income spent on housing rises about in proportion to income, the tax subsidy is relatively larger for higher income households. Indeed, it is hard to imagine a more perverse income subsidy scheme than the United States personal tax treatment of income from owner-occupied housing.

As a final example in the United States, consider the now dead and unlamented urban renewal program. During the late 1940s it was widely perceived that market imperfections inhibited private redevelopment of large U.S. cities. The Housing Act of 1948 thus authorized federal subsidies to local governments for the purpose of acquiring and demolishing existing properties in certain areas, redesigning the areas, and installing new public facilities, then reselling the cleared and redeveloped sites to private developers.

Such actions, it was believed, would spark the revitalization of large United States cities.

The sorry results of this programs are well known. Receipts from the resale of redeveloped land averaged only about 30 cents per doller of costs incurred (Anderson 1964:table A.1). In one city, St. Louis, large areas of the Mill Creek redevelopment project adjoining the downtown area still lie vacant almost twenty years after the inception of the project. Throughout the 1970s, as earlier in the postwar period, most large U.S. cities continued to lose population relative to their suburban areas, and some, such as St. Louis, have suffered absolute population losses. Though producing little or no benefit at substanial resource cost, urban renewal also resulted in the disruption of established neighborhoods. Many lower income families were forced to relocate, and because of the destruction of housing occupied by such families, they were forced to pay more for housing of given quality, at least temporarily.

If informed of the facts, many persons would probably agree that the results of housing policy in the United States to date have indeed been to reduce rather than improve our well-being. Few would probably support, however, the obvious conclusion from past experience that government should not attempt to influence the working of private housing markets. That is because most would no doubt argue that we have learned from our past mistakes and can do better in the future. Unfortunately this optimism may not be justified. Many past experiences with rent controls and the disruptions wrought by controls in New York City should serve as a warning to all. Yet with inflation in the 1970s in the United States, community after community has adopted new rent control ordinances. To take but one other example, housing allowances are now widely viewed as a promising vehicle for providing better housing for income families, as indeed they are. Yet if such a program were adopted, it would probably be encumbered by such severe restrictions on the eligibility of existing dwellings and requirements that a certain percentage of funds go to recipients living in newly constructed ones that it would be little improvement over past programs.

After all, the same politicial process and special interest groups that have taken good intentions in the past and produced such sorry result are still with us. To ensure better results, anyone proposing a new program should be required to produce evidence establishing beyond a reasonable doubt that the proposed intervention would improve on the private market's performance. Evidence on the latter's probable failure and the fond hopes of well-meaning people alone would not be accepted as grounds for intervention.

REFERENCES

Anderson, Martin. 1964. *The Federal Bulldozer.* Cambridge, Mass. MIT Press.

Buckley, Robert M. 1978. "On Estimating the Tax Loss of the Homeownership Incentive Plan." *American Real Estate and Urban Economics Association Journal* 6 (Spring):105–9.

Hendershott, Patric H., and Sheng Cheng Hu. 1981. "Inflation and Extraordinary Returns on Owner-Occupied Housing: Some Implications for Capital Allocation and Productivity Growth." In *House Prices and Inflation,* edited by John A. Tuccillo and Kevin E. Villani. Washington D.C.: The Urban Institute Press.

LESSARD, Donald. 1975. "Roll-Over Mortgages in Canada." In *New Mortgage Designs for Stable Housing in an Inflationary Environment,* edited by F. Modigliani and D. Lessard. Boston: Federal Reserve Bank of Boston.

Rosen, Harvey S., and Kenneth T. Rosen. 1980. "Federal Taxes and Homeownership: Evidence from Time Series." *Journal of Political Economy* 88 *(February):59–75.*

Rosen, Kenneth T. 1977. "The Housing Crisis and the Homeownership Incentive Plan." *American Real Estate and Urban Economic Association Journal* 5 (Fall):366–78.

Smith, Lawrence B. 1981. "Canadian Housing Policy in the Seventies." *Land Economics* 57 (August):338–52.

Weicher, John C. 1978. "How Home Affordability, Equity, and Housing Market Behavior." *American Real Estate and Urban Economics Association Journal* 6 (Winter):395–416.

———. 1979. "Urban Housing Policy." In *Current Issues in Urban Economics,* edited by Peter Mieszkowski and Mahlon Straszheim. Baltimore: The John Hopkins University Press.

———. 1980. *Housing: Federal Policies and Programs.* Washington, D.C.: American Enterprise Institute for Public Policy Research.

16 THE FUTURE OF NORTH AMERICAN HOUSING MARKETS
George W. Gau and Michael A. Goldberg

The chapters in this volume have examined, in some cases from quite different perspectives, the underlying trends and movements in North American housing markets. They have provided a thought-provoking commentary on the important demographic, economic, and political forces influencing housing and mortgage markets in both Canada and the United States. The authors have constructed a valuable framework for anticipating the likely future directions of these markets, as well as providing their readers with an opportunity to develop a better understanding of the functioning of these markets through comparative research in two different national settings.

The intention of this final chapter is to synthesize the analyses and findings contained in the previous chapters into a set of general conclusions concerning the important and unresolved issues facing North American housing markets in the future. Striving to do more than simply summarize the foregoing chapters, we focus on the more important implications of the research presented in this volume. Prognostication is treacherous in the best and most stable of times, and hazarding forecasts in the present volatile economic climate borders on folly. Nonetheless, we shall build on the foregoing chapters to develop a synthetic view of the prospects for these markets into the next century. We conclude this chapter by briefly describing what seem to be the most pressing unresolved questions that need to be addressed in future housing research.

OVERVIEW OF THE MARKETS

Mirroring the organization of this book, this overview of North American housing markets is divided into four sections: demand, supply, finance, and policy.

Demand

Given the data and analysis presented in Chapters 1 and 2, it is clear that a major demographic shift is underway in North America, a shift that could have a significant impact on the structure and scale of future housing demand. The aging of the children of the baby boom and the fall in fertility rates in both the United States and Canada imply substantial declines in the expected rate of household formation, especially after the 1980s. In the United States the annual growth rate of total households is projected to drop from the 1.8 percent level of 1975–1980 to 1.5 percent in 1985–1990, and down to only 0.9 percent by 1995–2000. The decline in Canada is expected to be even more precipitous, falling from a 3 percent rate of net household growth in 1976–1981 to 2 percent in 1986–1991, and subsequently to a 1 percent level by 1996–2001.

In support of these projections, Alonso's arguments concerning the improbability of another baby boom and the continuation of fertility rates below generational replacement are quite convincing. Women are unlikely to retreat significantly from their expanded role in the labor force. While traditional family formations will still be a major element of our societies, the size of these households will probably continue to decline as women seek other career objectives beyond the home. Of course, if large numbers of baby boom women decide to have children late in their reproductive years, the so-called echo resulting from even a small change in fertility rates could have a substantial impact on these projected rates of household formations and houshold size.

Fertility rates are ultimately behaviorally based and have not been readily amenable to forecasting in the past. If present forecasts are as much in error as those in the past have been, a radical change in the projections of household growth through the 1980s and 1990s could result from such an echo.

If natural increase is becoming less significant as a source of national population growth, the key element in the estimation of future housing demand is then migration, both interregional and international. As noted by Brown and by Alonso, international migration is the hardest component of population growth to forecast. Despite recent attempts in Canada and the United States to inhibit immigration, both could experience a repeat of past large inflows of economic migrants and political refugees. Although we North Americans may at times be pessimistic about our future economic conditions, our relative prosperity and stability when compared to underdeveloped countries still creates an attraction to a migrant flow that is often difficult to control. In addition, both countries have explicit or implicit ties with other politically less stable nations, which in a volatile world can lead to unexpected waves of refugees. Given such possibilities in Canada, it is likely that the immigration experience in the future will be in the upper rather than lower range of the figures in Tables 1–2 and 1–5 and the actual growth of households could be substantially higher than the projected 1–2 percent rates.

As indicated by Bourne in Chapter 3, the decline of the role of population growth means that migration at the interregional and interurban scale will become an increasingly important component of demand at the level of individual housing markets. The 1970s have been a period of stability in the rates of population movement across North America, the only shifts being in destinations: in Canada from the central to the western provinces and in the United States from metropolitan to nonmetropolitan areas. The remaining two decades, however, can be expected to be a period of more volatile rates of internal migration in both countries, with possibly even greater flows given the likely increase in economic instability, particularly at the regional level. Such shifts in locational preferences will cause major increases in the demand for housing in some markets, while others will simultaneously experience no increase and perhaps even falling demand, reflecting regional differentials in economic growth. As a result, despite ag-

gregate projections depicting declining national housing demand
due to slowing overall population growth, more buoyant demand
may in fact be brought on by interregional migration, necessitat-
ing considerably more new residential development than aggregate figures would suggest.

Supply

Ignoring for the moment the impact of interregional migration,
the projected decline in the rate of growth of housing demand in
the future should mean a reduced allocation of resources to the
construction of new housing supply. Assuming a 2 percent depreciation rate of the existing stock (the figure utilized by Chinloy in
Chapter 7), the necessary annual number of housing starts in the
United States to satisfy new and replacement demand is only 1.2
million units in 1995–2000, compared to 1.8 million per year in
1980–1985. Similarly, in Canada the required annual level of
starts drops from 242,000 units in 1981–1986 to only 141,000 in
1996–2001. These figures are well within the capacities of the existing housing production systems in both countries, which during
1976–1979 produced an annual average of 1.8 million units in the
United States and 236,000 units in Canada.

These aggregate figures, however, mask the potential supply
problem resulting from the future internal migration flows in
both countries. It is quite likely that some housing markets in
the future could still experience housing shortages caused by
rapid internal movements of population. The difficulty researchers have found in developing models to explain and predict interregional and interurban migration patterns contributes to
this supply problem. One missing explanatory variable in migration equations may be housing prices. If there is a price elasticity to these movements, rapidly rising house prices may well
deter continued migration inflows into a tight housing market.
Similarly, the attraction provided by low prices in declining areas
could serve to alter population flows considerably. House prices
as deterrents or attractions clearly need to be recognized in migration and housing supply forecasting exercises.

As discussed in Chapters 7 and 8, an important housing supply
issue that is too frequently overlooked in the traditional emphasis

on housing starts and new construction, is the management of the existing stock. Future supply deficiencies will be a concern for some areas, but an even more serious problem may be the housing surpluses likely in other markets. While a mobile labor force offers considerable economic benefits to a country, there are also significant costs associated with this mobility. Migration simultaneously causes the abandonment of valuable housing and social infrastructure in declining areas and the need for construction of new and expensive stocks of housing and infrastructure in growing areas. Whether it is better to demolish such units as suggested by Lowry, or instead attempt to maintain and redevelop the stock for future use, is not necessarily clear in a given situation. Historically, the general trend in the United States has been towards demolition, while in Canada greater emphasis has been placed on preservation, as Chinloy noted. Perhaps better interregional information flows on housing prices and availability would slow some of this mobility and reduce the attendant wastes of housing and social overhead capital that offset some of the gains from labor mobility and from an efficient national labor market.

Finance

The future housing finance system in the United States envisioned by Hendershott and Villani in Chapter 9 has many characteristics strikingly similar to those of the Canadian housing finance system during the 1970s. Without regulatory constraints, deposit and mortgage interest rates have been free in Canada to move with other capital market rates, and there are few distinctions between Canadian thrift institutions (trust and mortgage loan companies, as well as credit unions) and commercial (chartered) banks in their provision of household financial services. In addition, subsidiaries of Canada thrifts have been active participants in the real estate brokerage industry. The absence of prohibitions on branching by financial institutions has created a geographically integrated system without the need for a formal secondary mortgage market.

Given the expected evolution of the United States housing finance system, what can be learned from the Canadian experience with such a less regulated system? One important lesson is that disintermediation and credit unavailability are unlikely problems in a system with no interest-rate ceilings. Although the United States mortgage markets experienced a series of so-called credit crunches during the past two decades, there was no comparable nonprice rationing in Canadian markets at the time, despite similar restrictive monetary policies. A product of this absence of mortgage availability problems in Canada is a lower volatility of housing starts. From 1970 through 1979 the coefficient of variation of annual housing starts is 33.9 percent in the United States (see Table I–1 in the introduction of this book) compared to a Canadian coefficient during the same period of only 11.5 percent (Table I–2). Another lesson is that, unlike the United States thrift concerns, the financial viability and continuing existence of large numbers of the Canadian thrift industry has not been seriously threatened by the recent period of high and variable interest rates. Without regulatory interferences, the Canadian housing finance system has been able to respond effectively to this new financial environment.

Regarding this inflationary setting and alternative mortgage instruments, while the depth of the demand for non-level-payment designs is perhaps debatable, it is certain that different and more diverse financing arrangements are emerging to deal with interest-rate risk. In both countries there has been a widespread adoption by financial intermediaries of various forms of adjustable-rate mortgages (ARM). If the analysis of household risk preferences in Chapter 11 is correct, the risk levels inherent in ARMs may be higher than the desired portfolio risk levels of most borrowers, and we may very likely see in the future innovative mortgage arrangements evolving to reduce borrower's risk. Examples could include limits on rate adjustments for ARMs with offsetting interest-rate hedging by mortgage lenders or even a mortgage with some form of rate change insurance provided by a third party for a fee.

As described in Chapter 12, inflation and government taxation policies combined during the 1970s to increase significantly the after-tax returns from housing investment. What lies ahead for housing prices and homeownership as an investment in both countries is, of course, the interesting question. Even though Tuccillo's conclusion that a decline in the rate of inflation would lower investment returns from housing appears correct, it should also be noted that, even if inflation rates fall, the expected volatility of future migration rates discussed earlier can mean quite diverse investment experiences in different housing markets. While over-all housing prices across an economy may have an inflation elas-ticity of 1, changing migration patterns could cause individual markets in both countries to suffer price declines even in an infla-tionary environment or, conversely, price increases with low infla-tion rates. An implication of such price behavior in local markets is that the non-level-payment mortgage instruments may contain a higher level of default risk than generally anticipated. Designs such as graduated-payment and price-level-adjusted mortgages implicitly assume a uniform inflation elasticity across all housing prices. By building into their nominal payment schemes and mortgage balances an inflationary pattern that does not material-ize in some housing markets, there is a greater risk of increasing loan-to-value ratios and rising mortgage defaults when compared to level-payment instruments.

Future price trends in particular housing markets seem des-tined to become even more volatile and unpredictable. The diver-sity of forecasts over the medium term does not clarify the situation, as they range from continued high and variable infla-tion and interest rates to more stable times with correspondingly lower interest rates and house-price stability. Putting all of this together leads us to conclude that substantial volatility of house prices is likely at both the national and the local level. The need for flexible mortgage instruments and financial institutions is great as a result. Such instruments and institutional arrange-ments must be sufficiently resilient to deal not only with high and variable inflation rates but also with lower and more stable price levels and expectations as well. We must be careful not to over-react to present volatile conditions and preclude adjustment to more settled economic times.

Policy

Historically, governments in Canada and the United States have followed remarkably similar housing policies in an attempt to im-prove the shelter services provided their citizens. As examples, both countries have at various times operated programs in the areas of public housing, housing production incentives, and rent supplements. Despite a few differences, such as the lack of mortgage interest deductibility for homeownership in Canada, the goals and directions of Canadian and United States housing policies are basically the same. In addition, both countries have generally been very successful in raising the quantity and quality of available housing. As indicated by Fallis in Chapter 13 and Weicher in Chapter 15, by most measures of basic shelter standards (e.g., physical attributes, crowding), North American households are presently quite well housed.

Looking toward the future, the discussion of government housing policy supports the argument that there is no universal housing problem in Canada or the United States. Given the existing quality of the housing stocks and the continuing decline of population growth rates in both countries, there is no anticipated need for further massive government intervention in either the housing or mortgage markets. The affordability issue often pointed to as justification for an expanded government role in these markets should be separated into two types of problems. The first is the perceived payment difficulties created by the tilt problem inherent with the standard level-payment mortgages in an inflationary environment. Thoroughly analyzed in the housing finance section, the solution to this problem lies not in government assistance or subsidies but, rather, in the adoption of alternative non-level-payment mortgage designs. The second aspect of the affordability debates is the income problem. Some households in both countries may be viewed as not having sufficient disposable income to obtain a socially acceptable, minimum level of consumption of all commodities, including housing. As noted by Fallis in Chapter 13 and Smith in Chapter 15, this form of the affordability issue is really not a housing problem but, rather, a problem of inadequate income. The optimal government policy therefore is a direct income supplement instead of a new housing subsidy.

The absence of a national housing problem does not mean, however, that governments have no future role in North American housing markets. The volatility foreseen in the future, especially in the area of migration flows, will require a more directed and perhaps regionalized housing policy on the part of the federal governments in both countries. The federal level will need to assist state or provincial and municipal governments in monitoring and responding to the housing surpluses and shortages that can result from major population movements. The responsibility for growth and inventory management should not rest solely at the lower levels of government.

Correspondingly, however, local and regional governments must also adopt a more responsive approach to their housing policies, especially in the areas of land-use, subdivision, and development controls. These governments must ensure that regulatory constraints do not prohibit the density and land-use adjustments necessary for orderly housing markets. Edelstein's results in Chapter 5 indicate there is generally a high elasticity of substitution between land and nonland improvements in housing production functions. These findings suggest that shifts in demand can translate into changing densities and uses, thus mitigating the supply surpluses or shortages, if the housing and land markets in an urban area are allowed to adapt without major regulatory barriers.

SOME REMAINING QUESTIONS

Being prospective in nature, the chapters in this book cannot be definitive. They are not intended to be. Rather they are designed to raise important housing issues and analyze some of the likely (and unlikely) consequences of the trends and conditions influencing the future for North America housing markets. There are obviously many remaining unanswered questions. Outlined here are a few of the most pressing issues for future research.

External and internal migration are of critical importance to the demographic future of housing demand in both Canada and the United States. As Bourne points out in Chapter 3, studies of past migration behavior among Canada's major urban regions have failed to find any consistent or predictable pattern. The picture in the United States is not terribly different. Given lower birth rates, relatively small changes in regional preferences can lead to potentially dramatic changes in regional population and housing growth. Migration behavior, however, is only imperfectly understood and further research in this area would be quite valuable. The role of housing prices and of government policies (such as water development subsidies in the Southwest United States) in internal migration flows needs to be examined.

Another potential subject for research is urban spatial theory and the future shape of the urban landscape. In a number of chapters of this book interesting observations were made concerning the influence on interurban location decisions of factors such as demographic trends (Chapter 2), the housing production function (Chapter 5), and energy and environmental constraints (Chapter 6). The insights in these contributions should provide a useful framework for extending interurban location models. Traditionally, models of urban land use have been ill-equipped to deal with situations involving urban redevelopment and densification; yet these are precisely the circumstances envisioned for much of North America's urban landscape over the coming two decades. These chapters can provide considerable insight to the next generation of urban land-use modelers, so they can model cities of the 1980s and beyond instead of the 1960s and 1970s.

Although it is clear from the papers in the housing finance section that economists are thoroughly familiar with the problems of the fixed-rate, level-payment mortgage in an inflationary environment with high and variable interest rates, it is surprising that we do not better understand the actual instrument preferences of consumers. What are household life-cycle savings behaviors and how much interest-rate risk can they absorb in their wealth portfolio? To address these questions requires not only a theoretical analysis of consumer utility functions as in Chapter 11, but also an empirical study of the asset/liability composition of household portfolios and their portfolio adjustments over time. If the results of such a study show that the risk premiums of mortgage borrowers are high, greater attention must be given to alternative methods of dealing with interest-rate risk beyond adjustable-rate mortgages.

Finally, one of the more important outstanding topics is the competitiveness or efficiency of housing markets at a microlevel. The analysis of many housing issues revolves around the question of the speed and extent of the capitalization of information into housing and land prices. To give just one example in the area of housing policy, a variety of government assistance programs in both countries have aimed at increasing the construction of multifamily housing units through tax or interest-rate subsidies. Do these programs actually encourage multifamily development, or do competitive real estate markets simply capitalize into property values the benefits of such assistance programs and thereby reduce or eliminate any incentives? Despite the significance of such questions to policymakers and housing economists, thus far little empirical research has attempted to evaluate the competitiveness of housing markets.

CLOSING COMMENTS

Contributors to this volume were originally asked to develop broad and prospective views of the likely course of North American housing markets into the twenty-first century. They agreed to the almost impossible task of projecting the future and have succeeded in providing a broad range of information and ideas along with, in many cases, empirical support for their forecasts. However, as noted at the outset, such crystal ball gazing is always hazardous and subject to error, especially under the present circumstances with much uncertainty and flux surrounding most household and business decisions.

The purpose, though, has not been to derive a conclusive set of forecasts. Rather, it was the intent of this book and of this final chapter especially to suggest major themes about which the future will be unfolding. To these themes we have attempted here to provide a considerably broader context by sketching out areas of unresolved issues. By highlighting the as yet unknown, it has been our hope to stimulate discussion and research in order for today's questions to be tomorrow's findings. In short, we view this book and this final essay as being suggestive rather than decisive works. It is hoped that the book will serve as a foundation for future housing research and policymaking. As prospective pieces they should be seen as starting points for the coming generation of scholars and decision-makers and not as end points in our current accumulated knowledge. We have begun the process, it is very much up to the reader to continue the task.

CONTRIBUTORS AND SYMPOSIUM PARTICIPANTS

Robert T. Adamson, Vice President of the Policy Development and Research Sector of the Canada Mortgage and Housing Corporation.

William Alonso, Richard Saltonstall Professor of Population at Harvard University.

Morton Baratz, Associate of Management Account Reports, Columbia, Maryland.

Anthony E. Boardman, Associate Professor of Policy Analysis, Faculty of Commerce and Business Administration, University of British Columbia.

Larry S. Bourne, Director of the Centre for Urban and Community Studies and Professor of Geography at the University of Toronto.

Michael J. Brennan, Albert E. Hall Professor of Finance, Faculty of Commerce and Business Administration, University of British Columbia.

Philip W. Brown, Manager of the Housing Requirements and Conditions Unit, Market Forecasts and Analysis Division, Canada Mortgage and Housing Corporation.

Leland S. Burns, Professor in the School of Architecture and Urban Planning at the University of California, Los Angeles.

Dennis R. Capozza, Professor of Urban Land Economics, Faculty of Commerce and Business Administration, University of British Columia.

Jack L. Carr, Professor of Economics and Research Associate of the Institute for Policy Analysis at the University of Toronto.

Norman E. Carruthers, Assistant Professor of Policy Analysis, Faculty of Commerce and Business Administration, University of British Columbia.

Peter Chinloy, Associate Professor of Economics at the University of British Columbia.

Frank A. Clayton, President of Clayton Research Associates, Ltd., Toronto.

Robert H. Edelstein, Professor of Finance at the Wharton School, University of Pennsylvania.

George B. Fallis, Assistant Professor of Economics at York University.

Daniel H. Garnick, Associate Director for Regional Economics, Bureau of Economic Analysis, U.S. Department of Commerce.

Bernard I. Ghert, President and Chief Operating Officer of the Cadillac Fairview Corporation, Toronto.

Willam G. Grigsby, Professor of City and Regional Planning at the University of Pennsylvania.

Stanley W. Hamilton, Associate Professor of Urban Land Economics, Faculty of Commerce and Business Administration, University of British Columbia.

Patric H. Hendershott, John W. Galbreath Professor in Real Estate at Ohio State University.

Robert Hobart, Senior Research Associate at Clayton Research Associates, Ltd., Toronto.

Lawrence D. Jones, Associate Professor and Chairman of the Urban Land Economics Division, Faculty of Commerce and Business Administration, University of British Columbia.

Ira S. Lowry, Designer and Principal Investigator of the Housing Assistance Supply Experiment, The RAND Corporation, Santa Monica, California.

Jonathan H. Mark, Assistant Professor of Urban Land Economics, Faculty of Commerce and Business Administration, University of British Columbia.

Denton Marks, Assistant Professor of Policy Analysis, Faculty of Commerce and Business Administration, University of British Columbia.

Duncan Maclennan, Director, Housing Research Centre, University of Glasgow.

Richard Muth, Professor of Economics at Stanford University.

Lawrence B. Smith, Professor of Economics and Chairman of the Department of Political Economy at the University of Toronto.

Raymond J. Struyk, Senior Research Associate at the Urban Institute, Washington, D.C.

John A. Tuccillo, Senior Research Associate at the Urban Institute, Washington, D.C.

Keven E. Villani, Acting Deputy Assistant Secretary for Economic Affairs at the U.S. Department of Housing and Urban Development.

John C. Weicher, Associate of the American Enterprise Institute for Public Policy Research, Washington, D.C.

Index

elasticity of substitution
between land and nonland
improvements, 98–103
empirical estimates, 103–107
effect on future urban
development, 93–94
Production, housing, xxiii, 6, 127–
34, 136–37. *See also* New
housing construction
Property tax, 153
Public sector, 160
in Canada, 64
for management in declining
regions, 172–75
and price of housing, 266–67
in U.S. housing policy, 314–15,
319, 320–24, 333

Quality
hedonic index for, 102–103
housing, 49
Quebec province, 53, 58–59, 62,
67

Racial discrimination, 163, 327
RAMs (Reverse-annuity
mortgages), 224–26, 227
Reagan, Ronald, 332
Real estate brokerage industry,
193, 195, 357
Redman, A., 98
Regional growth
in Canada, 51–56, 62–66, 67–70
in U.S., 62, 74–79, 81, 83–86
Regions
changes in, 161–62, 167–75
in U.S., and price of housing,
262–63
Regulations, 179, 181–82, 184,
187–89, 192–96
Renshaw, Vernon, 79
Renters, 159, 165–66, 168–69, 171–
75,
in Canada, 16–17, 23–24, 296
Rent control, 348, 350
Repairs on housing, xvi, 89–90,
139–44
effect on depreciation, 144–45,
154–57
effect on new construction, 142,
148–53
Research, xxi–xxiv, 361–63

Residential Rehabilitation
Assistance Program (RRAP),
141–42
Risk, 177–79, 198
to borrowers, 214–15, 234–35,
243–45, 254
diversification, 191, 198
and financing, 359
and GPMs, 218
interest rate, xx, xxii, 177–78,
179, 246–52, 254–55, 357–58
and investment in other
countries, 271–75
to lenders, 214–18, 234–35, 246–
50
and VRMs, 216, 218, 235
Robinson, I., 52, 64
Rosen, Harvey, 98, 100, 341, 349
Rosen, Kenneth, 341, 349
Rydell, C. Peter, 174

SAMs (Shared-appreciation
mortgages), 226, 234, 246, 278
Samuelson, P.A., 239
Savings
effect of inflation on, 260
mortgages as, 238–42, 254, 271–
72, 275
in U.S., 275
Savings and loans (S&Ls), 177, 194
Schwert, G. W., 244
Security brokerage, 183, 198
Security underwriting, 183, 198
SES factors, 2, 38–40, 48–50, 51
Shannon,   , 327
Shared-appreciation mortgages.
See SAMs
Sharpe, C. A., 21
Shaw, Edward, 183
Sheshinski, E., 267
Silverman, L. P., 55, 64
Simmons, J. W., 52, 56, 64, 67, 70
Sirmans, C., 98–99
SLPM (Standard level-payment
mortgage), 244, 245, 254
Smith, B., 93, 109, 111
Smith, Lawrence, 51, 128, 209,
341, 345–48
Smolkin, H. M., 267
SMSA, 75–79, 98–100, 107, 116,
263–64. *See also* Urban areas
Solomon, Arthur P., xxi, 261

About the Editors

Michael A. Goldberg is currently the Herbert R. Fullerton Professor of Urban Land Policy in the Faculty of Commerce and Business Administration at the University of British Columbia. He is also the Associate Dean of the Faculty. He received his B.A. from Brooklyn college and his M.A. and Ph.D. from the University of California at Berkeley, all in Economics. He has written widely in areas of urban transportation planning, urban systems modeling, urban transportation and land use interactions, urban land and housing economics and policy, and on strategies for planning and decisionmaking in complex systems. His papers have appeared in *Transportation Research Record, Land Economics, Journal of Regional Science,* and the *Journal of the American Institute of Planners,* among others. He has co-authored a monograph on zoning, edited several volumes on urban land economics, and is in the process of co-authoring a textbook on *Urban Land Economics* as well as a book on decisionmaking and planning strategies.

George W. Gau is an Associate Professor of Urban Land Economics in the Faculty of Commerce and Business Administration at the University of British Columbia. He received his B.S., M.S., and Ph.D. in Finance from the University of Illinois, Urbana-Champaign. Prior to joining the Faculty at U.B.C. in 1978, he held positions at the University of Oklahoma and the University of Illinois. His research interests have primarily focused on mortgage, housing, and real estate investment markets. He has performed studies for the Canada Mortgage and Housing Corporation on alternative mortgage instruments and the feasibility of mortgage rate insurance. In addition, he has been involved in a major empirically based research project analyzing returns and risks in real estate markets.